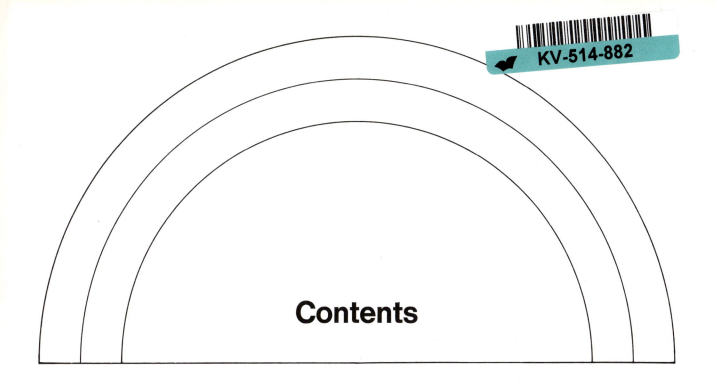

Contents

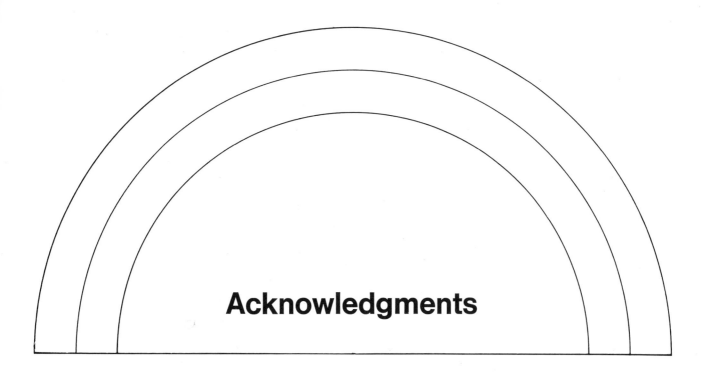

Acknowledgments

There were times during the two years spent researching and writing this book when we wished we were cataloguing Rhode Island instead of California. Were it not for the aid and comfort of numerous friends, colleagues, agencies, and editors, we could not have possibly begun to cover this vast state. We are particularly grateful to Art Finley, creator of "Art's Gallery," a daily feature in the *San Francisco Chronicle,* who let us borrow from his huge collection of engravings. Other historical graphics were furnished by Howell-North Books of Berkeley, the University of California's Bancroft Library, and Don McCartney. Numerous state agencies, such as the Department of Fish and Game and the Parks Department, helped us, as did chambers of commerce and visitors' bureaus across California. We are also grateful for the help of Debbie Goodman, Jon Carroll, Sandy Carroll, Ron Rapoport, Joan Rapoport, Stan Sesser, Rob Foss, Georganne Foss, Francesca Archer, Marcia Salner, and Buzz Wilms. Finally, we would like to thank our editors, Charles Sopkin and Susan Stanwood, who stayed with us long after the statute of limitations had expired.

Roger Rapoport
Margot Lind

Berkeley, California
March 3, 1976

California Series No. 9, April 16, 1894.   Published Weekly.   Price $25 per Year.

PICTURESQUE CALIFORNIA

California Series No. 9, April 16, 1894.

The J. DEWING COMPANY, Publishers,

SAN FRANCISCO   NEW YORK

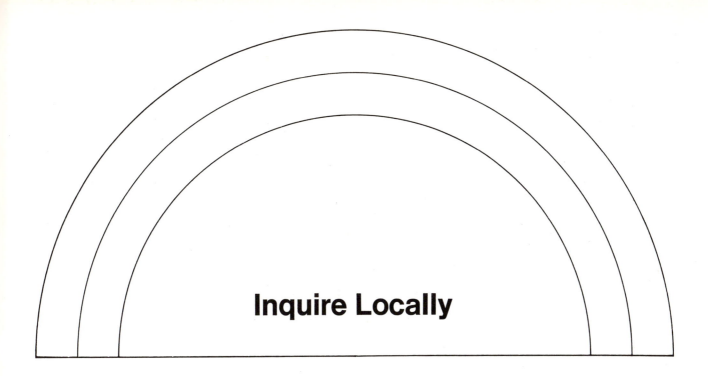

Inquire Locally

Within these pages we expect you'll find ideas that will lead you throughout California. But before taking off, please keep in mind that despite years of research we cannot guarantee you'll find everything in its place. To make the catalogue current, we have double-checked the accuracy of all our routes, locations, phone numbers, etc. But California is a restless place. What's here today may move tomorrow. Even some of the most important landmarks are inaccessible at times.

For example, in April 1974, threat of a high-speed avalanche triggered by a volcanic eruption or an earthquake forced closure of Lassen National Park's main campground, visitors' center, and museum. Similarly, several years back, landslides inundated a good share of the Big Sur community. And in the summer forest fires frequently make popular tourist areas completely inaccessible. So plan carefully before leaving home. Make sure that side road you're turning onto isn't flooded further on. Check with the ranger to be sure your hiking trail isn't blocked by snowdrifts. In fact, wherever you go in California, be sure always to inquire locally.

This magazine, published in 1894, was typical of the material that lured settlers to California.

New West. If you love *New York* magazine, chances are you'll adore *New West,* Clay Felker's entry into the Southern California publishing market. Investigative reports, service features, and columns (developed in part by some of *New York's* regular contributors) will appear in this biweekly. For subscription information, write *New West* Subscription Department, 9665 Wilshire Boulevard, Beverly Hills, CA 90212.

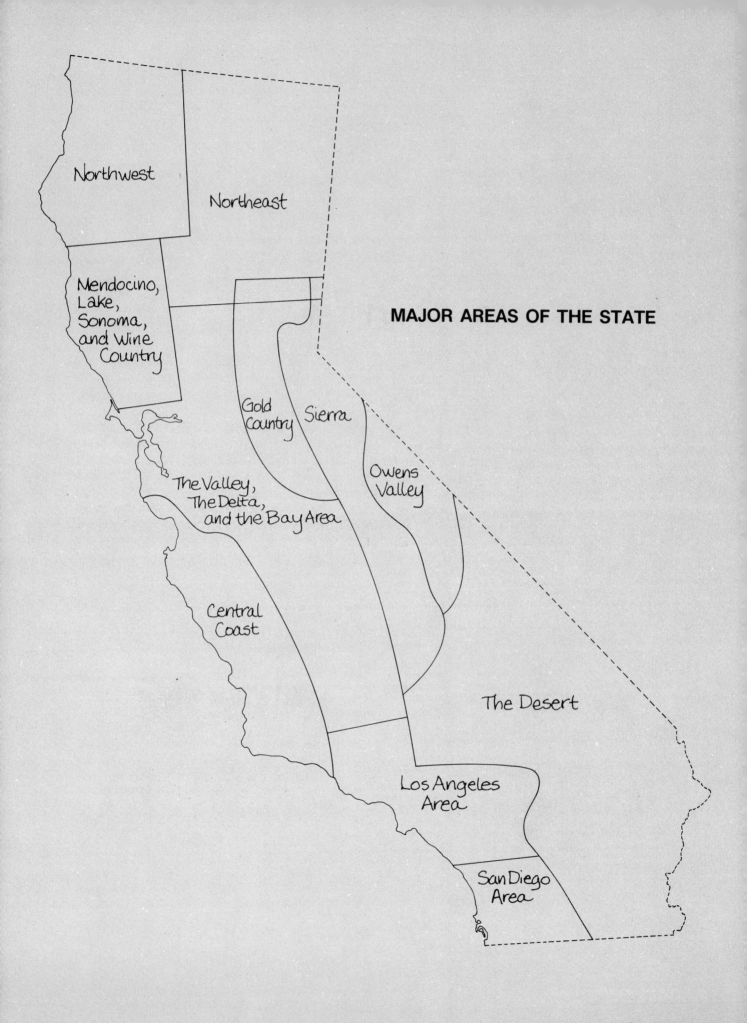

MAJOR AREAS OF THE STATE

Northwest

Northeast

Mendocino, Lake, Sonoma, and Wine Country

Gold Country

Sierra

The Valley, The Delta, and the Bay Area

Owens Valley

Central Coast

The Desert

Los Angeles Area

San Diego Area

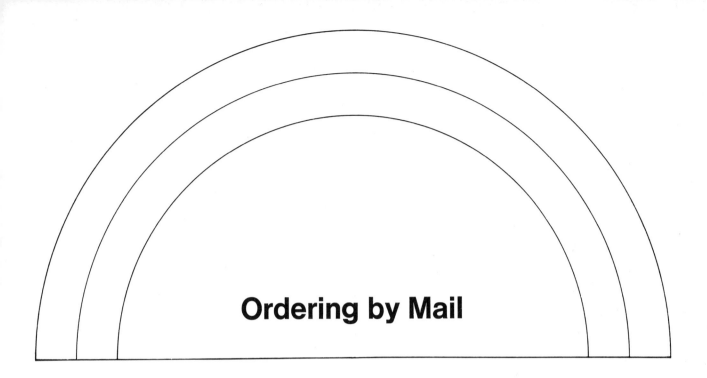

Ordering by Mail

Readers interested in ordering any of the items mentioned in *The California Catalogue* are urged to write suppliers for the latest catalogues, product information, and price lists before sending money. Prices listed were current at the time this book went to press and include handling and shipping charges. However, California residents must add 6 percent sales tax with all orders (6.5 percent for residents of Alameda, Contra Costa, and San Francisco counties). When placing your order, send a check or money order; do not send cash. Some firms impose a modest charge for their catalogues, which is usually refundable with any order; unless otherwise noted, catalogues are available free of charge.

CALIFORNIA

SHEEP RANCHE.

SACRAMENTO.

DESCRIPTION.

[*Area, 158,360 square miles. Population (1890), 1,208,130.*]

I. SITUATION AND EXTENT.

Situation. — California, the largest and most populous of the Pacific States, borders on the Pacific Ocean. It is included between 32° 31′ and 42° north latitude, and 120° and 124° 15′ west longitude.

Extent. — In shape it is an irregular oblong, about 750 miles long and 200 miles wide. It is three times as large as the New England States, and, excepting Texas, is the largest state in the Union.

II. SURFACE.

Physical Divisions. — California may be divided into five distinct sections: (1) the mountain region of the Sierra Nevada; (2) the plains of the Sacramento valley; (3) the coast belt; (4) the plateau east of the Sierra Nevada, on the border of the Great Basin; (5) the Colorado desert, in the south-east.

Mountains. — The Sierra Nevada Mountains extend north and south nearly two-thirds of the entire length of the state. The average width of this great range is about 70 miles. The western slope to the Sacramento valley is very gradual, and is 60 miles long; the eastern slope to the Great Basin, short and precipitous, not exceeding 10 miles in length.

The loftiest summits are Mount Whitney (14,887 feet) in the south, and Mount Shasta (14,440 feet) in the north. The average height of the crest summits is from 6,000 to 9,000 feet.

The higher peaks of this range are snow-clad all the year round, and are the retreats of numerous small glaciers, — the remaining fragments of a system of mighty glaciers that once covered the entire chain.

The Coast Range extends in parallel ridges, near the Pacific, the entire length of the state, 750 miles. It is from 20 to 40 miles wide, and is less than half the average height of the Sierra Nevada.

Its most noted peaks are Mount Hamilton (4,448 feet), the site of the

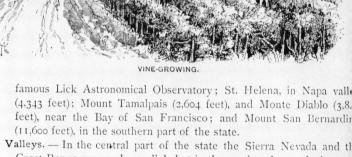

VINE-GROWING.

famous Lick Astronomical Observatory; St. Helena, in Napa valle (4,343 feet); Mount Tamalpais (2,604 feet), and Monte Diablo (3,8. feet), near the Bay of San Francisco; and Mount San Bernardir (11,600 feet), in the southern part of the state.

Valleys. — In the central part of the state the Sierra Nevada and th Coast Range are nearly parallel; but in the north and towards the sout the two chains run together, and inclose the Sacramento valley. Th great central valley is 400 miles in length and from 20 to 50 miles i width. It is drained from the north by the Sacramento River, an from the south by the San Joaquin. The Coast Range is intersecte

GEOGRAPHY OF CALIFORNIA AND NEVADA. *Copyright,* 1891, *by American Book Company.*

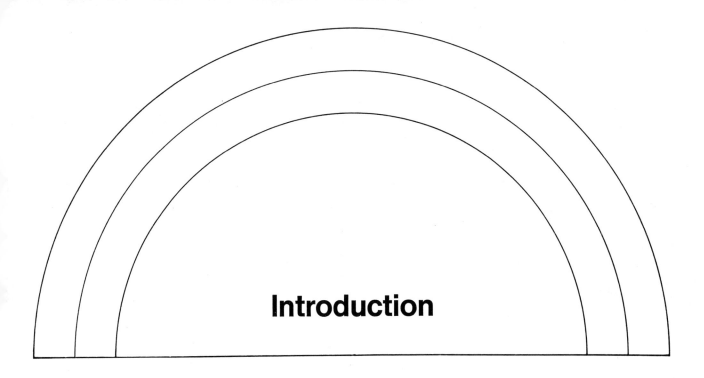

Introduction

Think about it. The beaches are better in Hawaii, the mountains are bigger in Alaska, the sunsets are finer in New Mexico. Colorado has superior skiing; you can eat better in New York restaurants and find far more lakes in Minnesota. Campgrounds are less crowded in Oregon, land is cheaper in North Carolina, and the cost of living is lower in Texas. So why do well over 21 million people choose to call California home? And why do another 9.9 million tourists annually make it one of the most visited states in the union?

What draws and keeps so many in California is not so much what the state has as what it suggests. Long after the mystery has gone from once popular destinations, California remains, almost inexplicably, America's promised land. Nothing—not the imminent possibility of calamitous earthquakes, poisoned air, oily beaches, packed freeways, or armies of symbionese liberators—can keep them away. The work of native sons like Richard Nixon and immigrants like Charles Manson, Sirhan Sirhan, and Donald ("Cinque") DeFreeze has prompted many to raise questions about the mental stability of our thirty-first state. And it certainly doesn't inspire confidence to realize that three of its better known residents—Marilyn Monroe, Janis Joplin, and Lenny Bruce—all ODed within a few miles of one another.

Yet the myth of California endures much as it did more than a century ago when companies began luring easterners to Lotus Land. Then the emphasis was on the fertile acreage, abundant sunshine, and friendly natives. No one talked about the desert heat, the lack of dependable water supplies, the high prices, and a citizenry that worked overtime to make sure California maintained the highest lynching rate of any state outside the Deep South. Caucasians, Negroes, and Orientals alike were strung up by angry mobs crazed at various times by obsession with instant retribution, racist frenzy, or sheer drunkenness. From 1849 to 1855 there were over 4000 murders in the state. San Francisco had 1200 murders between 1851 and 1855; yet there was only one conviction.

What has been the irresistible force that has lured so many to California? Some came after tangible objectives such as gold; others came to escape hated obligations like shoveling snow. But for most it has simply been the conviction that the grass really is greener west of Nevada. This belief springs not from objective criteria, but rather from blind faith in the mystical image of the Golden State.

The state's very name, given to the region by Spaniards who discovered the place in the sixteenth century, is based on a piece of fiction. These early explorers took it from a half-baked, long-forgotten Portuguese novel that described an imaginary island of Amazons called California. These was, of course, not an Amazon to be found in the new land. But the name stuck, as did the illusion that somehow everything grows bigger and better in the California sunshine. No less an authority than former Stanford University president David Starr Jordan boasted that "California college girls of the same age are larger by almost every dimension than are the girls of Massa-

What draws so many people to California?
(*American Book Co.*)

In the second half of the nineteenth century, California had
the highest lynch rate outside the deep south.
(*Wells Fargo History Room*)

Crossing the Sierras.

chusetts. They are taller, broader-shouldered, thicker-chested (with ten cubic inches more lung capacity), have larger biceps and calves and a superiority of tested strength."

Other early promoters insisted people could solve all their problems simply by stepping inside the state's boundaries. Physicians in the late nineteenth century spread the mistaken idea that Southern California's climate could help cure tuberculosis patients. Anxious to sell off some of its holdings, the Southern Pacific Railroad hired writers to churn out all manner of articles, stories, and books touting California. Ads promoted the vast potential of California agriculture by suggesting that squash and melons grew so large

they had to be picked on horseback. The fruit growers' exchange joined Southern Pacific in plastering Iowa with billboards crying, "Oranges for Health, California for Wealth."

These and similar campaigns were a dramatic success, but they failed to convince some cynics like the Jackson, Mississippi, editor who wrote in the 1870s: "California is a state of mind—exaltation is in the atmosphere. Birds of gorgeous plumage flit through the trees but they have no song. Flowers astound in size, gorgeous color and infinite variety but they have little perfume."

But such warnings were ignored as the millions poured in to dam up, pave over, chop down, bash in, or dig out much of what gave California its magical aura. A few voices like John Muir's were raised when, for example, the City of San Francisco sank one of the Sierra's loveliest valleys, the Hetch Hetchy, beneath a reservoir. Eastern California farmers vainly tried to dynamite the dam that diverted Owens River water to Los Angeles, drying up Owens Lake and destroying an entire agricultural region. Later generations tried to stop coastal oil drilling, contain redwood logging, protect the state's sole remaining wild river, and block freeway construction. But the victories were, for the most part, pyrrhic. Lady Bird Johnson flew out to dedicate a precious redwood grove, while loggers' buzz saws droned in the distance. Offshore oil wells were camouflaged with pastel paint. Freeway plans were cut back from eight lanes to six.

At the same time that California was cannibalizing itself, a series of man-made environments began springing up. The first of these, Disneyland, promoted on national television shows by the amusement park's cartoonist-founder, soon became the state's leading tourist destination. Overnight this semiautomated land of make-believe became the real thing. Indeed, no one could seriously claim that they had really visited California unless this artificial turf in Anaheim had been part of the itinerary. Khrushchev was furious when he couldn't get in.

Disneyland and other synthetic environments have given a new dimension to the California dream. Now people come to see not only what California is, but also what it is not. Jungle parks have sprung up in the suburbs, so the natives can drive through and let lions claw at their tires. The Matterhorn can be found rising just off the Santa Ana Freeway, the *Queen Mary* is docked at Long Beach, *La Pietà* is at Forest Lawn, and the Red Sea parts in Universal City.

Superimposing all these fantasies on the unreal world of California creates a peculiar identity crisis. No one, not even the natives, can tell you precisely what California is. The state by its very nature is an unfinished place, with earthquakes and even volcanos threatening to remake the landscape any day. Most of its residents are not indigenous; they have immigrated hoping to fulfill their own image of California. And the state's future is clouded by environmental, population, and developmental pressure. For there are those in power who see every river valley as a place for a reservoir, every farm as a subdivision site, and every national park as the perfect spot for taco stands.

All this means that anyone with a serious interest in California frequently finds that existing state information sources are inadequate. For example, an enjoyable visit to Los Angeles can't begin unless it is timed to avoid the worst smog season. Similarly, who wants to buy a house in the highest earthquake danger zone in California? And why should a college student attend a school where professors refuse to talk to undergraduates in groups of less than 500.

And that is precisely why this book inventories the best *and* the worst of California. We believe that a realistic California guide must chart both the highs and the lows of what the state offers today. Within these pages the selective person will find plenty to satisfy virtually every interest. In each category, we have tried to keep in mind the twin limitations of time and budget. And if you finish a section hungry for more, we'll recommend other sources that offer further details.

With the catalogue as your base, we expect you'll enjoy the best the state has to offer while steering clear of the obvious pitfalls. But please don't take us too literally. If you want trip tickets that map out your every mile, go see the auto club. Our primary purpose is to get you started. If, in following one of our leads, you cross a tempting new path, follow it. These spontaneous ventures are often the most rewarding. Bear in mind *The California Catalogue* is only a beginning. You'll have to write your own ending.

PART ONE:
ORIENTATION

The ideal northern approach to California leads through redwood forests like this one in Humboldt County.

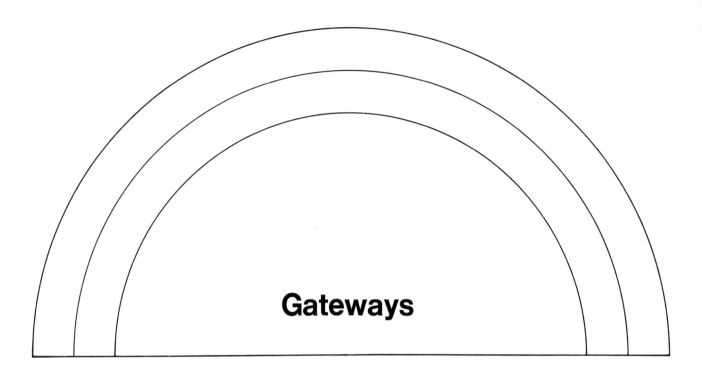

Gateways

California, of course, is located on the western edge of the United States just south of Oregon. This certainly comes as no surprise to students of geography, but we emphasize it because few visitors take advantage of the ideal northern approach. Most people seem to assume the logical route is through southern Nevada or Arizona.

They are wrong. Assuming you, like most people, are coming during the popular May–October season, the best way to get to California is through Oregon. To begin with, Oregon is prettier than Nevada. Reno may offer slot machines and easy access to bordellos, but it's no match for Coos Bay or Crater Lake. Why take the sweaty eastern gateway through Needles when you can come in along the cool North Coast at Crescent City?

There are a lot of good arguments for starting in northernmost California. For one thing, a lot of people don't realize it's there. Because it is far from population centers, lacks any Yosemite-style drawing cards, and has but one real freeway, the place is often overlooked. As a result, the region is seldom crowded and often empty. Indeed, there are places in Northeastern California where you can drive for hours without passing another car. And once you get off the road to explore on foot, you are really on your own.

There are several ways to reach California from Oregon. Coming out of Klamath Falls, you can head straight for Lava Beds, where you can walk for miles through scores of cool caves. Then you can head down to look at McArthur-Burney Falls and go on to Lassen National Park, which has as much to offer as Yosemite

but lacks the summertime hordes. Interstate 5 comes down into California through the Siskiyou Mountains and offers access to steelhead fishing on the Klamath River, backpacking in the Trinity Alps, and the back road to the small town of Peanut.

But best of all is the coastal route, which can be reached via either Highway 199 or Highway 101. Can you think of a better way to begin a visit to California than driving through seemingly endless groves of ancient coastal redwoods? Yes, there is some commercialization of the Immortal Tree, the Trees of Mystery, and the Avenue of the Giants. But you'll also find herds of wild elk, fern canyons, rhododendron trails through the redwoods, and little towns like Victorian-dominated Ferndale.

Farther south along Highway 1 is the Mendocino Coast, with its tidepools, blowholes, rocky headlands, abalone fishing, and probably the loveliest of the state's coastal parks, Russian Gulch. Keep on the coast road and you'll reach Point Reyes National Seashore, which offers grassy dunes, secluded bays, quiet lakes, remarkable tidepools, and over 300 species of birds. If you want to see California without the people, this is the place to come. Except for holiday weekends and a few peak periods in summer, crowds are never a serious problem. And even if one area seems busy, there are always secluded places a few miles away.

But if you simply can't take the northern approach, there are worthwhile alternatives. Coming in on Interstate 80 through Reno, cut off at Highway 89, skirt the western edge of Lake Tahoe, and then cut over to Highway 88, one of the most scenic of the trans-Sierra routes. It will set you down right in the midst of the Gold Country, where you can visit places like Volcano and Mokelumne Hill before heading on to the Bay Area metropolis. And in the wintertime an easy detour out of Las Vegas will enable you to start your California visit with a tour of Death Valley.

Unfortunately, there is not much to be said for the two most popular routes into California, Interstates 15 and 40. Even when the temperature does dip below 100 degrees, there is little to tempt nondesert buffs out of their cars aside from an ersatz ghost town called Calico. But we know a lot of you aren't going to listen to us. So go ahead, have it your way, and take Interstate 15 through Las Vegas into California. At Baker, the first significant town after the state line, you'll find the friendly service station attendants happy to help you and all the other destitute gamblers. They'll be glad to let you pawn your suitcase, tent, watch, or whatever else you have for the gas you'll need to make it into L.A.

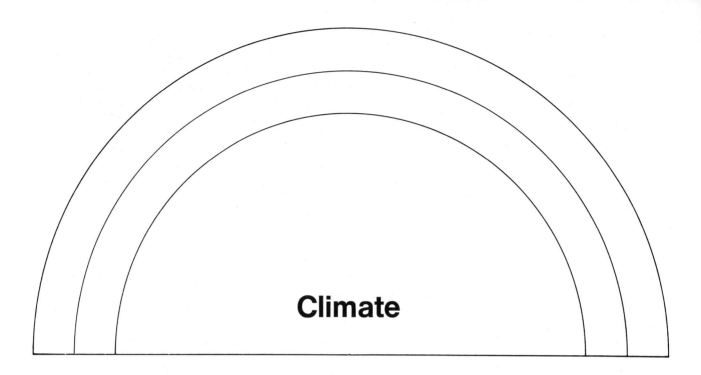

Climate

You can see them every summer, shivering in their shorts on Fisherman's Wharf as the cool fog rolls in off the bay. These are the tourists who come to San Francisco dressed for the summertime heat. After taking in the city's sights each day, they find it necessary to return to their hotels and thaw out. They are some of the many victims of various myths about the weather in California.

Climate has always been a major selling point for Golden State promoters. But newcomers are often victimized by fundamental misconceptions. For example, some early pioneers arrived in the Central Valley, sowed their crops in the late winter, and then sat back to wait for the spring rains. They never came. Even today, people arrive in Los Angeles singing about how it never rains in Southern California until they get caught in their first flash flood.

Characterized by winter rain and summer drought, California embraces twenty-one distinct climatic regions. The Los Angeles area alone has fourteen types, while eight are found in the Bay Area. It is frequently possible to leave 60-degree San Francisco, head across the Golden Gate Bridge, drive fifteen minutes, and find yourself in 95-degree weather. There is sufficient diversity that you can find four-season weather, complete with New England winters or desert living, within many individual counties. Table 1 shows the normal monthly temperature ranges in various areas of California.

Most of the precipitation in California comes between late October and early May (Table 2). The one major exception to this rule is the Northwest Coast, where rainfall is as high as 100 inches a year. This region, the mountains of Northern California, and the Sierra Nevada experience the state's heaviest precipitation. Rainfall generally tapers off as you move into the Central Valley, the South Coast, and the Desert Region.

It is this lengthy dry season that gives rise to California's designation as the Golden State. With the exception of certain coastal areas and mountain ranges, most of California is characterized by hot summers with temperatures frequently going into the 90s and 100s. Indeed, within weeks after the rainy season ends, the hills go golden brown and remain that way for at least half the year.

This two-season pattern—mild, wet winters followed by hot, dry summers—tends to predominate in most of the populous areas of California. In these regions there is no traditional spring and fall. As a result, many trees begin blooming in January or February, right in the midst of winter rains. And September is the hottest month of the year in many coastal areas.

Adjusting to the unusual climate is a major challenge to newcomers. "The coldest winter I ever spent was one summer in San Francisco," wrote Mark Twain. Every autumn millions of residents find they must survive without fall colors. Generally only those willing to drive the foothills along Highway 49 or head up into the mountainous regions get to see the leaves turn en masse. It also takes work to find snow. You must get above the snow line, which ranges from 3000 to 6000 feet, depending on the month and the mountain range you're talking about. In California only the higher

TABLE 1. NORMAL TEMPERATURES (Degrees Fahrenheit)

Station	January Max.	January Min.	February Max.	February Min.	March Max.	March Min.	April Max.	April Min.	May Max.	May Min.	June Max.	June Min.	July Max.	July Min.	August Max.	August Min.	September Max.	September Min.	October Max.	October Min.	November Max.	November Min.	December Max.	December Min.
Bakersfield	57.6	37.9	62.9	41.0	69.3	44.5	75.8	50.1	84.6	56.1	92.1	62.0	100.3	68.2	97.7	65.7	91.8	61.1	80.9	52.7	68.6	43.1	59.0	38.5
Bishop	53.7	19.8	58.1	24.3	65.8	29.3	73.5	36.7	81.9	43.2	90.7	48.9	98.0	55.2	96.3	52.2	89.8	46.5	77.5	37.3	65.0	26.5	56.1	22.4
Eureka	53.6	41.1	54.2	42.1	54.5	42.8	55.7	45.1	57.9	48.1	60.1	50.9	60.5	52.0	60.9	52.5	81.6	51.1	60.3	48.5	57.5	44.9	55.1	42.7
Fresno	55.4	36.7	61.3	39.6	67.9	42.0	76.1	46.4	84.5	51.8	92.1	57.2	100.0	62.6	97.6	62.0	92.1	56.3	80.7	48.5	67.5	40.0	56.5	37.5
Long Beach	65.3	40.8	65.7	43.1	68.1	43.3	71.2	48.8	73.9	53.1	77.2	57.7	82.0	61.1	82.6	62.0	82.1	60.4	77.8	55.1	73.9	48.4	68.0	43.9
Los Angeles	65.0	46.6	66.0	48.2	68.6	50.2	70.6	53.0	73.5	56.0	77.1	58.9	83.3	62.6	83.3	62.9	82.4	61.4	77.3	57.4	73.3	52.1	67.5	48.8
Oakland	55.4	40.6	58.7	42.6	62.5	44.7	65.5	47.7	68.2	51.1	71.3	54.2	72.7	55.9	72.4	56.0	74.6	55.5	71.1	51.1	63.9	45.4	57.1	41.8
Red Bluff	53.4	37.5	58.7	40.6	64.5	43.7	72.3	48.5	81.4	55.1	90.3	62.1	99.6	67.9	97.0	65.0	91.0	61.0	78.6	52.5	65.6	43.4	55.3	38.9
Sacramento	53.2	37.2	58.6	39.8	64.8	42.0	71.4	45.3	78.2	49.7	86.5	54.4	93.4	57.4	91.9	56.3	80.2	55.0	77.6	49.4	64.2	41.6	54.6	38.1
San Diego	64.6	45.3	65.4	46.9	67.7	50.2	69.2	53.8	70.9	57.0	72.6	59.8	76.8	63.4	78.0	65.6	77.6	62.2	74.4	57.8	72.1	51.4	67.0	47.2
San Francisco	55.8	45.5	58.6	47.3	60.7	48.6	61.9	49.5	63.4	51.3	65.0	53.1	64.3	53.3	64.9	53.9	68.9	55.1	68.3	54.4	63.7	51.0	57.5	47.4
Santa Maria	62.3	38.1	63.1	40.4	64.6	41.9	66.4	44.7	68.1	47.1	69.5	49.7	71.6	52.8	71.9	52.9	74.1	51.5	73.3	47.5	70.4	41.8	65.0	39.8
Stockton	52.4	37.0	58.2	39.7	65.0	42.3	72.8	46.5	80.6	51.7	88.6	56.9	95.4	60.9	93.1	59.3	88.6	56.7	77.7	50.2	64.6	41.3	53.9	37.9

Source: U.S. Department of Commerce.

elevations get four-season weather.

Living with California's two-season climate is impossible for some. They find it ridiculous to drive around the state searching for spring, winter, or fall. But once you've made the adjustment to California's climate, the weather in other parts of the country seems unnatural. There is, for example, the California executive who returned to the golden brown state from an Oregon summer vacation to tell a friend: "I was really kind of disappointed. Everything up there is so green this time of year."

Climate Notes

Rainfall: In the mountains and northern part of the state precipitation occurs 60 to 100 days per year, while there are as few as 10 days of rain in the southern desert. Throughout the state, the winter rainy season is composed of stormy periods alternating with longer periods of good weather. A typical winter storm brings intermittent rain from 2 to 5 days, followed by 7 to 14 days of dry weather. Occasionally there are periods of heavy, persistent rain in the north for 7 to 10 days. In the south similar patterns last 3 to 5 days.

Snowfall: Snow has been reported nearly everywhere in California at one time or another, but is seldom seen west of the Sierra Nevada, except at upper elevations in the Coast Range and the Cascades. Some snow is found as low as 2000 feet in the Sierra foothills each winter. Snow remains on the ground for appreciable periods each winter above 4000 feet. The heavy snow-pack begins at 7000 to 8000 feet.

Growing season: The average growing season ranges from 365 days on the South Coast to less than 50 days at upper Sierra elevations. The central and coastal valleys have a freeze-free season of 225 to 300 days. In the southeast desert basin the growing season ranges from 250 to 325 days.

Relative humidity: The lowest relative humidity is generally found in the Mojave and Colorado deserts. Along the coast moderate to high humidity is found year-round, while inland humidity is high in winter and low in summer.

Thunderstorms: Although thunderstorms can occur anytime, they are fairly rare over the coast and the Central Valley. They are most common at higher Sierra elevations, where they are observed at various locations 50 to 60 days a year.

Tornadoes: Usually only one or two tornadoes are reported each year. Generally they are little more than whirlwinds that damage a few trees or light buildings.

TABLE 2. NORMAL RAINFALL (Inches)

Station	Jan.	Feb.	Mar.	Apr.	May	June	July	Aug.	Sept.	Oct.	Nov.	Dec.
Bakersfield	1.17	1.14	1.06	0.81	0.22	0.09	0.01	0.01	0.08	0.32	0.49	0.97
Bishop	0.99	0.98	0.55	0.46	0.20	0.09	0.12	0.12	0.19	0.43	0.53	1.18
Eureka	6.70	5.53	5.25	2.67	2.18	0.74	0.11	0.10	0.64	3.19	4.61	6.71
Fresno	2.03	2.19	1.96	1.13	0.30	0.07	0.01	0.01	0.10	0.43	0.95	1.97
Long Beach	1.99	2.31	1.37	0.77	0.11	0.03	0.01	0.03	0.06	0.17	1.03	1.97
Los Angeles	3.07	3.33	2.26	1.17	0.16	0.06	0.01	0.04	0.23	0.41	1.08	2.87
Oakland	3.83	3.21	2.42	1.38	0.65	0.12	0.01	0.03	0.20	0.78	1.73	3.58
Red Bluff	4.29	3.31	2.70	1.83	1.13	0.45	0.04	0.06	0.37	1.37	2.29	4.21
Sacramento	3.18	2.99	2.36	1.40	0.59	0.10	0.01	0.02	0.19	0.77	1.45	3.24
San Diego	2.01	2.15	1.57	0.79	0.15	0.05	0.01	0.08	0.15	0.49	0.90	2.05
San Francisco	4.55	3.66	2.93	1.44	0.63	0.14	0.01	0.04	0.22	0.89	2.00	4.27
Santa Maria	2.84	2.50	2.06	1.19	0.22	0.14	0.03	0.03	0.16	0.60	1.02	2.58
Stockton	2.55	2.46	2.05	1.14	0.44	0.07	0.01	0.01	0.19	0.63	1.17	2.66

Source: U.S. Department of Commerce.

Know Your History:
Landmarks of California's Past

1542 Juan Rodríguez Cabrillo discovers San Diego Bay

1579 Sir Francis Drake discovers Drake's Bay

1769 San Diego founded

1776 San Francisco founded

1781 Los Angeles founded

1822 Spanish rule ends, Mexico assumes control of California

1846 Bear Flag Revolt, California declares independence from Mexico

1846–1847 Donner party stuck in Sierra, runs out of food

1848 Treaty of Guadalupe Hidalgo

1850 Statehood

1868 University of California chartered

1891 Stanford University opened

1902 First Rose Bowl game played

1906 San Francisco earthquake

1913 Richard M. Nixon born in Yorba Linda

1919 William Randolph Hearst begins construction of San Simeon

1933 Long Beach earthquake

1937 Golden Gate Bridge opens

1940 California's first freeway, the Pasadena, open to traffic

1942 Japanese evacuated to internment camps

1945 United Nations founded in San Francisco

1946 Richard M. Nixon elected to House of Representatives

1950 Richard M. Nixon elected to Senate

1952 Richard M. Nixon elected to vice-presidency

1955 James Dean dies in Porsche crash en route to Salinas

1962 Marilyn Monroe commits suicide

1962 Richard M. Nixon loses California governorship to Pat Brown; holds "last" press conference

1964 Free speech movement at Berkeley

1965 Watts riot

1966 Lenny Bruce commits suicide

1968 Robert F. Kennedy assassinated in Los Angeles

1968 Richard M. Nixon elected to presidency

1969 Sharon Tate, others, murdered by Manson gang

1970 Janis Joplin commits suicide

1972 Bay Area Rapid Transit (BART) opens

1974 Patty Hearst kidnapped

1974 Richard M. Nixon resigns presidency

1975 Patty Hearst captured

Rolling Stone. California's most successful national magazine gives you everything from the latest Gonzo raving of Hunter S. Thompson to the inside story on the Osmonds. Send $9 for eighteen issues to *Rolling Stone,* Box 2893, Boulder, CO 80302.

Los Angeles Magazine. Extensive coverage of Southern California with particular emphasis on the affluent sector. A one-year subscription to this monthly goes for $9.60. Write to 1888 Century Park East, Los Angeles, CA 90067.

California's
Top Ten Residents

Jerry Brown, Jr., Sacramento: Refusing to be weighed down by the trappings of status, California's chief executive has rejected the $1-million governor's mansion for a $250-a-month apartment. He dines at Shakey's Pizza Parlors, carouses in Berkeley with his bachelor friends, and vacations at the Tassajara Hot Springs Zen retreat in between efforts at whittling away the state bureaucracy. This onetime seminarian has proved far more parsimonious than his Republican predecessor as he holds down enrollment growth at state universities, stops new freeway construction, closes down the California Commerce Department, and halts the giveaway of free briefcases to state employees. With luck, Brown just may succeed in effectively wiping out California government in time to run for president in 1984.

Ed Davis, Los Angeles: Chief Davis, the state's most important right-wing figure, speaks loudly and carries a big stick as head of the Los Angeles Police Department. When he isn't cracking down on prostitutes, X-rated films, or rock concerts, the lawman is out spreading the bad word to civic groups. The chief is down on "Beverly Hills and Bel Air swimming pool Communists," considers the *Los Angeles Times* "a classic example of pink journalism," and firmly believes "today's law enforcement agencies cannot protect you."

Lew Wasserman, Beverly Hills: Chairman of California's largest and most successful entertainment corporation, Music Corporation of America, Wasserman enjoys global reach. Universal Studios, with its enor-mously successful television production arm, remains consistently in the black as it programs for the masses. Through a host of subsidiaries, the firm also is deep into the music and tourism industry. From the Universal City tour to Yosemite National Park, Wasserman is in charge.

Wilson Riles, Sacramento: Since moving into the hot seat as state superintendent of public instruction in 1971, Riles has earned the respect of both political parties. He judiciously wields his power over California schools and has worked well with both the Reagan and Brown administrations. Firmly entrenched, Riles enjoys more job security than virtually any politician in the state.

Otis Chandler, Los Angeles: As far back as the turn-of-the-century water-rights controversies, the Chandler family has been a potent state political force. Today, Chandler, the man responsible for remaking the *Los Angeles Times* into a paper for people who can read without moving their lips, is clearly the most important media figure in western America. As chairman of the well-integrated *Times-Mirror* conglomerate, he presides over activities ranging from pulp making to manufacturing Yellow Pages.

Ronald Reagan, Pacific Palisades: Star of such memorable screen epics as *Bedtime for Bonzo* (1951) and *Knute Rockne, All American* (1940), California's former governor remains a key figure on the national political scene. An opponent of gun control, big government, and the equal rights amendment (he's afraid it would lead to sexually integrated bathrooms), Reagan likes to relax by watching "Mission Impossible" reruns.

Richard M. Nixon, San Clemente: Don't overlook our only living ex-president. Residing quietly on a modest government pension, Mr. Nixon is plugging away at his memoirs, which promise to expose corruption in high places.

Herb Caen, San Francisco: Called "the most literate daily columnist in America," Caen's writing in the *San Francisco Chronicle* is required reading for the Bay Area. With one mention, he can make or break plays, films, and restaurants. A dependable source of scoops and amusement, Caen shows what Walter Winchell could have accomplished if he had ever learned to write.

Cesar Chavez, Delano: Head of the United Farm Workers Union, this tireless organizer has been the central figure in the state's longest and best known labor struggle. Fighting against growers, bureaucrats, and rival unions Chavez has been instrumental in improving the quality of life for the states' most oppressed minority—farm laborers. His campaign continues through boycotts, marches, picketing, and fasts.

Patty Hearst, San Francisco: The state's most celebrated kidnap victim–defendant appears destined to remain page one material for years. Her incredible story manages to embrace most of the major elements found in California's culture and counterculture. Look for many more explosive developments in the years to come.

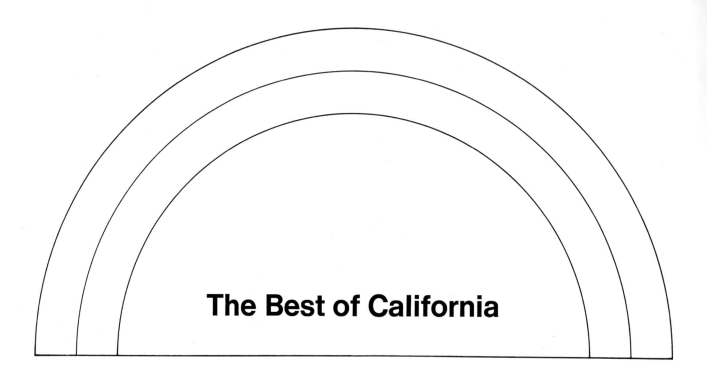

The Best of California

City zoning: Santa Barbara
Restaurant town: San Francisco
Hotels: Santa Barbara Biltmore, Bel Air
Prison: Lompoc
Private university: Stanford
Public university: University of California at Berkeley
National parks: Yosemite, Lassen
National monument: Death Valley
State park: Russian Gulch
State historic monument: San Simeon
Urban park: Golden Gate, San Francisco
Mission: San Juan Capistrano
Victorian buildings: Hotel Del Coronado, Coronado; Carson Mansion, Eureka
Victorian neighborhood: Pacific Heights, San Francisco
Shopping district: downtown Beverly Hills
Discount paint store chain: Standard Brands
Hardware store: Ace Foothill Hardware, Oakland
Fast food chain: Taco Bell
Candy store chain: See's
Breakfast: The Pantry, Los Angeles
Pizza: La Barbera's, Los Angeles
Ice cream: Bud's, San Francisco
Natural ice cream flavor: Gilbert H. Brockmeyer's banana walnut
Stadium hot dog: Polish sausage, Candlestick Park, San Francisco
Armenian bakeries: Fresno
Delicatessen: Canter's, Los Angeles
Wineries: Martini; Heitz; Freemark Abbey; Mondavi; Sebastiani
Port: Ficklin

Champagne: Schramsberg
Columnist: Herb Caen, *San Francisco Chronicle*
Sports columnist: Jim Murray, *Los Angeles Times*
Political cartoonist: Paul Conrad, *Los Angeles Times*
Radio newscaster: Dave McQueen, KSAN-FM, San Francisco
Gardens: Huntington, San Marino
Meadow: Tuolumne (Yosemite)
Hot springs: Grover
Caves: Lava Beds National Monument
Ghost town: Bodie
Archeological site: La Brea Tar Pits
Beaches: San Diego from Torrey Pines southward
Nude beach: Black's Beach, La Jolla
Surfing: the Wedge, Balboa Peninsula
Ski areas: Heavenly Valley; Mammoth Mountain
Sailing: San Francisco Bay
Biking: Santa Barbara; Sacramento Delta (summer excepted)
Clamming: Pismo Beach
Whale watching: San Diego
Zoo: San Diego
Pinball arcade: Knott's Berry Farm
Amusement park: Disneyland
Marine life park: Sea World, San Diego
Stadium: Chavez Ravine, Los Angeles
Fans: Los Angeles Dodgers
Opera: San Francisco
Repertory theater company: ACT, San Francisco
Art museum (collection): Los Angeles County Art Museum
Art museum (architecture): The Oakland Museum

Railroad museum: Laws
Newsstand: DeLauer News Agency, Oakland
Airport: Oakland
Amtrak station: Union Station, Los Angeles
Bridge: Golden Gate
Overpass: downtown Los Angeles intersection of Harbor, Pasadena, Santa Ana, and San Bernardino freeways
Drive: S.R. 1 from Carmel to San Simeon

Roadside rest: Nut Tree, Interstate 80, near Vacaville
Ocean view: Santa Barbara Biltmore lawn at dusk
Mountain view: Minaret Vista, Mammoth Lakes
Valley view: Napa Valley from Sugarloaf Ridge
Night view: San Francisco from Sausalito
Excursion train ride: the Skunks, Fort Bragg to Willits
Restrooms: Madonna Inn, San Luis Obispo
Coroner: Dr. Thomas Noguchi

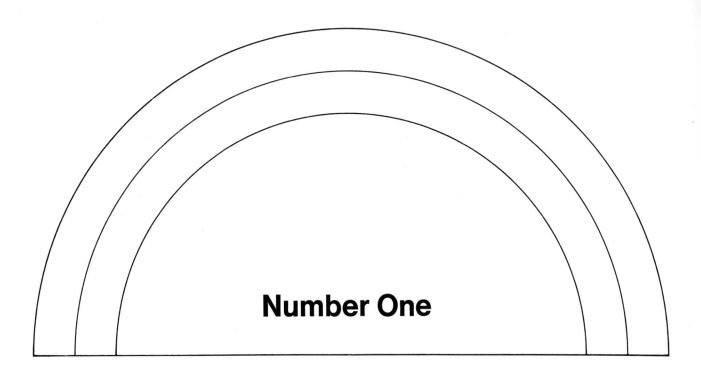

Number One

- California's 21.2 million residents make it the most populous state in America.
- California leads the nation in agricultural production.
- California has the largest aerospace industry in the United States.
- There have been more performances (28,500) of Disneyland's "Golden Horseshoe Revue" than of any other stage show in history.
- San Francisco-based Bank of America is the world's largest commercial bank.
- Los Angeles has the largest area of any city in the world.
- San Francisco Bay is the largest landlocked harbor in the world.
- The intersection of the Harbor, Pasadena, Santa Ana, and San Bernardino freeways in downtown Los Angeles is the busiest freeway interchange in the world.
- California leads the world in motion picture production.
- California's coast redwood, sequoia, and bristlecone pine are, respectively, the tallest, largest, and oldest living things.
- California has more national parks than any other state.
- San Francisco's Chinatown is the largest Chinese settlement outside the Orient.
- California leads the United States in gold production.
- The nation's largest municipal pool is Fleishhacker in San Francisco.

- California leads the nation in public beaches, business bankruptcies, major league athletic teams, cigarette consumption, freeway mileage, drug use, swimming pools, divorces, pleasure boats, cars, pets, bank robberies, and massage parlors.

Westways. This magazine, the official publication of the Automobile Club of Southern California (an affiliate of AAA), features first-rate travel writing on California and the West. Annual subscription to the monthly is $4 to club members and $6 to nonmembers. Remit to P.O. Box 2890, Los Angeles, CA 90051.

PART TWO:
TRANSPORTATION

California's love affair with highways knows no bounds,
as witness the Harbor and Santa Monica Freeway Interchange in Los Angeles.
(*State of California, Department of Transportation*)

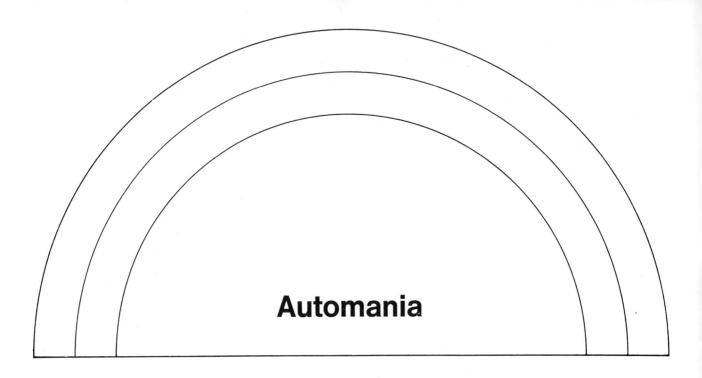

Automania

California is loaded with familiar symbols like the Golden Gate Bridge, Yosemite's half dome, and the Sleeping Beauty Castle at Disneyland. But if you really want to catch the spirit of the state, take the Ventura Freeway to the San Diego Freeway one night and head south. The route carries you through a steep canyon in the Santa Monica Mountains. Because virtually no homes are visible from the roadway, the canyon remains completely dark. For miles you'll see nothing except eight solid lanes of traffic rushing through this black passageway.

Forget Alcatraz, Fisherman's Wharf, and cable cars; this is the real California. Much like cows in India, autos are sacred in California. Some 12 million of them are driven by just about everyone over sixteen. Although public transit is decent and even good in many areas, people insist on driving everywhere. One of the strongest lobbies in the state is the auto club, whose publications have raised color pictorials of freeway interchanges to the level of erotic art.

California's love affair with highways knows no bounds. It is common for people to commute 80 miles a day, and some drive as many as 200. If you read Joan Didion's bestseller, *Play It as It Lays,* you know all about the class of Californians who frequently motor hundreds of miles for no reason whatsoever. They are out there on the interstates, driving in vast circles, with only enough time out for quick pit stops.

The fact is, if you're looking for someone in California, the chances are good you'll find him or her behind the wheel. For example, consider how Patty Hearst and her Symbionese Liberation Army friends,

Bill and Emily Harris, allegedly escaped police following the May 1974 holdup of an Inglewood sporting goods store. First, the desperate outlaws went shopping for a car. Then on the test drive they abducted the vehicle's young owner, drove to a drive-in, and spent the night watching *The New Centurions* as they munched buttered popcorn.

While Californians love the anonymity their cars provide, they also prize the status their vehicles confer. Several years back, a corporate-owned medical firm was having some difficulty recruiting new doctors to join its large group practice. Big salaries, plush offices, liberal vacation policies, and other inducements weren't working. Then the company hit on a terrific new way to win physicians—offer them their choice of a Cadillac or a Mercedes. This automotive fringe benefit worked immediately, for these luxury cars were what the physicians wanted more than anything else.

Here as nowhere else, business prospers off this automania. For example, in Los Angeles numerous companies are in the business of providing valet parking for private residential parties. At the door, each guest is met by an attendant, who parks the car down the street and picks it up when the party's over. Of course, people could walk down and retrieve their cars personally. But, like many Californians, they consider it a dangerous indulgence and cite traffic statistics to support their view: about 13,000 pedestrians are hit by cars each year, and more than 800 of these accidents are fatal.

Incredibly, this carnage comes despite the fact that California's motor vehicle code offers a remarkable

Invader VW Conversion Kits. Tired of driving around in your dull old VW beetle? Anxious to move up to a classy sports car? Well, there's no need to dream any longer. For just $2495, you can buy a conversion kit that will turn your old bug into a sleek sports car. With the simple removal of thirty-eight bolts, the VW bug body separates from the chasis, paving the way for installation of your new fiberglass sports car body. You get style without sacrificing any of the bug's great gas mileage. For a copy of the twenty-page catalogue send $2 to Autokit Industries, 2725 Magnolia Street, Oakland, CA 94607.

degree of protection to pedestrians. People on foot have the right of way at intersections, whether or not crosswalks are marked by painted white lines. Another law that distinguishes California from many states is that it is legal to turn right after making a full stop for a red light. The motorist is also permitted to turn left against a red light after stopping, provided he is going from a one-way street into an intersecting one-way

street where traffic moves left. Newcomers from flat states must also bear in mind that when two vehicles meet on a steep road where they cannot pass, the vehicle facing downhill must back up until the other vehicle can get by.

It's relatively easy to get used to these laws, but adjusting to California's freeways can be difficult. Although the state insists they are the safest roads of all, it takes some experience to feel comfortable going 55 miles per hour in close quarters. The problem is serious enough to persuade the Automobile Club of Southern California to offer ten-hour freeway and defensive driving clinics at no charge to members.

Probably the most common freeway problem of all is the missed off-ramp. It can generally be avoided by careful map study prior to leaving home (the best maps are published by the auto club, which supplies them free to members on request). If you pass your ramp, don't automatically assume you can get off at the next one, turn around, get back on the freeway, and return to your correct exit. Many off-ramps don't have corresponding on-ramps, and even if there is an on-ramp, you may return only to find no exit in this direction for the street you're seeking.

Even when you know where to get off, California's

legendary traffic tie-ups can pose serious problems. Los Angeles highway engineers have installed signal lights to control on-ramp flow during peak periods. This may force you to wait as long as ten or fifteen minutes just to get on the highway. To avoid running out of gas during these tie-ups, consider alternate routes or surface streets.

The first rain of the winter makes freeways particularly slick because it mixes with oil that has been accumulating on the roadway all during the dry season. Another problem is that California drivers tend to drive too fast during the rainy season, forgetting that they can end up hydroplaning if they go over 55 miles per hour. And all year, fog is trouble, particularly along the coast and down in the valleys. If you are planning a trip up and down the state, you may find U.S. 101 a good alternative when the valley routes (Interstate 5 or S.R. 99) are fogbound. Should you see a highway patrol car with an amber rear window flasher, four-way emergency flasher, and no siren approach you in a fog, slow down. This patrol vehicle is providing an escort to reduce the traffic flow due to dangerous conditions ahead. Don't pass him or you may find yourself in one of California's famous sixty-car chain collisions.

Despite all these precautions don't expect freeway driving to get any easier in the near future. Congestion is getting worse as the state's euphoric era of superhighway construction comes to an end. At one time, expressways were seen as the solution to California's highway needs. The massive road-building program got its start in 1939, when the state legislature passed the California Freeway Law, which permitted the highway commission to design limited-access routes. California's first expressway was a 6-mile section of the Pasadena Freeway (originally called the Arroyo Seco Parkway), which opened on December 30, 1940. An instant hit with motorists, the road led to similar roads throughout the state. A state plan envisioned that by 1980 these superhighways would crisscross California, carrying 59 percent of its highway load.

The projected centerpiece was Southern California, where 1540 miles of freeways were envisioned. But in the past few years, a shortage of highway funds, congestion, smog, and a growing interest in mass transit have virtually stopped construction of these expressways. Today the system is littered with half-built on-ramps leading to unfinished roadways that come to dead ends in clumps of weeds. More than $3 billion worth of partially completed roadway looks as if it will be abandoned. And now it seems doubtful that the Los Angeles freeway network will ever exceed 700 miles.

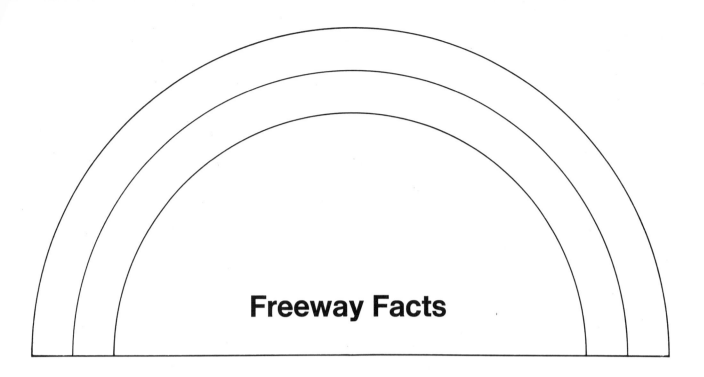

Freeway Facts

Best looking: Interstate 280 from San Francisco south toward San Jose.

Best view: Although much criticized for despoiling the downtown San Francisco landscape, the Embarcardero Freeway (S.R. 480) offers a terrific view of San Francisco Bay.

Best off-ramp: The Santa Monica Freeway off-ramp hooking up with the San Diego Freeway is a masterpiece.

Best mountain pass: The best freeway over the mountains is Interstate 80 through Donner Pass, closely followed by Interstate 5 through Tejon Pass.

Best hill: The first few miles of Interstate 5 south of the Oregon border provide a great ride down through the Siskiyou Mountains.

Most spacious: Except on weekends, the Interstate 880 Sacramento bypass is wide open and offers your choice of lanes. A close runner-up is the eastern edge of the Ventura Freeway (S.R. 134) coming out of Pasadena.

Ugliest: Interstate 5 from Wheeler Ridge to the Los Banos exit is the most boring ride in the state.

Worst intersection: Interstate 580 and S.R. 238 in Castro Valley. If you are coming from the east and want to continue on 580, you must cut directly across two lanes of on-ramp traffic carrying many cars heading left to get on S.R. 238. This leads daily to fascinating games of chicken.

Worst truck traffic: If you like being tailgated by speeding semis, try S.R. 99 in the San Joaquin Valley, between Fresno and Turlock. Runner-up is the Nimitz Freeway (S.R. 17) from Oakland down the east side of San Francisco Bay—big with diesels.

Worst on-ramps: Merging lanes are nonexistent at many points on the outmoded Pasadena Freeway. The short ramps dump you right into 55-miles-per-hour traffic.

Worst tie-ups: A lot of candidates here, but for sheer frustration try the San Diego Freeway in the vicinity of the Los Angeles Airport on the eve of a holiday weekend.

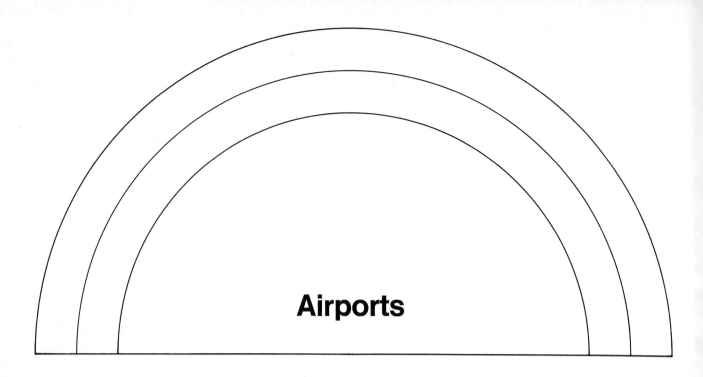

Airports

As long as you don't use Los Angeles International (LAX) late at night and avoid San Diego's Lindbergh Field whenever possible, you shouldn't have to fear flying in California. The former airport, which is blessed with long, long runways and a generally good reputation has recently driven pilots to apoplexy by requiring jets to land to the east from midnight to 6:30 AM, while others are taking off to the west. This strange rule, inspired by efforts at noise abatement, forces planes to fly toward each other in darkness with only a few thousand feet of separation.

Southern California's other major commercial terminal, San Diego, is, in the opinion of many pilots, America's worst major airport. Its short main runway lies at the bottom of a hill. To land, a pilot must navigate among downtown skyscrapers and skim numerous rooftops. Remarkably, the airport's accident rate isn't bad. Pilots attribute this to luck.

However, there is a positive side to this aviator's nightmare. San Diego offers a superb vantage point for seeing the planes come in. Many downtown office buildings and hotels like the El Cortez offer stunning closeups of the landing aircraft. The best of these is Mister A's, a restaurant atop an office building at Fifth and Laurel. This is jet-watching at its finest. The planes fly past at eye level just three to four blocks away, and at night they regularly illuminate the darkened dining room with their landing lights. If noise doesn't bother you, take a table out on the patio. Here it's almost as if you can reach out and touch the wings of airliners flashing past toward the runway below.

There's nothing comparable at Northern California's major terminal, San Francisco International. Here you'll find relatively unobstructed over-water approaches and lengthy runways. Unfortunately, traffic is heavy at times and many people prefer using the Oakland Airport, located 24 miles southeast of downtown San Francisco. In Oakland, as in San Jose, another regional airport 50 miles south of San Francisco, there are numerous in-state and some out-of-state flights. Facilities are excellent, waiting is minimal, the walk to the gate is shorter, and parking is cheaper.

Los Angeles also has a number of satellite airports with commercial traffic. The busiest is the Hollywood-Burbank terminal, about 20 miles northwest of downtown Los Angeles. This just may be the ugliest airport in America. Arrival is always a thrill because the airport is completely surrounded by subdivisions. Just when you think you're about to land at the deep end of some stranger's pool, the plane skips a fence and touches down on a short runway hemmed in by a Lockheed factory. Take a wrong door inside the terminal, and you may find someone trying to sell you a L-1011.

Although this facility is designed to offer a sane alternative to bustling Los Angeles International, it is often jammed at rush hours. More hospitable are the Ontario, Long Beach, and Orange County airports. All three offer in-state flights, and Ontario, located about 40 miles east of downtown Los Angeles, has service to a number of major destinations out of state. Ontario, in the heart of the region's worst pollution, is the perfect airport to choose if you want to get an introduction to Southern California smog. Orange County is the best airport for Disneyland, Knott's Berry Farm, California

Planes are forced to skim San Diego rooftops on landing approaches to Lindbergh Field. Many pilots consider it America's worst major commercial airport.

Alligator Farm, and the Movieland Wax Museum. Long Beach is convenient if you are heading out toward Catalina Island or the *Queen Mary.*

One word of warning about these satellite airports: all handle heavy general aviation traffic. In fact, Orange County is the second busiest airport in the United States from the standpoint of total traffic; Long Beach ranks fourth, and San Jose is tenth. While they are generally more convenient than the big terminals, it can be unnerving to watch some novice backing his single-engine flyswatter up to your window. This is no joke; at Orange County, one confused aviator misread the controller's instructions a few years back and dove straight for the tower. The terrified air traffic man abandoned his post and dove beneath a desk. The pilot missed—barely.

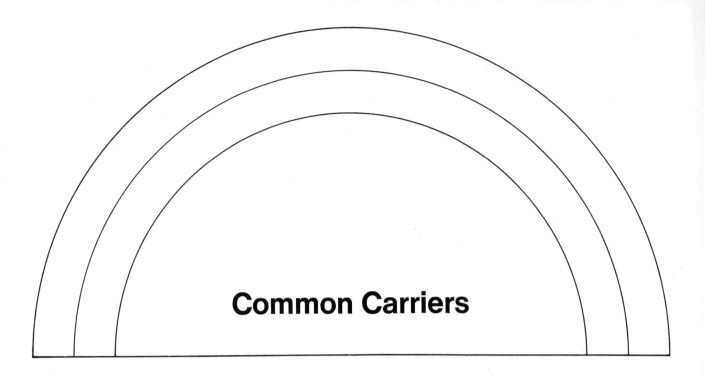

Common Carriers

With the cost of operating a private automobile pushing fifteen cents a mile, more Californians are turning away from jammed highways in favor of mass transit. Although service is still not up to the level once provided by such firm's as the Bay Area's Key Line or Los Angeles' old Pacific Electric, major improvements have been made in recent years.

The best urban mass transit in the state is found in the San Francisco region, where Bay Area Rapid Transit (BART), Southern Pacific Railroad, Golden Gate Transit's bus and ferry service, Greyhound, and A/C Transit all deliver commuters to San Francisco, where they can then pick up local MUNI buses, streetcars, and cable cars to their destinations. Despite frequent computer-caused delays and high prices ($1.80 round trip from Berkeley to San Francisco), BART remains a sensible alternative to driving during commuting hours. Resolution of safety problems, addition of new equipment, and development of more lines (the system is essentially a commuter line with only one route in San Francisco proper) will make BART a better bet in coming years. Another sore spot is the Southern Pacific route's weekday commuter service down the peninsula to San Mateo County. The railroad is hoping to turn this money-losing system plagued by limited, inefficient service over to a public agency that will expand the line.

One important plus in this area is Golden Gate Transit, which operates special weekend buses from San Francisco to popular Marin County destinations like the Point Reyes National Seashore. Golden Gate ferry service to Sausalito and the Harbor Tours ride to Tiburon are also good excursion trips. Inexpensive airport service is also provided from downtown San Francisco by the Airporter limousine. For more money, you can reach San Francisco Airport from Marin City, Emeryville (Berkeley), and Oakland via SFO Helicopter. During rush hours this approach is a good way to beat traffic jams, and naturally there's a great aerial view. Be sure to take advantage of special SFO discounts offered to those who buy their airline and helicopter tickets together before arriving at the airport. This line also operates excursion sightseeing trips over its regular route system.

Although it is possible to reach virtually all urban destinations by public transit in the Bay Area, transferring can be a problem, particularly at late hours. The San Francisco bus, train, and mass transit systems all use separate terminals, though there are plans to establish a common bus station. Complicating the situation is the fact that BART service has generally been limited to weekdays from 6 AM to about 11 PM. Extensive legal and safety problems have clouded plans for expanded service.

In Southern California, rapid transit remains in the planning stage, but both Los Angeles and San Diego have extensive bus services that can get you to most major destinations. Thanks to express service, bus lanes, and special subscription buses (where workers headed to the same place in effect charter their own bus), public transportation can compete effectively with the private car on many commuter rush hour runs.

Probably the best existing system is the El Monte Busway that links San Gabriel Valley commuters with downtown Los Angeles.

For visitors, express service makes it easy to get from the downtown terminal to major destinations like Disneyland. However, trips via local Los Angeles lines to lesser known destinations will probably send you reeling toward a rental car agency within a couple of days. The only sensible way around this problem is to keep moving your base of operation so that you are always within easy striking distance of all the local attractions.

In San Diego, much of this distance problem is eliminated. Most of the city's major attractions are within 10 miles of downtown. A plus is that the fare to any destination in the system is a modest thirty-five cents.

Although there are major inadequacies in California's urban transit network, interurban transit is excellent. Greyhound operates an extensive system throughout the state, and Amtrak links major coastal and valley cities through two major north-south lines. In addition, commuter train service is becoming a reality between San Diego and Los Angeles thanks to increased service on the scenic South Coastal run.

Scheduled intrastate airline service in California is probably the best in the nation. Although low air commuter fares pioneered by Pacific Southwest Airlines (PSA) have shot up in recent years, discount plans still make the Los Angeles–San Francisco run one of the most inexpensive air trips in the nation. In addition to hourly service operated between these cities by PSA and United, a number of other airlines have extensive schedules on this route. Additional flights from Oakland and San Jose to Burbank, Ontario, and Orange County (Air California has good service to this latter area) add to air travel flexibility between the two metropolitan regions.

Although PSA is the leading intrastate carrier, some travelers prefer using airlines with a lighter load factor on the Los Angeles–San Francisco trip. They find Western, TWA, or Air West flights frequently offer a bit more elbow room. The only problem is that none of these airlines match PSA's saturation scheduling.

California Parlor Car Tours. These deluxe bus tours to such places as San Simeon, Monterey, Yosemite, and the Lake Tahoe area run from three to five days. Routes include the Big Sur Coast, which is not served by scheduled commercial bus lines. For information write the firm's main office, c/o Jack Tar Hotel, Van Ness at Geary, San Francisco, CA 94101.

Extensive scheduled air service, via various airlines, links the San Diego, Palm Springs, Stockton, Sacramento, and the Lake Tahoe areas with Bay Area and Los Angeles airports at relatively modest fares. Air West also provides services to smaller communities like Eureka, Redding, Santa Maria, Monterey, and El Centro, while United flies to such San Joaquin Valley towns as Bakersfield, Visalia, and Merced. However, fares to these cities are considerably higher than those between the aforementioned towns. That's because there's little or no competition on these routes from low fare minded intrastate carriers like PSA.

Common Carrier Notes

The Southern California Rapid Transit District's *Guide for Going Places* is a useful map that will put you on the way to all major destinations. It's available through the District Ticket Office, 1060 South Broadway, Los Angeles, CA 90015. You can also get a transportation guide explaining how to use planes, trains, and buses to visit 155 cities in Southern California through the Southern California Visitors' Council, 705 West 7th Street, Los Angeles, CA 90017.

In the Bay Area, public transit information is available through the *San Francisco Walk-Ride Guide,* published by the San Francisco Convention and Visitors' Bureau, 1309 Market Street, San Francisco, CA 94102.

For a copy of the San Diego transit route map, write the San Diego Convention and Visitors' Bureau, 1200 Third Avenue, Suite 824, San Diego, CA 92101.

Transit Phone Numbers

Los Angeles
Rapid Transit District: 747-4455
Greyhound: 620-1200
Amtrak: 800-648-3850

San Francisco
San Francisco Municipal Railway: 673-6861
Bay Area Rapid Transit: 788-2278
Golden Gate Transit: 322-6600
A/C Transit: 653-3335
Southern Pacific Transportation Company: 981-4700
   (weekdays), 362-1212 (all other times)
Greyhound: 433-1500
Amtrak: 800-648-3850

San Diego
San Diego Transit: 239-8161
Greyhound: 279-1884
Amtrak: 800-648-3850

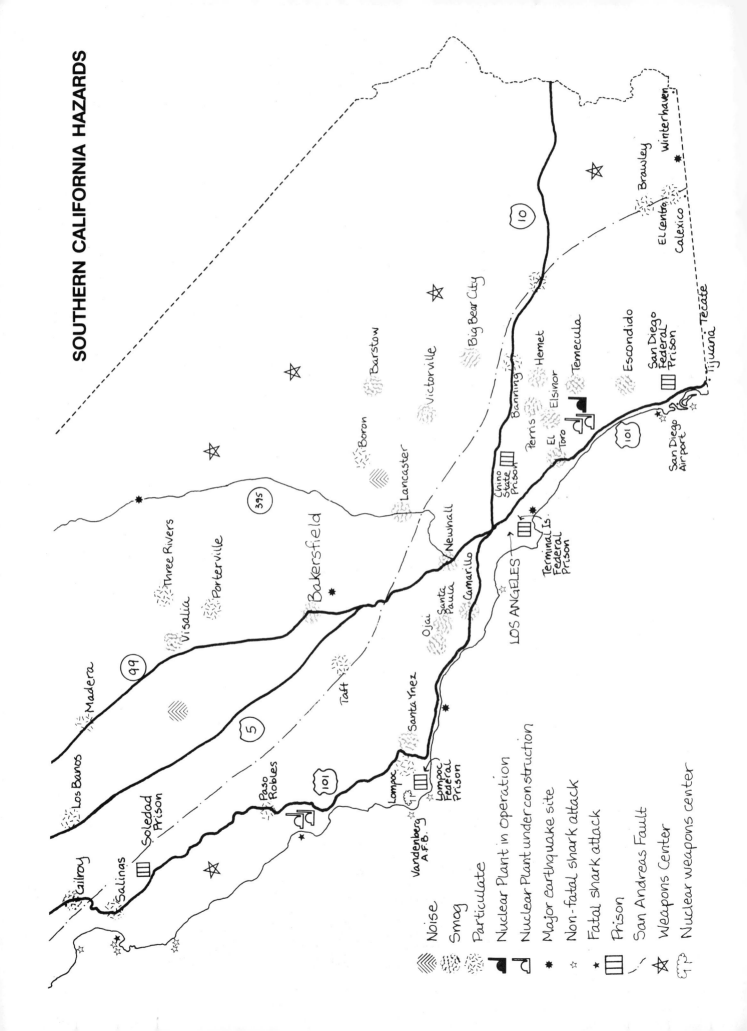

PART THREE: PARANOIA

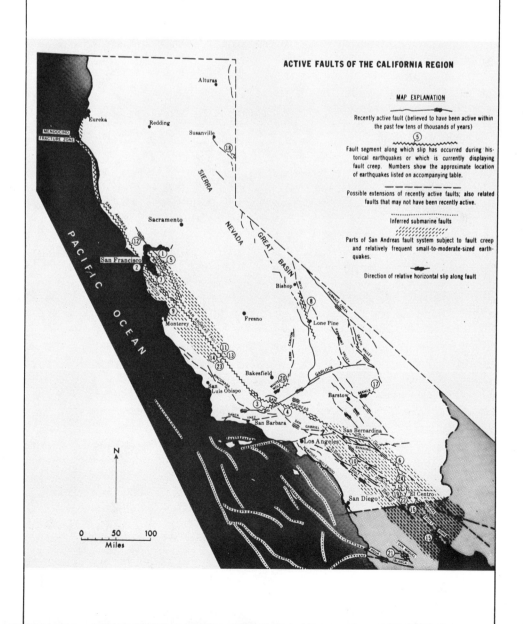

ACTIVE FAULTS OF THE CALIFORNIA REGION

MAP EXPLANATION

Recently active fault (believed to have been active within the past few tens of thousands of years)

Fault segment along which slip has occurred during historical earthquakes or which is currently displaying fault creep. Numbers show the approximate location of earthquakes listed on accompanying table.

Possible extensions of recently active faults; also related faults that may not have been recently active.

Inferred submarine faults

Parts of San Andreas fault system subject to fault creep and relatively frequent small-to-moderate-sized earthquakes.

Direction of relative horizontal slip along fault

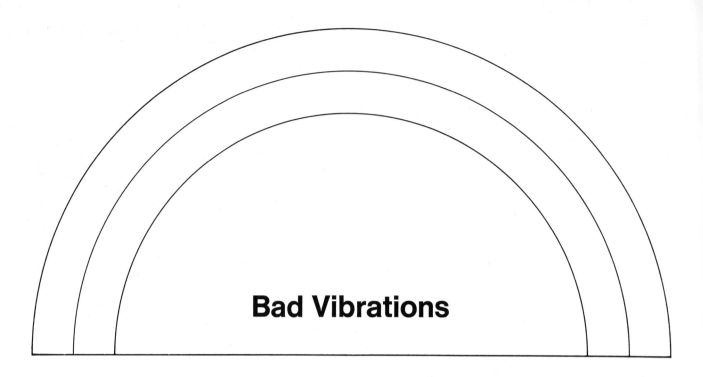

Bad Vibrations

When? Where? Why?

No one knows when the next big earthquake will hit, and it's doubtful that scientists will be able to develop predictive mechanisms before that catastrophe occurs. But most experts believe that a major quake could happen along the San Andreas fault zone at any time.

The San Andreas is the backbone of the state's fault system. It runs about 650 miles through most of the length of California, passing 33 miles east, at its closest point, of downtown Los Angeles and under the Gulf of the Farallones in the ocean just west of San Francisco. The land masses on opposite sides of the fault are moving in different directions: the land on the east side is moving southeast, and the land on the west is going northwest. Eventually, the land that is now Los Angeles and the land that is now San Francisco might be expected to converge. However, since the present rate of movement is only about 0.5 inch per year, it will be many millions of years before we can look forward to a new Golden Gate Bridge linking San Francisco and Burbank.

The northern part of the San Andreas fault zone has not moved significantly since 1906. But most experts think that the accumulating pressure caused by the opposing forces will eventually overcome the elasticity of the rocks along the fault. On that day, the masses of rock on either side will scrape past one another, producing another big earthquake. This quake could hit anywhere along the fault, but obviously its effects would be most disastrous in heavily populated areas. Many people have the impression that the San Andreas fault is responsible for all California earthquakes. In reality, the state is honeycombed with major and minor faults, any one of which is capable of producing a locally intense shock. There is, literally, no place in California where you can be completely "safe" from earthquakes, though some places may be safer than others. Wherever you live, you can help to minimize damage and prevent panic by taking some precautions before the next good-sized quake hits your area.

Buying a House

If you are buying a house in a new subdivision, you'll find relevant fault information in the California Division of Mines and Geology report that is part of the Department of Real Estate's *Final Subdivision Public Report*. Should the subdivision be located on a known fault, the builder must report it here.

If you are a second buyer of a home in a subdivision built after 1966, you can obtain a copy of the *Final Subdivision Public Report* by writing to the California Department of Real Estate, 714 P Street, Sacramento, CA 95814. Ask for the report by county and number of subdivision.

If you are buying a house built before 1966, information may not be easy to obtain. Until that time the state did not require builders to note fault information on subdivision reports. Your best bet would be to visit or write to the California Division of Mines and Geology, with main offices at 107 South Broadway, Los Angeles, and the Ferry Building, San Francisco. Twenty-seven regional maps showing approximate locations of known California faults are sold for $1.50 apiece. Unfortunately, these maps won't give you precise information.

But if you visit on Thursday afternoon or on Friday, you'll find a geologist on duty to answer public inquiries. He'll have his own detailed maps of certain areas that might help pinpoint the relationship of known faults to a house you have in mind.

Many people think that, in terms of earthquake resistance, the worst site for a house is high on a hill. Not necessarily, says UCLA structural engineering professor C. Martin Duke, who also heads the Earthquake Engineering Research Institute. Duke says that if you're looking for a homesite, "the best place to build is on top of a clear rock ridge." Of course, you probably won't be able to find one of those, but you should still opt for the hardest ground available. A solidly built house on a bedrock hillside is preferable to an identical structure built on flatland fill.

The U.S. Geological Survey rates metamorphic rock, greenstone, shale, chert, sandstone, gabbro-diabase, and serpentine as having high earthquake stability. Landslide deposits, artificial fill, bay mud, beach deposits, and sand all rate poor to fair. A competent geologist should be able to make sure your homesite is good solid ground.

Earthquake History of the United States. For a complete list of significant California earthquakes (above VI on the Mercali intensity scale), get a copy of the U.S. Department of Commerce's *Earthquake History of the U.S.* A fifty-two-page section gives extensive detail on quake activity in California and western Nevada. Send $2.80 to Superintendent of Documents, U.S. Government Printing Office, Washington, D.C. 20402. Stock number of the book is 0319–00019. Publication number is 41–1.

If you're planning a custom-built home, select a reliable architect and give him orders for a conventional frame house bolted down to a reinforced concrete foundation. No 20-foot ceilings, picture windows, parapets, big archways, or towering chimneys. You want a simple house with lots of medium-sized rooms, which mean more walls and bracing. Two diagonal braces should run the length of each wall. Rafters should be anchored into the walls. Roofing should be of some fire-resistant lightweight material rather than heavy tiles. Flexible utility connections will help prevent gas, power, or water leaks. Water heaters should be situated away from exits and as low in the house as possible, preferably in the garage. Under no circumstances should you allow unreinforced masonry to be used on or in the house. "The key thing to bear in mind when building an earthquake-resistant house in California," says Dr. Duke, "is to keep it simple."

Is Your Present Home Safe?

If you are not directly on top of a known active fault, the quality and foundation of your home are the most important safety factors. A solidly built house just 0.5 mile from the fault line is probably safer than a shoddily built one 10 miles away. But if you live in one of the thousands of structures that sit directly on top of the fault itself, even a moderate earthquake could break the building apart.

If you are certain that you live on a fault line, you should think about getting out. Someday it may be possible to convince the state or federal government to condemn these houses and compensate the owners. What would be done with the fault zone once the houses were torn down? Dr. Bruce Bolt, director of the University of California seismographic station at Berkeley, suggests that the San Andreas fault could be turned into a fine golf course.

Houses built of unreinforced masonry are dangerous anywhere in California, and residents of these structures should also move out, if they can. Old, unreinforced brick, cement, and adobe buildings have been responsible for most of the damage to people and property in earthquakes around the world.

High Rises

Are high-rise office buildings dangerous in a quake? It depends. If the structure is built of unreinforced masonry, it probably is a serious hazard in a quake. Even new buildings, like the Olive View Hospital, which collapsed in the 1971 San Fernando earthquake, are vulnerable if hit hard enough. Perhaps the best guidelines so far were provided by the July 1967 quake in Caracas, Venezuela. A report by California's Division of Mines and Geology points out that nearly all the estimated 1000 high-rise buildings erected there during the previous decade were "built on code provi-

sions that were based on California practice." Only four of these buildings collapsed; yet these failures accounted for 200 of the 277 fatalities in the quake. The point is that high-rise buildings are relatively safe, but like any structure, will fail if particularly hard hit. Dr. Charles Richter has argued for a thirty-story limit on buildings throughout the state, primarily to reduce density in downtown areas, where evacuation and falling debris could be critical problems.

If you live in an old, unreinforced masonry apartment building, try to move out. Your local building department should be able to tell you whether your building is reinforced. If you must live in a multistory building, choose an apartment on the upper floor of a wood frame or stucco structure. Ground floors did not fare well in the 1971 San Fernando quake.

Before the Earthquake

Dr. Charles Richter says: "There are only a few small steps an individual can take to reduce his risk in a

This collapsed overpass resulted from the February 9, 1971, San Francisco earthquake. (*U.S. Department of Interior, Geological Survey*)

future earthquake; but some of them are simple and may mean great savings."

Preparations begin with a fire extinguisher, first-aid kit, battery-operated lantern, and portable radio. Then invite the gas company or fire department to check for leaky gas connections or defective wiring that could be dangerous in a quake.

Next, brace the water heater and put all your bottled goods into securely latched cabinets. Remove brick and board bookcases, make sure shelves are securely fastened to the walls, and place big objects on the lower shelves. Anchor overhead lighting fixtures with wire; old, inverted-bowl chandeliers are particularly vulnerable. Deep plaster cracks should be investigated and repaired if necessary. Do not use the basement as a makeshift bedroom if it wasn't originally designed for occupancy. Make sure no beds are within range of a chimney that might come crashing through the house.

Sit down with your family, particularly with the children, and explain earthquake precautions. Everyone ought to know (and surprisingly few people do know) how to turn off electricity, gas, and water at the main connections. If wrenches are required, know which ones they are and keep them handy.

During the Earthquake

The best place to be during an intense earthquake is in an open field, as long as you are not wtihin range of falling debris. But if you are indoors, stay there. People who rush out of buildings when an earthquake begins may get clobbered by toppling facings, parapets, and chimneys. Getting under a doorway, table, desk, or other solid object is good protection as long as you are away from windows that may shatter. Watch out for falling plaster, bricks, light fixtures, high bookcases, china cabinets, and heavy furniture that might slide or topple. Try to remember that the earth does not open up and consume buildings. Think of yourself as being on the deck of a ship.

If you are in a busy store, don't rush for the doors because many other people will have the same idea. Don't get in the elevator; it may go out of order. If you are outside, get away from buildings whose facing could fall off and from power poles and big signs that might topple. Don't run through the streets. Try to move to an open area.

If you are driving a car, slow down, pull to the side of the road and wait. Do not get out of the car. The vehicle will jiggle a great deal, but it's a fairly safe place to be until the shaking stops.

If you're in the bathtub, stay put. Actually, it's not a bad place to be. One woman really did ride out the disastrous 1964 Alaska earthquake in her tub. Her house slid down a hill and broke up, but she just hung on to the tub and came out fine. The bathroom in general is a fairly secure location during a quake. It's usually a small room with solid walls and lots of piping to hold everything together. Even if the room does break up, you can jump in the tub and be fairly well protected.

After the Earthquake

- Check the family for injuries, but don't try to move anyone who is seriously injured unless he might be hurt by falling debris.
- Keep the family together if you can. After the February 9, 1971, quake, many parents took their children to a "safe place" and told them to stay there while the parents checked for damage. According to the San Fernando Valley Child Guidance Clinic, many children became terrified when parents left them alone. The clinic advises that children be told repeatedly, "Nothing is going to happen to us."
- Look for fires.
- If you smell gas in the house, follow these steps. Turn off the gas at the meter and open all the windows. Evacuate the house, and notify the gas company if possible. Do not use matches, lighters, or other open-flame appliances. Do not attempt to turn the gas back on by yourself. Wait for the gas company to check for damage.
- If you suspect damage to one of your utilities, don't use any of them until all have been pronounced safe. Even if your wiring is all right, you may get a shock if you use electricity before broken water lines are repaired. Activating electrical switches also can ignite leaking gas.
- Do not touch any wet appliances that are plugged in until you are sure that the electrical power has been turned off. Then unplug them and allow them to dry thoroughly before using them again.
- If you have any doubts about the safety of your water supply (the water probably is all right if it runs clear from your tap and smells and tastes the way it normally does), emergency drinking water can be taken from water heaters and softeners, toilet tanks, and ice trays. It's a good idea to keep a supply of drinkable water on hand stored in tightly covered, unbreakable containers.
- Wear sturdy, rubber-soled shoes while picking up debris. This protects you from shock hazards. Don't wander around barefoot or in bedroom slippers; your feet may be cut by broken glass.
- Use caution when cleaning up spilled flammable or toxic liquids.
- Check the chimney from a distance. If it appears cracked or wobbly, stay clear until you can have it dismantled by professionals.

- Do not eat anything from open containers near shattered glass. Liquids can be strained through a handkerchief or cloth to screen out glass debris.
- If the electricity is off, plan meals to use up foods that will spoil quickly in your freezer.
- Open closets and cupboard doors slowly to prevent objects from toppling to the floor.
- Do not flush the toilet before you are certain that sewage lines are intact.
- Don't touch downed power lines or anything that is in contact with them.
- Use a portable radio for emergency information.
- Do not spread rumors.
- If your telephone is working, use only for genuine emergencies.
- Remember that aftershocks are sometimes strong enough to cause additional damage.
- Help the police, firefighters, and relief organizations if (and only if) they ask for volunteers.
- Thou shalt not sightsee.

Animals

Roving packs of stray dogs were troublemakers after the San Fernando quake. Dr. Benjamin Hart, an animal behavior specialist at the University of California's Davis campus, suggests that family dogs and cats be confined to the house or yard for several days after a quake. Even after the animals have calmed down, watch them closely. Aftershocks could frighten them all over again and set them running. Be particularly careful with trained watchdogs that might get loose and attack at random in the post-quake confusion. Watch out for strange dogs in the neighborhood; they are more likely to bite you during these trying times. If you do get bitten, be certain to have the animal checked for rabies.

Insurance

In New Zealand, every homeowner pays a few dollars a year into a special government fund that insures against earthquake damage. California should—but doesn't—have a similar fund, because commercial earthquake insurance is of dubious value to most people. If you qualify, insurers will sell you quake protection at roughly twice the cost of regular homeowner's insurance. Since most policies contain a 5 percent deductible clause (which means that the first $2000 of damage to a $40,000 house isn't covered), normal light damage such as cracked walls and broken windows would not be covered. Policies also exclude damage to exterior masonry veneer (other than stucco), as well as any loss caused by a quake-related flood or tsunami

(tidal wave). Ask your congressman or state legislator to support provisions that would require earthquake insurance to be made widely available at reasonable cost.

Will California Fall into the Sea?

Not a chance. There will be no surfing off the coast of Nevada, because California will not tumble into the Pacific. This Armageddon myth has no basis in fact. However, there is a real danger of coastal landslides and an earthquake-generated tidal wave, which is one reason to keep clear of low-lying coastal areas immediately after an earthquake. Stay away from the beach until competent authorities have issued an all clear. In May 1960, sixty-one people in Hilo, Hawaii, heard a tsunami warning and decided to walk down to the shore to watch it come in. They all drowned.

Safety Pockets

No place in California is safe from earthquake danger. Dr. Richter says: "Every part of the state is shaken from time to time. Risk is less on solid rock, as in the mountains; but most cities, towns, and settled areas are on soft ground where the risk is relatively high." If you really want to avoid any risk, buy a trailer and move to Florida—but watch out for hurricanes.

Sunset. Home, garden, cooking, and travel information on California and the West. A year's subscription costs $5 in California, Oregon, Washington, Arizona, Idaho, Nevada, Utah, Hawaii, and Alaska. For all other American addresses, the price is $6. Send orders to *Sunset* Magazine, Menlo Park, CA 94025.

Light Earthquake
Reading and Viewing

Robert Iacopi's *Earthquake Country* (Lane Book Company, Menlo Park) is the best general book on California earthquake phenomenology. Peter Yanev's *Peace of Mind in Earthquake Country* (Chronicle Books, 870 Market St., San Francisco) offers excellent practical advice. Dr. Charles Richter's *Elementary Seismology* (W. H. Freeman and Company, 660 Market St., San Francisco) offers a more technical study, but Chapters 24 and 28 should be useful to the layman. William Bronson's *The Earth Shook, the Sky Burned* (Doubleday, Garden City, New York) offers good pictures and text on the 1906 San Francisco earthquake and fire.

Three good pamphlets are available locally from the U.S. Geological Survey. *Safety and Survival in an Earthquake* offers household hints; *Earthquake* discusses the general risk; and *The San Andreas Fault* explains California's prime quake threat.

Dr. Richter's pamphlet, *Our Earthquake Risk,* answers many general questions about the subject. Write to the Seismological Laboratory, California Institute of Technology, 1201 E. California Blvd., Pasadena, CA 91109.

For fifty cents you can get a special issue of *California Geology* magazine devoted to the 1971 San Fernando quake. It's available from the California Division of Mines and Geology, 1416 Ninth Street, Sacramento, CA 95814.

And if you want a good scare, go see a revival of the movie *San Francisco* with Clark Gable and Jeanette MacDonald, a reenactment of the 1906 earthquake and fire. When it was first released, it sent audiences screaming from the theaters.

California's Major Nineteenth-and Twentieth- Century Earthquakes

California Earthquake, December 21, 1812

Time of occurrence: About 11:00.

Epicenter: 34°N, 120°W, probably offshore in the province of the Transverse Ranges.

Area affected: Total felt area unknown.

Intensity: X (on a scale of I to XII).

Description: This shock was damaging in Santa Barbara, Ventura, and northern Los Angeles counties. A strong and damaging foreshock at about 10:30 alarmed inhabitants and sent them fleeing from buildings. This undoubtedly saved many lives when the main shock came. Some people were injured, but no deaths were reported. The church of Purisima Mission and many of the mission buildings were destroyed. At Santa Ynez Mission, a corner of the church fell, all roofs were ruined, walls cracked, and many new homes were demolished. At Santa Barbara, all mission buildings were severely damaged and the church was later rebuilt.

San Francisco Earthquake, June 1838

Time of occurrence: Just after noon.

Epicenter: 37°N, 122.5°W, San Francisco region.

Area affected: Considerable; total felt area unknown.

Intensity: X.

Description: This shock was comparable to the earthquake of April 18, 1906. Extensive displacements were reported along the San Andreas fault. At Yerba Buena, the shock was violent; walls were severely damaged at the missions of San Francisco, Santa Clara, and San Jose, and at the presidio of San Francisco.

Southern California Earthquake, January 9, 1857

Time of occurrence: About 08.00.

Epicenter: 35°N, 119°W, near Fort Tejon.

Area Affected: Considerable; total felt area unknown.

Intensity: X to XI.

Description: Violent shock. A ground crack 40 miles long was observed in the vicinity of Fort Tejon, an army post about 4 miles from the San Andreas fault between Los Angeles and San Francisco. Near Tejon, a corral was converted by horizontal dislocation of the ground into an open S-shaped figure; at the fort, buildings and large trees were thrown down. The roof of the mission church at Ventura collapsed. Artesian wells in the Santa Clara Valley (near Ventura) ceased to flow.

Owens Valley Earthquake, March 26, 1872

Time of occurrence: About 02:30.

Epicenter: 36°N, 118°W, Owens Valley, near Lone Pine.

Area affected: Felt strongly over 125,000 square miles; total felt area unknown.

Intensity: X to XI.

Description: The shock was felt over most of California, and probably most of Nevada and Arizona. It was very destructive in the Owens Valley and severe along the western slopes of the Sierra Nevadas, in the Mojave Desert, and in the eastern part of the Great Valley of California. The most disastrous effects of the earthquake were at Lone Pine, where twenty-seven were killed and fifty-six injured. Of fifty-nine houses, fifty-two were destroyed. Near Owens Lake, numerous depressions formed between cracks in the earth. In one place, an area 200 to 300 feet wide sank 20 to 30 feet, leaving vertical walls.

San Francisco Earthquake, April 18, 1906

Time of occurrence: 05:12.

Epicenter: 38°N, 123°W, northwest of San Francisco.

Area affected: Destructive intensity extended 400 miles; felt over 375,000 square miles, including water area.

Magnitude: 8.3.*

Intensity: XI.

Description: This was one of the greatest known shocks in California. It was associated with the largest known length of sideways slip along a fault plane in the contiguous United States. The observed extent of displacement on the San Andreas fault was about 180 miles in a N35°W direction. Assuming that the slip in the Cape Mendocino region is an extension of this, the total distance was 270 miles from San Juan in San Benito County to Telegraph Hill in Humboldt County. The greatest slip, 21 feet, was in Marin County. In many places, dislocation of fences and roads indicated the amount of movement. Motion of 10 to 15 feet was not uncommon.

The region of destructive intensity extended 400 miles. The total felt area included most of California and parts of Nevada and Oregon. On or near the primary rift, buildings were destroyed and trees uprooted or broken off. One house was torn apart. Roads crossing the fault line were rendered impassable, and pipelines were broken. This had an important effect in San Francisco, as lack of water supply let the fire get out of control, although it probably would have done so in

* The magnitude, as measured by the Richter scale, relates to the amount of energy actually released by an earthquake; the Mercali scale of intensity assesses the effects of a shock at a particular location. A quake of magnitude 2 is the smallest normally felt by human beings; the largest ever recorded was 8.9. Each whole number increase represents a ten-fold jump in earthquake size.

any case. The amount of damage was unevenly distributed owing to subsurface conditions.

Buildings and structures in all parts of the city and county of San Francisco were damaged. In small districts on man-made land, where the intensity was augmented, pavements were buckled, arched, and fissured; brick and frame houses of ordinary construction were severely damaged or destroyed; sewers and water mains were broken; and heavy streetcar tracks were bent into wavelike forms.

At Santa Rosa, although 19 miles from the rift, destruction was great, and the intensity was higher than at most other points at comparable distances. Vibrations from the shock were also felt on offshore vessels.

The great shock and resulting fires caused at least 700 deaths, including 50 in Santa Rosa. According to figures compiled many years afterward by John R. Freeman, earthquake damage was $20 million in San Francisco and $4 million outside the city, but these estimates appear low.

Imperial Valley Earthquake, May 18, 1940

Time of occurrence: 20:37.

Epicenter: 32.7°N, 115.5°W, southeast of El Centro.

Area affected: Some 60,000 square miles in the United States (including Arizona and Nevada) and an unknown area in Mexico.

Magnitude: 7.1.

Intensity: X.

The San Francisco earthquake of April 18, 1906— and the subsequent fires—caused at least 700 deaths. (*Courtesy, The Bancroft Library*)

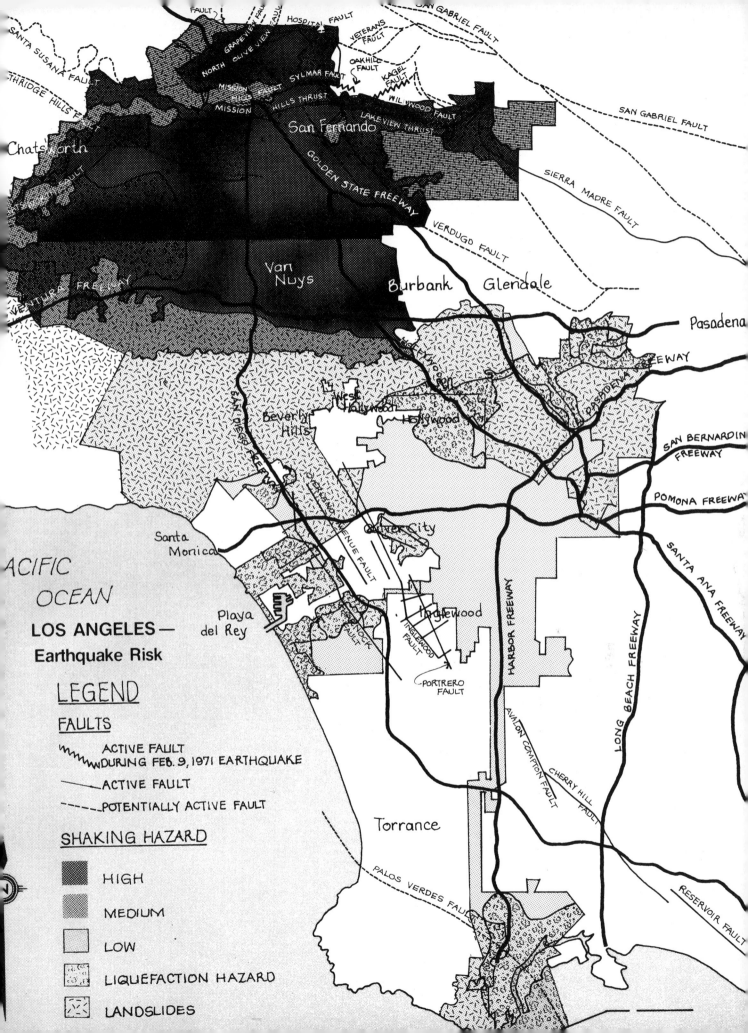

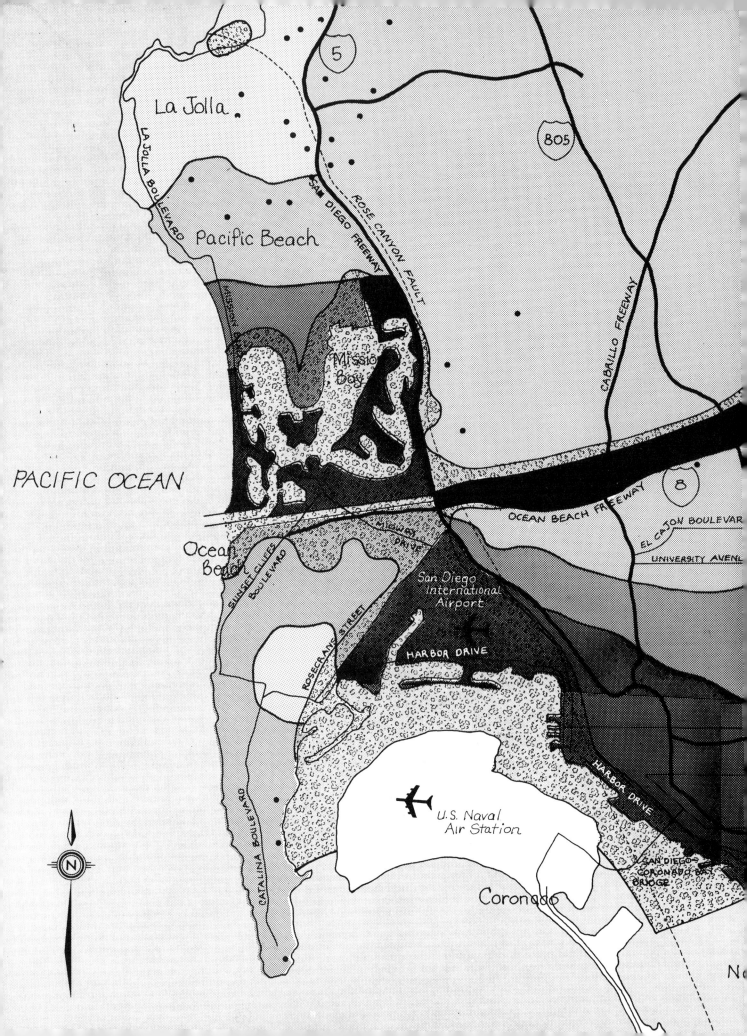

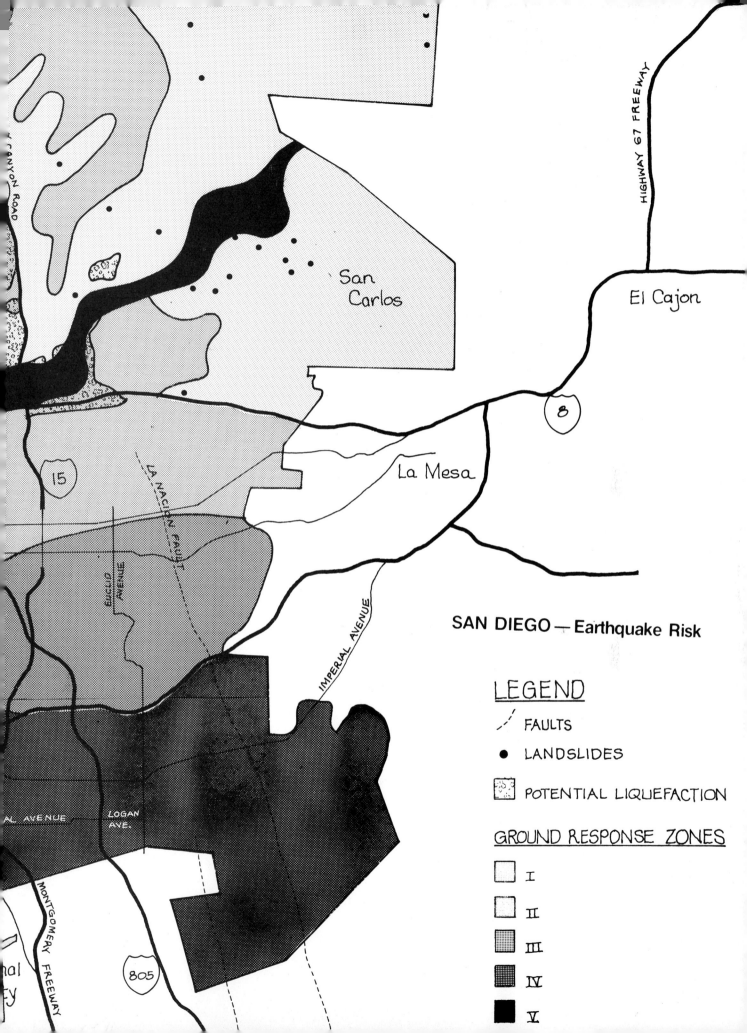

SAN DIEGO — Earthquake Risk

LEGEND

∕ FAULTS

● LANDSLIDES

▨ POTENTIAL LIQUEFACTION

GROUND RESPONSE ZONES

☐ I

☐ II

▨ III

▨ IV

■ V

SAN FRANCISCO — Earthquake Risk

LEGEND

DOTTED LINES ENCLOSE LANDSLIDE
LOCATIONS (AREAS OF
POTENTIAL LANDSLIDE HAZARD)

AREAS OF POTENTIAL
LIQUEFACTION HAZARD

STRONG

VERY STRONG

VIOLENT

MOST VIOLENT

Description: The epicenter was located southeast of El Centro, but there was surface slipping with surface rupture over a known distance of 40 miles. Horizontal displacement reached 15 feet near the border. Vertical displacements up to 4 feet were observed. There was damage at all towns in the Imperial Valley; canals were damaged, causing serious interruption to water service in a region that depends on irrigation for crops. Indirect loss of crops was considerable; direct earthquake loss in the United States was on the order of $6 million. Nine lives were lost.

At Imperial, the city water tanks collapsed, and 80 percent of the buildings were damaged. An estimated 40 percent of Brawley's buildings were damaged, and Holtville's water tank collapsed.

Kern County Earthquake, July 21, 1952

Time of occurrence: 03:52.

Epicenter: 35.0°N, 119.0°W, south of Bakersfield.

Area affected: About 160,000 square miles.

Magnitude: 7.7.

Intensity: XI.

Description: This was the main shock of the Kern County series and the largest earthquake in the United States since 1906. Damage to property was estimated at $50 million. Intensity XI effects were observed in a very small area on the Southern Pacific Railroad near Bealville. Reinforced concrete tunnels with walls 18 inches thick were cracked, twisted, and caved in. The distance between portals of two tunnels was shortened about 8 feet in 300 feet. Rails were shifted and bent into S-shaped curves. Urban intensities, however, did not exceed intensity VIII. Twelve persons were killed, nine of these at Tehachapi in the collapse of a brick wall. Eighteen persons were hospitalized, and several hundred were given first-aid treatment. Near Caliente, reinforced concrete railroad tunnels were demolished. South of Arvin, concrete irrigation pipe systems shattered, many fields required releveling, and hundreds of electric power transformers fell from elevated platforms. Near Wheeler Ridge, 10-inch-diameter steel pipelines were pulled apart and, in one case, telescoped 42 inches. Several million dollars' worth of damage resulted at the Paloma Cycling Plant from a fire ignited by a broken gas line. At Arvin, Bakersfield, and Tehachapi, old and poorly built masonry and adobe buildings were cracked; many collapsed. Reports of long-period wave effects were widespread. Water splashed from swimming pools in the Los Angeles area.

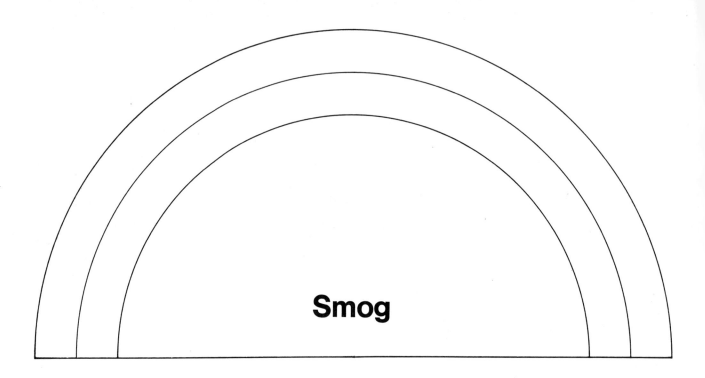

Smog

Although air pollution is a worldwide problem, in few areas is it more serious than in California. Virtually all urban areas in the state have some kind of air pollution. The situation is so bad in Southern California that sixty top doctors and scientists at UCLA have told residents to move out of the smoggiest sections (see maps and Tables 3, 4, and 5) for their own health. "The harmful effects of smog accumulating over another ten years may be physically intolerable," says the group's spokesman.

Adverse levels of photochemical oxidants, the principal air pollutant, have been recorded for the past twenty years. This is attributable primarily to high levels of auto exhaust, which become a serious pollutant when exposed to sunlight. This photochemical smog builds up and regularly becomes trapped in a temperature inversion. Making matters worse is the fact that the Los Angeles basin is often poorly ventilated. As a result, smog levels continue rising to the point where they become a serious health hazard. One UCLA physician estimates that 80,000 people, or 8 percent of the million residents living in the worst parts of Los Angeles, currently have respiratory trouble. According to the Los Angeles County Medical Association, Southern California doctors are currently advising at least 10,000 people a year to leave the polluted region for their own health, and one-third of the physicians are seriously thinking of going with them. The death rate from emphysema is doubling every four years, and physicians who specialize in diseases of the lungs are seriously overworked. Outsiders with respiratory difficulties are being urged to stay away, and healthy tourists are advised to avoid acute smog periods during summer and fall.

The greatest air pollution health hazard stems from photochemical oxidants. Despite the addition of emission-control devices on cars, oxidant levels actually increased in Southern California and the Sacramento region during 1974. Many cities counted over 1000 hours of oxidant above the state standard. The 1974 record was set by Upland, 40 miles east of downtown Los Angeles, which recorded 1771 hours of excessive ozone—the major component of oxidants—on 248 days. Carbon monoxide levels and suspended particulate matter also frequently exceed state standards in many communities. In addition, sulfur dioxide is becoming a more serious problem in some areas.

Although scientists have linked smog with everything from a runny nose to cardiac arrest, it is difficult to determine its precise effect. Admission of cardiac patients to hospitals does increase during smoggy periods, and experiments show air pollutants cause serious lung damage and lead to freeway accidents. But California mortality statistics don't conclusively prove a link between smog and disease. Explains one UCLA expert: "By the time the data accumulate into something that can actually be proved the result of air pollution, it may be too late."

A glance at the 1974 state smog records reproduced here gives some indication of the gravity of the problem. In communities like Riverside, high oxidant levels touch off dozens of smog alerts each summer, forcing parents to keep their children indoors. Doctors in that community of 150,000 estimate air pollution has ag-

The San Joaquin Valley, as seen from the Fresno Airport, on a clear day and in smog. (*Fresno Bee*)

gravated the conditions of 9000 patients during a recent five-year study.

Although the situation is worse in the Los Angeles area, you can find plenty of smog in other metropolitan regions like San Diego and San Francisco. Escondido has the highest ozone count in San Diego County, while the Bay Area's worst problem centers around the Livermore Valley and San Jose. San Francisco itself recorded particulate levels above the state standard in 1974, and high sulfur dioxide concentrations are also being found in some of the region's industrialized areas like Richmond, Pittsburg, and Martinez.

Residents of the most seriously polluted regions have a hard time escaping. In 1968, Frank Sinatra announced he was leaving Los Angeles for the clean desert air of Palm Springs, "where a man can get a breath of fresh air." Not long after he unpacked, a serious smog attack put Palm Springs over the danger level. Sinatra

subsequently pulled out of the desert resort, where the state oxidant standard was exceeded on 146 days in 1974.

Many other resort, recreation, and retirement areas like Lake Arrowhead, Perris, Hemet, Ojai, and Elsinore have recorded high oxidant levels during recent years because they are downwind from the major Southern California smog-generating counties. In addition, some agricultural regions (smog does about $250 million worth of damage to California crops each year) have a serious air quality problem. The San Joaquin Valley is particularly hard hit, with Bakersfield, Visalia, and Merced showing the highest 1974 oxidant levels outside Southern California. And two Sacramento Valley towns, Yuba City (population 14,700) and Redding (population 17,300) had worse oxidant records in 1974 than many Los Angeles stations.

Particulate matter, generated by farming machinery

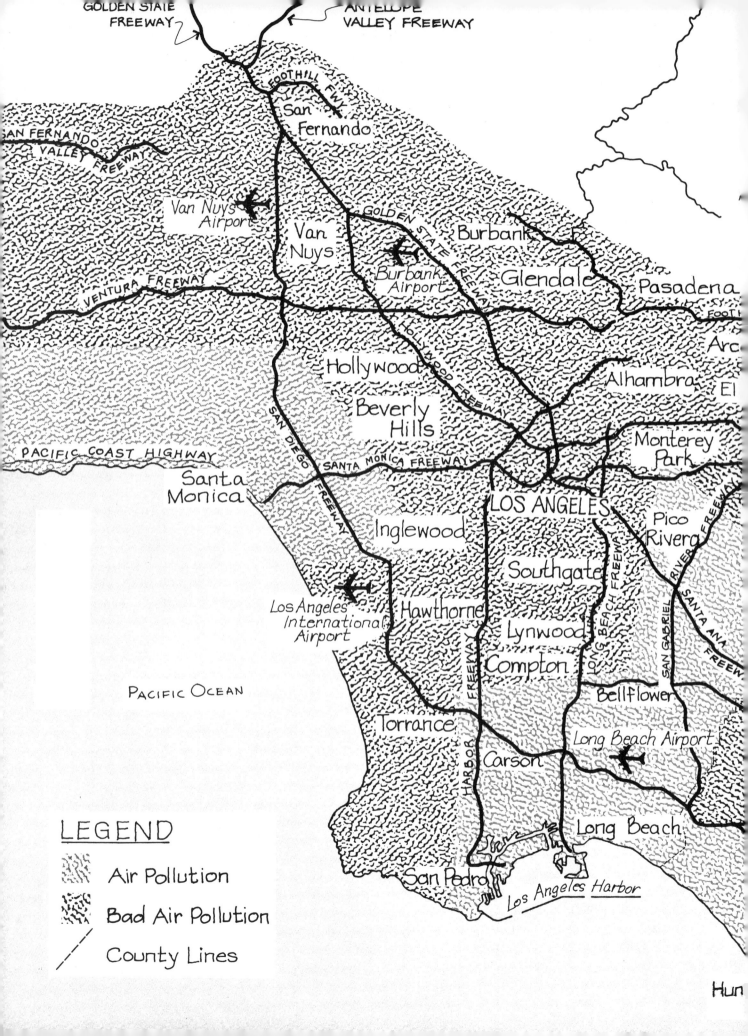

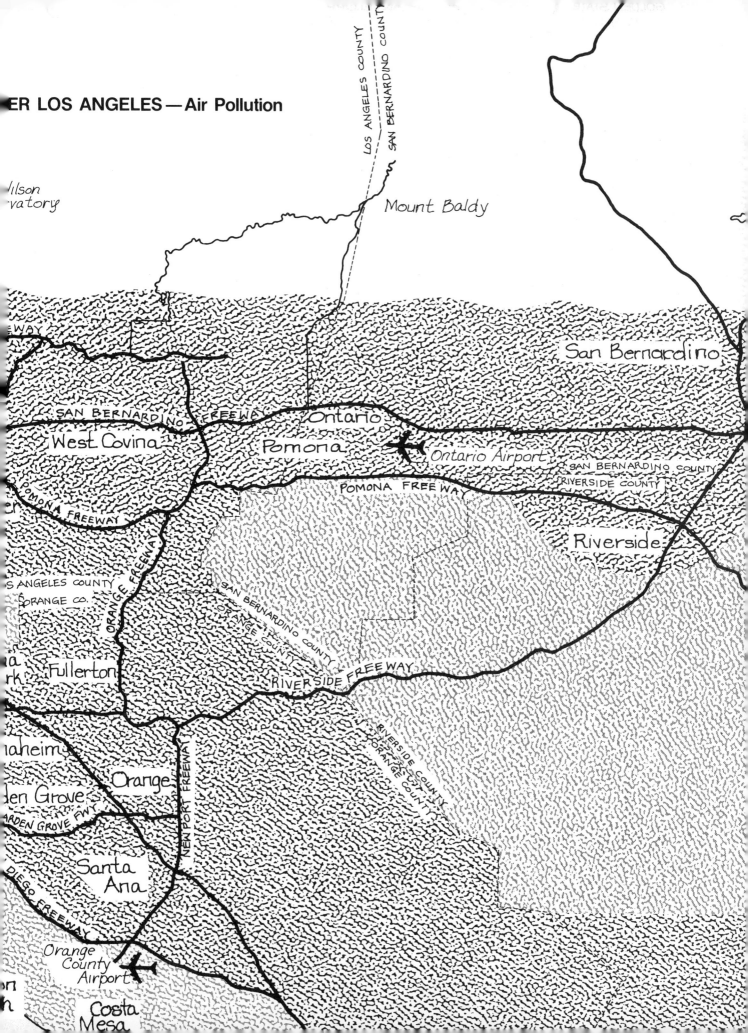

and autos, is, surprisingly, another persistent problem in many rural areas. In fact, this pollutant is actually more serious in some agricultural and lumbering areas than it is within big cities. The highest count in 1974 was recorded at Brawley (population 13,750) in the Imperial Valley, where levels were more than three times the state standard. Stations in other agricultural regions like the San Joaquin, Sacramento, Salinas, Santa Ynez, and Coachella valleys all routinely record high particulate levels, as do lumbering towns like Eureka-Arcata and Fort Bragg. Even fairly remote locations like Alturas, Mount Shasta, and Susanville are over the limit.

What can the concerned resident do about this problem? The first step is to limit your driving. Public transportation in California is better than most people think (for details, see Part Two, under Common Carriers). The impact of a voluntary reduction in car traffic appears to be dramatic. A University of California study during the worst of the 1974 fuel shortage showed that the death rate from chronic lung disease dropped 33 percent, while the death rate from heart disease fell off 17 percent and the death rate from all causes declined 13 percent. Although these statistics are not definitive, they do suggest the public health benefits of reduced exhaust emission levels.

During the peak summer and fall smog seasons, there are simple ways to minimize exposure to smog. Stay inside with the windows closed, especially during midday when smog is worst. Use air conditioning at all times; stay off the freeways and keep out of tunnels because they have a lot of carbon monoxide. When a smog alert is called, a person with respiratory disease should prepare to use oxygen, bronchodilator drugs, and positive-pressure breathing devices.

Visitors can spare themselves much of the smog problem by scheduling their trips to the state at the nonsmoggy time. The lowest oxidant levels are recorded from November through February. In terms of ozone, December is the best month for visiting Anaheim's Disneyland. It is also a good month for football fans to watch the Rams play at the Coliseum. On New Year's Day there shouldn't be any special pollution problem at the Rose Bowl in Pasadena.

If your vacation happens to fall at a smoggy time, you can still minimize your exposure to oxidants by being in the right place at the right time. During April, you're better off at the La Brea Tar Pits in Los Angeles than, say, at the NBC studios in beautiful downtown Burbank. During May, you'll be wise to pick Anaheim over Azusa. In June, see Marineland instead of the Huntington Gardens. And in July, you'll breathe easier at Forest Lawn in Cypress than at Forest Lawn in Glendale. For more information on this subject, obtain the quarterly California air quality data reports from the California Air Resources Board, Technical Services Division, 1709 11th Street, Sacramento, CA 95814. These documents include air quality data from throughout the state. Summary tables for the entire year are included in each fourth quarter (October, November, and December) report.

Smog Data

Oxidants: Federal air quality standards set a photochemical oxidant limit of 0.08 parts per million averaged over a one-hour period (Table 3). Oxidants come

TABLE 3. TOTAL HOURS AND NUMBER OF DAYS OXIDANT LEVEL EXCEEDED FEDERAL STANDARD (0.08 PARTS PER MILLION) IN CALIFORNIA COMMUNITIES, 1974

Air basin, station	Total hours	Days
San Francisco Bay		
Burlingame	44	18
Concord	104	35
Fairfield	141	38
Fremont	171	61
Gilroy	213	63
Hayward	206	48
Livermore	407	92
Los Gatos	281	69
Mountain View (Weisman Ave.)	38	18
Napa	78	30
Oakland	8	6
Petaluma	38	13
Pittsburg	32	14
Redwood City	56	20
Richmond	3	1
San Francisco (Ellis St.)	8	4
San Jose (Piedmont Rd.)	366	97
San Jose (4th St.)	351	87
San Leandro	80	31
San Rafael	12	8
Santa Rosa	13	6
Sonoma	52	10
Sunnyvale	127	46
Vallejo	75	27
Walnut Creek	92	31
North Central Coast		
Carmel Valley	18	8
Gonzales	16	5
Hollister	62	15
Monterey	2	1
Salinas (E. Alisal St.)	49	9
Santa Cruz	10	5
South Central Coast		
Paso Robles*	3	1
San Luis Obispo	36	11
Santa Maria	11	2
Santa Ynez*	247	56
South Coast		
Anaheim	280	77
Azusa	1118	206
Big Bear City*	972	151

Air basin, station	Total hours	Days
Burbank	837	168
Camarillo (Elm St.)	9	3
Camarillo (Palm St.)	686	143
Chino*	1071	197
Costa Mesa	350	94
El Monte*	18	3
Elsinore*	724	96
El Toro*	644	132
Fontana (Foothill Blvd.)	1423	200
Hemet*	553	97
Laguna Beach	327	68
La Habra	722	162
Lake Gregory	612	78
Lennox*	22	9
Long Beach	39	20
Los Alamitos*	515	126
Los Angeles	646	144
Lynwood	98	37
Newhall	867	167
Norco-Prado Park	1097	195
Ojai*	1477	202
Pasadena	1080	214
Perris	1525	210
Point Mugu	171	46
Pomona	814	160
Port Hueneme	306	62
Redlands*	1547	207
Reseda	912	175
Riverside (Magnolia Ave.)	1139	177
Riverside (Mission Blvd.)	1356	200
San Bernardino	1281	182
San Juan Capistrano*	392	100
Santa Ana Canyon*	21	7
Santa Barbara (Cathedral Oaks Rd.)	478	122
Santa Barbara (State St.)	148	46
Santa Paula*	630	129
Temecula	540	103
Temple City	638	116
Thousand Oaks*	863	156
Upland (San Bernardino Rd.)	1771	248
Ventura*	385	89
West Los Angeles	222	75
Whittier	333	84
San Diego		
Chollas Heights	123	35
Chula Vista	223	55
El Cajon	339	85
Escondido	530	112
Oceanside	173	48
San Diego (Island Ave.)	142	39
San Diego (Overland Ave.)	325	67
San Ysidro	116	31
Sacramento Valley		
Chico	364	76
Red Bluff	143	31
Redding (Market St.)	435	75
Sacramento (Creekside School)	51	19
Sacramento (P St.)	327	80
Yuba City	766	136
San Joaquin Valley		
Bakersfield (Chester Ave.)	846	142
Fresno (Courthouse)	461	92

Air basin, station	Total hours	Days
Fresno (1st & Olive Sts.)	52	15
Merced (W. 18th St.)	964	160
Modesto (J St.)	429	97
Parlier	28	9
Stockton	263	68
Visalia	1044	164
Southeast Desert		
Banning*	1216	155
Barstow	363	64
El Centro	135	50
Indio	1034	126
Lancaster	255	75
Palm Springs	1022	146
Victorville*	543	108

* Ozone only.

Source: California Air Resources Board.

from the reaction of hydrocarbons and oxides of nitrogen (primarily produced by cars) in the presence of sunlight. The major component of oxidants is ozone, a pungent, colorless, toxic gas; lesser components are nitrogen dioxide, peroxyacetyl nitrate (PAN), and trace amounts of other oxidizing substances. Oxidant concentrations are generally used to indicate the severity of photochemical smog. Studies have shown that exercising in air with a high ozone level can leave a relatively healthy person physically ill for several hours afterward. And relatively low levels of ozone may suppress the capacity of the body to combat infection.

Carbon monoxide: Federal air quality standards set a carbon monoxide limit of 9 parts per million averaged over eight hours (Table 4). This pollutant is an odorless, colorless gas primarily produced by automobiles. Studies have shown high carbon monoxide content can cause significant mental impairment and may contribute to heart disease. In addition, a committee of the National Research Council, Division of Medical Sciences, warns there is no level of carbon monoxide in ambient air known to be without negative effect.

Particulate matter: Airborne particulates are composed of finely divided liquids or solids like dust, aerosols, soot, fumes, and mist. They come from a wide variety of dust- and fume-producing industries, farming, auto exhaust, and photochemical reactions. Additional particulate matter enters the atmosphere from natural sources, such as dust storms. These particles can injure the respiratory tract and interfere with its clearance mechanism. Some are toxic to human beings or act as carriers for other toxic substances. Studies also indicate that the mortality rate for gastric cancer in white men and women aged fifty to sixty-nine is almost twice as high in areas where

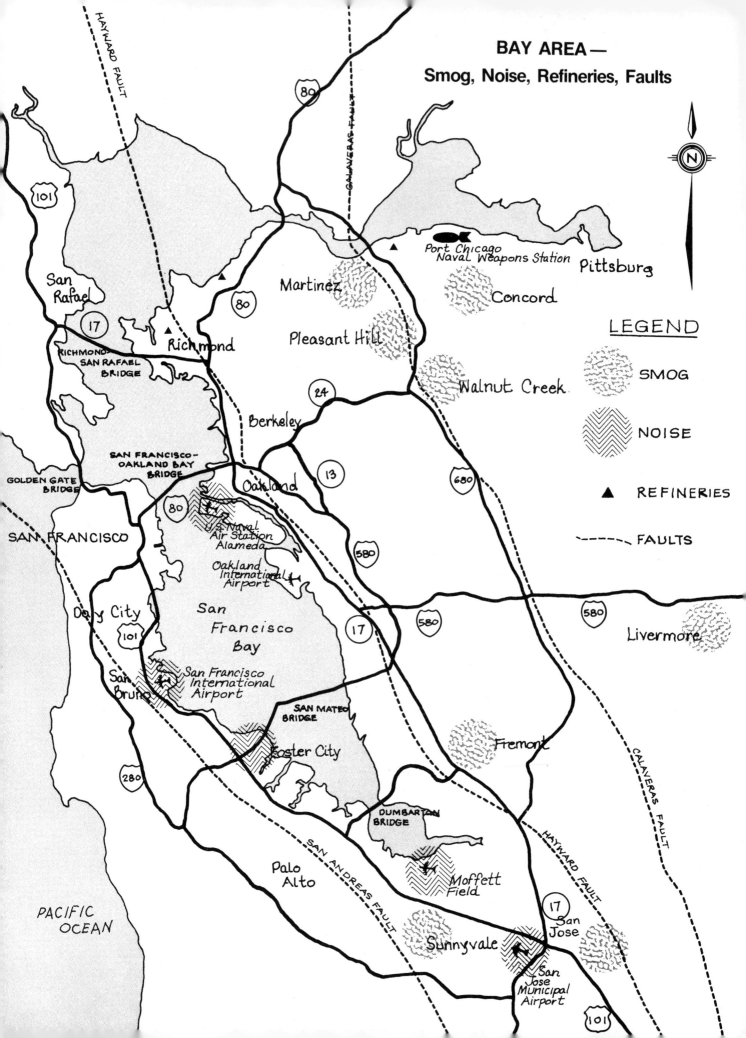

BAY AREA—
Smog, Noise, Refineries, Faults

N

HAYWARD FAULT

CALAVERAS FAULT

80

101

San Rafael

17

RICHMOND-SAN RAFAEL BRIDGE

Richmond

80

Martinez

Pleasant Hill

Port Chicago
Naval Weapons Station

Pittsburg

Concord

Walnut Creek

LEGEND

SMOG

NOISE

▲ REFINERIES

----- FAULTS

24

Berkeley

GOLDEN GATE BRIDGE

SAN FRANCISCO-OAKLAND BAY BRIDGE

Oakland

13

680

80

U.S. Naval Air Station Alameda

SAN FRANCISCO

Oakland International Airport

580

Daly City

101

San Francisco Bay

San Bruno

San Francisco International Airport

17

580

580

Livermore

SAN MATEO BRIDGE

Foster City

280

DUMBARTON BRIDGE

Fremont

Palo Alto

SAN ANDREAS FAULT

Moffett Field

HAYWARD FAULT

CALAVERAS FAULT

PACIFIC OCEAN

17

San Jose

Sunnyvale

San Jose Municipal Airport

101

TABLE 4. TOTAL HOURS AND NUMBER OF DAYS CARBON MONOXIDE LEVEL EXCEEDED FEDERAL STANDARD (9 PARTS PER MILLION) IN CALIFORNIA COMMUNITIES, 1974

Basin, station	Total hours	Days
San Francisco Bay		
Burlingame	9	2
Napa	11	1
San Francisco	10	2
San Jose (Fourth St.)	195	21
Vallejo	134	22
South Coast		
Anaheim	88	10
Azusa	21	2
Burbank	1712	125
Chino	165	14
Costa Mesa	241	28
La Habra	991	78
Lennox	2140	138
Long Beach	434	35
Los Alamitos	72	10
Los Angeles	1208	85
Lynwood	1768	113
Newhall	32	5
Norco-Prado Park	9	2
Pasadena	910	83
Perris	41	3
Pomona	126	18
Redlands	8	1
Reseda	783	63
Riverside (Magnolia Ave.)	410	33
Riverside (Mission Blvd.)	71	11
San Bernardino	103	14
Santa Barbara	98	14
Temple City	191	16
West Los Angeles	577	48
Whittier	423	40
San Diego		
El Cajon	18	4
Escondido	8	2
San Diego (Island Ave.)	54	8
Sacramento Valley		
Chico	47	5
San Joaquin Valley		
Bakersfield (Chester Ave.)	125	17
Fresno (1st & Olive Sts.)	10	2
Modesto (J St.)	8	2
Stockton	53	9
Visalia	27	2

Source: California Air Resources Board.

air pollution by suspended particulate matter is high as in areas of low pollution. Particulates also reduce visibility, help discolor and corrode buildings, and damage vegetation. The California standard for suspended particulate matter is an annual geometric mean of 60 micrograms per cubic meter (Table 5).

TABLE 5. STATIONS RECORDING PARTICULATE MATTER ABOVE CALIFORNIA STANDARD (60 MICROGRAMS PER CUBIC METER), 1974

Basin, station	Annual geometric mean (micrograms per cubic meter)
North Coast	
Arcata	60.8
Calpella	105.3
Eureka	62.4
Fort Bragg	103.0
Samoa	136.9
Ukiah (Court House)	77.2
Ukiah (Firehouse)	93.5
Willits	103.4
San Francisco Bay Area	
Livermore	70.8
San Francisco (23rd St.)	65.4
Vallejo	60.0
North Central Coast	
Salinas (Natividad Rd.)	79.8
Salinas (E. Alisal St.)	76.8
Watsonville	67.9
South Central Coast	
Lompoc	79.6
Paso Robles	76.3
Santa Maria	74.0
Santa Ynez	61.9
South Coast	
Anaheim	95.1
Azusa	104.7
Camarillo (Palm St.)	75.8
Costa Mesa	66.1
El Toro	69.2
La Habra	116.2
Lennox	119.0
Los Alamitos	102.8
Los Angeles	98.5
Moorpark	80.8
Oxnard	67.0
Pasadena	80.9
Point Mugu	62.7
Port Hueneme	102.0
Riverside (Magnolia Ave.)	134.5
Riverside (Mission Blvd.)	135.6
San Bernardino	114.8
Santa Barbara (State St.)	67.1
Santa Paula	81.1
Simi Valley	69.9
Sky Forest	88.8
Thousand Oaks	70.1
Ventura	75.8
San Diego	
Chula Vista	76.6
El Cajon	85.1
Escondido	92.1
Oceanside	89.1
San Diego (Island Ave.)	88.0
San Diego (Overland Ave.)	64.9
San Ysidro	161.5

Basin, station	Annual geometric mean (micrograms per cubic meter)
Northeast Plateau	
Alturas	69.8
Mount Shasta	101.8
Susanville	69.9
Sacramento Valley	
Anderson	61.4
Chico	77.6
Davis	62.0
Live Oak	79.3
Pleasant Grove	62.2
Sacramento (P St.)	67.1
Yuba City	77.6
San Joaquin Valley	
Bakersfield (Flower St.)	128.0
Bakersfield (Chester St.)	130.2
Corcoran	128.4
Five Points	71.3
Fresno (S. Cedar Ave.)	110.7
Goshen	136.5
Hanford	103.7
Kern Refuge	84.5
Los Banos	73.9
Madera-Library	88.9
Merced (W. 18th St.)	75.5
Modesto (J St.)	107.8
Modesto (Oakdale Rd. & Scenic Dr.)	92.2
Parlier	68.7
Patterson	75.2
Porterville	112.6
Salida	61.6
Stockton	83.9
Taft	83.9
Three Rivers	74.6
Tracy	77.0
Turlock	78.9
Visalia	119.3
Southeast Desert	
Banning	76.4
Boron	67.4
Brawley	226.4
Calexico	204.5
El Centro	127.6
Indio	120.0
Lincoln	67.9
Mojave	71.3
Placerville	82.8

Source: California Air Resources Board.

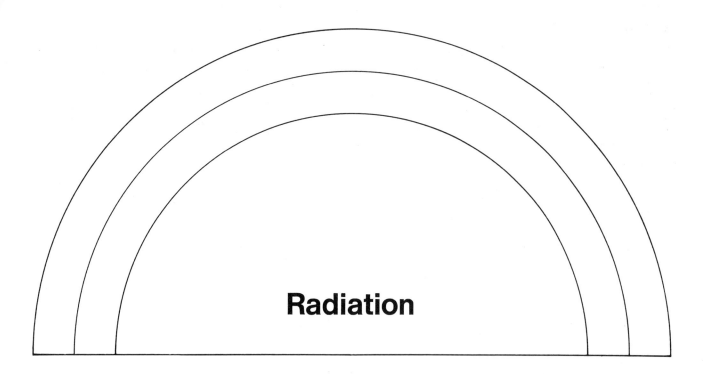

Radiation

Drive down Interstate 5 past San Clemente, and you'll see signs inviting you to visit a nuclear information center overlooking the San Onofre atomic reactor. Every day hundreds of visitors are taken through by guides working for the plant's co-owners, Southern California Edison and San Diego Gas and Electric. With the aid of films, charts, and models, they'll tell you how a nuclear plant is a safe, sensible way to generate electricity.

However, you will not see a copy of the plant's radiological emergency plan, which says: "In the event of any emergency condition involving potential hazard to Visitors Center personnel, the director of the Visitors Center shall be notified immediately in order that orderly evacuation of the public may be accomplished." Nor will you be told about the loudspeaker system designed to evacuate surfers and bathers "in the event of potential contamination of the beach and ocean area."

Depending on the winds at the time of a major accident, that evacuation area could embrace Richard Nixon's home. And an analysis by the Atomic Energy Commission shows that the melt down of a reactor roughly one-third the size of the one at San Onofre could release enough radiation to kill 3400, injure 43,000 and do $7 billion in property damage.

Definitely take these hazards into consideration before you move into the vicinity of an atomic installation. In addition to San Onofre (where two additional reactors are under construction), California has other operating nuclear plants at Humboldt Bay near Eureka

and at Ione southeast of Sacramento. Two more units are nearing completion at Diablo Canyon on the Pacific coast near San Luis Obispo; unresolved seismic questions have delayed the opening of this $1-billion operation.

The operating records of the San Onofre and Humboldt Bay plants raise serious concern about the proliferation of these atomic facilities. During its first six months of operation, San Onofre Number 1 was shut down six times due to various technical problems. There have also been two fires, including one that damaged 185 electrical circuits and closed the plant down for six months. At the Humboldt Bay plant there have been radiation leaks. Moreover, in early 1976, geologists charged that the nuclear plant is operating directly on top of an active earthquake fault. The unit's owner, Pacific Gas and Electric, has been criticized by government agencies for lax monitoring procedures that understated radiation readings around the facility. PGE has also been accused of doctoring data on rabbits which eat grass in the vicinity. As at other atomic plants, these animals are used to measure periodically the uptake of radionuclides from the nuclear unit. Instead of letting rabbits forage on grass alone, PGE management supplemented their diet with store-bought pellets, thereby watering down results.

For more background on the Humboldt Bay plant, you might want to take a look at Sheldon Novick's *The Careless Atom* (Houghton Mifflin). Details on activities at both the San Onofre and Humboldt facilities are contained in a March 1972 *Ramparts* magazine article. And a recent book, *We Almost Lost Detroit* (Reader's Digest Press), has more horrifying details on the current state of the nuclear power plant art.

If this added information proves worrisome, you might also want to consider avoiding the various California installations equipped with nuclear weapons. Although the chance that these devices might detonate spontaneously is remote, the consequences could be catastrophic.

All are filled with plutonium, the most carcinogenic substance known to man. One microgram (a millionth of a gram) injected intradermally causes cancer in mice. And inhalation of 300 tiny plutonium oxide particles (plutonium oxidizes in a fire) will double your risk of lung cancer. Were one of these nuclear devices to burn up in a plane crash, fire, or other accident, the entire downwind area would have to be evacuated and possibly condemned. Even if the weapon were simply to break apart in a trucking accident, there would be a massive cleanup problem. So bear this in mind before you move near an air force base equipped with nuclear arms. In California these facilities include Strategic Air Command bases at Marysville, Sacramento, Merced, Lompoc, and Riverside.

Beyond avoiding nuclear reactors and nuclear armaments, people who are really uptight about radiation might want to consider one additional warning from knowledgeable scientists. On the government's Nevada test site, just east of the California border, sit 250 square miles of land contaminated by plutonium. Some of the nation's top environmental experts fear that many of these cancer-inducing particles are slowly migrating toward California. Of course, there's no way to stop the drift until the government cleans up the plutonium mess and buries it. But in the meantime they suggest there is no reason to risk needless exposure. So if you're in the Las Vegas area and headed toward Death Valley, avoid U.S. 95, which approaches the test site's western boundary. Try Interstate 15 to S.R. 127 as an alternative approach.

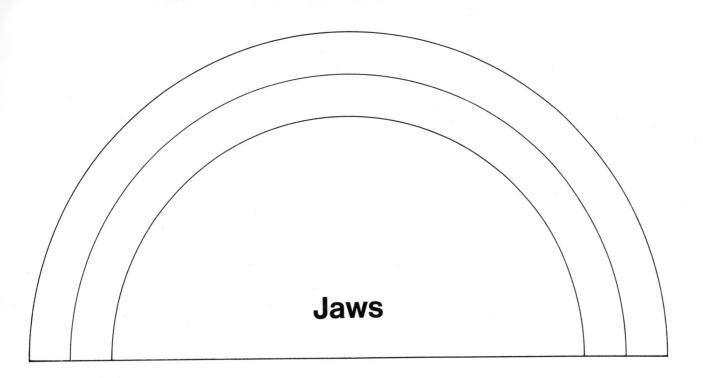

Jaws

Six kinds of large sharks found in the waters off the California coast—the great white, blue, tiger, mako, bull, and hammerhead—have attacked human swimmers or are considered capable of doing so. However, it is impossible to pinpoint precisely how many people have been bitten or swallowed by these local predators. Official state records show that since 1950, twenty-eight people have been attacked by sharks. Four of the attacks are listed as fatal, but only two of these have been confirmed by visual examination. On the other hand, there are doubtless other shark victims missing and unaccounted for whose deaths were erroneously attributed to accidental drowning.

Surprisingly, most of the shark attacks have come in the cold waters off Central and Northern California, where little serious swimming is done without a wet suit. Since 1950, only four swimmers have been attacked along the popular Southern California beaches. And of these victims, just one, a young man swimming at La Jolla Cove, died.

But don't let these statistics make you overconfident. The most serious potential hazard is posed by the great white shark. This gray-backed, white-bellied species, which had star billing in *Jaws,* is believed to have been responsible for nine of the twenty-four non-fatal California attacks since 1950. Although blue sharks generally don't come as close to shore as the great whites do, they are numerous off the California coast and can become menacing at feeding time.

The tiger, mako (also known as bonito), bull, and hammerhead visit the state's waters infrequently, but keep an eye out for them. In particular the mako, which has a gray back and white belly like the great white, is a fish to stay away from. Although other species such as the leopard, swell, horn, smoothhound, and angel (all told thirty kinds of sharks live in or visit California waters each year) are not considered dangerous, treat them with respct. Shark expert Robert Lavenberg has commented in the *Los Angeles Times* about a diver who made the mistake of grabbing the angel shark's tail in waters off Catalina Island. The shark immediately turned around and bit the diver in the crotch. "All he suffered was a very bad, painful bite in the upper thigh," explained Lavenberg, "but he came awfully close to losing a lot more."

Shark damage can generally be avoided by taking a few simple precautions, according to authorities. Because sharks are consummate bloodhounds, never enter the water when you are bleeding from a cut or sore. Stay out of regions where seals, otters, sea lions, and other marine mammals abound because they attract great whites and other man-eating species. Experts say the higher concentration of these mammals off Northern California beaches is a major reason why that part of the state records a higher rate of shark attacks on humans than Southern California. If you're going spear fishing, don't carry wounded or bleeding fish on your belt. Don't thrash about needlessly, and last of all, heed the word of *Jaws* author, Peter Benchley: "Swimming at night, far from shore is . . . plain crazy."

NORTHERN CALIFORNIA HAZARDS

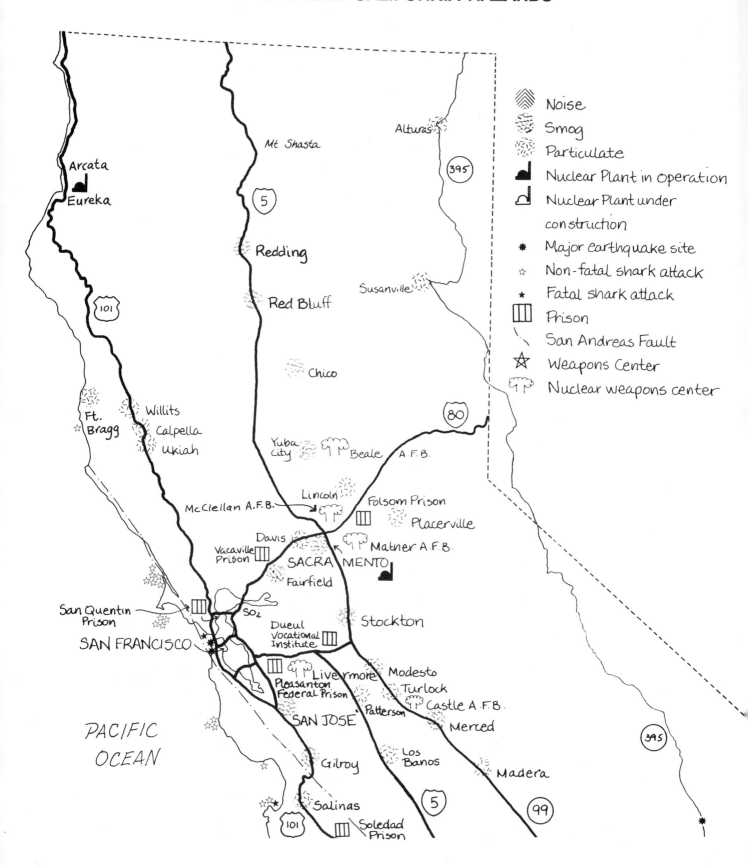

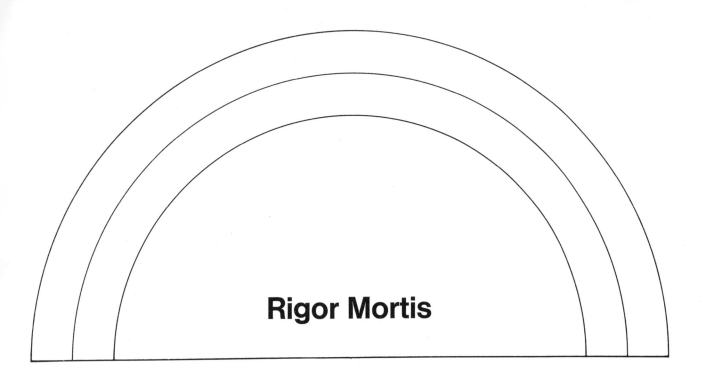

Rigor Mortis

As in everything else, California traditionally leads the country in accidental deaths. Unfortunately, it takes years to total the data. The State Health Department's most recent accidental death statistics cover 1971 (Table 6).

TABLE 6. ACCIDENTAL DEATHS IN CALIFORNIA, 1971

Type of accident	Number of deaths
Transport accidents	
Motor vehicle	4919
Other	495
Nontransport accidents	
Poisoning by solids and liquids	925
Poisoning by gases and vapors	104
Falls	1581
Fire and flames	519
Drowning	683
Other	1854
Late effects of accidental injury	129
Suicide	3783
Homicide	1758
Legal intervention (by police)	61
Accident, suicide, or homicide undetermined	470
Operations of war	3

Source: California State Health Department.

CATHAY
SING CHONG
CHINESE BAZAAR
FAR EAST
FOUR SEAS
GOODS
Far East CAFE

PART FOUR: IMMIGRATION

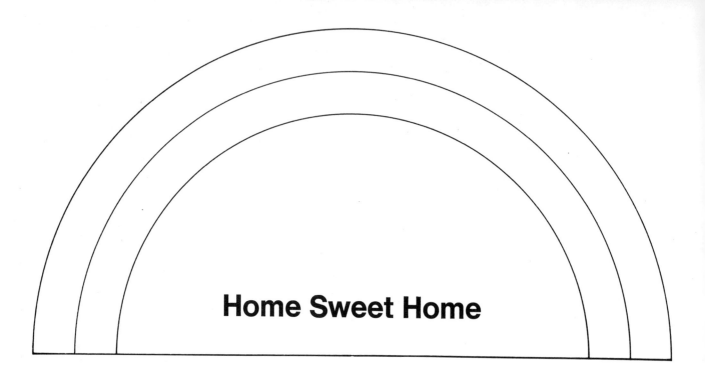

Home Sweet Home

Because newcomers arrive in California with such widely varying expectations, there is no common approach toward choosing a new home. Most people naturally select a given area because of job, educational, or family considerations. As a result, their real problem is finding the right locale in a given region.

The only practical way of deciding is to drive around all potential areas and make a first-hand examination. (For some ideas about where to get started, check Part Seven of this book.) Do this before you actually begin shopping for a house or apartment. Many newcomers make the common mistake of letting realtors sway them into the wrong neighborhood. In sizing up potential areas, start by putting aside your zeal for a hillside setting, majestic ocean view, and prestige address. Make sure you are not looking at a seismic danger area (see Part Three, under Bad Vibrations). Check on the availability of mass transit to your job (the rising price of gas is becoming a serious economic threat to long-distance commuters). Unless you want to be a slave to your car and a chauffeur to your children, make sure schools, stores, and other services are within walking distance. Finally, and most important, talk to as many people as you can about the neighborhood.

Of course, not everyone who comes to California finds himself confined to choosing a house in a specific geographical area. The following discussion gives some general ideas to help those searching for areas that are compatible with their climatic, educational, employment, and political prerequisites. In addition, we've listed towns that are favorites with the well-to-do, students, artists, and assorted professionals.

Good weather: The South Coast has the balmiest weather, with San Diego traditionally enjoying the most sunshine.

Four-season weather: The Sierra Nevada and northern mountains.

Job opportunities: Skilled workers will find the greatest range of employment prospects in the metropolitan Los Angeles area. Unskilled workers will have trouble just about anywhere. White collar and professional workers should consult Part Five, especially Table 11.

Low-cost housing: Smaller towns away from the major urban and resort areas generally have the fairest housing prices. This is particularly true in the San Joaquin Valley. Bargains can also be found in outlying Los Angeles suburbs.

Cheap colleges: Tuition is free at community colleges throughout the state after you meet a one-year residency requirement. Living costs are generally lower at schools away from major urban centers.

Retirement: Although the state is loaded with suburban and rural retirement developments, transportation costs should be a major consideration. In general, you'll do best in metropolitan areas with good public transit and services within walking distance. Mild weather makes Southern California the leading choice with most retirees, and in recent years there has been a steady exodus toward the desert. But before moving to a remote area, make sure your life will not be totally dependent on the car. Also, bear in mind that escalating housing costs are beginning to price resort areas like Carmel, Newport Beach, and Santa Barbara out of the market for all but the affluent retirees. Once again, the Los Angeles area offers the widest variety of options.

Singles: Marina Del Rey, Redondo Beach, Hermosa Beach, Manhattan Beach, San Francisco.

Beach towns: La Jolla, Del Mar, Laguna Beach, Newport Beach, Santa Monica, Santa Barbara, Monterey, Santa Cruz.

Mountain living: Depressed economic conditions make this a tough one. The two major mountain centers, Lake Tahoe and Mammoth Mountain, are filling up. Others have extremely limited employment opportunities. Unless you are a doctor or a dentist or are independently wealthy, you may encounter difficulty supporting yourself. A possible compromise might be some of the mountain regions near Los Angeles and San Diego, where commuting is possible (but expensive).

Urban living: Apartment projects in downtown Los Angeles, San Francisco, and Oakland are a good bet for those who want to walk to work. The central areas of all three cities are gaining favor with families who want some independence from their cars. Self-contained areas like Westwood Village, Park LaBrea, and Century City in Los Angeles are also a practical alternative to suburbia.

Oil rights: Many Los Angeles residents have the good fortune to live over drilling areas that provide them with a fair amount of royalties each year. This can be a major home-buying incentive, particularly when oil revenues are enough to cover your property taxes. Be sure to ask your realtor what, if any, oil money comes with the house you're considering.

Posh: Ross, Piedmont, Orinda, Hillsborough, Woodside, Carmel, Montecito, Malibu, Pacific Palisades, Beverly Hills, Bel Air, San Marino, Palos Verde, Balboa, La Jolla, Palm Springs, Sugar Bowl.

Right-wing: If you are down on Marxist professors, the drug culture, and underground publications like *ZAP* comics, you'll find plenty of company in the San Marino, Orange County, and San Diego areas. The last region has been particularly popular with paramilitarists and hate mailers.

Left wing: The state's greatest concentration of old and new leftists is found in the Bay Area. Here you can work with like-minded radicals on virtually every cause of the day. Among your colleagues will be some of the nation's sharpest undercover agents.

Outdoor life: The Gold Country, the northern mountains, rural San Diego County, Mammoth Lakes, the coast from San Luis Obispo to Santa Barbara.

Artist colonies: Carmel, Ojai, Bolinas, Mendocino, Ferndale.

University towns: La Jolla, Santa Cruz, Davis, Berkeley, Santa Barbara.

Pilots: Saratoga, Los Gatos, Palos Verdes, Marina Del Ray, San Diego.

Stewardesses: San Bruno, San Mateo, Marina Del Ray, Manhattan Beach, Hermosa Beach, Redondo Beach.

Rock stars: Marin County, Laurel Canyon, Topanga Canyon.

Movie stars: Beverly Hills, Bel Air, Laurel Canyon, Topanga Canyon, Hollywood Hills, Malibu.

Los Angeles vs. San Francisco

The rivalry between the state's two major urban centers takes on special significance when you're getting ready to move to California. Even those who can live anywhere they want generally end up choosing between the Los Angeles and San Francisco areas. There's no simple formula for making up your mind. Southern California offers warmer weather, ocean swimming (it's too cold in San Francisco), a wider variety of housing and job opportunities, and a slightly lower cost of living. The air is cleaner in the Bay Area, and you can survive without a car and enjoy better views, parks, and restaurants. The following list compares the two areas in a number of respects:

Mass transit: San Francisco
Beaches: Los Angeles
Sailing: San Francisco
Sunshine: Los Angeles
Views: San Francisco
Amusement parks: Los Angeles
Downtown: San Francisco
Freeways: Los Angeles
Seafood: San Francisco
Delicatessens: Los Angeles
French bread: San Francisco
Pizza: Los Angeles
Ravioli: San Francisco
Bagels: Los Angeles
Topless: San Francisco
Massage parlors: Los Angeles
Celebrities: Los Angeles
Rock groups: Both cities

Movie stars: Los Angeles
Opera: San Francisco
Museums: Los Angeles
Hotels: San Francisco
Discount stores: Los Angeles
Bars: San Francisco
Stadiums: Los Angeles
Chinatown: San Francisco
Japantown: Los Angeles
Bridges: San Francisco
Overpasses: Los Angeles

People who have lived in both areas find Los Angeles somewhat more open to newcomers, insisting that San Francisco is stratified, insular, and downright unfriendly at times. The high cost of housing in the fashionable areas of both cities forces most families out into the suburbs, where commuting is a way of life. Indeed it is often difficult to tell suburbs of the two areas apart, particularly since many of them are built by the same construction companies. It sometimes seems as if the two areas are becoming more alike every day. Both are encircling their downtown regions with tall skyscrapers despite the warnings of earthquake experts. Each is assaulting the last remaining undeveloped mountainsides (San Bruno Mountain and the Santa Monica Mountains) with vast housing developments. San Francisco freeway congestion is fast approaching Los Angeles levels, and on some days Bay Area smog levels actually exceed those in the Southern California metropolis.

Although you may find it hard to choose between

the two areas, consider yourself fortunate. Geological forces are in the process of eliminating the option. You see, San Francisco and Los Angeles sit on two distinct land masses on opposite sides of the San Andreas fault. Because the area to the east of the fault is moving southeast and the area to the west is moving northwest, the land that is now Los Angeles and the land that is now San Francisco will one day come together. Of course, there's no need to worry at the moment since at the average shift rate of 0.5 inch per year, the two areas won't be joined for another 50 million years or so.

Electronic Meditation Timer. This instrument operates with total silence during the meditation period. At the end of the selected time period a pleasant tone is emitted which slowly increases in volume in a startleproof manner. The manufacturer, Anand Electronics (Box 831, Berkeley, CA 94701) points out that the $24.50 device (which includes shipping and handling charges) is not only useful for timing meditation but "it may also be applied to catnapping, cooking, parlor games, photography, etc." A six month warranty is included.

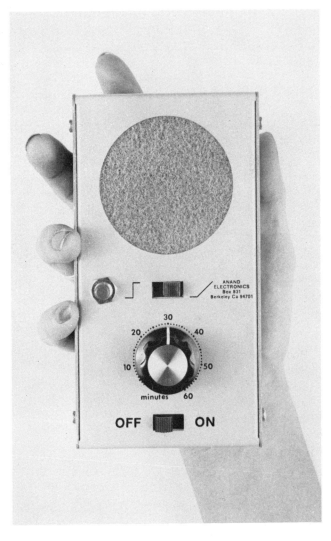

Consumer Price Index

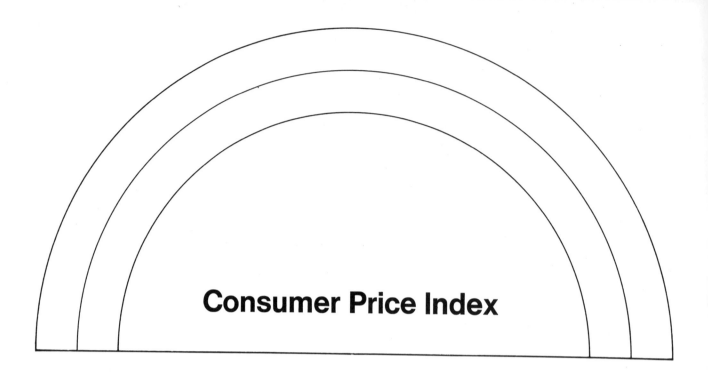

The U.S. Department of Labor, Bureau of Labor Statistics, regularly surveys prices of a wide variety of goods and services throughout the country. This information is averaged to provide a consumer price index. By comparing the current price index level against a base year, you can tell how much prices have risen in the intervening year. The following price index levels for fall 1975 show how much prices have risen since 1967, when the index stood at 100. In other words, between 1967 and fall 1975, the index rose 63.6 percent. These figures show that prices in California are slightly below the national average:

United States: 163.6
California: 161.1
Los Angeles–Orange Counties: 160.4
Bay Area: 161.5
San Diego County: 162.5

The Evergreen Press, Inc. This firm publishes an unusually attractive line of bookplates that can be customized to make a gift. The plates range from fifteenth-century German woodcuts to astrological signs. For a catalogue send 25¢ to the Evergreen Press, Inc., P.O. Box 4971, Walnut Creek, CA 94596.

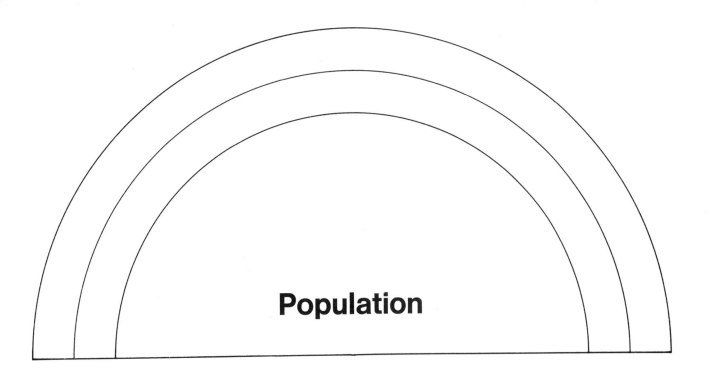

Population

Before choosing an area to live in, you may want to give some thought to population trends during the next decade. As Table 7 shows, major growth gains over the next decade are anticipated in San Diego, suburban Los Angeles, suburban San Francisco, Sacramento, Santa Cruz, San Luis Obispo, Santa Barbara, Mendocino, Monterey, Stanislaus, and Tulare counties as well as in the Lake Tahoe area (El Dorado and Placer counties). Population is dropping in Los Angeles and San Francisco counties, reflecting the continuing exodus to suburbia.

Mountain Travel, Inc. This California-based firm runs trips to the great wilderness areas of the world. Trek to Annapurna, Everest, and the Valley of Swat. Take a Sahara camel expedition, go overland through Patagonia, or take the Aconcagua expedition via the Polish route. For a catalog, write Mountain Travel, Inc., 1398 Solano Avenue, Albany, CA 94706.

See's Candy. California's leading candy store chain sells by mail at $2.80 per pound plus shipping. To get your memorable buttercreams, nougats, milk chocolates, toffees, bonbons, etc., write for an order form to See's Candy Shops, Inc., 3423 South La Cienega Boulevard, Los Angeles, CA 90016.

TABLE 7. TOTAL POPULATION OF CALIFORNIA COUNTIES, PROJECTED, 1970–1985

County	July 1, 1970	July 1, 1975	July 1, 1980	July 1, 1985
Alameda	1,074,400	1,103,600	1,143,800	1,194,800
Alpine	500	600	700	800
Amador	12,400	15,500	18,100	20,400
Butte	102,000	115,900	129,400	143,000
Calaveras	13,600	16,300	18,800	21,100
Colusa	12,400	12,400	12,500	12,900
Contra Costa	558,100	602,100	652,800	715,200
Del Norte	14,600	15,400	16,400	17,700
El Dorado	44,000	53,900	64,200	76,100
Fresno	414,200	447,200	477,200	513,500
Glenn	17,600	18,200	19,100	20,300
Humboldt	99,700	103,600	108,300	114,400
Imperial	74,900	80,200	86,300	94,100
Inyo	15,600	17,700	19,900	22,400
Kern	331,000	347,100	365,200	386,000
Kings	66,800	67,300	69,500	74,400
Lake	19,700	24,400	28,200	31,600
Lassen	16,800	18,800	20,300	22,000
Los Angeles	7,045,200	6,924,500	6,963,200	7,122,900
Madera	41,600	45,400	49,600	54,000
Marin	207,500	217,800	233,200	249,200
Mariposa	6,100	7,900	9,300	10,700
Mendocino	51,500	57,800	65,100	73,000
Merced	105,500	115,500	126,300	138,900
Modoc	7,500	7,900	8,100	8,400
Mono	4,100	7,600	10,500	13,100
Monterey	249,000	271,600	299,000	329,800
Napa	79,700	90,800	101,600	113,800
Nevada	26,600	32,500	37,200	42,100
Orange	1,432,900	1,712,000	1,970,500	2,233,900
Placer	77,900	93,500	109,500	125,000
Plumas	11,800	13,800	15,400	17,100
Riverside	461,200	527,100	596,900	676,700
Sacramento	637,700	695,900	753,600	820,400
San Benito	18,300	19,600	21,000	23,000
San Bernardino	685,500	711,000	765,100	836,400
San Diego	1,358,500	1,573,100	1,801,300	2,022,400
San Francisco	714,300	671,700	661,100	653,500
San Joaquin	292,200	308,600	330,200	352,500
San Luis Obispo	106,700	126,400	147,500	164,300
San Mateo	557,400	572,000	593,100	616,300
Santa Barbara	264,700	283,300	305,800	333,700
Santa Clara	1,073,200	1,213,000	1,342,800	1,487,800
Santa Cruz	124,100	152,800	177,200	203,400
Shasta	77,900	88,200	98,200	108,100
Sierra	2,400	2,600	2,700	2,800
Siskiyou	33,300	35,700	38,200	41,100
Solano	173,600	183,600	198,400	220,800
Sonoma	205,200	250,200	300,500	349,300
Stanislaus	195,300	214,800	235,400	256,700
Sutter	42,000	45,700	49,900	54,700
Tehama	29,600	32,300	34,500	37,100
Trinity	7,700	9,200	10,500	11,900
Tulare	189,400	206,900	224,300	245,500
Tuolumne	22,400	27,400	32,200	36,100
Ventura	381,200	446,200	523,300	612,100
Yolo	92,200	104,900	118,800	133,000
Yuba	44,800	45,000	47,300	50,800
Total	20,026,000	21,206,000	22,659,000	24,363,000

Source: California Department of Finance.

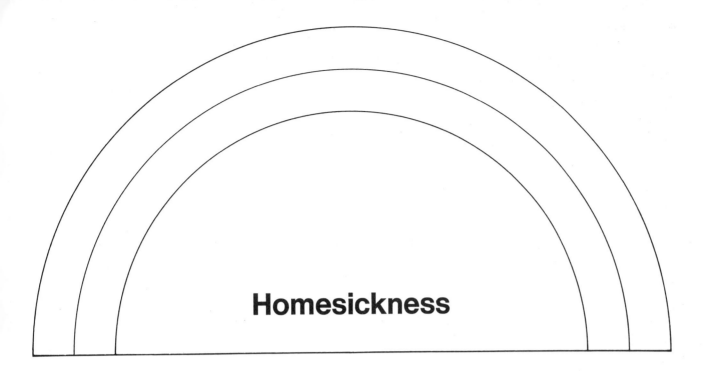

Homesickness

It seems as though every other person you meet in California comes from somewhere else. And all these immigrants suffer from homesickness of one kind or another. Of course, no place is exactly like home. But within California's borders you can find neighborhoods, landscapes, streets, stores, restaurants, and other places reminiscent of almost any place you can name in America. There's no need to panic over a sudden thirst for Dr. Brown's cream soda when there's a delicatessen around the corner on Fairfax. In California, it's easy to ward off that rootless feeling.

Inner city Detroit, Chicago, Cleveland, Baltimore, Philadelphia, or Buffalo: When you tire of suburban monotony and yearn for a decaying midwestern-style scene, try downtown Oakland. Follow San Pablo Avenue from the Greyhound Bus Depot at 21st Street down to Broadway. Even better, follow Brush Street from 16th Street to the Nimitz Freeway. You'll see lots of fine boarded-up buildings, winos, empty lots, condemned houses. Another possibility is Broadway in downtown Los Angeles, walking south from Second Street, where you'll find a teeming, neon-lit scene filled with bargain emporiums.

West 42nd Street, Manhattan: Walk through San Francisco's downtown Tenderloin area near Market Street to catch that sordid feeling.

Fifth Avenue, Manhattan: San Francisco's Union Square and downtown Beverly Hills have branches of many leading New York stores like Tiffany's, Saks, F.A.O. Schwarz.

Southern River Towns: The Sacramento Delta northeast of San Francisco.

Iowa: San Joaquin Valley, particularly the Oakdale-Manteca region on Highway 120.

Florida: San Diego.

Topeka: Stockton.

West Texas: Interstate 5 out of Kettleman City.

Gary, Indiana: Richmond or Wilmington County.

Amarillo: Bakersfield.

Oklahoma City: Sacramento.

New England Coast: The Mendocino Coast from Point Arena to Westport.

New England Winters: Thanks to Interstate 80, there's easy access to the frequent blizzards on Donner Pass. Carry chains.

San Francisco Magazine. A wide range of features on prominent Bay Area personalities as well as the inside story on assorted cause célèbres are published in this Bay Area Monthly. A subscription is $12 per year. Send your money to the magazine at 120 Green, San Francisco, CA 94111.

PART FIVE:
EMPLOYMENT

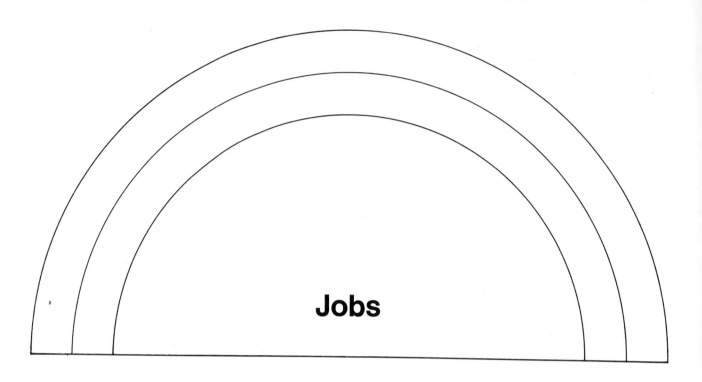

Jobs

Looking for work in California? Your prospects are good if you're an experienced engineer, machinist, machine tool operator, tool and die maker, diesel mechanic, nurse, secretary, clerical worker (with training in bookkeeping, payroll, banking, legal, and medical work), insurance salesperson (willing to work on commission), waitress, dinner cook, specialty cook, or fry cook. But if you don't have training in these areas or a job already waiting, there are a few facts you should bear in mind.

California's unemployment rate as of August 1975 was 10.2 percent, considerably higher than the 8.4 percent national average. Roughly 898,400 Californians can't find work and forty-seven of California's fifty-eight counties have substantial or persistent unemployment problems (Table 8). Among them are every major urban center except San Jose.

Between August 1974 and August 1975, the state's nonfarm employment fell 1.2 percent to 7,824,000. Employment fell in every major category except finance, insurance, real estate, services, and government. The manufacturing work force was down 149,600 to 1,602,900, while transportation and utilities workers declined 14,700 to 469,400, and trade employment dropped 7300 to 1,775,700. Agricultural employment also slipped 20,000 to 329,100.

These numbers mean the great job boom of the 1950's and 1960's has slacked off in recent years. And while the situation is bad in urban areas (Table 9), it is even worse in agricultural and rural sectors (Table 10). You know things are bad when 14.5 percent of El Dorado County is out of work.

But depressing as these statistics may look, skilled workers do have a reasonable expectation of finding work. The data presented in Table 11 suggest there is a variety of openings in specific areas for trained personnel. Tables 12, 13, and 14 supply some idea of the relative wage rates in various jobs and locales. The State Employment Development Department updates these data regularly in the *California Labor Market Bulletin.* Write for it in care of the agency's Employment Data and Research Division, P.O. Box 1679, Sacramento, CA 95808. This agency is also a good place to write for job information before selling your house and calling the movers.

One final note. Business is done a little more casually in California than in the rest of the country. The boom-bust cycle is a way of life. As the current unemployment rate suggests, California's job market is particularly vulnerable to swings in the economy. A cut in defense spending, a dip in air travel, or a sudden rise in mortgage rates can have drastic consequences here. The region attracts more than its share of entrepreneurs with wild new schemes. Sometimes they work out, but often they collapse before new employees get a chance to unpack. So don't let your zeal to escape another bad winter get in the way of common sense. Make sure to check out your new employer carefully and nail down terms of employment before moving your whole family to the coast. Just because a job is in California doesn't mean it's any good.

TABLE 8. AREAS OF SUBSTANTIAL AND PERSISTENT UNEMPLOYMENT, 1975

Substantial unemployment[a]

Alturas (Modoc)[b]
Anaheim–Santa Ana–Garden Grove (Orange)
Bakersfield (Kern)
Fresno (Fresno)
Hanford (Kings)
Jackson (Amador)
Los Angeles–Long Beach (Los Angeles)
Loyalton (Sierra)
Madera (Madera)
Oxnard–Simi Valley–Ventura (Ventura)
Riverside–San Bernardino–Ontario (Riverside, San Bernardino)
Sacramento (Placer, Sacramento, Yolo)
Salinas–Seaside–Monterey (Monterey)
Santa Cruz (Santa Cruz)
Santa Rosa (Sonoma)

Persistent unemployment[c]

Angeles Camp (Calaveras)
Chico–Oroville (Butte)
Crescent City (Del Norte)
El Centro (Imperial)
Eureka (Humboldt)
Grass Valley (Nevada)
Hollister (San Benito)
Lakeport (Lake)
Mariposa (Mariposa)
Merced (Merced)
Modesto (Stanislaus)
Placerville (El Dorado)
Quincy (Plumas)
Red Bluff (Tehama)
Redding (Shasta)
San Diego (San Diego)
San Francisco–Oakland (Alameda, Contra Costa, Marin, San Francisco, San Mateo)
Sonora (Tuolumne)
Stockton (San Joaquin)
Susanville (Lassen)
Ukiah (Mendocino)
Weaverville (Trinity)
Yreka (Siskiyou)
Yuba City (Sutter, Yuba)

a An area is classified as having "substantial" unemployment when unemployment is equal to 6 percent or more of the work force, discounting seasonal or temporary factors, and it is anticipated that the rate of unemployment during the next two months will remain at 6 percent or more, discounting temporary or seasonal factors.

b The area is the labor market area or standard metropolitan statistical area. The names of counties included in each area are shown in parentheses.

c An area is classified as having "persistent" unemployment when unemployment during the most recent calendar year averaged 6 percent or more of the work force and has been at least (1) 50 percent above the national average for three of the preceding four years, (2) 75 percent above the national average for two of the preceding three calendar years, or (3) 100 percent above the national average for one of the preceding two calendar years.

Source: U.S. Department of Labor, February 1975.

TABLE 9. UNEMPLOYMENT, BY COUNTY, 1975

County	Percent unemployment
Alpine	Not available
Amador	6.6
Butte	10.8
Calaveras	12.1
Colusa	5.0
Contra Costa	9.0
Del Norte	15.9
El Dorado	14.5
Glenn	6.7
Humboldt	17.4
Imperial	8.5
Inyo	11.1
Kern	8.5
Lake	12.6
Lassen	14.5
Los Angeles	9.3
Madera	8.0
Marin	8.0
Mariposa	2.8
Mendocino	9.7
Merced	6.9
Modoc	9.5
Mono	12.3
Monterey	6.8
Napa	4.5
Nevada	12.3
Placer	10.1
Plumas	10.5
San Benito	5.4
San Francisco	10.9
San Luis Obispo	7.5
San Mateo	7.0
Santa Barbara	7.3
Santa Cruz	10.5
Shasta	12.6
Sierra	9.5
Siskiyou	10.9
Solano	7.1
Sonoma	8.5
Stanislaus	8.5
Sutter	7.6
Tehama	12.6
Trinity	8.2
Tuolumne	14.0
Ventura	9.0
Yuba	9.0

Source: California Employment Development Department, August 1975.

TABLE 10. UNEMPLOYMENT, BY CITY, 1975

City	Percent unemployment
Alameda	8.5
Alhambra	6.4
Anaheim	8.8
Bakersfield	6.9
Bellflower	9.0
Berkeley	13.9
Buena Park	9.3
Burbank	9.5
Carson	11.1
Chula Vista	10.9
Compton	15.4
Concord	8.5
Costa Mesa	8.6
Daly City	7.8
Downey	7.2
El Cajon	10.2
El Monte	9.4
Fremont	8.3
Fresno	7.3
Fullerton	8.6
Garden Grove	8.8
Glendale	7.4
Hawthorne	9.9
Hayward	11.0
Huntington Beach	8.1
Inglewood	9.3
Lakewood	9.1
Long Beach	10.1
Los Angeles	11.3
Modesto	6.4
Mountain View	5.8
Newport Beach	7.3
Norwalk	10.6
Oakland	11.3
Ontario	13.4
Orange	7.3
Oxnard	9.4
Palo Alto	5.4
Pasadena	13.2
Pico Rivera	9.3
Pomona	12.2
Redondo Beach	10.4
Redwood City	7.2
Richmond	12.4
Riverside	10.2
Sacramento	8.9
San Bernardino	12.4
San Diego	11.0
San Jose	8.5
San Leandro	8.4
San Mateo	7.1
Santa Ana	9.4
Santa Barbara	6.8
Santa Clara	8.2
Santa Monica	9.9
Santa Rosa	9.2
Simi Valley	10.3
South Gate	8.8
Stockton	7.6
Sunnyvale	7.0
Torrance	7.6
Vallejo	5.8

City	Percent unemployment
Ventura	7.1
West Covina	7.3
Westminster	8.5
Whittier	6.5

Source: California Employment Development Department, August 1975.

TABLE 11. OCCUPATIONAL SHORTAGES, 1976[a]

Occupation	Anaheim–Santa Ana–Garden Grove	Los Angeles–Long Beach	Sacramento	San Bernardino–Riverside	San Diego	San Francisco–Oakland	San Jose
Professional, technical, managerial							
Accountant (degree)							X
Electrical or electronics engineers		X				X	X
Electronic technician		X				X	X
Mechanical drafter						X	X
Mechanical engineer						X	
Nurse, licensed vocational	X	X	X	X	X	X	X
Nurse, registered	X	X	X	X	X	X	X
Programmer (experienced)	X	X					X
Clerical, sales							
Bookkeeper, full charge (experienced)	X	X					X
Insurance sales agent			X			X	X
Keypunch operator (experienced)					X	X	X
Payroll clerk	X	X		X			
Secretary	X		X		X	X	X
Teller, bank		X		X	X	X	
Services							
Cook (experienced)	X		X				X
Waiter/waitress	X						X
Industrial occupations							
Diesel mechanic		X		X			
Electronics assembler							X
Machine tool operator	X	X			X		X
Machinist	X	X	X		X	X	X
Office machine repairer			X			X	X
Refrigerator mechanic			X				
Sewing machine operator	X	X		X		X	
Television repairer (color)							X
Tool and die maker					X		

[a] X indicates continuing shortage of qualified applicants during January–March, 1976.

Source: California Employment Development Department, 1976.

TABLE 12. EARNINGS AND HOURS OF WORKERS IN MANUFACTURING, BY AREA, 1975

Area	Average weekly earnings ($)	Average hours per week	Average hourly earnings ($)
Los Angeles–Long Beach	192.76	39.1	4.93
San Francisco–Oakland	243.04	38.7	6.28
Anaheim–Santa Ana–Garden Grove	192.55	39.7	4.85
San Diego	195.20	38.2	5.11
San Jose	210.72	37.9	5.56
Riverside–San Bernardino–Ontario	210.80	40.0	5.27
Sacramento	222.52	38.3	5.81
Fresno	176.43	37.3	4.73
Bakersfield	197.98	38.0	5.21
Oxnard–Simi Valley–Ventura	176.61	37.9	4.66
Stockton	211.87	37.7	5.62
Santa Barbara–Santa Maria–Lompoc	180.32	39.2	4.60
Salinas–Seaside–Monterey	188.50	37.7	5.00
Vallejo–Fairfield–Napa	215.95	38.7	5.58
Modesto	190.09	37.2	5.11
Santa Rosa	190.39	37.7	5.05
California	203.97	39.0	5.23

Source: California Employment Development Department, July 1975.

TABLE 13. EARNINGS AND HOURS OF WORKERS IN MANUFACTURING, BY TYPE OF WORK, 1975

Industry	Average gross weekly earnings ($)	Average hours per week	Average gross hourly earnings ($)
Total manufacturing	199.41	39.1	5.10
Nondurable goods	182.09	37.7	4.83
Durable goods	209.08	39.9	5.24
Nondurable goods			
Food and kindred products	198.60	37.9	5.24
Fish canning and preserving	126.47	32.1	3.94
Meat products	223.78	37.8	5.92
Dairy products	262.68	40.6	6.47
Fruit and vegetable canning and preserving	169.92	37.1	4.58
Grain mill products	246.93	42.5	5.81
Bakery products	220.34	37.6	5.86
Sugar	203.41	40.6	5.01
Confectionery and related products	169.89	38.7	4.39
Beverages	228.00	37.5	6.08
Textile mill products	153.75	41.0	3.75
Knitting mill products	142.39	40.8	3.49
Apparel and other textile products	115.75	36.4	3.18
Men's and boys' furnishings	110.35	36.3	3.04
Women's and misses' outerwear	118.26	36.5	3.24
Women's and children's undergarments	105.33	38.3	2.75
Children's outerwear	105.94	37.7	2.81
Paper and allied products	210.60	39.0	5.40
Miscellaneous converted paper products	193.27	38.5	5.02
Paperboard containers and boxes	209.13	38.8	5.39
Printing and publishing	210.45	34.9	6.03
Newspapers	226.46	33.7	6.72
Commercial printing	221.33	34.8	6.36
Chemicals and allied products	207.37	39.2	5.29
Industrial chemicals	239.57	40.4	5.93
Plastics materials and synthetics	207.36	40.9	5.07
Drugs	177.58	39.2	4.53
Soaps, cleaners, and toiletries	210.14	38.0	5.53
Paints and allied products	209.37	38.7	5.41
Agricultural chemicals	217.74	40.1	5.43
Petroleum refining and related industries	266.02	40.8	6.52
Petroleum refining	272.33	41.2	6.61
Rubber and plastic products	167.11	39.6	4.22
Tires and inner tubes	222.08	39.8	5.58
Rubber footwear and other fabricated rubber products	147.43	38.9	3.79
Miscellaneous plastic products	161.59	39.8	4.06
Leather and leather products	136.29	38.5	3.54
Durable goods			
Ordnance and accessories	263.94	41.5	6.36
Lumber and wood products	200.59	39.8	5.04
Logging, sawmills, and planing mills	216.14	40.4	5.35
Millwork, plywood, and related products	202.36	39.6	5.11
Wooden containers	174.09	37.6	4.63
Furniture and fixtures	160.93	37.6	4.28
Household furniture	155.91	37.2	4.18
Partitions and fixtures	201.00	37.5	5.36
Stone, clay, and glass products	225.76	39.4	5.73
Glass and glassware	229.60	40.0	5.74
Cement, hydraulic	277.01	41.1	6.74
Structural clay products	167.28	40.9	4.09
Pottery and related products	132.47	36.9	3.59
Concrete, gypsum, and plaster products	265.87	38.7	6.87
Primary metal industries	227.08	39.7	5.72
Blast furnaces and basic steel products	261.86	39.2	6.68
Iron and steel foundries	189.68	39.6	4.79

Industry	Average gross weekly earnings ($)	Average hours per week	Average gross hourly earnings ($)
Nonferrous rolling and drawing	220.19	40.7	5.41
Nonferrous foundries	179.79	39.0	4.61
Fabricated metal products	216.01	40.3	5.36
Metal cans	297.93	42.5	7.01
Cutlery, hand tools, and hardware	189.24	39.1	4.84
Plumbing and heating, except electric	164.81	40.1	4.11
Fabricated structural metal products	244.21	40.1	6.09
Screw machine products, bolts, etc.	206.99	41.9	4.94
Metal stampings	196.43	40.5	4.85
Coating, engraving, and allied services	170.91	40.5	4.22
Miscellaneous fabricated wire products	165.84	38.3	4.33
Machinery, except electrical	228.52	41.7	5.48
Farm machinery	195.13	39.5	4.94
Construction and related machinery	227.28	41.1	5.53
Metalworking machinery	222.68	41.7	5.34
Special industry machinery	247.67	39.5	6.27
General industrial machinery	224.17	41.9	5.35
Office and computing machines	195.02	40.8	4.78
Service industry machines	181.23	37.6	4.82
Electrical equipment and supplies	199.80	39.8	5.02
Electric test and distributing equipment	215.90	41.6	5.19
Electrical industrial apparatus	187.73	40.9	4.59
Household appliances	175.54	36.8	4.77
Electric lighting and wiring equipment	161.09	39.1	4.12
Radio and television receiving equipment	171.86	39.6	4.34
Communication equipment	238.39	39.6	6.02
Electronic components and accessories	176.36	39.9	4.42
Transportation equipment	232.66	39.5	5.89
Motor vehicles and equipment	225.81	38.6	5.85
Aircraft and parts	253.37	40.8	6.21
Ship and boat building and repairing	202.13	35.4	5.71
Instruments and related products	175.78	39.5	4.45
Mechanical measuring and control devices	183.19	40.8	4.49
Miscellaneous manufacturing industries	154.45	39.2	3.94
Toys and sporting goods	141.77	39.6	3.58

Source: California Employment Development Department, Spring–Summer, 1975.

TABLE 14. EARNINGS AND HOURS OF WORKERS IN NONMANUFACTURING JOBS, BY TYPE OF WORK, 1975

Industry	Average gross weekly earnings ($)	Average hours per week	Average gross hourly earnings ($)
Mineral extraction	184.96	41.6	6.85
Oil and gas extraction	282.76	41.4	6.83
Nonmetallic minerals, except fuels	305.12	40.2	7.59
Contract construction	341.96	35.4	9.66
General building contracting	331.93	35.5	9.35
Heavy construction contracting, except building	351.82	38.2	9.21
Special trade contracting	344.27	34.6	9.95
Plumbing, heating, air conditioning	369.20	35.5	10.40
Painting, paper hanging, decorating	343.04	33.5	10.24
Electrical work	361.79	35.4	10.22
Masonry, stonework, plastering	316.47	33.0	9.59
Transportation and utilities			
Electric, gas, sanitary services	295.26	39.9	7.40
Trade			
Wholesale	217.95	39.2	5.56
Retail	154.25	33.9	4.55
Services			
Motion picture production	285.85	42.3	6.76

Source: California Employment Development Department, Spring–Summer 1975.

PART SIX:
LAW AND ORDER

Critics and inmates contend that state prisons are the most dangerous places to be in California. Among the most troubled—San Quentin. (*Redwood Empire Association*)

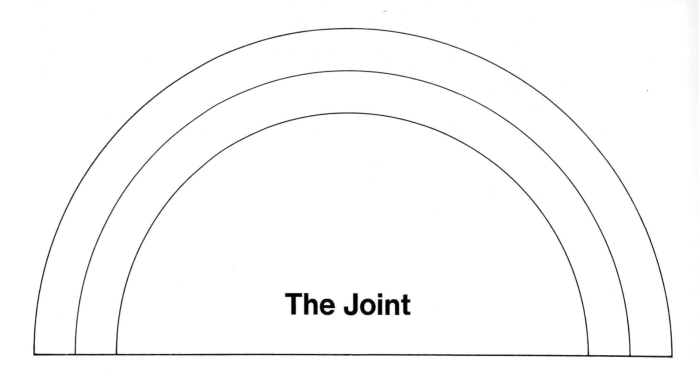

The Joint

California's prisons have hosted some of the best-known inmates in the world. Caryl Chessman, Eldridge Cleaver, George Jackson, Donald ("Cinque") De-Freeze, Timothy Leary, Angela Davis, Huey P. Newton, Sara Jane Moore, Lynette ("Squeaky") Fromme, Sirhan Sirhan, Charles Manson, Juan Corona—the list is virtually endless. Many of these inmates have been critical of the California Department of Corrections. They contend that the prison agency's policies have led directly and indirectly to the death of many an inmate. There are widespread reports of torture, dope rings, prostitution, and shameful health conditions within the prisons. Some critics, like Jessica Mitford, have documented cases in which inmates have been used as guinea pigs for drug testing by pharmaceutical companies. Others complain about brutal, sadistic guards who create riotous conditions within institutions they are supposed to protect.

Prison corruption of this kind is hardly a new phenomenon. When San Quentin became the state's first penitentiary in 1852, three bars set up for the inmates' pleasure were also frequented by the guards. Fourteen months and 110 escapes later, the state issued a report criticizing guard drunkenness. Although residents feared rape by gangs of roving escapees, the only proven rapist at San Quentin turned out to be an off-duty guard.

In an attempt to keep the prisoners down, the whip was introduced (sixty lashes for escape, thirty for weakening chains or insubordination, eighteen for fighting, twelve for stealing, and ten for lying). Subsequently, a form of water torture was initiated for incorrigibles. Under this system, the inmate was handcuffed, bound in a tightly laced jacket, hooked to a block and tackle and lifted off the floor. While one guard kicked the prisoner in the kidneys, another sprayed a high-pressure water jet in his mouth.

Over the years a continuing capital improvement led to a wide range of new accommodations, including dungeons and 6-foot by 5-foot cells for incorrigibles. Racially segregated San Quentin put all Blacks and Indians in the basement of a factory building and 168 Chinese in a 58-foot by 39-foot room. No effort was made by prison officials to stop the heavy addiction of many Chinese prisoners to opium.

After the turn of the century, a series of reforms helped curb some of the grossest inequities. But the murder of three unarmed black convicts by a guard at Soledad Adjustment Center in 1970, the death of George Jackson in the yard of San Quentin, the long series of shootings, stabbings, muggings, rapes—all these add up to the fact that state prisons are the most dangerous places to be in California.

Probably the worst institution to be committed to these days is San Quentin. It receives large numbers of unpredictable inmates who are considered inappropriate for most other institutions. It is also subject to large population fluctuations owing to its traditional role as the department's overflow facility. The old, rambling layout further complicates life there. State officials hope to close the prison and scatter its 3400 inmates to a variety of smaller, more personalized sites.

Another bad scene exists at Soledad, where violence

against inmates is a way of life. In recent years there have been repeated complaints about the "adjustment center," where patients have been confined to filthy security cells and periodically sprayed with tear gas. Perhaps this institution's best known alumnus was the late Donald ("Cinque") DeFreeze, who escaped in March 1973 and went on to form the Symbionese Liberation Army.

DeFreeze also served for a time at the California Medical Facility in Vacaville, where he was active in the Black Cultural Association. A group of young Bay Area men and women frequently visited the institution to help the fledgling organization along. After the cultural association meetings ended, some inmates led women beneath the auditorium stage, where they celebrated by making love. This kind of behavior was frowned upon by Vacaville officials, who pride themselves on maintaining tight control of the aggressive homosexuals, chronic psychotics, and all the rest of the 1450 patients held in the facility's psychiatric hospital (another 400 to 600 inmates are also held at any one time for analysis in the prison's reception center).

Vacaville has been criticized for letting pharmaceutical companies test a wide range of new drugs on inmates. If you are committed here, stay away from these programs. In her book, *Kind and Usual Punishment,* author Jessica Mitford likens the medical experiments to those conducted in Nazi Germany. She cites the case of a Vacaville inmate who was seized by four prison guards who forcibly injected a test drug in both his arms.

Not far from Vacaville is yet another troubled correctional institution, Folsom. Opened in 1880, this venerable penitentiary has traditionally served as the state's maximum security institution. Folsom's first major influx came in 1891, when the state decided to take all hangings away from the counties. Executions began here and continued until December 1938, when the gas chamber was introduced at San Quentin. Although capital punishment is no longer administered at Folsom (or any other state prison), officials there do their best to maintain discipline among the 2200 inmates serving lengthy sentences. In a lawsuit a few years back, militant prisoners complained that they were being punished for their politics with long-term solitary confinement.

There have been serious problems at a number of other state prison units, such as Deuel Vocational Institution, California Institute for Men (Chino), and California Men's Colony at San Luis Obispo (whose best-known escapee is Timothy Leary). Officials concede that "dangerous and unsatisfactory overcrowding" along with "oppressive" solitary confinement have made matters worse.

Until these scandalous conditions are rectified, the prudent California criminal is well advised to avoid state correctional institutions. If you've been apprehended, ask your lawyer to try to get you into a federal prison. A good bet for pretrial confinement is the new twelve-story Metropolitan Correctional Center at San Diego. This is where Sara Jane Moore stayed prior to trial on charges of trying to assassinate President Ford. Free of steel grilles and high noise, this pleasant unit has a rooftop recreation center, where you can enjoy the fine San Diego weather.

If you are convicted, try serving your term at the Federal Correctional Institution in Lompoc. Considered the country club of California prisons, this institution offers vocational training in everything from small engine repair to air conditioning. Convicts between the ages of eighteen and twenty-six should also consider the Federal Youth Center at Pleasanton. This modern facility looks like a college campus; all the inmates are called "residents." Conditions are so good there that some older convicts have taken to lying about their age just to get in the place.

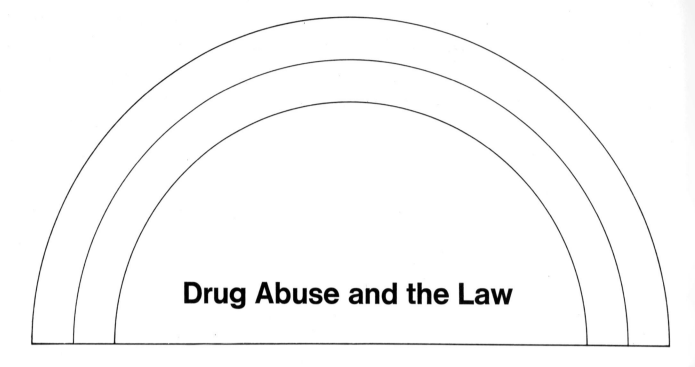

Drug Abuse and the Law

Tables 15, 16, and 17 outline the steps the state of California takes in dealing with possessors, transporters, sellers, and users of various psychedelic and narcotic drugs. Table 18 indicates the penalties incurred by driving under the influence of alcohol and/or drugs.

California's Marijuana Laws Made Simple

- If you are found holding less than 1 ounce of marijuana other than concentrated cannabis, you are fined not more than $100.
- If you are picked up for the fourth time in two years for the above offense, you are sent to a drug rehabilitation program.
- If you give away or transport 1 ounce of marijuana other than concentrated cannabis, you are fined not more than $100.
- If you are caught with more than 1 ounce of grass other than concentrated cannabis, you get a fine of up to $500 and six months in jail.
- If you are picked up with concentrated cannabis (a separated resin obtained from marijuana), you get up to five years in state prison.
- If you are convicted of any other offense associated with transporting, importing, selling, or giving away grass, you get five years to life in state prison and are ineligible for parole for three years.
- If you are convicted under the above item subsequent to a previous marijuana conviction, you get five years to life in state prison and are ineligible for parole for five years.
- If you are convicted under the above item subsequent to two previous marijuana convictions, you get ten years to life and are ineligible for parole for ten years.

Los Angeles Smog Postcards. These postal cards feature a fine color picture of southern California smog at its very worst. For the minimum order of ten cards, send $2.50 to Chinook Winds, P.O. Box 794, Mill Valley, CA 94941.

Crazy Cooking with Almonds and Chocolate. This cookbook contains 80 recipes covering everything from exotic Caribbean and Moroccan cookery to simple chocolate cake. Send 60¢ to the Almond Board of California, P.O. Box 15920, Sacramento, CA 95813.

TABLE 15. LAWS RELATING TO HEROIN, AMPHETAMINES, AND LSD

Crime	Number of prior convictions	Sentence (years)[a, b]		Years before parole eligibility or release
		Min.	Max.	
Possession (felony)	0	2	10	2
	1	5	20	5
	2 or more	15	Life	15
Possession for sale (felony)	0	5	15	2.5
	1	10	Life	6
	2 or more	15	Life	15
Sale, gift, transporting, furnishing, etc. (felony)	0	5	Life	3
	1	10	Life	10
	2 or more	15	Life	15
Person over 18 who involves a minor in these crimes or who furnishes to a minor (felony)	0	10	Life	5
	1	10	Life	10
	2 or more	15	Life	15
Person under 18 who involves a minor in these crimes or furnishes to a minor (felony)	0	5		
	1 or more	10		
Use of or being under influence of a drug (misdemeanor)		90 days	1 year	90 days
Knowingly being in a place where drug is being used (misdemeanor)		15 days, $30	180 days, $500	

[a] In state prison for felonies; in county jail for misdemeanors.

[b] In the case of a felony committed by a person over 18 years of age, a fine of up to $20,000 may also be imposed.

TABLE 16. LAWS RELATING TO BARBITURATES

Crime	Number of prior convictions	Sentence (years)[a]		Years before parole eligibility or release
		Min.	Max.	
Possession (felony)	0	1	10	
	1 or more	2	20	2
Possession for sale (felony)	0	2	10	2
	1	5	15	3
	2 or more	10	Life	6
Sale, gift, transporting, furnishing, etc. (felony)	0	5	Life	3
	1	5	Life	5
	2 or more	10	Life	10
Person over 18 who involves a minor in the crimes or furnishes to a minor (felony)	0	10	Life	5
	1	10	Life	10
	2 or more	15	Life	15
Agreeing or offering to violate drugs laws (felony or misdemeanor, at judge's discretion)		5[b]		
Use of or being under influence of a drug (misdemeanor)		90 days	1 year	90 days

[a] In state prison for felonies; in county jail for misdemeanors.

[b] Or 1 year in county jail.

TABLE 17. LAWS RELATING TO GLUE

Crime	Sentence (jail, fine)[a]	
	Min.	Max.
Inhalation of poison, including glue, for purposes of intoxication (misdemeanor)		6 months, $500
Sale or delivery of poisonous glue to a minor (misdemeanor)	90 days, $100	1 year, $500

[a] In county jail.

TABLE 18. LAWS RELATING TO ALCOHOL, NARCOTICS, DRUGS, AND DRIVING

Crime	Number of prior convictions	Sentence (jail, fine)[a, b]	
		Min.	Max.
Driving on a public highway under influence of alcohol or of alcohol and a narcotic drug (misdemeanor)	0	30 days, $250	6 months, $500
	1 or more	5 days, $250	1 year, $500
Causing injury by unlawful act while driving under influence of alcohol or of alcohol plus narcotic or drug (felony or misdemeanor, at judge's discretion)		1 to 5 years in state prison or 90 days to 1 year in county jail; fine not less than $250 or more than $5000	
Driving under influence of a drug, including marijuana	0	30 days, $250	6 months, $500
	1 (within 7 years)	5 days, $250	1 year, $1000
	2 or more (within 7 years)	5 days, $250, no probation	1 year, $1000, no probation
Causing injury by unlawful act while driving under influence of narcotic or drug (felony or misdemeanor, at judge's discretion)		1 to 5 years in state prison or 90 days to 1 year in county jail; fine of $250 to $5000	

[a] In county jail, except as specified.

[b] If convicted person is under 21 years of age and vehicle he was driving is registered to him, vehicle may be impounded for 30 days at his expense.

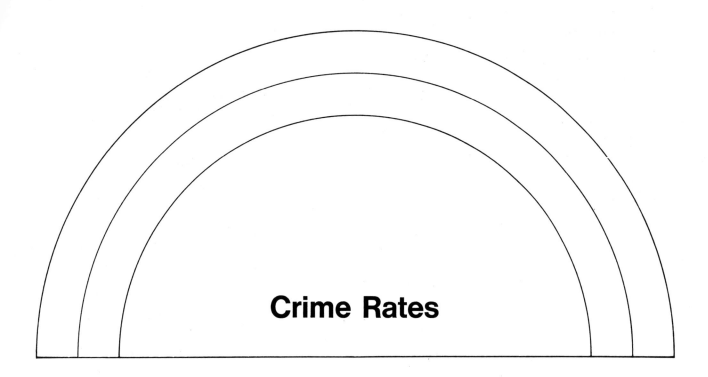

Crime Rates

Crime is a serious problem in most parts of urban California—and getting worse. As you'll see in tables 19 and 20 both major and medium size metropolitan areas are seriously affected. Although you'll find the total crime rate tends to be somewhat higher in areas like Bakersfield and Stockton, the highest number of felony arrests are in the Los Angeles and San Francisco area. Of course within given areas the figures vary widely. As a result we have pinpointed the high crime sections of Los Angeles, San Francisco, and San Diego on the maps on pages 79–83.

Unity Records. This independent record company's catalogue features "New Age Music" developing primarily in the Bay Area. Artists include the Sufi Choir, Blue Aquarius, the Khalsa String Band, Rada Krishna Temple, Uncle Vinty, Shanti, the Guru Blanket Band, and many others. For a catalogue, write to Unity Record, Dept. SR, Box 12, Corte Madera, CA 94925.

Eipper-Formance. This catalogue of hanggliders contains everything necessary to get you off the ground. Send the firm $1 for a copy c/o P.O. Box 246, Lomita, CA 90717.

TABLE 19. ARRESTS IN MAJOR COUNTIES, 1973

	Rate per 100,000 residents		
County	Adult felony arrests	Adult misdemeanor arrests	Juvenile arrests
Los Angeles	1545.0	4846.1	1522.8
State less Los Angeles	956.5	3220.5	1862.4
Alameda	1252.5	4914.9	1733.1
Contra Costa	795.2	2426.5	2246.6
Fresno	986.5	5591.2	2097.3
Kern	915.5	3130.7	3398.5
Marin	452.7	2713.2	2045.4
Monterey	1104.4	4144.6	1890.2
Orange	1068.6	2556.6	2098.2
Riverside	1009.4	3587.5	1812.1
Sacramento	959.2	3359.2	1428.7
San Bernardino	993.7	2478.4	1974.5
San Diego	1063.1	3116.8	1981.9
San Francisco	1478.7	4704.3	1152.8
San Joaquin	888.5	4549.3	1613.8
San Mateo	590.8	2432.1	1439.7
Santa Barbara	875.7	2503.1	1938.4
Santa Clara	634.2	2112.5	2048.8
Sonoma	511.4	1667.1	1906.9
Stanislaus	1159.8	3877.3	2001.0
Tulare	820.9	3903.7	1983.5
Ventura	833.6	2453.0	2211.6
Balance of state	879.2	3149.3	1465.2
Total	1154.2	3766.6	1748.3

Source: California Department of Justice, 1973.

TABLE 20. CRIME RATE IN METROPOLITAN AREAS, 1974

Area	Rate per 100,000 residents
Bakersfield (includes Kern County)	8105.9
Stockton (includes San Joaquin County)	7579.3
San Francisco–Oakland (includes Alameda, Contra Costa, Marin, San Francisco, and San Mateo counties)	7477.5
Modesto (includes Stanislaus County)	7282.8
Riverside (includes Riverside and San Bernardino counties)	7145.7
Santa Cruz (includes Santa Cruz County)	7098.9
Sacramento (includes Placer, Sacramento, and Yolo counties)	7098.8
Los Angeles–Long Beach (including Los Angeles County	6992.1
San Jose (includes Santa Clara County)	6848.5
Anaheim–Santa Ana–Garden Grove (includes Orange County)	6644.8
Santa Rosa (includes Sonoma County)	6235.8
Vallejo–Fairfield–Napa (includes Napa and Sonoma counties)	6176.2
San Diego (includes San Diego County)	6121.7
Salinas–Seaside–Monterey (includes Monterey County)	5632.3
Santa Barbara–Santa Maria–Lompoc (includes Santa Barbara County)	5508.8
Oxnard–Simi Valley–Ventura (includes Ventura County)	5430.2

Source: Federal Bureau of Investigation Index of Crime, 1974.

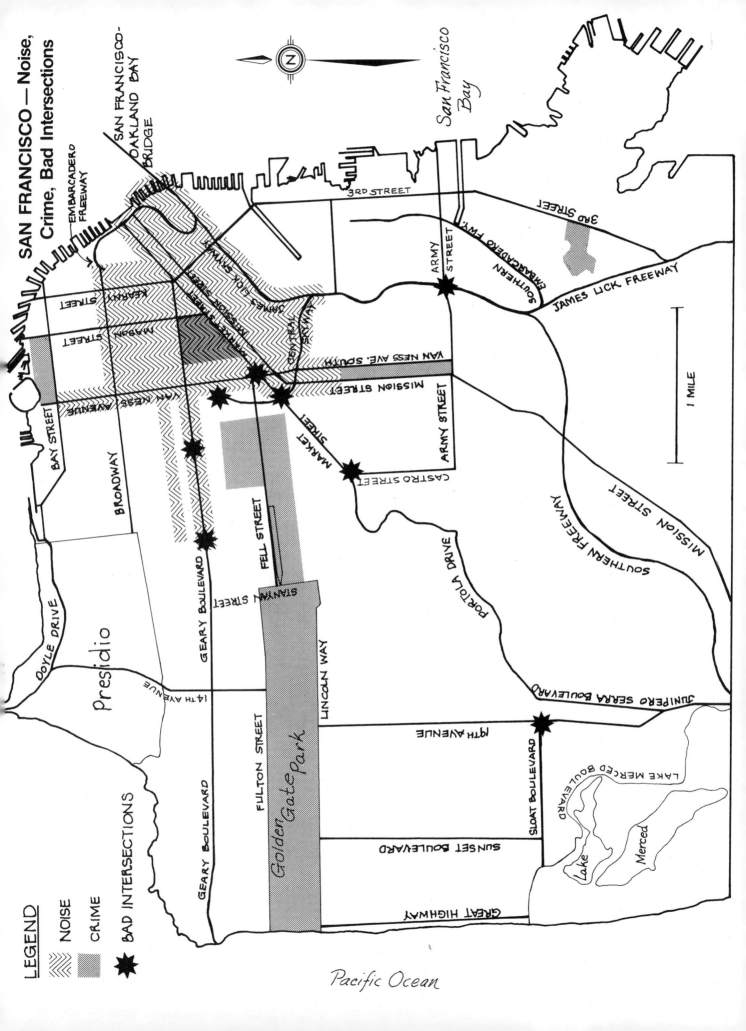

SAN FRANCISCO — Noise, Crime, Bad Intersections

LEGEND

NOISE

CRIME

BAD INTERSECTIONS

San Francisco Bay

San Francisco-Oakland Bay Bridge

Embarcadero Freeway

3RD STREET

3RD STREET

ARMY STREET

SOUTHERN EMBARCADERO FWY.

JAMES LICK FREEWAY

1 MILE

KEARNY STREET

MASON STREET

JAMES LICK SKWY.

CENTRAL SKYWAY

VAN NESS AVE. SOUTH

MISSION STREET

ARMY STREET

BAY STREET

VAN NESS AVENUE

MARKET STREET

CASTRO STREET

MISSION STREET

SOUTHERN FREEWAY

BROADWAY

FELL STREET

PORTOLA DRIVE

DOYLE DRIVE

Presidio

14TH AVENUE

GEARY BOULEVARD

STANYAN STREET

LINCOLN WAY

19TH AVENUE

JUNIPERO SERRA BOULEVARD

SLOAT BOULEVARD

LAKE MERCED BOULEVARD

FULTON STREET

Golden Gate Park

SUNSET BOULEVARD

Lake Merced

GREAT HIGHWAY

Pacific Ocean

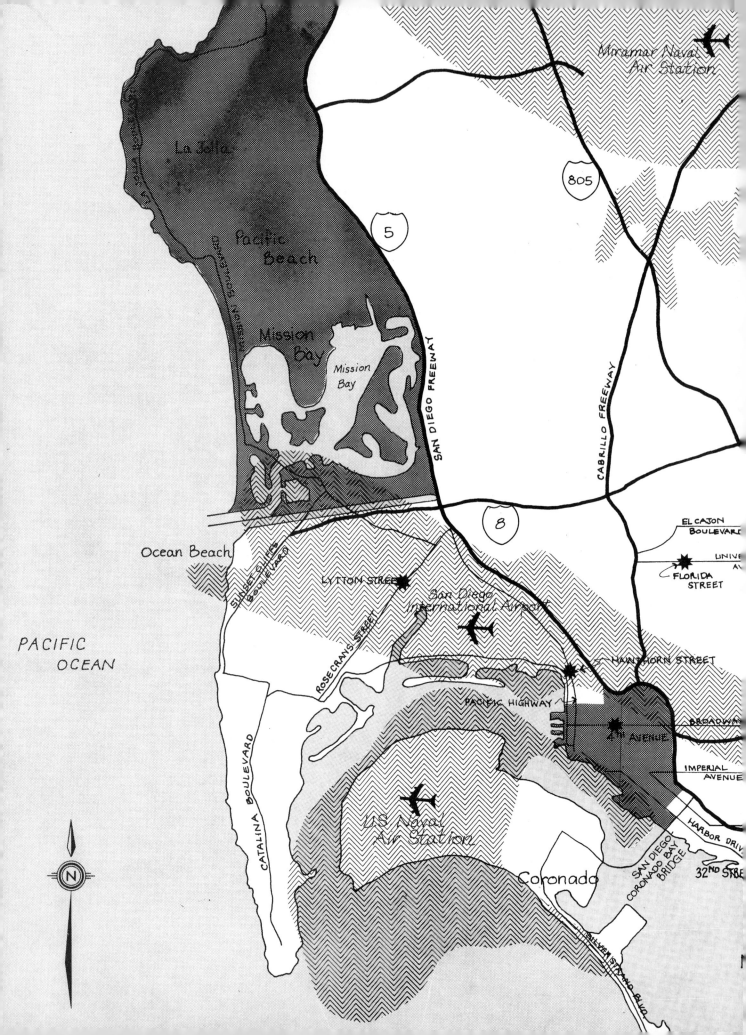

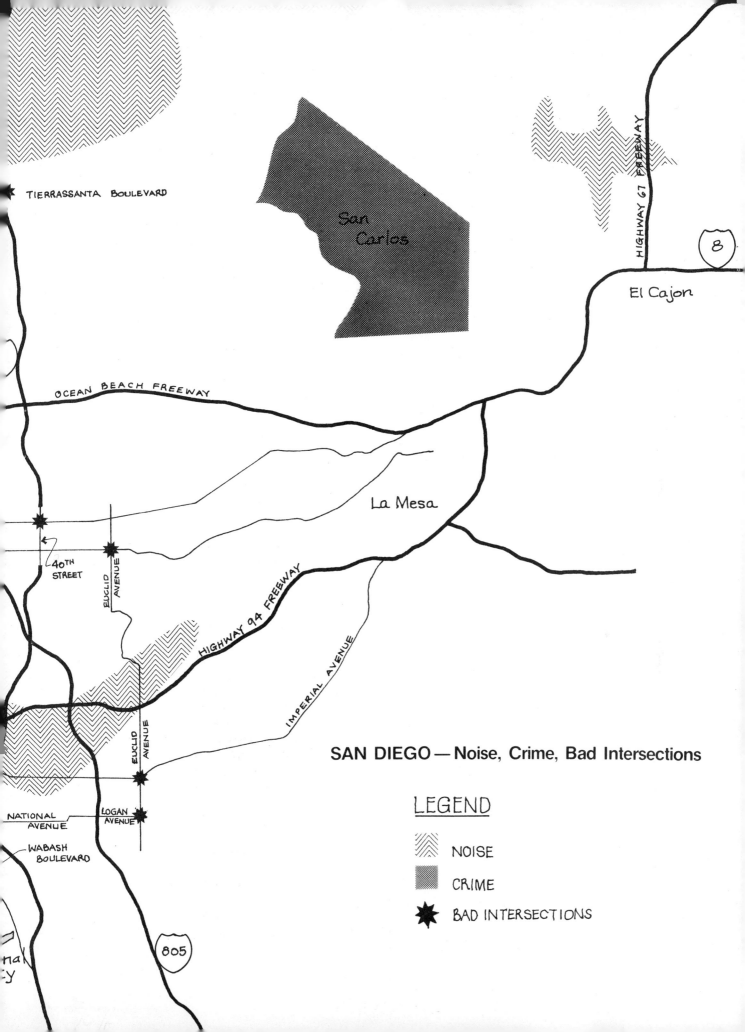

SAN DIEGO — Noise, Crime, Bad Intersections

LEGEND

NOISE

CRIME

★ BAD INTERSECTIONS

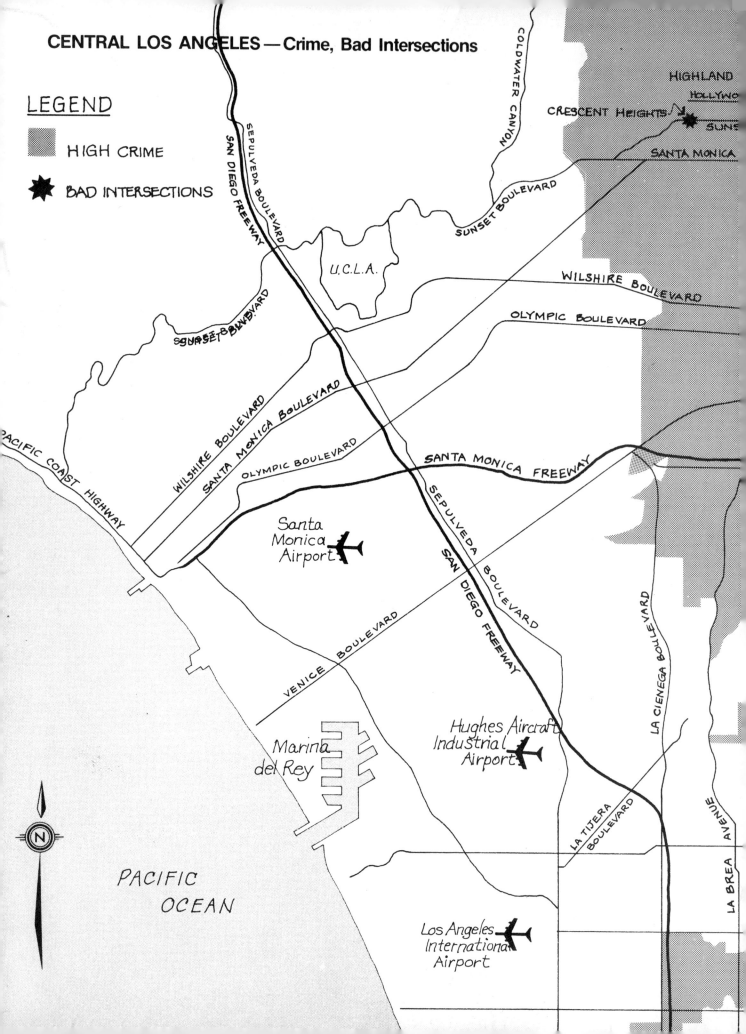

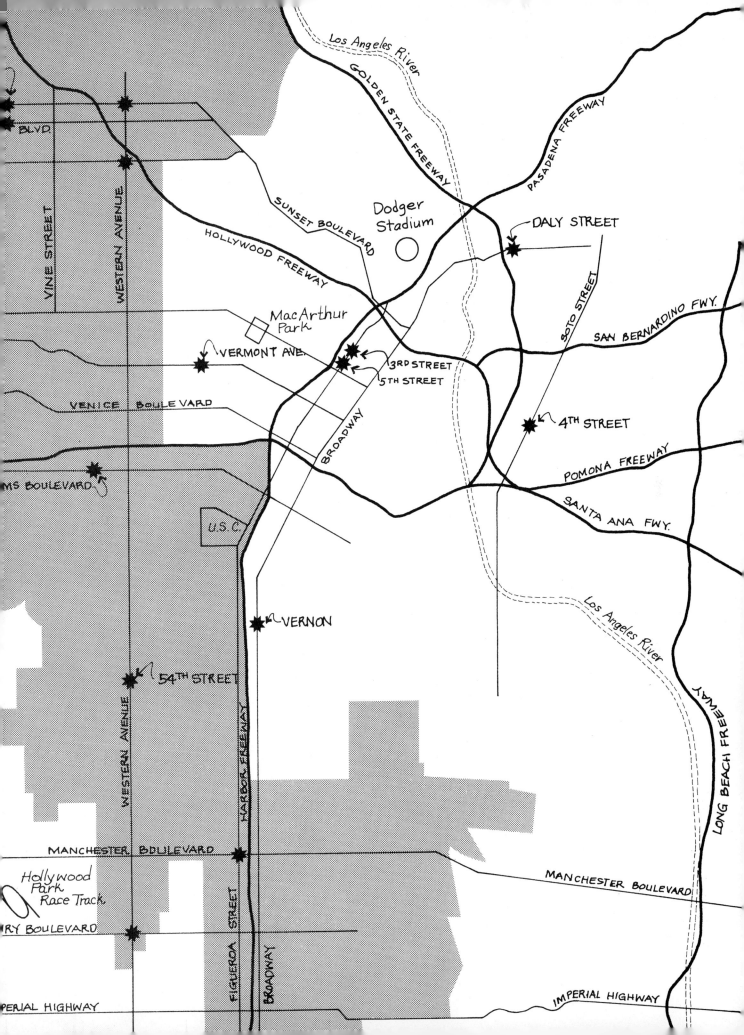

The Small Claims Court:
A Simplified Checklist

- Determine the full, legal name and address of the person (or persons) you are suing. This will help you decide where you must file your claim, which may not be larger than $500.

- Visit the clerk of the small claims court, and fill out the form he gives you. You must pay him a fee of $2.00.

- Arrange for the order to be served on the defendant (but not by yourself). The clerk will mail it for a $1.50 fee, or you may authorize someone to serve it personally.

- While waiting for the trial, gather and ready all important documents. Contact all potential witnesses and arrange for them to come with you to the trial, or obtain a subpoena from the clerk for any witness who will not come voluntarily.

- Come to the court building early and ask the clerk where your case is being heard. When you get to the courtroom, check the calendar to see that your case is listed.

- Give your testimony, presenting only the facts. Be brief. Submit all papers and documents you think will help your case.

- If you win, ask the defendant courteously for the money awarded you in the judgment.

- If you have difficulty collecting your money, ask the clerk to assist you.

- As plaintiff, you are not allowed to appeal if you lose (unless you must pay as the result of the counter-claim).

PART SEVEN:
REGIONS

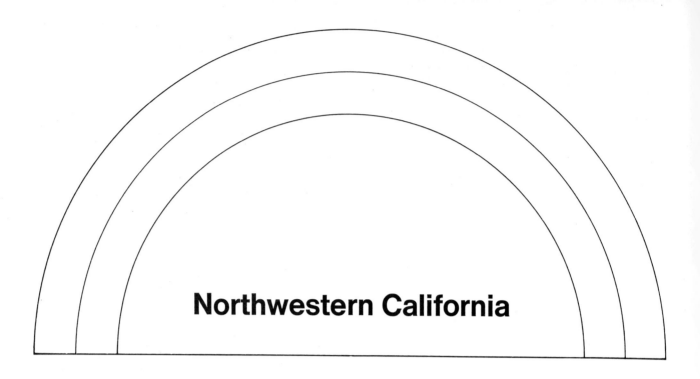

Northwestern California

The Best of Northwestern California

State park: Jedediah Smith
Redwood groves: Humboldt Redwoods State Park; Redwood National Park
Camping: Prairie Creek Redwoods State Park
Hiking: Marble Mountains Wilderness; Trinity Alps
Jet boat: Klamath River (leaving from Klamath)
Houseboating: Shasta Lake
Waterskiing: Shasta Lake
Sailing: Whiskeytown Lake
Tidepools: Luffenholtz Beach, near Trinidad
Driftwood: Centerville Beach, near Ferndale
Elk herd: Prairie Creek Redwoods State Park
Azaleas: Azalea State Reserve, near Arcata
Lilies: Crescent City
Wildflowers: Del Norte Coast Redwoods State Park
Cookhouse food: Samoa
Victorian building: Carson Mansion, Eureka
Town square: Arcata
Redwood drive: Avenue of the Giants
Mountain drive: S.R. 299
Harbor: Trinidad Bay
Historic site: Chinese joss house, Weaverville
Museum: Jackson Museum, Weaverville
Gold rush town: Shasta
Company town: Scotia
Small town: Ferndale

Names don't seem to mean much in the northwestern part of the state—even to native Californians. Once you get past Crescent City, Eureka, and Redding, few places seem to ring a bell. Hoopa, Weaverville, Petrolia, Trinity Center, Willow Creek, Yreka, Etna, and Ferndale—none of these places is widely known. For unlike the rest of California, this sector has few famous landmarks.

And that, of course, is its primary appeal. While it does not have the tallest mountains, the bluest lakes, the biggest waterfalls, or the most famous monuments, the Northwest lacks the congestion that marks many of California's better known areas. And because those who do frequent this area generally stick to a few easily accessible locations like the redwood parks or Shasta Lake, those willing to venture into the back country will find plenty of room anytime outside the peak summer vacation period.

There are two basic reasons why this scenic sector remains so well preserved. First, heavy winter rains along the coast and snow in the mountains make it undesirable to most people for about half the year. Second, it lacks the well-publicized destinations that draw so many to other parts of the state. Main roads are decent, but much of the rugged region is accessible only on foot or horseback.

Although you'll want to approach this area with some kind of plan in mind, keep yourself flexible. One day your path may lead through an Indian reservation; the next you may find yourself collecting jade. Turn off interstate 5 and an hour later you may be hiking through an alpine wilderness. There are jet boats that take you up major fishing streams and steam trains that carry you through the redwoods. Victorian architecture abounds in this region, where you may discover a Chinese joss house around the bend.

En route north, you'll want to make your first stop at Red Bluff, where a Chamber of Commerce map will lead you to a number of distinguished Victorian buildings, including the Kelly-Griggs House, now a museum. Just north of town, Adobe Road leads to a state historic monument commemorating William B. Ide, the first and only president of the California, or Bear Flag, Republic. This chief executive's rise to power was remarkably swift. After Ide and his family completed the long overland journey from Missouri to California in October 1845, he joined up with pioneers determined to secure their rights as settlers. As rumors spread that Mexico was about to drive all the Americans out of California, Ide led a party to Sonoma, where they staged the Bear Flag Revolt on June 14, 1846. After the group locked up the Mexican leaders, Ide issued a proclamation declaring California an independent republic. But Ide's career ended less than a month later, when California was taken by the American military and declared part of the United States.

After the Bear Flag Republic ended, Ide settled and later purchased part of a Mexican land grant known as the Red Bluff Ranch, where he promptly made a fortune mining gold. At the Ide monument you can visit his adobe house, smokehouse, and carriage house, which have been carefully restored. You'll find this riverside park with its huge oak trees a welcome contrast to the crowded, noisy, often hot rest areas of Interstate 5. It's an ideal place for a picnic lunch.

Farther north at Redding, you can make the short drive up to Shasta Lake, one of California's more popular boating, fishing, waterskiing, and swimming areas. Houseboat rentals are popular here, as are a wide variety of lakeshore resorts, campgrounds, and trailer parks. Although this man-made reservoir can be busy, numerous coves along the lake's 370-mile shoreline make seclusion easy to find. Some of the campgrounds in quieter sectors like the Pit River Arm are accessible only by boat. If you're planning a visit here, try to avoid the peak summer season, when the heat can be oppressive and fishing is not at its best.

At Redding you can also pick up S.R. 299 westbound, the best of the three highways linking Interstate 5 with the Eureka area. Just a few minutes after you pick up this route, you'll come to Shasta, the first community established in this part of California. Today the onetime mining center is a state historic monument, where you can visit the old courthouse, Masonic hall, gallows, and jail ruins.

After leaving Shasta, you'll come to Whiskeytown Lake, another popular reservoir, where you can camp, swim, or rent a small sailboat. Just beyond the west end of the reservoir, you may want to take a short detour to the tiny town of French Gulch. There are a number of historic buildings in this old town, which was once a stop on the Shasta-Yreka Turnpike. Among them are an old Catholic church and the French Gulch Hotel, which has been reopened for dinner (call first for reservations).

Continuing over Buckhorn summit on S.R. 299, you'll soon reach Weaverville, the seat of Trinity County. Citizens of this onetime gold rush center have done an admirable job of preserving their old Victorian and commercial buildings. Walking through the center of town, you'll come upon the old Pacific Brewery building as well as the yellow bandstand where the ladies' band used to play. Nearby is the small but selective Jackson Museum, featuring collections of clothing, toys, dolls, and other heirlooms of everyday life. Here, too, you'll learn about important events in the community's past, such as the 1854 Chinese Tong War between rival factions of Oriental miners.

The museum sits next door to Trinity Historic Park, which is distinguished by relics retrieved from local gold mines. Across the way is the famed joss house, built to serve 2500 Chinese who hunted for gold along the Trinity River here in the 1850s. Generally, these prospectors did well despite the fact that they usually worked the less profitable claims, sent much of their earnings back to relatives in China, and had to pay a monthly $4 tax imposed on them as foreign miners.

When the mining business began slacking off in the mid 1860s, many Chinese left Weaverville to work on the Central and Union Pacific railroads. Another mass exodus occurred in 1906, when the heart of Weaverville's Chinatown burned down. Yet to this day, descendants of those who built the original joss house continue using it as a house of worship. Chinese come from all over California to pray in this ornate structure. Indeed, there is considerable competition for the post of temple attendant, and the job is auctioned off to the high bidder for as much as $500.

Present-day worshippers stand before three elaborately carved wooden canopies portraying images of the saints of medicine, decision, and mercy. There they place offerings such as incense, candles, paper money, or food. Strict rules proscribe prayers for material rewards or revenge on an enemy.

A few miles northwest of Weaverville, you'll find Lewiston and Clair Engle lakes. The latter, which is also known as Trinity Reservoir, is virtually surrounded by campgrounds, marinas, boat ramps, and resorts. On the northwest side you'll find Trinity Center, the only community on the lakefront. Here tiny Scott's Museum gives you a look at the region before it was flooded. Since this area can get busy in the summer, you may want to venture out back along Coffee Creek Road,

The Weaverville Joss House, built in the 1850s, to serve Chinese prospectors for gold on the Trinity River. (*State of California, Divisions of Beaches and Parks*)

Whiskeytown Lake.

where there are several guest ranches as well as trails that lead into the adjacent Salmon-Trinity Alps. One of the state's more popular wilderness areas, this back country is also easily accessible by several routes off S.R. 299 west of Weaverville. There's some excellent hiking in this alpine lake country, but the trails can get congested in summertime. Once again, this is a region where you'll do better in the late spring or early fall as long as you check out weather conditions in advance.

From Weaverville, you can head south to Douglas City and then pick up S.R. 3 westbound. Just before the town of Hayfork, Wildwood Road leads you to a small picnic area from where you can hike to Natural Bridge, a limestone arch that crosses Hayfork Creek. This region was originally the home of several Indian tribes, who got along fine with new settlers until they were accused of murdering a white man in 1852. It was here at this picturesque formation that the white men took their revenge by massacring some 100 Indians.

Passing on through Hayfork pick up S.R. 3 through the tiny hamlet of Peanut. A few miles further on you'll hit S.R. 36, which connects with U.S. 101 south of Eureka. Heading back east, the same highway provides access to a number of trails leading into the Yolla Bolly–Middle Eel Wilderness. This wild, rugged route along the headwaters of the Eel River's middle fork can be challenging for the inexperienced hiker or backpacker. Yolla Bolly, incidentally, was the designation applied to the region by its original residents, the Wintun Indians. It means "high snow-covered peaks."

Although S.R. 36 is certainly a picturesque way to travel toward the coast, most drivers find S.R. 299 a quicker, easier way across the mountains to the ocean. En route you'll pass through the Big Bar region, where remains of one of the world's largest hydraulic gold mines, the La Grange, can be seen from the highway. Nearby you can also take the steep hike to the Burnt Ranch Falls in the Trinity River Gorge.

A more roundabout way across this part of the state is S.R. 96, which begins north of Yreka near the Oregon border. The quickest way to reach this road is via Interstate 5, which passes through Castle Crags State Park a few miles south of Dunsmuir. The dramatic crags have been a famous regional landmark for travelers since the pioneer California-Oregon toll road opened up this region in the mid-nineteenth century. Subsequent arrival of the Southern Pacific Railroad opened this area to a number of resort hotels built around local mineral springs. One called Soda Springs can be found near the park picnic area, not far from the Sacramento River. For many years water from this spring was bottled and sold as Castle Rock Mineral Water.

In Yreka, you may want to visit some of the gold rush era buildings still standing on Miner Street.

Among them is the Arcade Saloon where the singing and dancing of rising California star Lotta Crabtree was such a hit with local miners that they threw her a $1500 bag of gold dust. Yreka is also the site of the Siskiyou County Museum, which is crowded with Indian exhibits, mining day relics, and $80,000 worth of gold nuggets taken from the local area.

Although Interstate 5 is the most popular way to reach Yreka and nearby S.R. 96, you can also take the back route via the Scott Valley. Pick up S.R. 3 northbound at Weaverville, skirt the edge of Trinity Lake, and head on into Callahan (population 80), an old mining center where a few buildings remain. Here is the first of two turnoffs into the popular Salmon River fishing country. The other is 12 miles north, at Etna, where you'll want to stop off at the local museum.

The towns of Etna, Sawyers Bar, and Forks of Salmon all provide easy access for hiking and horseback trips into the 400,000-acre Marble Mountains Wilderness, where there are over 200 lakes, virgin forest, waterfalls, and fishing streams. But you don't have to hike into this remote territory to enjoy some of the region's best features. Heading north on S.R. 3 out of Etna, there's a cutoff at Greenview to the picturesque Quartz Valley mining district. And history buffs can explore the Chinese cemetery in the ghost town of Oro Fino. There's also good swimming at Jones Beach on the nearby Scott River.

From here, you can loop back into Fort Jones, the site of an army outpost established in 1852 after skirmishing between local settlers and Indians. The local museum features "rain rock," which the Indians used to douse whenever they wanted the gods to end a local drought. Leaving Fort Jones, you can hook up with S.R. 96 via Yreka, but before heading west you may want to make a short detour north to Hornbrook, the home of a remarkably diversified radio museum. And

Indians of California. A twenty-page pamphlet produced by the U.S. Department of Interior provides some general background on the state's Indian tribes. Those seeking an overview of native California life (there were once forty major tribes with twenty-one major languages) will find this booklet useful. Of particular interest is the mission period, during which Spanish law effectively put the Indians into de facto slavery. A pint of maize per day was considered an adequate daily ration for an Indian man, woman, or child laborer. For a copy of this pamphlet, send fifteen cents to the Superintendent of Documents, U.S. Government Printing Office, Washington, DC 20402.

Castle Crags, a landmark for travelers since the California–Oregon toll road opened up the region in the mid-nineteenth century.
(*Mrs. B. Beauchamp, Redding, California*)

during the summer, you may also want to venture a few miles over the Oregon border to Ashland, home of a popular Shakespeare festival. Just be sure to come carrying reservations.

Picking up S.R. 96 at Interstate 5, you'll parallel the Klamath River for the next 130 miles. Most people come here for the famed steelhead and trout fishing. But within this region you'll also find a number of old gold rush towns, among them Horse Creek, Happy Camp, and Seiad Valley. Happy Camp is best known for its jade mine, discovered by a Chinese prospector named Wong Chan. Unfortunately, while celebrating his great find, the pioneer fell or was shoved (accounts vary) into the shaft.

Following this tragedy, mining operations began, and thousands of tons of jade were shipped to China. Although the Wong Chan Mine is much too dangerous for exploration today, you may be able to get permission from a local landowner to hike along Indian Creek, where jade pieces ranging from fragments to boulders lie by the riverbed.

Following the highway south near the edge of the Marble Mountain Wilderness, you may want to take a short detour to Ishi Pishi Falls, just north of Somes Bar. Here you may see steelhead jumping the falls and an occasional fisherman trying to catch them with a net.

Farther along on S.R. 96 you'll pass through the 87,000-acre Hoopa Valley Indian Reservation, home to 5000 Indians, mostly Hupas and Yuroks. Just south of the reservation there is camping at Tish Tang on the Trinity River.

About 12 miles beyond Hoopa is the lumbering community of Willow Creek, which touts itself as the gateway to Big Foot Country. Since the late nineteenth century, there have been reports of giant 350- to 800-pound humanoids wandering the regional forests of Northwestern California and Southern Oregon. In 1958, a road construction crew working in the Bluff Creek area found giant footprints that were first dismissed as a joke. But when more tracks were discovered on steep banks and rough terrain that would have discouraged pranksters, casts and photos were taken. Wire services carried the Big Foot story worldwide.

Since that time more than forty separate sightings of Big Foot prints have kept the legend alive. Although skeptics refuse to take the story seriously, local Indian families talk about the "tribe of big people" that has lived in the hills for generations. And one zoologist points out: "We know there were primitive men on this continent before the last ice advance and during the last million years. . . . Why couldn't the hairy sub-men or ape-men of China (like the Abominable Snowman) have emigrated southward from the ice regions? If they survived, to where would they retreat? Obviously to those inaccessible areas not populated by modern man. And one such place is this primitive area of California . . . where water, berries, and small game are plentiful."

Cutting west at Willow Creek onto S.R. 299 soon brings you to Blue Lake. Here you can take an hourlong train ride on the Arcata and Mad River Railroad, which hauls lumber to North Arcata. The tracks roughly follow the state highway that terminates at the junction of U.S. 101. If time is not a problem, you should head north to the coastal redwood parks, pausing long enough to visit the first community established on the North Coast, Trinidad. This village started as a supply center for the mining country you've just visited. Later it developed into a lumber town, and today it's a popular ocean fishing locale (Table 21). Trinidad is adjacent to some of the state's best tidepools, such as Luffenholtz Beach, but the state is encouraging visitors not to be acquisitive, lest this popular area be stripped of its sealife. Look at the starfish, sponges, crabs, sand dollars, and squid—but don't touch.

North of Trinidad you may want to fish or beachcomb at Dry Lagoon State Park before passing through Orick to visit Redwood National Park. Perhaps the most controversial unit in the entire federal system, this 56,025-acre site is not so much a park as a logging pathway. You share the roadways with lumber trucks carrying away the giant redwoods. You can wake to the music of chain saws cutting down groves immediately adjacent to the park boundary. In one section erosion from a logged-out area is dumping so much silt in Redwood Creek that streambed overflow has undercut the root system of the tall trees grove that includes the world's first, third, and sixth highest trees. Correcting the problem will take twenty years at a cost of $1 million; officials of the state Conservation Department are now working on it.

The situation is more favorable in the nearby Prairie Creek, Del Norte, and Jedediah Smith redwood state parks, which are ultimately supposed to be incorporated in the national park unit. The coastal Prairie Creek Park has several tall trees groves easily accessible by foot trails and is also distinguished by the presence of two Roosevelt elk herds. Del Norte is a particularly good place to visit in the spring when the azaleas and rhododendrons are in bloom or in the fall when the alder leaves turn. Jedediah Smith, just west of Crescent City, is named for the first white man to cross overland from the Mississippi to the Pacific. After leading his first trip in 1828, Smith brought many subsequent parties of trappers west before being killed by Comanches in 1831. Today you'll find eighteen memorial redwood groves in this park, which is popular with campers who enjoy fishing and swimming

TABLE 21. OCEAN FISHING PORTS WITH CHARTER BOAT FACILITIES

Port	Number of charter boats	Reported season	Most sought-after species
Crescent City	3	May–Sept.	Salmon, rockfish, lingcod
Trinidad	4	June–Sept.	
Eureka	5	Mar.–Nov.	
Fort Bragg	10	Feb.–Dec.	
Point Arena	1	Aug.–Sept.	
Bodega Bay	9	Feb.–Dec.	
Dillon Beach	2	Feb.–Nov.	Salmon, rockfish, striped bass, sturgeon
Sausalito	28	All year	
Tiburon	1	Jan.–Nov.	
San Rafael	2	Feb.–Apr.	
Vallejo	2	Jan.–Mar.	
Rio Vista	2	Feb.–Apr.	
Crockett	5	Jan.–Nov.	
Rodeo	7	All year	
Richmond	8	All year	
Berkeley	26	All year	
Oakland	2	Feb.–Nov.	
Alameda	5	Feb.–Oct.	
San Francisco	42	All year	
Princeton	8	Jan.–Nov.	
Santa Cruz	4	All year	Salmon, rockfish, lingcod
Moss Landing	1	Feb.–May	
Monterey	9	All year	
San Simeon	5	Apr.–June	
Morro Bay	13	All year	Salmon, albacore, rockfish, lingcod
Avila Beach	4	All year	
Santa Barbara	6	All year	
Ventura	1	Feb.–Dec.	Albacore, rockfish, halibut, yellowtail, barracuda, rock and sand bass, bonito
Oxnard	11	All year	
Port Hueneme	3	All year	
Paradise Cove	3	All year	
Malibu	5	All year	
Santa Monica	2	All year	
Playa del Rey	2	All year	
Redondo Beach	3	All year	
Avalon	1	July	
San Pedro	23	All year	
Wilmington	4	July–Aug.	
Terminal Island	1	June–Sept.	
Long Beach	19	All year	
Seal Beach	3	All year	
Sunset Beach	1	Sept.–Oct.	
Huntington Beach	2	Jan.–Oct.	
Newport Beach	21	All year	
Dana Point	12	All year	
Oceanside	9	All year	
Mission Bay	18	All year	
San Diego	74	All year	
Imperial Beach	2	May–Oct.	
Salton Sea	9	Mar.–Nov.	Corbina, sargo

in the Smith River, where there are sandy bathing beaches.

Leaving this park, you can head east along S.R. 199 to Gasquet, a popular fishing resort area, or return in the other direction to Crescent City. Like Trinidad, Crescent City got its start as a port serving the needs of nearby gold miners and is now a fishing center. Here you can visit the old Battery Point Lighthouse at low tide, see a number of marine aquariums, the county historical society museum, and the McNulty Pioneer Memorial Home completely furnished with antiques. At the south end of Pebble Beach is the site of an old Indian Village, and nearby is the Brother Jonathan Cemetery, where many of the 213 victims of an 1865 shipwreck are buried. Downtown you can visit the mall built after a tidal wave touched off by the 1964 Alaska earthquake destroyed a twenty-one-block area of Crescent City. Here too is the Redwood National Park headquarters, which provides visitors' information. After making your tour of the town, drive north to Smith River, another popular fishing site. Growers in this region produce 90 percent of the nation's lily bulbs and join each summer to stage an Easter in July festival.

Returning south on S.R. 101, you can pick up a jet boat in Klamath which runs 65 miles up the Klamath River, or you can head on to Arcata, settled in 1850 as Union Town. Today this onetime supply center for the Trinity and Klamath river mines is the home of

Northern Coastal redwoods.

Fern Canyon, a scenic highlight near the town of Orick.
(*Redwood Empire Association*)

Some of the finest Victorian houses in the state are in Eureka, including the ornate Carson Mansion. (*Redwood Empire Association*)

Humboldt State University, which adjoins the community's 600-acre redwood forest. A few miles north is the Azalea State Reserve, which shouldn't be missed when the flowers bloom in late spring.

At the Arcata city hall you can pick up a tour map of the city's architectural past. The route begins at the town plaza, which originally served as the loading center for pack trains carrying supplies to inland mining camps. If you don't have time for the entire tour of all the Victorian buildings, be sure to stop at 927 J Street, where Bret Harte lived while editing the *Northern Californian*. In 1860, the twenty-four-year-old journalist got himself in trouble by condemning a group of white men who had massacred innocent Indians on Humboldt Bay Island. With his life in danger, Harte jumped a ship to San Francisco. He drew on Union

Town as the setting for many of the stories that later brought him fame.

From Arcata, S.R. 255 takes you through the onetime company town of Samoa—here you can stop off at the Samoa Cookhouse which, as you might expect, serves food in the old cookhouse style—and across Humboldt Bay into the region's major commercial center, Eureka. This lumbering and shipping center abounds with Victorian architecture, including the ornate, often photographed Carson Mansion. Originally the home of an 1880s lumber baron, this great green house is now a private club unavailable for tours. But visitors can still walk inside the mansion gate for a closeup look at its gingerbread features.

Another popular site here is Fort Humboldt State Historic Monument. This garrison was built in 1853 in response to the hysterical demands of settlers who claimed to be defenseless against the very Indians they were harassing. While no fighting took place here, the fort served as a major supply center for military installations established inland. Among the military leaders stationed at this Eureka outpost was Ulysses S. Grant. Separated from his family and unable to relate to the discipline of the fort commander, a depressed, hard-drinking Grant resigned his army commission in 1854. From California, he headed back to meet his wife and children in Missouri and didn't rejoin the military until 1861.

While in the area, you may want to visit the Eureka Oyster Farms plant (Humboldt Bay is the source of nearly all California's Pacific oysters), take a fishing cruise, and stop at the Tudor-style Eureka Inn or the Clarke Museum. However, a tour of the local Pacific Gas and Electric nuclear power station at the south end of Humboldt Bay is not recommended (see Part Three, under Radiation).

South of Eureka, detour off S.R. 101 to Ferndale, an old dairy farming center dominated by a wide variety of distinguished Victorian homes. Here you'll want to visit the home of town founder Seth Louis Shaw, which he built in 1856 as a rough copy of Hawthorne's house of the seven gables. Also be sure to see the Skim Milk, Gum Drop Tree, and Hart houses. On the main street, many of the old commercial buildings have been taken over by artists, craftspeople, and antique dealers. Centerville Beach, west of town, is an excellent place to collect driftwood.

Continuing south from Ferndale, a rough winding road leads through farmland and timberland toward Cape Mendocino, the westernmost point on the Pacific Coast south of Alaska. Although the cape has long served as a navigational landmark, heavy fog conditions in the area have led to over 200 shipwrecks. Leaving this locale that was once the home of an Athabascan Indian tribe, you'll drive on to tiny Petrolia, where California's first successful oil wells were drilled in the 1860s. From here, the road loops back to U.S. 101 via the Mattole River Country. This demanding drive is not recommended during inclement weather, and you should inquire in Ferndale about road conditions before heading out at any time of year.

Instead of taking this long way around, most people double back to U.S. 101 at Fernbridge, which is in the midst of one of many popular salmon and steelhead fishing locales along the Klamath River. In town you can visit the cider factory or cheese works, and south off Highway 36 rides are offered on the Alton-Pacific Steam Railroad. Farther south along U.S. 101, you can visit Scotia, an old company town built entirely of redwood. After touring the old part of town, you may want to visit the museum and the Pacific Lumber Mill, one of the world's largest. It has been operating con-tinuously since 1869. Here you can watch California's precious redwood being chopped up year-round except during Christmas and Fourth of July weeks.

A few miles farther on is the turnoff for the Avenue of the Giants bypass, which winds through a 33-mile-long stretch of redwood country. The heart of this district is the Humboldt Redwoods State Park, which includes seventy memorial groves. Among the best parts of the park is the Rockefeller Forest, preserved thanks to a $2 million gift from the family of the same name.

After rejoining U.S. 101 at the end of the Avenue of the Giants, several more redwood parks, such as Richardson Grove (where there is swimming in the Eel River) and Standish-Hickey, can be found between Garberville and Leggett. Briceland Road out of Garberville also leads to Whittemore Grove, through the Mattole River Country, to Shelter Cove and the King Range Conservation Area. This district has been popular in recent years with young urban refugees determined to escape to the country. But there has been some tension between local authorities and the newcomers. Although this is good fishing country, the roads are rough, campgrounds are few, and fog often obscures the beaches. Ambitious development plans at Shelter Cove were interrupted a few years ago when a plane carrying land salesmen crashed at the site.

Continuing on the main highway south of Garberville, you'll come to Benbow Lake State Recreation Area, a good place to cool off on a warm summer day. The lake adjoins the Tudor-style Benbow Inn, which has hosted such celebrities as Eleanor Roosevelt, Herbert Hoover, John Barrymore, and Charles Laughton. If you've grown tired of hot dog cookouts and takeout stands, you may want to try the good restaurant here.

Northwestern California Notes

Mike Hayden's *Guidebook to the Northern California Coast,* Vol. 2, offers comprehensive information on Humboldt and Del Norte counties. Although this title, published by Ward Ritchie Press of Los Angeles, is out of print, copies can be found in some bookstores and many libraries. It is highly recommended. Additional information is available on Siskiyou County from the Associated Chambers of Commerce, Yreka, CA 96067. You can also write the Trinity County Chamber of Commerce, P.O. Box 517, Weaverville, CA 96093; the Humboldt County Chamber of Commerce, 1112 5th Street, Suite D, Eureka, CA 99692; and the Del Norte County Chamber of Commerce, P.O. Box 246, Crescent City, CA 95531. The *Redwood Empire Visitors Guide* (Redwood Empire Association, 476 Post Street, San

Francisco, CA 94102) offers additional information on Humboldt and Del Norte counties.

Pier Fishing

The following coastal cities in California maintain public piers open to fishing: Crescent City, Trinidad, Eureka (jetties), Point Arena, Point Reyes, Princeton, Santa Cruz, Capitola, Aptos, Moss Landing, Monterey, San Simeon, Cayucos, Morro Bay (jetties), Avila, Pismo Beach, Gaviota, Goleta, Santa Barbara, Ventura, Port Hueneme, Malibu, Venice, Playa del Rey (jetties), Manhattan Beach, Hermosa Beach, Redondo Beach, San Pedro, Long Beach, Seal Beach, Huntington Beach, Newport Beach (pier and jetties), Balboa, Aliso Beach, Dana Point, Capistrano Beach, San Clemente, Oceanside, Pacific Beach, Mission Bay (jetties), Ocean Beach, Imperial Beach, and Avalon.

Remote Shelter Cove has attracted young urban refugees in recent years. (*Redwood Empire Association*)

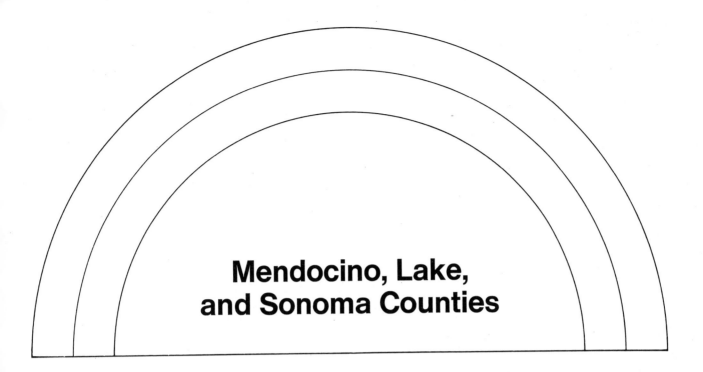

Mendocino, Lake, and Sonoma Counties

The Best of Mendocino, Lake, and Sonoma Counties

State park: Russian Gulch
Redwood grove: Armstrong Redwoods
Camping: MacKerricher State Park
Tidepools: MacKerricher State Park
Tidal lagoon: Cleone Lake, MacKerricher State Park
Hiking: Van Damme State Park; Sonoma Coast State Beaches
Swimming: Russian River
Canoeing: Russian River
Waterskiing: Clear Lake; Lake Mendocino
Sword ferns: Van Damme State Park
Pygmy forest: Russian Gulch State Park
Rhododendrons: Kruse Rhododendron State Reserve
Gardens: Burbank Gardens; Mendocino Coast Botanical Gardens
Geothermal site: the Geysers
Bay: Bodega
Historic site: Fort Ross
Small museum: Ripley Memorial, Santa Rosa
Small town: Mendocino
Victorian buildings: Mendocino
Port town: Bodega Bay
Adobe building: Petaluma
Excursion train ride: the Skunks, Fort Bragg-Willits
Big meals: Occidental
Farm shopping: Sonoma Coast farm trails
Drive: S.R. 1
Route from U.S. 101 to S.R. 1: S.R. 128
Ocean view: Russian Gulch

Mendocino, Lake, and Sonoma counties north of the San Francisco area offer a comfortable mix of developed and undeveloped attractions. Areas like Russian River, Clear Lake, and Mendocino have been popular with nearby Bay Area residents for years. But once again, the tendency of people to funnel into a few centers leaves most of the region relatively uncrowded. And if you come in fall, winter, or spring, hardly anyone will be around to interrupt your privacy.

Except for logging in the coastal mountain ranges and the urbanization of southern Sonoma County, this area remains largely unspoiled. U.S. 101 and S.R. 1 form the two major north-south arteries, linked by half a dozen east-west routes. The lack of commercial or agricultural activity in much of the rugged inland country leaves a large share of the area without the wide variety of back roads and small towns found in other parts of the state. Most of the tourist activity centers along fairly narrow corridors.

One starting point for a tour of the area is the town of Leggett, in the northern part of Mendocino County. Here you can pick up S.R. 1 for the winding drive down to the old coastal lumber town of Rockport. Nearby is the area's leading attraction, 2.5-mile-long Westport–Union Landing State Beach, popular with fishermen when the smelt are running. At the south end of this park is another former lumbering center, Westport. Just before reaching this community you'll find Branscomb Road, leading inland to the Admiral William H. Standley Recreation area, a quiet 45-acre redwood area with frontage on the Eel River's south fork.

Continuing on to Cleone, you come to MacKerricher, the first of several popular state parks in this coastal

Off Laguna Point, California gray whales can be spotted on their annual winter migration from Alaska to Baja, California.

region. Named for the original settlers in this district, this forested park is covered with wildflowers, berries, and plants. Nearby Cleone Lake, a formal tidal lagoon, is surrounded by willows, alders, sedges, and cattails. It is also home to ninety species of birds. There is easy access to the sandy beach, where you can see seals living year-round on the nearby rocks. Off Laguna Point, you can occasionally make out gray whales on their annual 5000-mile winter migration between Alaska and Baja California.

Immediately to the south is Fort Bragg, the largest community on the coast between San Francisco and Eureka and home of a busy lumber mill. Founded as an army post in 1857, this town has a number of good seafood restaurants and is headquarters of the California Western Railroad. Originally built as a logging railroad to serve the Union Lumber Company, the California Western acquired the first of several self-powered, gas-driven cars in 1925. They were promptly dubbed "skunks" by local people who liked to joke: "You can smell 'em before you can see 'em." The name has stuck ever since, and today the Skunk and Super Skunk (a half-century-old steam-locomotive-powered train) regularly take tourists on the 80-mile round-trip through the Noyo River redwood country to Willits. The trip is a casual one, with frequent stops to drop off mail or groceries to residents and tourists along the route. Reservations are a must.

Continuing on Highway 1, you can turn off into the fishing village of Noyo, stop at the Mendocino Coast Botanical Gardens with its acres of rhododendrons, fuchsias, azaleas, and other plants, or continue on to Russian Gulch State Park. Endorsed earlier in these pages, this coastal park includes headlands, beach, and the heavily forested Russian Gulch Creek Canyon.

Be sure to see Devil's Punch Bowl, a 200-foot-long sea-cut tunnel that has collapsed at the inland end, leaving a hole 100 feet wide and 60 feet deep. The bowl's steep walls are lined with wildflowers and plants. Although technically considered a blowhole, you won't see any blowing except under storm conditions. While here, also visit the Pygmy Forest in the northeast section of the park. This is one of several areas along the North Coast where vegetation is stunted because of bad soil conditions.

Just beyond the park is Mendocino, a charming coastal community that had twenty-one saloons, eight hotels, and two hospitals in its lumbering heyday. Today it is popular with artists, urban escapees, and tourists, who value its carefully preserved architectural heritage and picturesque oceanfront setting. Movie directors frequently choose it for a New England coastal location. The best entertainment here is simply walking the streets to gaze at the old homes, Masonic temple, newspaper office, Presbyterian church, and the Mendocino Hotel, where residents once came to pick up their mail from steamers just in from San Francisco. A number of inns are available in town and at nearby Little River. Unfortunately, Mendocino's growing popularity has brought on new subdivision development as the area makes the gradual transition from retreat to resort.

South of town is the Van Damme State Park, where you can explore the tidal pools, hike to Sword Fern Canyon, and visit another small pygmy forest area. Continuing on, you pass the fishing village of Albion and then hit S.R. 128, which cuts inland along the Navarro River. About 6 miles past the cutoff is Paul M. Dimmick State Recreation Area, where campers avoid coastal fog and enjoy winter fishing for steelhead. Farther east is the Hendy Woods State Park, which includes two primeval redwood groves and offers swimming in the Navarro. Nearby is Indian Creek, another state redwood reserve.

The next major community on S.R. 128 is Boonville, the small commercial center of the Anderson Valley, best known as home of an obscure language called Boontling. The whole thing began at the end of the nineteenth century, when local residents tried to one-up each other with new words. Within a few years, the game turned into a semiserious business, and Boontling became the "native tongue" of 500 residents (about 1000 people live in Boonville today). The 1000-word vocabulary was developed primarily on the strength of community names, familiar sounds, or corruption of other languages. Thus, pie was renamed "charley brown" after a local farmer who ate the dish after every meal; the phone was called a "walter" because the first resident to acquire one was Walter Levi. Many animals were renamed for the sounds they created (a squirrel was a "squeekyteek"). "Gorm" (to eat) was taken from the French *gourmand.* Boontling flourished in the Anderson Valley until World War I, when many citizens moved away. But in the 1960s a

Boontlingers' club was founded to revive the unique language. Thanks to the efforts of members, over 200 local residents have taken up the local language again, and it is now being taught in the Anderson Valley elementary school.

From Boonville, either head on to U.S. 101 or double back to the coast on winding Mountain View Road. You'll hit S.R. 1 just south of Manchester State Beach, where dip netting for surf fish is popular. Nearby is the Point Arena light station, a major coastal landmark, and the old milltown of Point Arena. Farther

Redwood Home. Pacific Frontier Homes, Inc., will provide everything necessary to build your own California redwood home. The package price includes drawings, posts, beams, and rough-sawn redwood. For literature, send $1 to the firm, P.O. Box 1247, Fort Bragg, CA 95437.

The "Super Skunk," an old-time steam train, regularly carries tourists through redwood country between Fort Bragg and Willits, forty miles inland. (*Redwood Empire Association*)

Rhododendrons. (*Edward Freitas*)

down the coastal road, there's good camping at Anchor Bay and Gualala, another old lumber town best known for steelhead fishing and first made famous by Jack London.

After passing the private Sea Ranch second-home development, you'll reach Stewarts Point, once a busy lumber port, where you'll still find an intriguing general store. There's also an old stage route hotel here that has become a private home. A few miles farther down the road, you'll find fishing, hiking, and camping at the Salt Point State Park. Once coastal Indians visited this beach annually to gather salt left in the sandstone honeycombs by wave action. Adjacent to the park is the Kruse State Rhododendron Reserve, at its best in the spring.

After passing the old port town of Timber Cove, distinguished by a towering sculpture completed by California's popular Benny Bufano shortly before his death a few years ago, you'll come to Fort Ross, set on a dramatic coastal bluff. Here, in 1812, some ninety-five Russians and forty native Alaskans came ashore to build the wooden fortress and adjacent housing. The newcomers planned to use this base for trade with Spain and for hunting sea otter and growing wheat to supply Russian communities in Alaska. Gradually, the Russian-American Company, which ran the fort, added a number of buildings, including the Russian Orthodox chapel. To help these entrepreneurs corner the regional market, the Czar issued a ukase closing the Pacific Coast north of San Francisco to all non-Russian ships.

This move, as well as the presence of Fort Ross, was answered by the Monroe Doctrine of 1823, which

Fort Ross, built by the Russian-American Fur Company in 1812, served as a sea otter hunting base until 1841 when it was abandoned. You'll find it on Highway One, eighteen miles north of Bodega Bay. (*Redwood Empire Association*)

declared that the New World was no longer open to aggression. Although this American policy had little practical effect, the Russians became discouraged after systematic slaughter virtually wiped out the sea otters and the agricultural operations failed to meet expectations. In 1839, Moscow ordered the Russian-American Company to sell out. Two years later the fort was purchased for $30,000 by Captain John A. Sutter, and the Russians returned to Alaska.

The fort was subsequently held by several other private owners before being taken over by the state just prior to the great 1906 earthquake. Although fires in 1970 and 1971 wiped out much of the Fort Ross complex, the church has been carefully reconstructed. Adjacent are a pair of blockhouses as well as the commandant's house, which now serves as a small museum with background on the Russian occupation. To pass this historic site without stopping is unthinkable.

Leaving the fort, S.R. 1 leads down a steep switchback to Jenner and the Sonoma Coast State Beaches. The 11 miles of public beach frontage here is popular with fishermen as well as hikers, who enjoy exploring the Salmon Creek sand dunes. From November to April, it is sometimes possible from several vista points to see whales migrating. At the south end of the Sonoma Coast beaches is picturesque Bodega Bay, sport and commercial fishing center and home of the University of California Marine Biology Laboratory,

which can be visited by appointment. Out at the end of Bodega Head, you'll find a vast hole dug out by Pacific Gas and Electric as the site for a nuclear power generating station. The project was canceled after environmentalists pointed out that serious seismic hazards precluded safe siting at this location. As a result, the area remains an ideal site for a day of fishing, beachcombing, or hiking along the ocean bluffs. Limited camping facilities are available, as well as some motel and rental units. From Bodega Bay, you can head inland back to U.S. 101 or continue south via S.R. 1 into the San Francisco area.

An alternate route through Mendocino and Sonoma counties is U.S. 101, offering access to a number of resort areas and historic sites in the region. At Longvale, S.R. 162 leads east off U.S. 101 to the historic frontier town of Covelo and the adjacent Round Valley Indian Reservation. Farther south, near U.S. 101, is Lake Mendocino, with ample camping facilities for visitors who come here to fish, swim, and waterski. Its proximity to the main highway makes it an excellent place to stop and cool off on a hot summer day. Just beyond Lake Mendocino, a cutoff north leads to the Lake Pillsbury resort region, while southward, S.R. 20 gives access to Clear Lake. Today people flock to this, California's largest natural lake, for much the same reasons that made the area home to Indian tribes in earlier days. Here they found fishing in the lake, hunt-

Clear Lake, California's largest natural lake. (*Redwood Empire Association*)

The "Valley of a Thousand Smokes" has attracted such distinguished tourists as U. S. Grant, Mark Twain, and Theodore Roosevelt. (*Redwood Empire Association*)

ing in the nearby mountains, and mineral springs believed to have curative powers. Now a growing recreation, second-home, and retirement area, Clear Lake offers good bass fishing and is popular with waterskiers. On the west side of the lake is Lakeport, the county seat, where you can visit the old vine-covered stone courthouse and Indian museum.

Leaving the lake, you can either head south via S.R. 175 through the Cobb Mountain resort area, with its old Indian hot springs, and into the Napa Valley, or you can return to U.S. 101 by driving west on S.R. 175. This route passes through Hopland, best known for its hopfields and towering oasthouses used to cure hops. About 13 miles south on U.S. 101 is the cutoff to the Geysers. Such distinguished tourists as U.S. Grant, Mark Twain, and Theodore Roosevelt have come to visit the steam spouts and cauldrons still visible at this remote site, now the home of geothermal power plants. You can loop back to the main road at Geyserville, just a few miles south of Asti, home of the Italian Swiss Colony Winery started as a utopian cooperative by Swiss and Italians from San Francisco.

This same Russian River region of Sonoma County was also home to three other utopian communities. One, a French-speaking community known as Icaria Speranzia, bought 885 acres of vineyard and orchard land here in 1881. Its fifty-five members pooled their possessions and credited each other with labor premiums for time worked. At the end of the year, part of the surplus was retained by the community and the remainder divided equally among the members. Unfortunately, a recession cut into the dream of these utopians, and the colony closed in 1886.

Another community, Altruria, organized by a group of egalitarian-minded Bay Area residents inspired by an obscure William Dean Howells novel, was even shorter-lived. In 1894, they acquired 185 acres on Mark West Creek, just west of Santa Rosa and embarked on plans to dam the creek, thereby creating a lake that would provide hydroelectric power for the community as well as a new tourist hotel. With financial support from Altrurian clubs in cities across the state, the colony moved ahead, ignoring the carping of San Francisco *Examiner* columnist Ambrose Bierce, who wrote: "Of the amiable asses who have founded the Altrurian colony at Mark West it ought to be sufficient to explain that their scheme is based upon the intellectual diversions of such humorists as Plato, More, Fourier, Bellamy, and Howells. That assures the ludicrous fizzle of the enterprise." And indeed, by June 1895, the community had run out of money and was forced to disband.

While Altruria flopped, Fountain Grove, another utopian experiment started in a valley just north of Santa Rosa, proved more prosperous. The project began in 1875, when Thomas Lake Harris, "primate"

Thomas Lake Harris, founder of the utopian community Fountain Grove.

Waring, to the ridicule of the San Francisco press, which ran headlines like "No More a Celibate." Fountain Grove continued producing wine after Harris left, and in 1900 the pivotal man sold out his interest to five colony members. The winery closed in 1934, and today all that remains of Fountain Grove is a red barn that new developers have promised to save as they carve up the onetime utopia for homes and factories.

While in Santa Rosa, you'll want to visit monuments to the city's two best-known residents, Luther Burbank and Robert L. Ripley. At the Burbank Home and Memorial Gardens are the greenhouses where the naturalist developed many hybrid flowers as well as larger fruits and vegetables. He credited much of his success to this locale. "I firmly believe," he once wrote, ". . . that this is the chosen spot of all the earth, as far as nature is concerned. The climate is perfect . . . everything is like a beautiful spring day all the time." Burbank is buried here, at the foot of a 118-foot cedar of Lebanon he planted himself. Also interred in Santa Rosa is Ripley of "Believe It or Not" fame. You can visit the worthwhile Ripley Memorial Museum situated on the edge of Julliard Park in a century-old church made from the wood cut from a single redwood.

Before leaving Santa Rosa, you may want to stop off at the Chamber of Commerce and pick up a Sonoma County Farm Trails Map. More than 100 farmers, processors, and growers shown on this map invite visitors to their farms and shops to buy apples, cherries, eggs, zucchini, honey, raspberries, and dozens of

of the Brotherhood of the New Life, began construction of an impressive complex that would become home to his minions. This utopian creed was based on an amalgam of Christianity, mysticism, spiritualism, Swedenborgianism, and antimonopoly socialism, with Harris serving as the focal point. As Robert V. Hine explains in *California's Utopian Colonies,* Harris proclaimed himself a "pivotal man . . . within whom the cosmic forces of good and evil battled for predominance on a physical plane. Christ would appear again on earth, but his coming would be announced through the pivotal personality. The concept of the primate or pivotal man worked on Harris's mind until he came eventually to associate, if not identify, himself with Christ. God was conceived of as bisexual, and Christ revealed himself as the Divine Man-Woman. . . . Through sex, in its purely spiritual aspects, man came closest to God."

These and other theories were widely misinterpreted and led critics to allege that free love was a way of life at this self-proclaimed "Eden of the West." In fact, Harris remained celibate during his seventeen years at Fountain Grove, which supported itself through production of some excellent wines. But in 1891, publication of a biography that implied Harris was both corrupt and immoral led to a storm of criticism that persuaded him to leave Fountain Grove. Just before doing so, he married his longtime secretary, Jane Lee

Former headquarters at Fountain Grove. (*Brotherhood of Life Museum*)

COMMON WATER AND

Check	Time Seen	WHERE SEEN USUALLY	Size	GENERAL BODY COLOR	
* 1. Grebe, Eared	R.	1. On ponds, lagoons, or ocean	M.	1. Dark gray above, white below	1. W s o
* 2. Grebe, Western	W.V.	2. On the ocean	L.	2. Black above, white below	2. T
* 3 Grebe, Pied-billed	R.	3. On ponds, lagoons or sloughs	M.	3. In winter, brownish above, whitish below; in summer, blackish-brown above.	3. P
‡ 4. Pelican, White	R.	4. Inland on lakes or ponds	V.L.	4. White above and below	4. W
* 5. Pelican, Brown	R.	5. On ocean or bays	V.L.	5. In winter, brownish above and below; in summer, gray streaked with brown above, brown below.	5. M n
‡ 6. Cormorant, Double-crested	R.	6. On ocean, bays or inland	L.	6. Black. Immature brownish	6. T
‡ 7. Cormorant, Brandt's	R.	7. On ocean or bays, never inland	L.	7. "	7.
‡ 8. Cormorant, Pelagic	R.	8. " L. Smaller than the others.	L.	8. "	8.
* 9. Heron, California	R.	9. On marshes, sloughs, beaches or fields.	V.L.	9. Gray-blue on back, white streaked below. Immature gray.	9. T in
*10. Egret, American	R. or W.V.	10. On marshes, sloughs or fields	V.L.	10. White all over	10. L d
*11. Egret, Snowy	W.V.	11. "	L.	11. "	11.
*12. Heron, Green	R. or S.V.	12. On marshes, ponds or ditches	L.	12. Back and wings greenish or bluish, under parts, brown. Immature brown above, white below streaked with brown.	12. T di
*13. Heron, Black-crowned Night	R.	13. Feed mostly at night time on marshes. Roost in trees or in tules during the day.	L.	13. Gray and white. Young brown streaked with white.	13. B w se
†14. Goose, White-fronted	W.V.	14. On marshes, ponds or fields	L.	14. Brown.	14. B
†15. Goose, Canada	W.V.	15. "	L.	15. Back brown, under parts gray	15. H c
16-21. River and Pond Ducks					
†16. Mallard Duck, Common	W.V. or R.	16. Rivers, ponds, lagoons, bays, etc.	L.	16. Brown above, gray below. Female brown all over.	16. M ha si
†17. Baldpate or American Widgeon	W.V.	17. "	L.	17. Pinkish-brown above, on chest and flanks, abdomen white. Female brownish, heavily streaked.	17. B th o
†18. Pintail or Sprig	W.V.	18. "	L.	18. Back gray with fine black lines, white below. Female brownish, much streaked.	18. H ne
†19. Teal, Green-winged	W.V.	19. "	M.	19. Grayish-brown with brownish wash on chest. Female brownish, abdomen white.	19. C ey
†20. Teal, Cinnamon	W.V. or S.V.	20. "	M.	20. Cinnamon-red mostly. Female brownish, much streaked.	20. B
†21. Shoveller	W.V.	21. "	L.	21. Reddish-brown, black and white. Female brownish, mottled.	21. H w
22-26. Sea or Diving Ducks					
†22. Redhead	W.V.	22. Found in ponds, lagoons, etc., or in the ocean.	L.	22. Red head and neck, gray back and flanks Female uniform brown.	22. B a
†23. Canvasback	W.V.	23. "	L.	23. Red head and neck, white back and flanks. Female with brownish head, gray back and flanks.	23. B
†24. Lesser Scaup Duck or Bluebill	W.V.	24. "	L.	24. Head and breast black, lower back and flanks white. Female brownish with white abdomen.	24. S wh
†25. Scoter, White-winged	W.V.	25. Mostly seen on the ocean	L.	25. Black. Female solid dark brown	25. L blo be
†26. Scoter, Surf	W.V.	26. "	L.	26. "	26. W Fe in

R.—Resident.
S.V.—Summer Visitor.
W.V.—Winter Visitor.
V.L.—Very Large (30 inches or more).

L.—Large (about size Mallard Duck—20-25 inches).
M.—Medium (from 12-18 inches).
S.—Small (about the size of a Killdeer—8-11 inches)
V.S.—Very small (about size of Western Sandpiper— 5-7 inches).

...ACTERISTIC MARKINGS	REMARKS	BILL	LEGS AND FEET
on cheeks and in each wing. In ...d is black and crested with a tuft feathers on each side.	1-3. Expert divers, sometimes called "Hell Divers." All grebes commonly leap forward and then dive head first.	1. Slender, black, longer than head.	lobed webs.
of black and white is conspicuous. ...ck on throat in summer	2. Neck long and slender	2. Slender, yellow, longer than head.	"
	3. Neck slender, head and neck somewhat snake-like.	3. Shorter than head, black band in middle in summer.	"
...k-tipped	4.	4. Huge, yellow with pouch below.	webbed between all four toes.
...s with white on top of head and	5. Dive into water with a splash when fishing.	5. Huge, yellow above, gray below.	"
...h naked, orange	6-8. Cormorants have long slender necks, wings set far back on body, and a short tail. Fly with bill held at an upward angle.	6-8. Cormorants have bills as long as or longer than head.	"
" , blue			
" , red; white patch in each ...ing.			
...l white when mature, black when	9-11. Herons crook their necks when flying. Necks long, slender. Miscalled "Cranes" by some. Cranes fly with outstretched necks.	9. Slender, sharply-pointed, longer than head.	large, without distinct webs. Comb on middle toe.
...s of white feathers in a cascade ...n spring.		10. Slender, yellow, longer than head.	" black.
_____ " _____		11. Slender, black longer than head.	legs black, feet yellow.
black, back and sides of neck red-	12. Solitary birds as a rule. Eyes yellow	12. Longer than head, dark with yellow on sides.	greenish.
...nd back; forehead white; two long ...ers on back of head in breeding	13. Feed mostly at night time	13. Sharply pointed, black, longer than head.	yellow.
...hite around bill	14. Formerly more abundant	14. Shorter than head, pink	orange yellow, webs between 3 toes only.
...eck black; white patches on cheeks ...ther on the throat.	15. _____ " _____	15. Shorter than head, black	black.
...een head with white collar. Female ...n speculum with white bar on each	16-21. All river and pond ducks have a small unlobed hind toe. Dabble or tip for food.	16-21. Flattened often with straining device on sides.	feet webbed between 3 toes.
	16. The ancestor of most domestic ducks, formerly our most common duck.	16. Yellow	orange legs and feet.
...a area on top of head in male, hence ...a name. Large white patch in top ...male, smaller in female.	17.	17. Bluish	grayish.
...with white stripe extending up ...le.	18. Neck and wings long and slender. Middle tail feathers much elongated in male.	18. Bluish	grayish.
...rown head with green stripe through ...Green speculum in both sexes.	19. Rapid flight and small size	19. Black	brown in male, gray in female.
...um in both sexes	20. _____ " _____ ; red eyes	20. Black in male, gray-black in female.	orange in male, yellow in female.
...nish-black, flanks reddish, breast ...ale. Female brownish.	21. Shovel-shaped bill is characteristic	21. Black, longer than head, broader at tip. Female has lighter bill.	orange.
	22-26. Sea or Diving Ducks have lobed hind toe and are expert divers. Are more often seen in deep water.		
...reast and tail. Female has gray ...ge of wings.	22. Rounded head	22. Bluish-gray with black tip	grayish.
...k. Female has brown breast	23. Long low sloping forehead and long bill are diagnostic. Eyes red in male.	23. Black	grayish.
...white in both sexes. Female has ...at base of bill.	24. Purplish reflections on head of male. Eyes yellow.	24. Bluish	black.
...e patch in wing. Male has white ...nd eye. Female has white blotch ...nd another in front of eye.	25. Scoters are large heavy birds with swollen bills and long sloping foreheads.	25. Orange in male, dusky in female.	black and flesh color or orange.
...h on forehead and back of neck. ...white patch below eye and another ...eye.	26. _____ " _____	26. _____ " _____	"

The arrangement of this list is according to the relationships of the birds as accepted by the American Ornithologists Union.

Prepared by Adele Lewis Grant, Ph.D., and Blanche Vignos.—Reviewed by California Academy of Sciences, Santa Barbara Museum of Natural History, State Dept. of Fish and Game.

For LAWS in full, see **Fish and Game Code.** Secure **Abstract California Sporting Fish and Game Laws** and **Migratory Birds,** where annual hunting and fishing licenses sold, or State **Department of Fish and Game, Resources Bldg.,** Sacramento, or **Ferry Bldg., San Francisco 11,** or **State Bldg., Los Angeles, Calif.**

Check	Time Seen	WHERE SEEN USUALLY	Size	GENERAL BODY COLOR	
†27. Ruddy Duck	R.	27. In ponds, lagoons, bays or in the ocean.	M.	27. Reddish-brown in summer; brown in winter. Female brown.	27. C
†28. American Coot	R.	28. Ponds, bays, rivers, etc.	M.	28. Grayish-black	28. B
29-42. Shore Birds					
*29. Plover, Snowy	R.	29. On beaches, shores of ponds or lagoons.	V.S.	29. Gray-brown above, white below	29. A a
*30. Killdeer	R.	30. On beaches, ponds, shores, cultivated fields, pastures, etc.	S.	30. Back and wings black, under parts white	30. T re
*31. Plover, Black-bellied	W.V.	31. On beaches, shores of ponds, lagoons, etc.	S.	31. Dark brown barred with white above; white below in winter, black in summer.	31. I b.
*32. Wilson or Jack Snipe	W.V. or R.	32. Wet meadows or marshes	S.	32. Brown streaked with black above; under parts mostly speckled brown.	32. B re
*33. Curlew, Long-billed	W.V.	33. Ocean shores and borders of lagoons, ponds or bays.	L.	33. Light cinnamon-brown barred and streaked with dark brown above, underparts light brown.	33. T
*34. Curlew, Hudsonian	W.V.	34. "	M.	34. Brown above and below, barred with darker brown.	34. B tl
*35. Sandpiper, Spotted	W.V.	35. Rocky ocean beaches or lagoons or inland bodies of water.	S.	35. Brown above, white below spotted with black in summer, unspotted in winter.	35. L
*36. Willet, Western	W.V.	36. On sandy beaches or shores of lagoons or bays, etc.	M.	36. Gray above, unspotted; grayish-brown below.	36. W w
*37. Yellow-legs, Greater	W.V.	37. Marshy shores and mud flats, often wading in water.	M.	37. Grayish-brown above, barred with white; white below.	37. W
*38. Sandpiper, Least	W.V.	38. Sandy beaches and open mud flats.	V.S.	38. Grayish-brown above, white below	38. B
*39. Dowitcher, Long-billed	W.V.	39. "	S.	39. Dark gray above, light gray below	39. W w
*40. Sandpiper, Western	W.V.	40. "	V.S.	40. Grayish-brown above, white below	40. D
*41. Godwit, Marbled	W.V.	41. "	L.	41. Reddish-brown above, paler below	41. ...
*42. Sanderling	W.V.	42. Sandy beaches, shores of ponds, etc.	V.S.	42. Gray above, white below; chestnut bars on upper part in summer.	42. ...
43-48. Gulls					
*43. Glaucous-winged Gull	W.V.	43. On any body of water on or near the coast, beaches, etc.	L.	43-48. Immature gulls have uniform dark plumage the first year; mottled, the second. 43. Back bluish-gray, under parts white	43. H w
*44. Western Gull	R.	44. Water front, beaches, ponds, etc.	L.	44. Back dark gray, under parts white	44. H pe
*45. California Gull	W.V.	45. Water front, beaches, ponds, bays, lawns, and inland.	M.	45. Back bluish-gray, under parts white	45. H st w
*46. Ring-billed Gull	W.V.	46. "	M.	46. Back light gray, under parts white	46. ...
*47. Heermann's Gull	W.V.	47. Water front, beaches, bays, lagoons.	M.	47. Back deep grayish-black, under parts gray	47. H br
*48. Bonaparte's Gull	W.V.	48. Water front, beaches, ponds, etc.	S.	48. Back light gray, under parts white	48. H w ba pa
49-50. Terns					
*49. Forster's Tern	W.V. or S.V.	49. Ocean shores, lagoons, ponds, marshes, irrigation areas, etc.	M.	49. Back pearl gray, under parts white	49. To w
*50. Black Tern	W.V. or S.V.	50. "	S.	50. Summer, upper parts black, dark gray; under parts black. Winter, upper parts dark gray; under, forehead, back of neck - white.	50. In

*Protected at all times.
†Open season at certain times.
‡Not protected in California.
R.—Resident.
V. L.—Very Large (30 inches or more).

L.—Large (about the size of a Mallard Duck—20-25 inches).
M.—Medium (from 12-18 inches).
S.—Small (about the size of a Killdeer—8-11 inches).
V. S.—Very small (about the size of the Western Sandpiper—5-7 inches).

THE CALIFORNIA CONSERVATION C
other agencies in sponsoring: Californ
Good Manners campaign, and Conferer

...ACTERISTIC MARKINGS	REMARKS	BILL	LEGS AND FEET
...area under tail white	27. Short stiff tail, usually held up at a sharp angle.	27. Short, broad, blue or dusky	blue or dusky.
...eld on forehead white	28. Eyes red. Toes with scalloped webs	28. Shorter than head, broad, white.	greenish with scalloped webs.
...lack on each side of throat, just ...ad and back of eye.	29-31. Most plovers have a white forehead. 29. Commonly follows the waves back and forth gleaning food.	29. Black, shorter than head	gray.
...ars across breast. Tail and rump ...n.	30. Jerks head and body when standing. Very noisy. Often heard during nights.	30. .... "	gray.
...breast and flanks streaked with ...ck patch on body under wings; ...se of tail.	31.	31. .... "	black.
...buff stripes on head. Tail short, ...n.	32. Hides in vegetation. Corkscrew type of flight.	32. Greenish-gray, straight, much longer than head.	greenish gray.
..., cinnamon-brown	33. Very long decurved bill. More often seen on muddy shores of ponds, etc.	33. Pink and black, at least 3 times as long as head, decurved	gray.
			gray.
...line over eye; narrow light line ...wn; top of head blackish.	34. Long decurved bill. More often seen on sandy beaches.	34. Black mostly, at least twice as long as head.	
...te spots through wing	35. Teeters or bobs vigorously	35. Orange-yellow in summer, gray in winter.	pinkish-gray in summer yellow-green in winter.
...k, crossed with broad band of ...p white.	36. Bobs. Color pattern on wings very conspicuous in flight.	36. Black, longer than head	greenish-gray.
...mp and base of tail	37. Bobs and nods head. Legs long and yellow.	37. .... "	yellow.
...ked with darker gray	38. Occurs in great flocks. The smallest of our shore birds.	38. Black, shorter than head	greenish.
...down lower back; rump and tail ...line over eye.	39. Usually seen in flocks..........	39. Black, at least twice as long as head.	black.
...on breast	40. Often seen with Least Sandpipers. Most readily separated by the color of the legs.	40. Black, as long or longer than head.	black.
	41. Long upturned bill, pink at base, black at tip.	41. Longer than head, upcurved	gray.
	42. Follows waves in and out; the whitest of our sandpipers.	42. Black, much longer than head, straight.	black.
	43-48. Wings long	43-48. Bill thickened, the upper mandible longer and hooked.	webbed between 3 of the 4 toes.
...c and breast white in summer, ...h dark gray in winter.	43. This is the only gull we have which has no black on wing tips.	43. Light yellow with red spot on lower mandible.	pinkish.
...and breast white, wings black tip-...with white.	44. The only gull with us in winter having a pure white head and neck.	44. Deep yellow with red spot on lower mandible.	pinkish.
...c and breast white in summer, ...th dusky in winter, wings tipped	45. One of our most common gulls	45. Yellow with a red spot on lower mandible and a black spot in front of this.	greenish.
... " "	46. Lighter gray than the California Gull and more agile.	46. Yellow with black ring near tip.	yellow.
...pper neck white in summer, grayish-...inter; tail black, tipped with white.	47. Our darkest gull. The red bill is distinctive.	47. Red tipped with black	black.
...black hood in summer, white in ...a dark spot before eye and another ...e. Large patch of white in outer ...g, this edged with black.	48. Our smallest gull .... 49-50. Legs shorter than gulls. Plunge into water with a splash when fishing. Wings slender, long pointed.	48. Black	orange-red.
...d black in summer, white in winter ...k stripe from bill through eye.	49. Tail deeply forked	49. Orange at base, rest black	orange.
...black spot back of eye	50. Feed on insects even more than on fish..	50. Black	blackish.

...o-operates with Federal and State Departments, Schools, and ...ation Week, March 7-14 annually, and Year-Round Outdoor

THIS IS LEAFLET C-659, 3¢ each. Stamps accepted for small orders. Please add mailing costs—6¢ for each 4 Leaflets or less. Address: **CALIFORNIA CONSERVATION COUNCIL** (Leaflets Office) 912 Santa Barbara Street, Santa Barbara, California, 93101.

20th Printing revised—170,000—

The forested Russian River is a favorite resort of Bay Area vacationers.
(*Redwood Empire Association*)

other items in bulk at considerable discounts. Even if you don't happen to need smoked meat or rhododendrons, you may enjoy poking around the back country, where a number of farmers have set up picnic tables and offer you a chance to see their animals and operations. Some of these historic farms date back to the days of the Russian-American Company.

Santa Rosa also offers easy access to the Russian River region, long a favorite of Bay Area vacationers. This forested resort area has everything from the exclusive Bohemian Grove (where famous businessmen and politicians retreat each summer) to public beaches jammed on weekends. You can rent a canoe, fish, or visit the Armstrong Redwood Grove north of Guerneville. There are also a number of worthwhile side trips to such places as Occidental, known for its generous Italian restaurants that serve gargantuan meals at modest prices (historically, the most interesting of these eating emporiums is the charming old Union Hotel), and Sebastopol, an old apple-growing center now, unfortunately, being urbanized, that is distinguished by the Enmanji Buddhist temple, one of the

area's leading architectural attractions. From here, you can return south to U.S. 101 and the community of Petaluma, onetime egg basket of the world and home of the Petaluma adobe. This two-story structure with wide balconies served as the base for Mexican General Mariano Vallejo's agricultural operations in Sonoma County. Each summer the general brought his family down here from the Sonoma hacienda to lead a fiesta at sheepshearing time. Leaving the adobe, you can head to the old part of town, which features a number of fine Victorian buildings. But over on the west side of U.S. 101 you'll see the latest wave of subdivisions installed by ambitious developers. Here, in southern Sonoma County, rural California yields to the urban Bay Area.

Mendocino, Lake, and Sonoma Notes

Barbara Mullen's *Mendocino Coast* ($1.95, CM Publications, P.O. Box 3330, San Rafael, CA 94902) and *Sonoma County Crossroads* ($3.00 same publisher) provide good introductions to their respective areas. You can also write the Fort Bragg/Mendocino Coast Chamber of Commerce, P.O. Box 1141, Fort Bragg, CA 95437; the Lake County Chamber of Commerce, Lakeport, CA 95453; the Santa Rosa Chamber of Commerce, 637 First Street & Santa Rosa Avenue, Santa Rosa, CA 95404; and the Russian River Region, Inc., Armstrong Woods Road and 3rd, Guerneville, CA 95446. More details on the area are available from the *Redwood Empire Visitors' Guide* (Redwood Empire Association, 476 Post Street, San Francisco, CA 94102).

Boontling Made Simple

Before venturing into Boonville you may want to pick up some of the local vocabulary to impress the "natives." Here are a few everyday words:

Kimmie: man
Dame: woman
Tweed: child
Gorms: food
Zeece: coffee
Wee: small
Hairk: haircut
Schoolch: school teacher
Highheeler: police officer
Charley balled: embarrassed
Bucky walter: pay phone
Tweeds: hippies
Minks: girls
Moshe: car
Burlap: to make love
Spat: .22-caliber rifle
Skipe: preacher
Skipe region: church

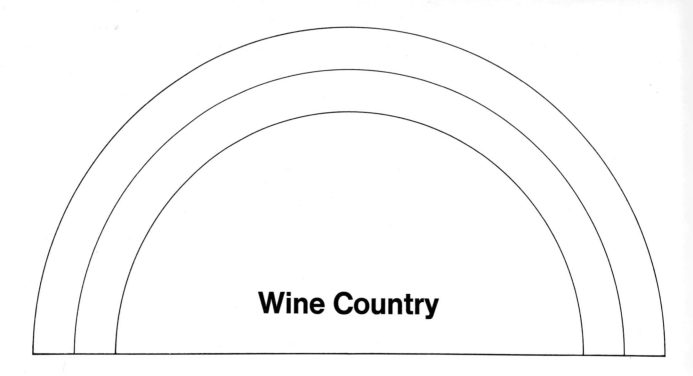

Wine Country

The Best of Wine Country

State park: Sugarloaf Ridge
Camping: Sugarloaf Ridge
Hot springs: Calistoga
Historic site: Jack London State Historic Park
Museum: Silverado, Saint Helena
Historic building: Vallejo home, Sonoma
Town square: Sonoma
Veranda: Mark West Springs
Ruin: Wolf House, Jack London State Historic Park
Main road: S.R. 12
Side road: Warm Springs Road, Glen Ellen to Kenwood
Historical winery tour: Christian Brothers' Mount La Salle Vineyards
Modern winery tour: Sterling Vineyards
Wine tasting: Christian Brothers' Mount LaSalle; Sterling; Louis M. Martini; Charles Krug; Freemark Abbey; Mondavi; Sebastiani
Small winery: Heitz Wine Cellars
Champagne: Schramsberg
Valley view: Napa Valley from Sugarloaf Ridge

Although California has nine wine districts spreading from Mendocino County to Riverside, most people associate the state's Wine Country with the Napa and Sonoma valleys just north of San Francisco. This region has the heaviest concentration of wineries and boasts premium labels like Martini, Schramsberg, Mondavi, Heitz, and Freemark Abbey.

But even if you don't know the difference between a Chardonnay and a Sauvignon blanc, a special visit to this historic region is in order. With their sloping vineyards, aging wineries, and tree-lined byways, these two valleys fulfill everyone's preconception of a wine-producing region. Unlike the San Joaquin Valley, where some of the giant wineries have all the warmth of oil refineries, the Napa and Sonoma valleys have retained a human scale and the rich character that has attracted such diverse residents as Robert Louis Stevenson, Jack London, and Arthur Hailey.

What brings most people to this region is a chance to drink fine wines for nothing. Of course, you can spend hours weaving your way among the wineries. But you'll be making a mistake if you don't take time out to visit some of the area's numerous little communities, hot springs, parks, and historic sites. Instead of making a day trip, plan on staying over a couple of nights. This way you'll be able to avoid the most common pitfall of Wine Country visits—intoxication.

Before starting your Wine Country trip, set your priorities. Some wineries that are generous in the tasting room sell a second-rate product. On the other hand, a number of premium establishments have no tasting rooms. And even places that have fine wines and good tasting programs don't put out their best vintages.

Regardless of your interests, don't overlook the historical and technical aspects of the business. A number of wineries offer excellent tours of their total operations. A worthwhile one is the Christian Brothers' Mount La Salle Vineyards located in the redwoods 8 miles northwest of Napa. Although most tourists stop at the brothers' Greystone Cellars near Saint Helena, you'll be better off here at headquarters. Not only is Mount La Salle less crowded, but it gives you a look at the Christian Brothers' novitiate, winery, and vineyards filled with European pedigreed varietal grapes. Eventually the mature grapes are harvested, crushed, and bottled here into Christian Brothers' table wines as well as the Mount La Salle sacramental wines. Keep an eye out for the winery's esteemed cellarmaster, Brother Timothy.

Another excellent historical tour is the Buena Vista Winery, 2 miles northeast of Sonoma. Here you can explore one of the state's older wineries, visit its cellars, and enjoy a picnic. For contrast, visit one of the region's most recent additions, Sterling Vineyards, south of Calistoga. Here, a tramway takes you from the parking lot up to the new Moorish winery. The ride costs $2, but you can apply it to any vintage wine you buy. Instead of rushing visitors through, Sterling offers self-guided tours and lawns and picnic tables where people can sample in a leisurely fashion.

If your primary interest is tasting, consider the afore-

Napa Valley wine country. (*Redwood Empire Association*)

Tiburon Vintners. This Northern California winery sells an extensive line via mail within the state only. Personalized label service makes these wines an ideal gift. You must be over twenty-one to order, and the firm can only ship to homes or offices with California addresses. Wine can not be sent to post office boxes. For information, write Tiburon Vintners, Windsor Vineyards, Windsor, Sonoma County, CA 95492.

---

mentioned Christian Brothers' Mount La Salle Vineyards and Sterling Vineyards as musts. Two other Napa Valley establishments traditionally generous with a wide variety of wines are Louis M. Martini south of Saint Helena and Charles Krug on the north side of the same community. You won't leave either place thirsty. In the Sonoma Valley the Sebastiani Vineyards has been thoughtful about letting people sip a wide variety of offerings.

You'll have a hard time getting two people to agree on where to buy the best wine in this region. But in the Napa Valley, Martini, Heitz, and Freemark Abbey wineries near Saint Helena plus the Robert Mondavi operation near Oakville all get high marks. And in Sonoma, the generous Sebastianis are credited with a first-rate product. But this is a subjective evaluation; ultimately you'll do best to move about and be your own judge.

One subject that does not draw much disagreement among connoisseurs is Schramsberg champagne. Perhaps you remember this is the brand Richard Nixon took along when he went to visit Chairman Mao a few years back. Jerry Ford likes to serve it to his guests also. In fact, just about everyone is high on this product, produced 4 miles north of Saint Helena. This winery was founded in 1862 by Jacob Schram, who aged his wines in limestone tunnels dug out by coolies. Although these champagne cellars are now a state historic landmark, it's not easy to get inside. If you call 707-942-4558 and give Schramsberg owner, Jack Davies, a convincing story, he may let you in for a tour. Because his champagne is produced in limited quantities, tasting is not allowed. But be polite and you'll be allowed to purchase some of this premium product to take home.

After your visit to Schramsberg, you may want to stop off at the Silverado Museum in Saint Helena, commemorating one of the winery's earliest boosters, Robert Louis Stevenson. In his book *The Silverado Squatters,* Stevenson describes how he managed to sample eighteen of Jacob Schram's vintages in a single day. The author's wine-tasting tour was a highlight of the two-month honeymoon-convalescence Steven-

son spent on Mount Saint Helena with his new wife, Fanny Osbourne.

The writer, who was then thirty, had met this California woman in a Grez, France, artists' colony and followed her back to the United States, where he persuaded her to divorce her husband. By the time they married in San Francisco on May 19, 1880, Stevenson was broke and seriously ill with tuberculosis. So the couple moved into the abandoned bunkhouse of the old Silverado Mine, accompanied by Fanny's twelve-year-old son, Samuel. Not only did the writer regain his health here on the mountain, but he also won parental acceptance of his marriage. Now blessed with an annual allowance, Stevenson took his wife to Scotland, where he resumed his writing career.

Although Stevenson's stay in the Napa Valley was relatively brief, it had an important impact on his subsequent work. Descriptions of the region abound in his writing. For instance, Mount Saint Helena formed the basis of descriptions of Spy-Glass Hill in *Treasure Island.* Also "Juan Silverado," a Mexican slang description of the mine where he stayed, is believed to have inspired the name "Long John Silver."

For the full story of Stevenson's days in this region, you can read *The Silverado Squatters,* visit the Silverado Museum, drive the Silverado Trail through the Napa Valley, or visit the largely undeveloped Robert Louis Stevenson State Park north of Calistoga. Here you can hike the steep 1-mile-long trail to the old Silverado Mine and site of the honeymoon cabin.

Although there are no camping sites at the Stevenson park, you can pitch a tent nearby at the Bothe-Napa Valley State Park south of Calistoga. There is also good camping at Sugarloaf Ridge State Park, reached via the Sonoma Valley town of Kenwood. If you prefer a bed, there is a variety of accommodations in Napa and Sonoma, including a few small inns. Or consider staying at one of several hot springs resorts around Calistoga, where you can revitalize with a volcanic mud bath.

While you're in the area, don't miss a second state park dedicated to one of California's best-known writers, Jack London. Located just west of Glen Ellen, this 48-acre ranch offers excellent views of London's beloved Valley of the Moon. Near the entrance is a museum located in the House of Happy Walls, which the writer's widow, Charmian, built as a memorial in 1919. Here, you'll find London's old office, manuscripts, brass bed, and south seas collection gathered during a twenty-seven-month honeymoon trip on his 42-foot ketch, *The Snark.*

On their return to California, the couple bought this ranch and hired work crews to build a twenty-six-room mansion with nine fireplaces, a courtyard, a reflecting pool, and a fireproof vault for manuscripts. Draft horses hauled in big boulders of volcanic lava, which were combined with redwood to erect the Wolf House. On August 22, 1913, just before the Londons planned to vacate their nearby cottage and move into the house, a fire consumed the place, leaving only the stone foundation, walls, and chimney. Today you can visit the ruins of the Wolf House and London's grave by taking an easy 1-mile walk down from the museum.

Although London's career was cut short in 1916, when he died of uremic poisoning at the age of forty, he left an extensive legacy. Besides his fifty books, which have been translated into thirty languages, he wrote hundreds of short stories that are standard reading in literature classes throughout the world. "I would rather be a superb meteor," he once wrote, "every atom of me in magnificent glow, than a sleepy and permanent planet. The proper function of man is to live, not to exist. I shall not waste my days in trying to prolong them. I shall use my time."

One other major historic site in this region is the town of Sonoma. It was here in 1846 that California declared its independence from Mexico and established the Bear Flag Republic. Mariano Guadalupe Vallejo, the resident Mexican general who had been advocating annexation of California by the United States, was arrested by the rebels at his Casa Grande home. Then the Mexican Flag was lowered and re-placed with the republic's new flag emblazoned with a grizzly bear.

One month after this nonviolent revolt, American naval forces took Monterey and declared that the republic was now United States property. In 1848, after the Mexican government signed the Treaty of Guadalupe Hidalgo with Washington, Vallejo turned to wine making, served two terms as mayor of Sonoma, and eventually became the region's first state senator. Today you can visit Vallejo's home, the Sonoma barracks where his soldiers drilled, and the Bear Flag Monument. Most of these sites are clustered around the Sonoma Plaza, where you can also stop at Mission San Francisco Solano, which was partially outfitted with gifts from Russian fur traders. When you're done sightseeing, be sure to walk over to the half-century-old Sonoma Cheese Factory for lunch (tours are available here).

By this time you may have noticed that we have refrained from mapping any specific routes through the Napa and Sonoma valleys. That's because the area is particularly serendipitous. If you take our advice and spend several days here, you'll inevitably do some doubling back and forth between these two regions. While this may seem unnecessary, it actually provides you with an excellent excuse to drive many of the

The House of Happy Walls, a memorial to Jack London. (*Redwood Empire Association*)

scenic back roads linking the valleys. One of the best pastimes in this region is simply winding through the hills and up the mountains, where you'll find a variety of Wine Country vantage points. The countryside is particularly fine in the spring and fall, but no matter when you go, schedule a leisurely trip. For instance, on the ride from the Calistoga area to Fulton (just north of Santa Rosa), you'll want to stop at the small petrified forest. Further on, you can pick up the road to Mark West Springs, where an old stage stop has been converted into a pleasant restaurant with a wide, shady veranda. In Glen Ellen, cut off on Warm Springs Road, which takes you to Kenwood via the scenic long way. And if your car has good brakes, try the mountainous route from Glen Ellen to Oakville. Should you run out of roads, park your car and go hiking in the undeveloped, uncrowded Annadel Farms State Park near Santa Rosa. It's a good way to clear your head after a hard day's tasting.

Wine Country Notes

Before heading for this region, get a copy of *California's Wine Wonderland,* a free thirty-page booklet on all the state's growing districts put out by the Wine Institute, 165 Post Street, San Francisco, CA 94108. For a more comprehensive treatment of the subject, you can get the beautifully photographed *California Wine* ($14.95, Lane Publishing Company, Willow and Middlefield Roads, Menlo Park, CA 94025). Other good information sources are the Sonoma Valley Chamber of Commerce, 461 First Street West, Sonoma, CA 95476; the Napa Chamber of Commerce, P.O. Box 636, Napa, CA 94558; and the Calistoga Chamber of Commerce, 1339 Lincoln Avenue, Calistoga, CA 94515.

For a comprehensive evaluation of hundreds of California vintages, get *The Buying Guide to California Wines* ($8.95, Wine Consultants of California, P.O. Box 19062, San Diego, CA 92119). Included are details on fine wines bottled in such small quantities they never even leave the state.

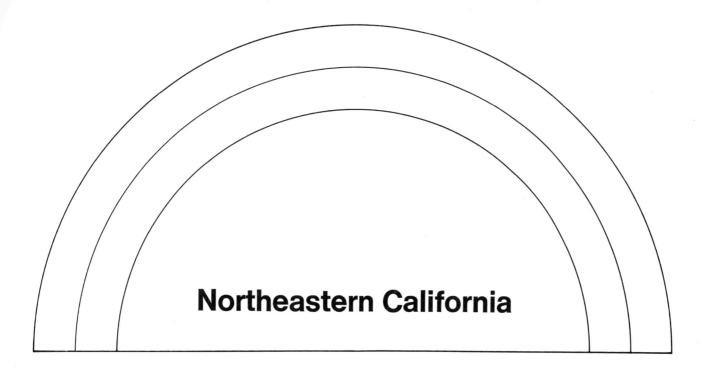

Northeastern California

The Best of Northeastern California

State park: McArthur-Burney Falls

Camping: McArthur-Burney Falls

Hiking: Lassen National Park

Waterskiing: Lake Almanor

Swimming: Lake Almanor; McArthur-Burney Falls State Park

Sailing: Lake Almanor

Mountain climbing: Mount Shasta

Volcano: Mount Lassen

Cinder cone: Lassen National Park

Caves: Lava Beds National Monument

Ice caves: Skull and Merrill, Lava Beds National Monument

Bird-watching: Tulelake

Gold panning: Feather River, above Upper Thermalito Bridge, Oroville

Geothermal activity: Bumpass Hell Trail, Lassen National Park

Obsidian: Glass Mountain

Waterfalls: McArthur-Burney

View: Lassen Peak; Mount Shasta

Drive: S.R. 70 along Feather River Canyon

Company town: Tennant

Chinese temple: Oroville

Pioneer museum: Oroville

Gold rush town: Cherokee

Private estate: Wyntoon (closed to public)

One great frustration in traveling through California is the feeling that you've arrived a generation too late. Often you come upon a new locale and find yourself thinking what a place it must have been back then before the postwar population influx, before subdivision, before freeways. However, there is one portion of the state that remains pretty much the way it's always been —scenic, spacious, and uncrowded—Northeastern California.

Most residents think of this region in terms of a few specific areas: Lassen National Park, Mount Shasta, McArthur-Burney Falls State Park, and the popular resorts of the Feather River Country. But beyond these and a handful of other vacation favorites, Northeastern California offers a variety of inexpensive, secluded attractions. Here you can pan for gold, explore obsidian mountains, visit national wildlife refuges, have beaches to yourself, fish in privacy, walk through miles of caves, climb volcanic cinder cones, visit old company towns, and hike through wilderness lake valleys. Most of these areas have so few visitors you may actually wind up feeling a little lonely.

The easiest way into the region from the central part of the state is through the town of Oroville, a community of 7500 that was once the state's busiest mining town with over 100 saloons and 25 hotels. Its appeal stemmed from the fact that it was situated directly above the richest placer deposits of gold in California. Even now experts estimate millions in gold ore lie beneath the city streets.

The town grew steadily as entrepreneurs set up the world's largest hydraulic gold mine at nearby Cherokee

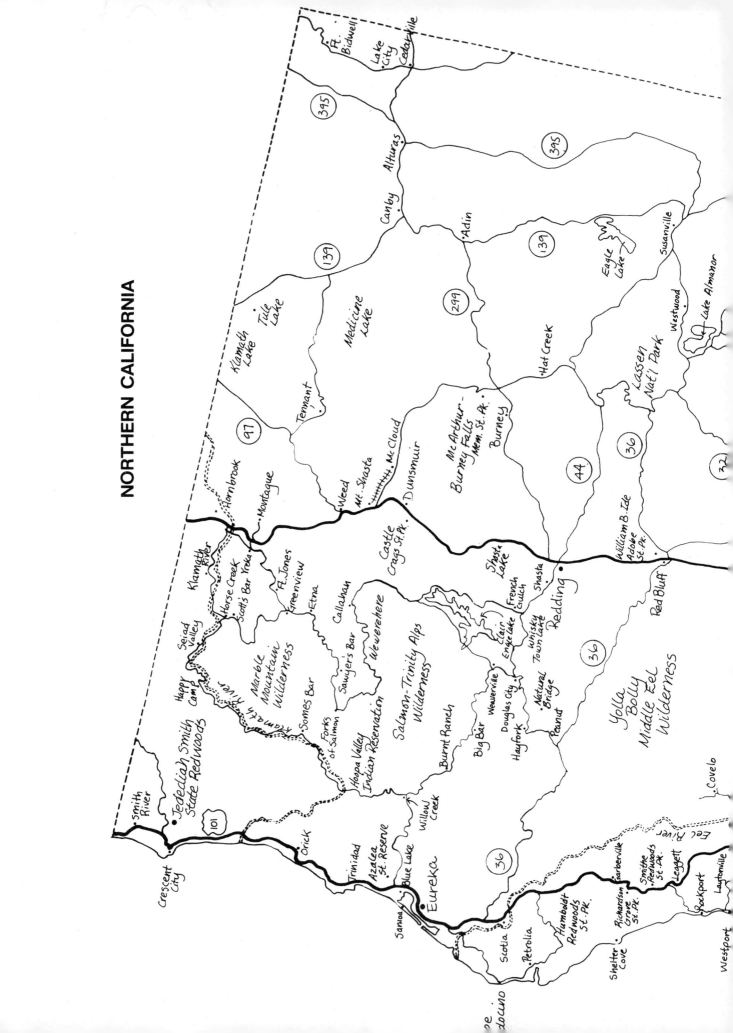

NORTHERN CALIFORNIA

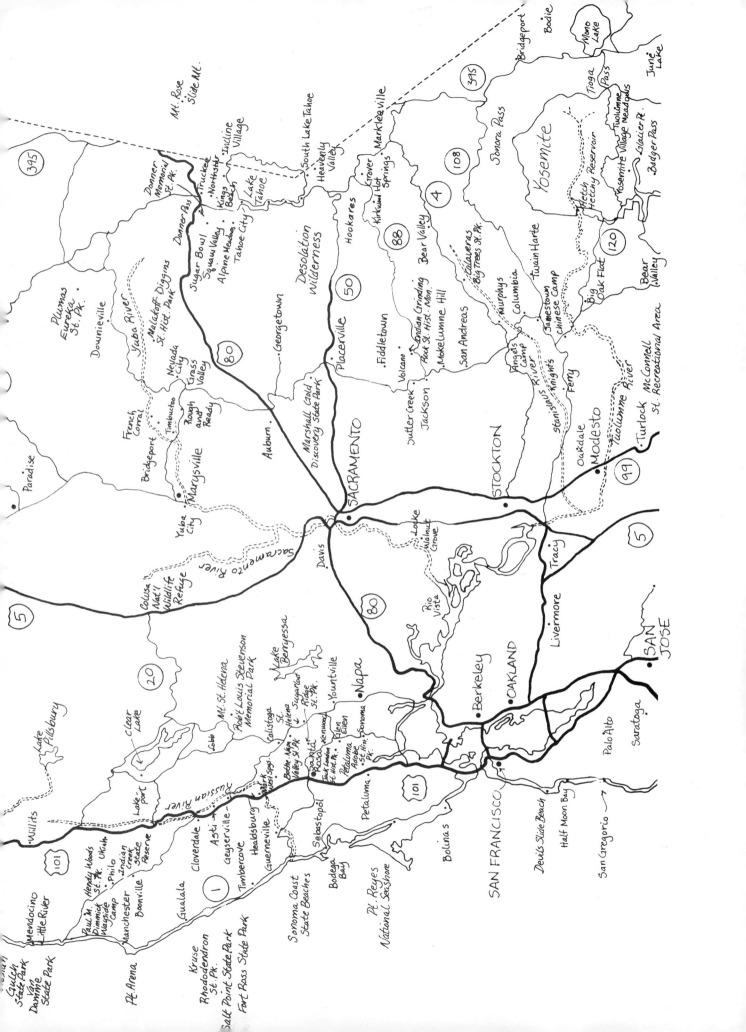

and established the first of forty-seven dredges along the Feather River. By 1875, Oroville's Chinese community alone exceeded 10,000. Although the town can no longer boast the largest Oriental population in the West, you can still visit the city's Chinese temple built with foreign aid from Emperor Quong She of the Ching dynasty.

While in Oroville, you may also want to visit the Pioneer Museum for its collection of artifacts from mining days, as well as some of the fine gold rush era homes such as the Lott House, now part of a city park. And at the corner of Oak Avenue and Quincy Road, you'll find a monument marking the site of the slaughterhouse where Ishi, the last of the Yahi Indians, was discovered in 1911. For thousands of years this tribe roamed the foothills between Mount Lassen and the Sacramento Valley. But white settlers eventually wiped the Indians out through a combination of disease, gunfire, and starvation. By the end of the nineteenth century, only a few Yahis remained; Ishi was the last known survivor. University of California anthropologists took the man back to Berkeley, where he died of pneumonia in 1916. *Ishi: In Two Worlds* by Theodore Kroeber (University of California Press) explains how this brave Yahi managed to remain apart from the white world for so many years.

A few miles north of Oroville is the once prosperous Cherokee mining center. Although only a few residents live here today, you can visit the museum, the pioneer cemetery, and the remains of the assay office, and see the 700-foot-high bluffs once blasted daily with 40 million gallons of water by ambitious hydraulic miners. The rock was swept into sluices, where gold was separated out. Like Malakoff Diggins, these operations were halted in 1884 when the state banned this destructive practice.

Although there is no active mining here today, rock hounds and gold panners still work the Cherokee region and about a dozen other popular sites in the Feather River Country. One area that regularly puts gold color in the amateur's pan can be found near Oroville on the Feather River just above the Upper Thermalito Bridge. The Oroville Chamber of Commerce offers a regional gem and mineral map and can put you in touch with the Feather River Gem and Mineral Society, which offers helpful panning tips.

When you're finished hunting for gold in the Cherokee region, take the short drive over to Chico. Here is the mansion built by John Bidwell, the man who started the regional boom by discovering gold on the Feather River just below Oroville. Today, the home is part of a 2400-acre city park which extends almost 10 miles long Chico Creek. The Bidwell Mansion, one of the state's finer Victorian buildings, is also part of the Chico campus of California State University.

From here, scenic S.R. 32 will take you north to Lassen National Park, but if you're not pressed for time, consider a circuitous route that will give you a broader view of the area. First, make the short trip east to Paradise, the birthplace of Crunchy Granola. Although Lassen Foods, the pioneering manufacturer of this breakfast cereal, does not offer tours, the 18-square-mile unincorporated city is worth visiting. Located on the edge of one of the state's more abundant recreation areas, Paradise is a relaxed town particularly popular with retirees. Today it has one of the highest ratios of Social Security pensioners of any community in the state.

Leaving Paradise, you'll want to head into the Feather River Country. East of Oroville you can take the 3-mile hike in to 640-foot-high Feather Falls. But if this trip, which takes at least five hours, sounds excessive, head up S.R. 70 northeast along the Feather River Canyon. It's easy to exhaust superlatives in California, but this cliff-hanging drive up into the Plumas National Forest is, quite simply, one of the state's finest. You can take it all the way to Paxton, where the best bet is to pick up S.R. 89 northwest toward the region's major body of water, Lake Almanor. Or if you don't mind driving a tough dirt road (not for campers), cut off just north of Belden toward Caribou, a tiny community maintained for Pacific Gas and Electric employees who help operate extensive hydroelectric generating facilities in this region. After passing through this little town, you can take the steep, narrow dirt road down to Butte Valley Reservoir, where there are camping, swimming, and waterskiing. From here, you can head directly to Lake Almanor or take the steep, somewhat treacherous way around through Seneca, a tiny settlement catering to fishermen determined to get away from it all. This route is not recommended for inexperienced back road drivers.

Lake Almanor is a commendable family resort area offering a wide variety of accommodations. While you're here, be sure to take the drive over to Westwood, founded in 1913 by the F. B. Walker family of Minnesota. They established the Red River Lumber Company and administered it on utopian precepts. Everyone earned the same basic wage, and food, medical services, schooling, and recreational facilities were provided at minimal cost. Unions and alcoholic beverages were outlawed. But ultimately the arrival of outside labor agitators and the departure of thirsty socialists cut into the community feeling. The family sold the enterprise in the mid-1940s, and the huge mill was finally closed down in 1956. The company-owned homes were sold off to individuals, and today the community is enjoying a resurgence as a popular recreation area.

From here, you'll want to take S.R. 36 and S.R. 89 to the southwest entrance of Lassen Volcanic National Park. Unlike **California's other four** national parks,

Lassen Peak.

Lassen's season lasts only from June to the end of October. Heavy snows keep most of the 30-mile park road closed the rest of the year. Frequently you cannot go much beyond the winter sports area (which operates tow lifts and serves as a base for cross-country skiing), just past the southwest entrance.

And as we've mentioned earlier, the threat of a high-speed avalanche triggered by a volcanic eruption or earthquake forced the closure of Lassen's campground museum and concession facilities at the popular Manzanita Lake area in 1974. The campground was reopened in the summer of 1976. But, as of press time, park officials have not decided whether to continue using the Manzanita Lake camping area during future summers. Regardless of the final decision, other fine campgrounds such as Summit Lake, Sulphur Works, and Butte Lake remain open.

You'll probably want to stay several nights at one of these facilities because the park offers such fine views of the volcanic forces that have shaped California. Although it's been over sixty years since the last major eruption of Lassen Peak, many geologists believe this California volcano is the one most likely to erupt in the near future. The prospect frightens the National Park Service, since the last eruption knocked off the mountain top, devastated the immediate area, and sent up ashes that buried city streets more than 100 miles away.

To get some idea of why the National Park Service has taken precautions in the Manzanita Lake area, you need only pass through the devastated area of the park. Here you can see giant trees smashed by the hot volcanic blast and meadows inundated by as much as 20 feet of mud. Even on the mudflow's edge, bark was ripped off trees to a height of 18 feet.

Although some key attractions can be seen from your car, plan on doing considerable hiking at Lassen. Of course, you won't want to miss the Bumpass Hell Trail, which takes you through an area that includes hot springs, fumaroles, mud pots, and mud volcanoes. From this hydrothermal area, you can continue on to Boiling Springs Lake, which remains at a constant 125 degrees, thanks to steam rising through underground vents and fissures. Bear in mind as you visit this territory that Bumpass Hell was discovered by Kendall Vanhook Bumpass, who lost a leg after he made the mistake of stepping in a thermal pool. You'll be secure as long as you stick to the designated route and observe warning signs.

Many other trails lead to scenes of major volcanic activity on such peaks as Red Cinder Cone, Ash Butte, Brokeoff Mountain, and Crater Butte. One you shouldn't miss on the northeast side of the park is the safe but strenuous Cinder Cone Trail. Here, you walk past fantastic lava beds to the base of a 700-foot-high cone.

The slope is about 35 degrees, and loose cinders make it hard to maintain your footing. But if you remain patient and rest frequently, you'll make it to the top, where there's a good view of the entire region. After you come down, head for nearby Bathtub Lake, whose temperature is considerably warmer than most of the park waters.

Leaving this part of Lassen, you can pick up S.R. 44 east, which leads over toward Eagle Lake. Although this is one of the largest natural lakes in California, it is almost never busy. This fishing haven north of Susanville has warm waters that make it comfortable for swimmers. The remote location and barren setting keep the lake wide open for those who enjoy privacy.

If Eagle Lake isn't what you have in mind after leaving Lassen, take S.R. 44 over to S.R. 89 north, which passes through Hat Creek, a popular fishing region. Soon you'll come to McArthur-Burney Falls Memorial State Park. As the name suggests, the falls are the star attraction. But there's also good swimming and hiking here. This popular state park unit is also one of the few that rents small sailboats.

From here, head over to S.R. 299 and north and east through Adin to Canby. If you're the kind of person who is determined to see all California, here's your chance to check out a region few people ever touch. Continuing on S.R. 299, you'll pass through Alturas, the Warner Mountains, and down into Cedarville, hub of the Surprise Valley. Once a trading post for emigrants passing through to the coast, this community is now the gateway to the near–ghost town of Lake City and the decaying settlement of Fort Bidwell, set up in the 1860s to help defend settlers from Indian attacks.

This entire corner of the state is bleak country, with hot summers and freezing winters. But if you're seeking privacy, no place in California can offer anything less. Indeed, it is the sheer lack of activity that gives this sector its greatest appeal. While you're in the region, you should double back on S.R. 299 to S.R. 139 and drive over to Lava Beds National Monument. Because of its remote location near the Oregon border, most Californians never visit here. But those who do realize they have discovered one of California's great sleepers.

On ground level Lava Beds offers a look at a wide variety of lava flows, cones, and chimneys that were the scene of the only major Indian war ever fought in California. In 1872, following several years of disputes with settlers, Indian leader Captain Jack and his Modoc tribe took refuge here. In an area now called Captain Jack's Stronghold, the small band held out against federal troops for almost six months. The military forces finally managed to drive the Indians out of their lava bed hideout, but losses were heavy. This war ended in 1873 with the capture and hanging of

Captain Jack and three of his Modoc braves at Fort Klamath.

Visit the Lava Beds Monument today, and you'll probably want to spend most of your time exploring dozens of fascinating caves. Unlike commercially owned caverns you may have visited, Lava Beds doesn't force you to follow a predetermined path behind a loquacious guide. You borrow a flashlight at park headquarters and make your own way. In the cave loop area you can enter almost any place you choose. You may emerge at Mushpot, Blue Grotto, or Hopkins Chocolate Cave. And then again you may not. For where you emerge from the labyrinth depends on how far you feel like walking. Lava Beds regulars have their favorite caves, but most agree that any trip would be incomplete without a stop at Valentine, Skull, and Merrill ice caves. Be sure to keep an eye out for rattlesnakes in this area.

While you're in this region, you may want to stop off at nearby Tulelake National Wildlife Refuge. Experts estimate that as many as 70 to 80 percent of the waterfowl on the Pacific Flyway pass through this refuge. The 13,000-acre lake and surrounding 24,000 acres of grainland make the region a perfect feeding ground for the pintails, mallards, ducks, and geese migrating through here. Tulelake and the nearby Lower Klamath Refuge have been known to support simultaneously as many as 2 million ducks.

Leaving this area, you'll probably want to head west toward S.R. 97. The easiest way to link up is via S.R. 161. However, if you have courage or a four-wheel-drive vehicle, you may want to head south of the Lava Beds headquarters to Glass Mountain. It's a dusty, dirt-road drive, but it gives you a chance to pick up obsidian to take home. Backpackers who cherish their privacy enjoy a number of fine trails in this remote volcanic region. There's also camping, fishing, and swimming at Medicine Lake, the center of a now-collapsed volcano. Nearby, you can visit the pumice stone well and paint pot craters.

From Glass Mountain, the rough Tennant–Lava Beds road provides a back way out of this area for those headed west. First inquire locally to ensure conditions are suitable for your vehicle. As the name suggests, this remote route leads to the old company town of **Tennant,** which was abandoned by its owner, the Long Bell Lumber Company, in 1957. After the lumber firm pulled out, it gave the community to the Veterans of Foreign Wars; they sold the place to a drama teacher, who made an unsuccessful effort to turn it into a theater school. He, in turn, peddled it to an elderly grain broker, who unsuccessfully tried to convert the place into a millionaires' retreat. Finally, elderly citizens began moving in and buying up the 100 old loggers' homes for prices ranging from $3000 to $6000. Al-

though vandals have stripped the wood from many of the unoccupied buildings, residents are gradually putting the town back together. The 100-room hotel is not open for visitors, but there is a campground in the vicinity.

Unfortunately, one of this area's most remarkable assets, a Bavarian village left by William Randolph Hearst at Wyntoon (near McCloud), is not open to the public. Still used as a vacation retreat by the chief's heirs, the complex includes a stone castle called the Gables and three smaller units known as the Angel, Cinderella, and Bear houses, each adorned with fairy-tale murals. Hearst's wartime retreat, the place was despised by his mistress, Marion Davies, who hated the remote location. She nicknamed it "Spittoon."

At McCloud, you can take the steam railroad excursion to the nearby town of Mount Shasta. The ride gives you an excellent look at the 14,162-foot peak popular with skiers and hikers. If you're an experienced climber in good shape, you may want to make the long hike to the top of this dormant volcanic peak (August is generally the best month to make the trek). Don't worry if you've forgotten your ice ax and crampons; you can rent some in Mount Shasta. Just be sure to check with the Forest Service office in town to make certain you're a good match for this mountain crowned with five permanent glaciers.

Experienced climbers do not even consider making this difficult ascent alone. Those who approach the mountain with a hiking background and plenty of stamina can make it from Bunny Flat to the top in about nine hours. Just be sure to follow the Forest Service route information. Do not head up the steep slope leading to the left of the Heart. Four deaths have occurred there in recent years.

Northeastern California Notes

Jim Martin's *Guidebook to the Feather River Country* provides a good introduction to this popular vacation region. (The publisher, Ward Ritchie Press, 3044 Riverside Drive, Los Angeles, CA 90039, is closing out a limited number of copies for 50¢ each.) Other information can be obtained from the Oroville Chamber of Commerce, 1789 Montgomery Street, Oroville, CA 95965; the Butte County Development Commission, 175 Cohasset Road, Chico, CA 95926; and the Plumas County Chamber of Commerce, 500 Jackson Street, Quincy, CA 95971. Farther north, you can write the Lassen County Chamber of Commerce, P.O. Box 338, Susanville, CA 96130, or the Modoc County Chamber of Commerce, P.O. Box 1690, Alturas, CA 96101. Information on the Mount Shasta area is available from the Chamber of Commerce, P.O. Box 201, Mount Shasta, CA 96067.

What Is a Trout?

Trout fishing is a popular activity throughout California. But if you've never done it before, you may have difficulty distinguishing trout from salmon or whitefish. To help avoid unnecessary embarrassment, *The California Catalogue* asked the State Department of Fish and Game to explain precisely what a trout is. Here is the reply.

"Trout are members of the great family of fishes known as Salmonidae, which includes the salmon. They are typically inhabitants of the colder streams and lakes of North America, Europe, and Asia. Under suitable conditions, many kinds migrate to sea, but all spawn in fresh water.

"There is nothing so very unusual about the appearance of a trout, except perhaps the adipose fin, which grows from the back about half way between the dorsal fin and the tail, or caudal, fin. All members of the family Salmonidae have this adipose fin.

"All trout have bodies shaped a good deal like the illustration. The mouth is never located on the underside of the head as in the suckers and carp. It is always at the tip of the head and it is quite large, the maxillary bone projecting back to the eye or behind it. It is never small, as in the whitefish. Trout have the usual number of fins, but their location on the body is not quite the same as in many other fishes.

"From the illustration it can be seen that the pectoral fins, one on each side just behind the head, are set low, almost down to the belly. The pair of ventral fins is located about half way between the tip of the head and the tip of the tail. In a bass these fins are much farther forward.

"All trout have scales after they have grown to be a couple of inches long; even the brook trout has scales, though they are so small they are difficult to see.

"In most of the lakes and streams of California there are no whitefish, which are relatives of trout. They are found only on the eastern slope of the Sierra Nevada in the Truckee, Carson, and Walker river drainages. The whitefish has a small mouth, the maxillary bone extending back barely to the eye.

"Salmon are often confused with steelhead trout, and in the water it is difficult to tell them apart. Only after they have been caught and compared side by side can the layman see how they differ. In many coastal streams fishermen catch young silver salmon and call them trout. Actually yearling silver salmon up to five inches look so much like steelhead that it is no wonder they are often confused with them.

"In these small fish one should count the rays of the anal fin; the salmon has more than 12, whereas the trout has 12 or fewer, as shown in the illustration.

"After these small trout and salmon have migrated to the ocean and returned to the stream as mature fish ready to spawn, they are still a little difficult to distinguish. A quick way to tell them apart is to grasp the fish around the base of the tail (caudal peduncle)—if it slips through your hand it is a steelhead trout, and if it can be held quite easily it is a salmon."

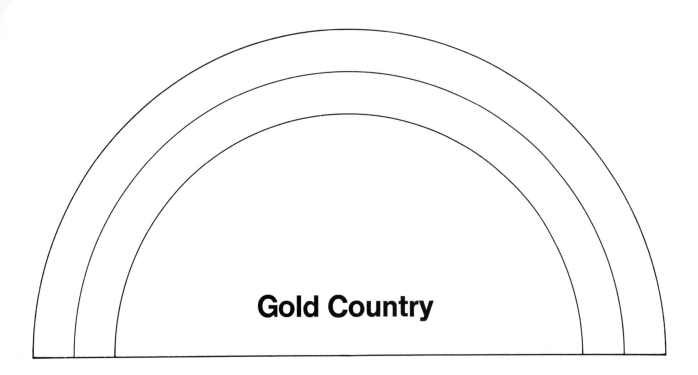

Gold Country

The Best of Gold Country

State park: Plumas-Eureka

Camping: Plumas-Eureka

Hiking: Malakoff Diggins State Park

Swimming: Stanislaus River, Knight's Ferry; Consumnes River at S.R. 49

Whitewater rafting: Stanislaus River, Camp 9 to Parrot's Ferry; American River, Chile Bar to Folsom Lake (experienced guides required on both runs)

Caves: Mercer Caverns

Old hotels: Saint George, Volcano; Leger, Mokelumne Hill; Gunn House, Sonora

Museums: Tuolumne County, Sonora; Amador County, Jackson

Mining site: Malakoff Diggins State Park

Mine ruins: Kennedy and Argonaut

Chinese community: Chinese Camp

Covered bridges: Knight's Ferry; Bridgeport

Small town: Volcano

Flowers: Daffodil Hill

Railroad: Sierra Railroad, Jamestown

Gazebo: Volcano

River town: Downieville

Historic site: Sutter's Mill

Frog jump: Angels Camp

Drive: S.R. 49, Nevada City to Downieville

"When I came to California," explorer, politician, and entrepreneur John C. Frémont once observed, "I hadn't a cent. Now I owe two million dollars." Like many who rushed to the Sierra Nevada foothills following James Marshall's discovery of gold at Coloma in January 1848, Frémont ended up hopelessly in debt. Although his Mariposa mines were productive, expenses overtook profits and he was forced to sell them at a fraction of their value.

Today, as you visit the Gold Country, a region centered around 300-mile-long Highway 49, you'll find countless remnants and artifacts of the mass hysteria that overwhelmed this part of California in the mid-nineteenth century. Over 500,000 tourists, mostly Californians, visit the area each year. Out-of-state visitors generally pass it up in favor of big-name attractions like Disneyland, Yosemite, and San Simeon. Even those who do come follow the well-established route to the Mother Lode's few sizable communities. They miss the covered bridges, Chinese settlements, Indian monuments, French hotels, mine workings, and pioneer cemeteries away from the tourist centers.

The cosmopolitan flavor you'll find in this region suggests the extent to which gold fever cut across racial, religious, ethnic, and national lines. The territory was packed with whites, blacks, Orientals, Catholics, Jews, Mormons, Protestants, Irish, French, Mexicans, Chileans, and English. The Mother Lode also had the toughest gunslingers, the meanest bandits, the worst lynch mobs, the hangingest judges, and the wickedest whorehouses around. The greed of these forty-niners knew no bounds. One day several miners

The 49'er. (*Hutchings' California Magazine,*
from "Scenes of Wonder and Curiosity," Howell-North Books)

the voyage or overland journey to California. On arrival, they set about searching for the precious mineral by every means possible. If mining, panning, or dredging didn't work, they used powerful water jets to shoot down hillsides and wash the earth into sluice boxes that retained the gold.

No period in California history can match the excitement of this gold rush era extending through the 1850s. The state cemented its reputation as the place where a man could make an overnight killing. No matter that the system worked in reverse for people like James Marshall. Those who couldn't make enough to afford Gold Country prices, like $16 for a fifth of whiskey, $3 for an egg, $10 for pills (without advice), and $100 for pills (with advice), simply moved to another part of the state to farm, raise cattle, chop lumber, or go into commerce. And slowly they became reconciled to the idea that California was not going to make them independently wealthy overnight.

To see the area these would-be millionaires left

In his declining years, James Marshall, the man who started the gold rush, was reduced to selling his autograph. (*Wells Fargo Bank, History Room, San Francisco*)

in Rough and Ready were standing at a friend's funeral when they noticed gold in the ground dug out for the grave site. Without even waiting for the eulogy to end, they all immediately jumped in to start working their newly staked claims.

First on the scene were state residents who succumbed to promotional efforts of speculators, walked off their jobs, and headed for the mines. "The whole country from San Francisco to Los Angeles, and from the sea shore to the base of the Sierra Nevada resounds with the sordid cry of gold, GOLD, GOLD! while the field is left half-planted, the house half built and everything neglected but the shovels and pickaxes," complained the San Francisco *Californian* in May 1848.

Soon afterward, the paper itself declared it was suspending operations because employees, advertisers, and readers had all split for the gold-laden hills. In San Jose, a jailer released all ten of his prisoners so they could come along and do his gold digging. The army and navy were beset by hundreds of desertions after word spread that one soldier had made more on a three-week furlough ($1500) than the army paid him in five years.

As gold fever spread across America and throughout the world, families parted with their life savings to make behind, begin on Highway 49 at Mariposa, the southern gateway to the Mother Lode. A good starting point is the entrance to one of John C. Frémont's mines located behind Saint Joseph's Catholic Church. And when you're finished looking at Mariposa's historic courthouse, Odd Fellows hall, and Schlageter Hotel (now a commercial building), head 11 miles north to view the ruins of Frémont's home at Bear Valley.

An unusual side trip from this point is the 13-mile drive west to Hornitos. This community was built by Mexicans who had been driven out by racist miners in nearby Quartzberg. A number of old buildings remain in rustic Hornitos today, including the jail, Mason's lodge, Catholic church, and ruins of the Ghirardelli store, built by the man who eventually made his chocolate a household word in California.

The candy man was only one of several entrepreneurs who got their start in the Mother Lode. Levi Strauss sold clothes to fellow passengers on his New York–San Francisco passage and began mass marketing his famous pants in the Gold Country. In Placerville, John Studebaker got into the transit business making wagons and carriages, and Philip Armour ran a butcher shop before heading to Chicago, where he got into the meat-packing jungle.

Hornitos is also the best place to pursue the legend of infamous Joaquin Murieta, the Mother Lode's leading bandito, who supposedly swore revenge after being tied to a tree where he was forced to watch the rape of his wife and the lynching of his brother. Romanticized over the years by novelists and Hollywood screenwriters, Murieta has emerged as the Gold Country's Robin Hood. Allegedly, his wild exploits took him through Volcano, Sonora, Mokelumne Hill, and numerous other towns. Murieta frequently showed up in Hornitos, where he made use of a tunnel beneath the local fandango hall to escape lawmen.

Finally, the tale goes, California hired a Texan gunslinger named Harry Love to lead a twenty-man posse in pursuit of the elusive Mexican. They got their man, cut off his head, and stuck it in a bottle of formaldehyde, which was sent off on a statewide tour. Today, historians disagree on the authenticity of the Murieta saga. True, Harry Love did kill a Mexican bandit, but there is no proof that his victim was really Joaquin Murieta.

Heading north again on Highway 49, the next essential stop is Chinese Camp, one of the best-preserved small communities in the Gold Country. About 4500 Chinese miners lived here during the peak of the gold rush, and about 125 people remain today. A number of stone-walled buildings with iron doors remain, including the old post office, which is still in use. Like other gold rush towns, Chinese Camp had its share of random violence emanating from mining quarrels. The worst occurred in October 1856, when 2000 mem-

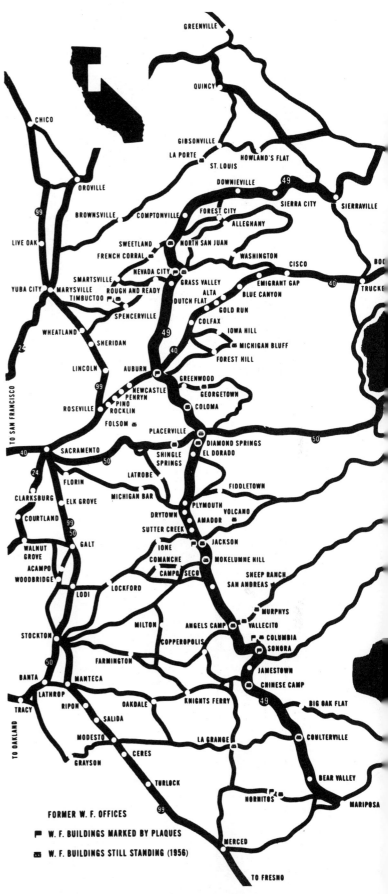

This map of Wells Fargo Bank-Express offices suggests the extent of Mother Lode commerce during the gold rush heyday. (*Wells Fargo Bank, History Room, San Francisco*)

Joaquin Murietta, the Mother Lode's leading bandito. (*Wells Fargo Bank, History Room, San Francisco*)

One of the many Chinese mining camps that sprang up during the gold rush. (*Wells Fargo Bank, History Room, San Francisco*)

bers of the Sam Yap and Yan Wo factions took on each other in a battle that left 4 dead and 250 in jail.

If you go west from Chinese Camp on S.R. 120, you'll reach Knight's Ferry in about twenty minutes. This community was founded in 1848 by William Knight, who promptly began making $500 a day ferrying miners across the Stanislaus River. He died in a gunfight the following year, and five years later the community erected a covered bridge over the river; you can drive through its successor today. This side trip also gives you a chance to cool off in the clear Stanislaus River just above the town.

Back on Highway 49, head to Jamestown, home base for the Sierra Railroad, which offers the most extensive railroad schedule in the state, with round-trip tours running from one to four hours. The Mother Lode Cannonball, Sierra Supper Chief, Twilight Limited, Spring Flower Special, and Indian Summer Special provide easy ways to see the countryside. These trains, which are available for charter, have been used in over 100 movies and television shows, ranging from *My Little Chickadee* to *Petticoat Junction.* Be sure to take the roundhouse tour, visit the history room, and see the antique carriage collection. If you don't have time for a train ride, have lunch in the air-conditioned California Zephyr dining car parked on a station siding.

Just north of Jamestown is Sonora, a regional commercial center founded in 1848 by Mexicans soon driven out by Americans who stole their mines. What made it impossible for the original settlers to stay was a $20 per month tax on foreigners passed by the state legislature. The act turned out to be shortsighted, as the mass exodus of Mexicans cut the town's population from 5000 to 3000. Finally in 1851, hard-pressed merchants persuaded the legislature to repeal the special levy, and the Mexicans began drifting back into town.

Today, Washington Street, Sonora's historic main drag, is crowded with traffic headed into the Sierras. But step over a block and you'll find some of the finest Victorian buildings in California. To see them, pick up the Heritage Homes tour brochure at the county museum located in the century-old jail on West Bradford Street. Although only one of the private homes on this walking tour, Cady House, is open for inspection, all fifteen have striking exteriors and most have flourishing gardens that bloom year-round. Toward the end of the tour you'll come to the Gunn House, which has been restored to a fine hotel completely furnished with antiques.

After leaving Sonora, you pass into the central Mother Lode region and come to Columbia State Historic Park. Formerly one of the region's most produc-

tive mining towns, Columbia today is the place for people who like packaged tours. In the process of restoring the town, the state has brought in a dozen concessionaires who cater to visitors with stage rides, saloons, snack bars, and gift shops. Although the main street is closed to traffic from May through September, commercial development in the vicinity of the park undermines the official preservation effort. You'll probably be better off just giving this crowded tourist center a quick look and heading on to other Gold Country attractions.

One of them can be found 8 miles east of Angels Camp, site of the famous Calaveras County frog jump held each May. This is Murphys, which abounds with many gold rush era stone and brick structures still in use today. Towering locust trees shade the carefully restored buildings and elegant Victorian homes that make the community a highlight of any Gold Country visit. There's a museum in the P. L. Traver building, and you can stay at the Murphys Hotel, where the presidential suite includes a grand piano. Previous guests here include Mark Twain, Horatio Alger, Jr., Ulysses S. Grant, J. Pierpont Morgan, and the infamous Black Bart, who pulled off twenty-eight stage coach robberies between 1877 and 1883.

A cordial fellow, he would frequently get the job done by asking a confronted driver: "Will you please throw down your treasure box, sir?" Bart turned out to be a socially prominent San Franciscan, who was traced by police after dropping one of his laundry-marked hankies during a Copperopolis getaway. He was eventually tried, convicted, and sent off to San Quentin, where a six-year sentence was cut short by an early parole. In 1888, Bart disappeared, and the parole board has never seen him since.

Just north of Murphys you'll find Mercer Caverns, where stalactites, stalagmites, helictites, and other colored limestone formations grace such caverns as the Fairies Grotto, Gothic Chamber, and the Chinese Meat Market. More of the same can be seen at Moaning Cave, 2 miles south of nearby Vallecito. Unfortunately, addition of a staircase has wrecked the sound effects, and the cave moans no longer.

After returning to Highway 49, head for Mokelumne Hill, where murders ran as high as five a week during the gold rush era. And 2 miles south of town, you'll find Chile Gulch, where local citizens were victorious in their fight against a Chilean doctor using forbidden slave labor to do his mining. This Chilean War, as it is known today, nearly touched off real combat between the United States and Chile.

Mok Hill has many gold rush era structures on its winding streets, including the luxurious Hotel Leger, a

Black Bart:
"Will you please throw down your treasure box, sir?"
(*Wells Fargo Bank, History Room, San Francisco*)

Mother Lode landmark that remains open today. On summer weekends you can stay in one of the Victorian rooms and walk to the old courthouse, now a theater offering live entertainment.

Although Mok Hill is rich in historic landmarks, you probably won't find any signs pointing out that it is also the birthplace of a lasting Mother Lode institution, the E. Clampus Vitus Society. It was founded here in 1850 by J. H. Zumwalt to ridicule elitist, secretive, fraternal organizations like the Masons and the Odd Fellows. Ruled by a Noble Grand Humbug, the society was dedicated to helping "widders and orphans—especially widders." Calling itself the "fraternity for non-joiners," the society liked to say its sole function was recruiting new members. It is still active today, and you can find a number of historical markers put up by the organization when it wasn't busy making mischief—or doing an anonymous good deed, for it had its serious side as well. Periodically, you can still catch a glimpse of the Clampers riding back roads in fire engines and other emergency vehicles as they head off to stage their latest practical joke.

From Mok Hill, it's a short drive to Jackson, where the Amador County Museum, one of the region's finest, is found in a century-old home overlooking the town. While here, you can also visit the headframe, tailing wheels, water tanks, and office buildings of two of the nation's most successful gold mines, the Kennedy and the Argonaut. After exploring the remains of these mines that collectively produced gold worth $80 million, take S.R. 88 for the 13-mile trip east to Volcano.

Throughout this region you'll find tourist towns billing themselves as "Queen of the Sierras," "Gem of the Southern Mines," or "Paradise of the Mother Lode." But none can compete with Volcano (population 109). This quiet, uncommercialized community on Sutter Creek maintains the remnants of its gold rush civili-

Wells Fargo. For a booklet on the early days of the Wells Fargo Express and Banking Company, stop by the firm's history room, 420 Montgomery Street, San Francisco, or write Wells Fargo Bank, San Francisco, CA 94120. The booklet is especially useful for children, who may also want to have a miniature replica of the century-old Wells Fargo office at Columbia for $3.95. In addition, the firm sells official Wells Fargo belt buckles at $9.50 each. You can get the last two items by writing Wells Fargo Bank Customer Services, Room 500, 274 Brannan Street, San Francisco, CA 94107. The prices include tax, but be sure to add $1 per order to cover handling and postage.

zation in a careful state of arrested decay. Here you will find the old express office, Sibley Brewery, Odd Fellows–Masons' hall, numerous abandoned bars, and several commercial buildings that once served a population of 5000. Some buildings, such as the vine-covered Saint George Hotel, have been completely restored and accommodate guests today. Others, like the Wells Fargo building, consist of nothing but the bare stone walls. But wherever you go in Volcano, from the bookshop housed in the old bandstand, to the home made out of a former schoolhouse, you'll be rewarded. Everything done wrong in restoring tacky Columbia has been done right in Volcano.

While in the area, be sure to make the short trip north on Ram's Horn Grade to Daffodil Hill. Maintaining an old tradition, the McLaughlin Family has covered an entire hillside with over 200,000 daffodil bulbs. The best time to see these flowers in bloom is late March or early April, and the McLaughlins have provided a picnic area free of charge near their home.

Turning back south, you can head to Indian Grinding Rock State Historic Monument, which has one of the first conveniently located public campgrounds you've passed since entering the Mother Lode at Mariposa. Here you'll want to take a look at the 7700-square-foot rock used by the Northern Miwok Indians as a primary tool to pulverize various seed-bearing plants into palatable food. Scattered around this outcropping are over 1100 mortar holes and 363 petroglyph designs. Don't walk on the rock because your shoes will wear away the petroglyphs.

Heading back to Highway 49, you can take the short route to Sutter Creek, where Leland Stanford struck it rich in the mining business and went on to start a university at Palo Alto. On Fridays you can also visit the Knight Foundry, which has been in continuous operation since 1873. Here were made the waterwheels that powered numerous gold stamp mills as well as the dredges used to help dig Seattle and San Francisco harbors. A wide variety of industrial products continues to be cast here today.

From Volcano you can also loop back to the main highway via Fiddletown. While adjacent communities like Hogtown, Helltown, and Suckertown have disappeared, Fiddletown remains alive as a modest farming-tourist village. A number of old buildings, including a blacksmith shop, are here, and a giant fiddle stretches across the roof of the modern-day firehouse.

After picking up Highway 49 at Plymouth, you'll soon come to the Cosumnes River. Although we don't recommend doing the Gold Country in the hot summertime, this is an excellent place to cool off on a warm day. Here you can swim in clear pools glittering with fool's gold. And when you've dried off, look about the bank for some wild blackberries.

The next major stop is Placerville, formerly known

as Hangtown. Mark Hopkins, Philip Armour, and John Studebaker lived here in this major gateway to forty-niners en route to the mines and millions. But perhaps the most illustrious resident of all was Ulysses S. Grant, who did his best to keep the community's bars in business. Today Placerville has 6000 residents, and its historic business section is a busy commercial district. After taking a look at the old city hall, pioneer building, pony express office, and Masonic temple, you may be tempted to try the town's culinary specialty at a local restaurant. It was invented in response to a miner who had just struck it rich and insisted on having the two most expensive items on the menu—eggs and oysters. The chef mixed in a little bacon and christened it the "Hangtown fry." Today, you can find this dish at many restaurants throughout the state.

Moving on to Coloma, you'll want to stop briefly at the Marshall gold discovery site. Looking at the towering monument atop the founder's grave, you get no sense of his tragic fate. It was all downhill for James Marshall after he discovered gold in 1848 at Sutter's mill. Miners who rushed to the scene refused to honor Marshall's and Sutter's joint property rights or to pay royalties on gold they took away. Marshall complained so bitterly that the other miners finally drove him off. His subsequent efforts to find a new site were disrupted by hangers-on convinced he would discover a new lode. Tired of interference and unable to make another strike, Marshall eventually gave up mining. By the end of his life, he was reduced to living off odd jobs, an occasional handout, and the spare change brought in by his scrawled autograph.

After passing through Pilot Hill and Cool, you'll dip down to the American River, and then make the steep climb up to Auburn, the region's largest city and gateway to the northern Mother Lode. Unlike Placerville, this community of 7000 has set aside an old section of town as a preservation area. Most of the important original structures such as the firehouse, post office, Wells Fargo office, and shops can be found here. The old public hanging yard has been replaced by the county courthouse.

Grass Valley comes next, and here the Kiwanis offer an annual tour in the summer of the region's mines, including the Empire, Gold Center, Scotia, and North Star. Most important of the historic buildings is the cottage in which the legendary Lola Montez lived. A theatrical star in Europe, she came to America in 1852, fresh from affairs with Franz Liszt, Victor Hugo, Alexander Dumas, and Mad Ludwig of Bavaria. After her dancing failed to draw crowds in San Francisco, she moved with her pet bears and monkeys to this small Grass Valley home in the heart of the booming Gold Country. Here she threw frequent parties for adoring miner friends. After one minister complained about Lola's antics, she danced in full view of his home.

When he ran out to complain, she promptly gave him a good whipping.

During her stay in Grass Valley, Lola began baby-sitting for a seven-year-old neighbor, Lotta Crabtree. The child quickly picked up a little singing and dancing from the star; within a year she was performing in Rough and Ready. Lotta's career continued to flourish in the mines; Lola made an abortive attempt to come out of retirement, subsequently failed at lecturing, and finally died in New York in 1861, at the age of forty-three. A few years later Lotta had become a star, eventually going on to storm America and the Continent. When she died in 1924, Lotta left a $4 million estate.

While you're in Grass Valley, take a look at the stretch of freeway that links it with nearby Nevada City. This four-lane road is a mere 6.5 miles long and does not connect with any other superhighway in the region. Probably the worst single piece of expressway in the entire state, it is a vivid demonstration of California's freeway mania. Not only is the road unnecessary, but it manages to dissect the heart of picturesque Nevada City, one of California's most historic communities. For over a century, citizens of this town have worked to preserve the Victorian buildings, gazebos, old wooden sidewalks, hotels, and commercial districts. And now the highway department has split the town in half with a senseless freeway.

North and east of Nevada City along the Yuba River you'll find the Gold Country's best camping sites. There are numerous tiny towns to explore, such as the

---

Ladybugs. If you've become uncomfortable about spraying poisons on your garden, consider the alternative—ladybugs. Bio-Control Company, a small Auburn enterprise, is one of a growing number of firms supplying biological control agents that work with instead of against nature. Increasingly, agricultural experts are finding natural methods of control preferable to poisonous sprays. Ladybugs, which devour aphids, fruit scales, mealybugs, bollworms, leafworms, leafhoppers, fleahoppers, corn earworms, and other plant-destroying insects, also often prove cheaper than sprays. A gallon of 75,000 hardy young ladybugs goes for $17, but you can get them in quantities as small as a half pint for $4. To obtain information, write Bio-Control Company, 10180 Ladybird Drive, Auburn, CA 95603. Incidentally, the firm also sells the Chinese praying mantis, another biological control agent that works well alongside the ladybug. Mantises seldom eat ladybugs due to their bitter taste.

The legendary Lola Montez and her protegee, Lotta Crabtree. (*Wells Fargo Bank, History Room, San Francisco*)

hillside community of Alleghany, Bridgeport with its covered bridge, and Frenchville where a handful of old buildings remains. At Rough and Ready, you can learn about the community's decision in 1850 to secede from the United States because of opposition to a special mining tax. Although the town did rejoin the union, this fight didn't officially terminate until the late 1940s, when the government was allowed to open a Rough and Ready post office.

Although it's on a dirt road and difficult to reach, the Malakoff Diggins State Park at North Bloomfield offers camping on the edge of what once were the state's most controversial hydraulic mining sites. This technique employed huge jets of water that ate away at hillsides. The earth was carried off into sluices, where the gold was extracted. Not only was the process hideously destructive, but it also fed so much silt into the region's rivers that disastrous flooding occurred in the Sacramento Valley. After the state outlawed this mining method in 1884, the diggings were abandoned. For many years the badly eroded site resembled an open pit mine. But with time, the scarred hillsides have weathered to colorful pinnacles reflected in small lakes on the valley floor.

The last major Gold Country town you'll want to see is Downieville, where old stone houses cling to the hillsides above the converging Downie and Yuba rivers. A popular area for swimming, camping, fishing, hiking, and gold panning, Downieville bears the dubious distinction of being the first community in California to

hang a woman, a dancehall girl named Juanita, who stabbed a miner to death. Although she claimed self-defense, the enraged community strung her up within hours.

Beyond Downieville, there is one more eminently worthwhile side trip through the Sierra Buttes region north of Sierra City. It can be reached by taking Gold Lake Road off Highway 49. Along the way you'll pass a string of small mountain lakes ideal for fishing and boating. There's also good swimming at Sand Pond. Farther north, there is more camping at Plumas-Eureka State Park, which includes the remarkably well-preserved mining town of Johnsville. State ownership of the community has helped protect the wide array of frame homes restored by private owners. Walking the streets of Johnsville today, you'll also see the former boardinghouse, stamp mill, and fair-sized collection of mining tools and wagons. There's also skiing in the park during the winter.

Bear in mind when planning a trip to Johnsville or any other part of the Gold Country that spring and fall are the best times to come. Heat and heavy traffic on Highway 49 make the trip more complicated in summer. Autumn is especially good if you want to see the leaves turning along Highway 49 north of Nevada City. If you do come at a busy time, try to escape the traffic by taking side roads leading to some of the smaller communities like Ben Hur, Smartville, or Timbuctoo. These and other drives lead through oak-studded foothills, down into deep river gorges, up

COMMON LAND BIRDS

THIS CONSERVATION LEAFLET
Originally devised for School Use by
California Conservation Committee
Garden Club of America

Check	Where	NAME	Time Seen	WHERE SEEN MOSTLY	Size	GENERAL
....	....	Turkey Vulture	R.	Soaring	L.	Black
....	....	Cooper Hawk	R.	Soaring or hidden in trees	L.	Back dark, strea...
....	....	Sparrow Hawk	R.	Open country, wires, posts	M.	Reddish brown a...
....	....	Sharp-shinned Hawk	R. or W.V.	Soaring	M.	Back dark, strea...
....	....	Red-tailed Hawk	R.	Soaring	L.	Brown streaked...
....	....	Red-shouldered Hawk	R.	Soaring	M.	Brown streaked,
....	....	California Quail	R.	Open country, brushy areas	M.	Brownish
....	....	Mourning Dove	R.	Open areas	M.	Brownish
....	....	Roadrunner	R.	Brushy areas	L.	Brown speckled..
....	....	Barn Owl	R.	Brushy areas	L.	Tawny, white or
....	....	Screech Owl	R.	Brushy areas	M.	Gray streaked w
....	....	Allen's Hummingbird	S.V.	Around plants	Tiny	Iridescent green.
....	....	Anna's Hummingbird	R.	Around plants	Tiny	Iridescent green.
....	....	Black-chinned Hummingbird	S.V.	Around plants	Tiny	Iridescent green.
....	....	Acorn Woodpecker	R.	In oak trees and on telephone posts	M.	Black above, bla...
....	....	Red-shafted Flicker	R.	Trees and brush near open land	I.	Brownish above..
....	....	Western Kingbird	S.V.	Open places, on wires and fences	I.	Ashy gray
....	....	Black Phoebe	R.	In trees and on ground	M.	Head, neck and
....	....	Western Wood Pewee	S.V.	In woods	S.	Brownish gray....
....	....	Western Flycatcher	S.V.	In woods	S.	Brownish gray....
....	....	Horned Lark	R.	Open fields and roadsides	I.	Brownish gray....
....	....	Barn Swallow	S.V.	In air; mud nest on buildings	S.	Glossy blue black
....	....	Cliff Swallow	S.V.	In air; mud nest on buildings and bridges	S.	Glossy blue black
....	....	Violet-green Swallow	S.V.	In air; nest in holes in trees or cliffs	S.	Glossy bottle gree
....	....	§Scrub Jay	R.	Trees and shrubs; chaparral	M.	Blue and gray br
....	....	§Stellar Jay	R.	Coniferous forests	M.	Dark purplish-bl
....	....	§Crow	R.	Open areas	L.	Black
....	....	Plain Titmouse	R.	In trees	S.	Brownish gray..
....	....	Bush-tit	R.	In trees	S.	Brownish gray..
....	....	Wren-tit	R.	In chaparral, low bushes or on ground	S.	Brownish gray...
....	....	Bewick Wren	R.	In woods, brush	S.	Brown
....	....	Canyon Wren	R.	In canyons	S.	Brown
....	....	House Wren	S.V.	In woods, brush	S.	Brown
....	....	Mockingbird	R.	Abundant in warmer parts of California	M.	Dark gray
....	....	California Thrasher	R.	Brushy areas, gardens	M.	Brownish
....	....	Hermit Thrush	R. or W.V.	Coniferous forest and brushy undergrowth	I.	Brownish
....	....	Swainson's Thrush	S.V.	Damp, shaded thickets	I.	Brownish
....	....	Robin	R. or W.V.	Everywhere	M.	Brown
....	....	Western Bluebird	R.	Foothills and open fields	I.	Male deep blue,
....	....	Ruby-crowned Kinglet	R. or W.V.	Coniferous forests, woodlands and gardens	S.	Olive gray
....	....	Loggerhead Shrike	R.	In open or in trees, on wires or poles	M.	Gray
....	....	Audubon Warbler	R. or W.V.	Trees, bushes	S.	Bluish gray
....	....	Yellow Warbler	S.V.	In trees and higher bushes	S.	Yellow
....	....	Wilson's Warbler	S.V.	Trees, bushes	S.	Yellow
....	....	*Brewer Blackbird	R.	Yards, fields	M.	Male iridescent bl
....	....	*Red-winged Blackbird	R.	Swampy areas, fields	M.	Male black, femal
....	....	Western Meadowlark	R.	Open fields	M.	Brown, streaked...
....	....	Hooded Oriole	S.V.	In trees	I.	Male yellow, fema
....	....	Bullock's Oriole	S.V.	In trees	M.	Male yellow, fema
....	....	Black-headed Grosbeak	S.V.	In trees	M.	Black, brown and
....	....	§House Finch (Linnet)	R.	Orchards, weedy fields, telephone wires	S.	Brown streaked..
....	....	Lesser Goldfinch	R.	In trees, fields or gardens	S.	Olive green
....	....	American Goldfinch	R.	In trees, fields or gardens	S.	Male bright yellov
....	....	Brown Towhee	R.	Yards, brushy areas	M.	Dark reddish brov
....	....	Rufous-sided Towhee	R.	Brushy places	M.	Black and white..
....	....	Junco	R. or W.V.	On ground, in bushes	S.	Head, neck and b
....	....	§English Sparrow	R.	In towns, barnyards	S.	Brown streaked..
....	....	Fox Sparrow	R. or W.V.	Brushy places	M.	Grayish brown....
....	....	White-crowned Sparrow	R. or W.V.	On ground, in bushes	S.	Grayish brown....
....	....	Golden-crowned Sparrow	W.V.	On ground, in bushes	S.	Grayish brown....
....	....	Song Sparrow	R.	On ground, in bushes	S.	Brown streaked..

*Protected only in parts of Southern California
§Not protected in California
Others protected

R — Resident
S.V. — Summer Visitor
W.V. — Winter Visitor

Time varies in different parts of State

L. — Large birds larger than a Jay
M. — Medium (birds between a Jay and

CALIFORNIA CONSERVATION COUNCIL LEAFLETS: NATIONAL PARKS AND MONUMENTS IN CALIFORNIA 5c; COMMON LAND BIRDS, WATER AND SHORE BIRDS, and WILD FLOWERS OF CALIFORNIA, at 3c each; other leaflets at 2c and 1c each. *Leaflets price less than cost; to help cover mailing, please add 6c for each four Leaflets or fewer.*

CONSERVATION COUNCIL LEAFLETS D
STATE AND EDUCATIONAL AGENCIES.
SEND FOR FREE COPY OF CURRENT PR
SEND ORDER FOR LEAFLETS WITH REM
CALIFORNIA CONSERVATION COUNCIL, 9

STATE BIRD—CALIFORNIA QUAIL
Selected by popular vote 1929,
by legislative enactment 1931.

R	CHARACTERISTIC MARKINGS	BILL	FOOD
	Gray under wings; head naked, red	Hooked	Scavenger
	Streaked light breast; long rounded tail; short rounded wings	Hooked	Birds and small mammals
	Black cheek bars; long narrow wings; short tail	Hooked	Grasshoppers and beetles chiefly,
	Heavily streaked light breast; long square tail; short rounded wings	Hooked	Birds mostly mice, voles
	Tail reddish	Hooked	Mice and squirrels
and breast	Short, square tail, barred black and white, rounded wings	Hooked	Mostly rodents, mice, insects
	Plume on head points forward	Short and thick	Seeds and insects
	Long pointed tail edged with white	Slender	Weed seeds
	Tail as long as body; crest	Long, curved at tip	Lizards, mice, snakes, insects
ow	Characteristic "monkey face" with white area around each eye	Hooked	Gophers, mice, rats
	Two tufts of feathers on sides of head	Hooked	Mice chiefly
	Gorget copper-red; tail and flanks reddish-brown	Long, slender, curved	Nectar and insects
	Gorget and top of head deep red	Long, straight	Nectar and insects
	Gorget black edged with violet band, narrow white collar	Long, slender, curved	Nectar and insects
te below	White rump and white wing patches	Long and straight	Insects and acorns
	Black necklace on breast; reddish under tail and wings	Long, straight	Ants and other insects
	Yellow under parts, black tail	Flattened, slender	Flying insects
s black	White belly	Flattened, slender	Flying insects
	Two white wing bars; white line down the breast	Flattened, slender	Flying insects
	Two white wing bars; white eye ring	Flattened, slender	Flying insects
	Two tufts over eyes; black band on throat	Short, thick	Seeds, insects
	Forked tail	Flattened, slender	Flying insects
	Rufus rump	Flattened, slender	Flying insects
	Under parts white, white on sides of rump	Flattened, slender	Flying insects
	Throat and breast whitish; tail long	Chisel like	Eggs, nestlings, insects, fruit
	Crest, head and upper back blackish, wing and tail with black bars	Chisel like	Eggs, nestlings, insects, fruit
	Tail square — that of raven rounded	Chisel like	Grain, mice, eggs, insects
	Crest	Slender, short	Insects
	Slender tail	Slender	Insects
	Long slender tail	Slender	Insects
	Short, perky, barred tail; whitish line over eye	Slender	Insects
	White breast; tail short, barred	Slender, long	Insects
	Short, perky, barred tail; without white line over eye	Slender	Insects
	White wing patches; outer tail feathers white	Long, slender	Insects chiefly
	White throat	Long, curved	Insects chiefly
	Reddish brown tail; breast spotted	Slender	Insects chiefly
	Upper parts reddish brown; breast spotted	Slender	Insects chiefly
	Rusty brown underparts	Slender	Insects chiefly
der	Rusty brown underparts	Slender	Insects
	White eye ring; two white wing bars	Slender	Insects
	Black wings with white spots; rump white; black line through eye	Hooked	Grasshoppers, beetles, some birds
	Yellow rump patch; yellow spots on top of head, throat and upper flanks	Slender	Insects
	Breast streaked with brown	Slender	Insects
	Black cap	Slender	Insects
ale brown	Male — eyes white	Sharp pointed	Insects, seeds, and some grain
d	Red shoulder patch	Slender	Insects and grain
	Yellow below; black necklace on breast; tail short, outer feathers white	Slender	Insects and grain
sh	Black face, wings and tail, white wing bars	Slender	Insects and fruit
	Top of head black; white wing patches	Slender	Insects and fruit
	Black head; cinnamon brown on flanks; white patch in wing	Thick	Insects chiefly
	Male red on head, throat, breast, rump; female no red, breast streaked	Short, thick	Seeds and fruit
	White wing patches; top of head black	Short, thick	Weed seeds
greenish	Wings and tail black or dusky with white wing bars	Short, thick	Weed seeds chiefly
	Cinnamon area under tail	Short, thick	Insects and seeds
	Cinnamon flanks	Short, thick	Seeds and insects
ck	White outer tail feathers	Short, thick	Seeds and insects
	Black bib on male; breast gray; not streaked; female without black bib	Very thick	Seedlings, fruit seeds
	Heavily spotted breast	Short, thick	Seeds and insects
	Three white lines on top of head	Short, thick	Seeds and insects
	Dull yellow patch bordered with black on top of head	Short, thick	Seeds and insects
	Breast streaked with brown and with dark spot in middle	Short, thick	Seeds and insects

I. — Intermediate (birds between the Blackbird and
Linnet)

S. — Small (birds about size of Linnet or smaller)

Originally compiled by DR. ADELE LEWIS GRANT and BLANCHE VIGNOS

Common names as approved by American Ornithologists Union, 5th Edition

TED IN COOPERATION WITH FEDERAL,

GUIDE AND LEAFLET LIST.

E, to

A BARBARA ST., SANTA BARBARA, CALIF. 93101

YOU ARE INVITED TO AID IN THE YEAR-ROUND EDUCATION MOVEMENT. JOIN THE CALIFORNIA CONSERVATION COUNCIL (Individual $3.00 up; Organzation $5.00 up). A CONTRIBUTION, IN ANY AMOUNT, MAY BE SENT WITH LEAFLET ORDER.

This is Leaflet C-58, 3c. 20th printing, revised 1966.

Hydraulic mining was outlawed by California in 1884 because of its destructiveness. (*Courtesy, The Bancroft Library*)

through pine forests, and past snow-covered mountain peaks. You're close to the giant sequoia in Calaveras Big Trees State Park (on S.R. 4), mountain lakes in the Eldorado National Forests, and river running on the Stanislaus.

But no matter when you come, remember you're probably better off concentrating on one Mother Lode section at a time. If you have just a few days, pick a base like Sonora, Jackson, or Nevada City and fan out from there. These communities, as well as towns like Murphys, Volcano, Amador City, and Coloma, have beautifully restored inns you can stay at. Should you prefer to camp, bear in mind that there are only a handful of sites in the southern and central Mother Lode. But no matter how you go or where you stay, enjoy the Gold Country selectively. Don't worry about what you're missing. You'll be back, just like everyone else.

Gold Country Notes

Sunset's Gold Rush Country is the best general guide on the subject ($1.95, Lane Magazine and Book Company, Menlo Park, CA 94025). Also helpful is *Exploring the Mother Lode Country* by Richard Dillon (50¢, Ward Ritchie Press, Los Angeles, CA 90039). The Automobile Club of Southern California (AAA) publishes a *Guide to the Mother Lode Country*. You can get a map of the region from Golden Chain Council of the Mother Lode, 217 Maple Street, Auburn, CA 95603. Cyclists should get *Bicycling Through the Mother Lode* (California Department of Parks and Recreation, P.O. Box 2390, Sacramento, CA 95811).

Rattlesnakes

Although you can find rattlesnakes in many parts of the country, few states offer better opportunities to see them than California. Here are such subspecies as the Pacific, Great Basin, Panamint, western diamondback, red diamondback, and Mojave rattlers, as well as the sidewinder. Although many residents have never viewed one of these poisonous reptiles, if you do any serious exploring you're bound to encounter one or more of these snakes averaging 3 to 4 feet in length. They are there waiting for you along the coast, down in the valleys, up in the mountains, and out on the desert. The fact is, almost anywhere you go in California, from the Lava Beds caves to the suburbs of San Francisco, you'll never be far from a rattler.

But the proximity of all these snakes is no reason for alarm. Most of them hibernate during the winter, emerging in the late spring, then sunning during the daytime and hunting squirrels, rabbits, mice, or lizards at night. If you give them distance, they won't bother you. Generally, rattlers withdraw when they are disturbed. But if they sense they are being cornered, these snakes will strike.

Should you be bitten, you can suck out some of the venom with an inexpensive snakebite kit routinely carried by people who frequently travel the back country. You should also apply a lightly constricting tourniquet above the wound. The bites are generally not fatal, provided you remain calm and get prompt medical attention. Some physicians will treat you with an antivenin, although bad reactions to this substance have caused many doctors to limit its use.

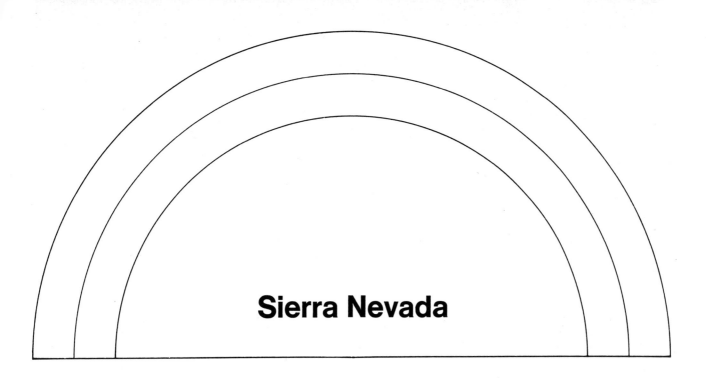

Sierra Nevada

The Best of the Sierra Nevada

National park: Yosemite
State park: Calaveras Big Trees
Camping: Grover Hot Springs State Park; Calaveras Big Trees State Park
Swimming: Shaver Lake
Sailing: Huntington Lake
Hiking: Kings Canyon National Park; Mineral King; Tuolumne Meadows, Yosemite National Park
Hot springs: Grover
Valley: Mineral King
Meadow: Tuolumne, Yosemite National Park
Waterfall: Yosemite falls
Wilderness: Mokelumne; Desolation
Small lake: Donner
Old hotel: Ahwahnee, Yosemite National Park
Pioneer history center: Wawona, Yosemite National Park
Historic monument: Donner Memorial
National park entrance: S.R. 180 into Kings Canyon
Views: Lake Tahoe from Desolation Wilderness; Yosemite Valley from Glacier Point
Pass (winter): Carson
Pass (summer): Tioga
Trans-Sierra route: S.R. 88
Norse-style fortress: Vikingsholm, Lake Tahoe
Sequoia: General Sherman

Probably the best way to explore California's principal mountain range, the Sierra Nevada, is to strap on a backpack and start hiking the John Muir Trail. You can walk more than 200 miles through the best of the rugged High Sierra without passing over one road or seeing a single community. But if limitations of time and endurance make this impractical, don't worry. There are plenty of other ways to reach the best of this 400-mile-long mountain range that stretches roughly from the north fork of the Feather River down to Tehachapi.

One good place to begin a Sierra visit is the tiny community of Mineral King, the southernmost of the important Sierra attractions. Not only is this the jump-off point to some of the best hiking, fishing, and camping in the Sierras, but it will give you first-hand insight into one of the state's major conservation battles.

To reach Mineral King, you must go off S.R. 198 just east of Three Rivers and navigate a winding 22-mile road (closed in winter) with 322 turns. This drive, which is not suitable for campers or trailers, cuts through the southwest corner of Sequoia National Park, runs along the Kaweah River, and stops at the edge of the wooded, 2-mile-long Mineral King Valley. From here, you must walk or rent a pack horse to reach the lakes (there are twenty-two), fishing streams, waterfalls, and dramatic Sierra peaks. Using Mineral King as your base, you can hike up to a different lake each day, take a three-day saddle trip, or go backpacking into neighboring Sequoia National Park.

While you're in the area, be sure to talk with some of the summer residents who live in cabins without phones, electricity, or gas; cook on wood stoves; and put rubber tubes in the clear Kaweah to draw their water. They'll tell you about the lengthy Sierra Club legal effort that has thwarted Walt Disney Enterprises from turning this spectacular mountain region into a major ski area.

This is not the first time Mineral King has been a development target for outsiders. Greedy speculators and promoters and their political allies gave the valley its first economic jolt a century ago. In 1872, a spiritualist named James Crabtree claimed he was guided by an Indian spirit to Mineral King's White Chief Mine, which he duly staked and recorded in 1873. Soon Crabtree and a group of investors formed the Mineral King Mining District, which quickly lured prospectors; speculators rushed in to form mining companies.

Although Mineral King's population eventually soared to 3000, it soon became clear that the beckoning Indian spirit didn't have much grasp of mineralogy. The ore turned out to be a "rebellious" brand that lacked enough gold, silver, zinc, lead, or sulfur to support extraction. By 1877, the mining enterprises began declaring bankruptcy; a year later, a series of disastrous slides crushed a bunkhouse and damaged mining equipment at the big Empire Mine.

The town dwindled until Tom Fowler, a state senator and cattle baron from Visalia, bought the Empire Mine and recharged the boom in the 1880s. To spur his miners on, he left the Empire with a load of raw ore and returned with a handsome silver bar that spelled big money for everyone. Unfortunately, the same bar was used over and over again. It was a bogus piece made from melted-down silverware. Ultimately, Fowler's efforts at upgrading the mine were undone, not by his chicanery, but by a series of avalanches that destroyed the entire settlement. These frequent avalanches, which continue to this day, lead Mineral King summer residents to suggest their valley is a dangerous site for a major ski area.

After acquainting yourself with the Mineral King region, head back to S.R. 198 and return to Three Rivers, where you'll find a 2.5-mile road leading to the tiny settlement of Kaweah. Today there's not much left of the utopian community, the Kaweah Cooperative Colony, begun here in 1885. On settling, the founders filed claims with the federal government for a series of 160-acre timber tracts extending along the Kaweah River up into the Giant Forest. Among the huge sequoias in the stand was the General Sherman Tree, which, at 272.4 feet high and 30.7 feet in girth, measures in as the largest living thing.

Even though the federal government rejected Kaweah's claim and withdrew the land the founders sought from the market, these utopians remained optimistic about ultimately winning title. Accordingly, in 1886, they embarked on the monumental job of

constructing an 18-mile logging road into the forest. Instead of being paid cash, all members of the colony received time checks computed at an identical rate. In return, these vouchers were accepted as currency at the Kaweah store.

During the four years it took to complete the job, the utopians mapped plans to build a private railroad down to the valley, from where their logs could be floated to San Francisco via private canals and rivers. There stevedores would load the timber along with colony-produced wine, honey, marble statuary, and selected California fruits into Kaweah-owned ships. Then socialist skippers would sail forth to major ports, bringing home immense profits to plow into furthering the utopian dream. The Kaweahans were so confident of their bountiful future that they even renamed the General Sherman Tree for Karl Marx.

But the days of the socialist sequoia were numbered. On September 25, 1890, President Benjamin Harrison signed a bill establishing Sequoia National Park. A week later Congress surprised local Tulare County residents by signing another bill that tripled the size of Sequoia National Park and established adjacent Grant Grove as a new national park. This effectively destroyed any possibility that the colonists could successfully live and work in this region, where they had built their road and homes. It subsequently turned out that the second bill was passed at the behest of the Southern Pacific Railroad, which saw the Kaweah colonists as serious competition for their own timberland operations in Northern California. The railroad also expected to pick up considerable business hauling tourists to the new national park.

Not only did the colony fail to win title to the timberlands, it was never even compensated for building the road, which for many years was the only route into Giant Forest. Even worse, the government arrested five colony leaders and took them to a Los Angeles court, where they were fined $100 to $300 apiece for cutting down five small pines worth $2 each during construction of the road.

By 1891, the utopian group abandoned its lumbering plans and began breaking up. Nearly half the members went off the time-check system, took personal possession of property owned in the Kaweah community, and absolved themselves of responsibility for the debts of others. Meanwhile, the federal government stripped Karl Marx's name from the largest sequoia and restored the tree's original name, General Sherman.

Despite the humiliation, many colonists stayed in the Kaweah area, and some of their descendants can be found in the region today. Generally, they like to cite the judgment of one of Kaweah's founders, Burnette Haskell, who summarized the disastrous colonization experience this way: "The capitalist press used their banal reporter's English to stab us to death;

the lumber monopoly of the San Joaquin went to Congress behind our back and made a 'Park' of the Forest we had saved from flame. The machinery of the law was used to take us three hundred miles to meet charges in court without one single jot of evidence while gigantic lumber thieves were looting the forests of Humboldt [County] and the authorities winked their eye. We were poor. We were ignorant. We were jeered at. But no man dare say but we were honest.''

If you're interested in pursuing the history of this utopian group, check with Sequoia National Park rangers for permission to drive the old route from Kaweah to Old Colony Mill. Today the easiest way into the park is S.R. 198. It quickly leads to the Giant Forest area, which is the center of activity inside Sequoia Park. Here you can rent a cabin at the Giant Forest Lodge or camp at the Lodgepole area not far from the visitors' center. Aside from the obligatory drive through Tunnel Log, you'll find it best to park your car and explore the Giant Forest area on foot. Pick up a trail map and take your choice of eight walks through the forest. They range from the easy 1.4-mile Sunset Rock Trail loop to the moderately strenuous 9-mile Lakes Trail.

A good choice for families is the 1-mile-long Congress Trail, which begins near the General Sherman Tree and leads past some of the forest's better known sequoias. You'll note many of these thriving giants have been charred, scarred, and otherwise damaged by fire. Their ability to survive the perils that destroy lesser species has long been a subject of fascination. "I never saw a big [sequoia] tree that had died a natural death," wrote naturalist John Muir, who gave the Giant Forest area its name during one of his long trips through the Sierra in the mid-nineteenth century. "Barring accidents they seem to be immortal, being exempt from all the diseases that afflict and kill other trees. Unless destroyed by man, they live on indefinitely until burned, smashed by lightning, or cast down by storms, or by the giving way of the ground on which they stand."

A somewhat more ambitious, 5-mile walk is the Trail of the Sequoias. Although it's considered a moderate walk, allow five hours for this hike that takes you through an open forest of pine, fir, and sequoia. You might also consider the 4.6-mile Moro Rock–Soldiers Trail loop. It's fairly level except for the climb to the top of the rock, where you'll get a good view of the 13,000-foot peaks of the Great Western Divide as well as the frequently smoggy San Joaquin Valley. But you can also get much the same view without climbing huge Moro Rock. Just before reaching the big landmark, you'll find a good overlook on level terrain. Since there's no railing here, be sure not to get too close to the edge. Trite as this warning may sound,

it is one that should be heeded throughout the mountains of California. What seems like firm ground often has a tendency to give way.

After you've finished hiking, consider a trip to Crystal Cave, where you can explore the limestone caverns. Be sure to see the curtain formations in Marble Hall and the fairy pool in the Dome Room. When you're done, it's time to head on to the Grant Grove area of Kings Canyon National Park. Owing to its location halfway between Giant Forest and the popular Cedar Grove section of Kings Canyon, (via S.R. 180), Grant Grove's campground or lodge makes a practical place to stay.

While at the grove you'll want to visit the General Grant Tree, second in size only to the General Sherman. Nearby is the Fallen Monarch, a hollow tree that entrepreneurs used as lodging for their work crew while cutting down one of the giant sequoias. They expected to make big money by exhibiting part of the huge tree at the 1876 Centennial Exhibition in Philadelphia. After carefully cutting out two 16-foot sections, the men sent them cross-country to the extravaganza. There the pieces were cemented together and a doorway carved out so visitors could go inside. But as soon as spectators saw the seams, they charged the whole thing was an assemblage of several trees and dismissed it as a hoax. Today, the stump of this great tree is known as School Stump because loggers' wives and children used it for Sunday school classes.

Continuing east on S.R. 180 (closed in winter), you'll begin heading down into Kings Canyon. This descent down the steep, walled valley of the Kings River's south fork, with its switchback along sheer canyon walls, is among the most dramatic in California. Campgrounds in the Cedar Grove area serve as the base for backpacking and pack-horse trips into the surrounding high country, where you can visit Evolution Basin, Tehipite Valley, or Kern Canyon, or even hike all the way back into Sequoia Park. But don't consider approaching this rugged country before checking with park rangers.

On the canyon floor itself, you can make the easy hike to Roaring River Falls, Mist Falls, or Zumwalt Meadows. At the last site, there's a 1.5-mile-long loop trail past old Indian rock mortars, popular fishing sites on the Kings River, and an abundant marsh. Rattlesnakes and mountain lions both roam this meadow for food. But there's no need to be paranoid. No one has been bitten by a snake here in recent years, and mountain lions are hardly ever seen due to their secretive nature. Another popular trip is the 3.5-mile Cedar Grove Motor Trail. Although this route is designed for cars, you'll get a much better view of the river, marsh, glacial moraine, cliffs, forest, and old Monachi Indian camp on foot or on a horse rented at the nearby corral.

After visiting Sequoia and Kings Canyon National Park, you may want to head north to Yosemite. Gen-

Yosemite Valley. (*Hutchings' California Magazine, from "Scenes of Wonder and Curiosity," Howell-North Books*)

erally, people make this trip by returning to Fresno via S.R. 180 and then picking up S.R. 41 to the park's south entrance. But for a more scenic alternative that leads through the Sierra foothills, take S.R. 180 and cut north on Academy Avenue, just north of Sanger. Then pick up S.R. 168 to Auberry Road just east of Prather. In Auberry pick up Powerhouse Road to Road 222, which takes you through to North Fork, along the west side of Bass Lake, and finally hooks up with S.R. 41 at Yosemite Forks.

If you're not pressed for time, there is a side trip worth including in this route. Instead of cutting off S.R. 168 to Auberry, consider taking S.R. 168 up to the popular Huntington Lake–Shaver Lake region. Long a favorite family vacation spot, there are five mountain lakes in this area, which is a base for pack trips into the High Sierra. There's good swimming and water-skiing at Shaver Lake, while Huntington Lake's dependable winds make it popular with sailors. In addition to a variety of campgrounds and lakeside cottages, this region boasts Camp Sierra, which offers accommodations for organized groups of 30 to 250 people.

Returning to Auberry and picking up the previously mentioned route brings you to Yosemite's south door, through which you'll enter one of California's most complicated recreational habitats. Once bears were the only things you had to worry about on a trip to Yosemite. But today more than 2 million visitors annually crowd into this 1189-square-mile geological wonderland that cynics have begun calling Yosemite National Park and Shop.

Most tourists insist upon spending their visit on the floor of Yosemite Valley. The resultant traffic congestion, pizza stand lines, and smoke make the place difficult to enjoy during peak summer months. Part of the problem is that Music Corporation of America (MCA), the park concessionaire, wants to develop Yosemite into a convention center with a variety of new attractions. Among the come-ons suggested by MCA have been a nightclub, a tramway from the valley floor to Glacier Point, hundreds of new hotel units, two golf courses, and more expensive campgrounds. Conservationists have criticized these plans as well as an MCA decision that allowed a sister television division to paint over park rocks so they would blend in better during filming of an unsuccessful series called "Sierra."

Don't get us wrong. Yosemite Valley is wonderful when the leaves turn in fall, when the snow comes in winter, and when the waterfalls peak in the spring. But if you must come during the summer, plan on spending most of your visit outside the crowded valley floor. The easiest way to do this is to head up into the park's high country on Tioga Road (S.R. 120), which offers easy access to Tuolumne Meadows, Tenaya Lake, Smokey Jack campground, and the White Wolf area. Although this region is also popular, you'll find it easy to escape the crowds by hiking or taking a pack trip into the interior. If you're hiking and don't want to carry your own tent, you can make arrangements to stay at a series of tent camps spotted across the high country. Breakfast and dinner are included at a package rate of $14.50 per day; box lunches are available at additional charge.

If you don't want to sleep on the ground, the park offers a wide variety of accommodations, ranging from bathless tent-cabins at $5 per person to the elegant Ahwahnee Hotel, where prices start at $22 and privileges at the pitch-and-putt golf course, tennis court, and swimming pool are available. Somewhat less expensive is the comfortable Yosemite Lodge. As with camping, you are probably better off staying in accommodations outside the valley floor during peak summer months. An alternative to the Ahwahnee is the Wawona Hotel, with its wide verandas, wicker chairs, and rates that begin at $8.75 for those willing to live without a private bath. This old hotel at the south end of the park is near the Wawona Pioneer History Center and Mariposa Grove of big sequoias. Modest tent cabins are also available at Tuolumne Meadows and White Wolf lodges.

After you've seen Half Dome, Glacier Point, Happy Isles, Mirror Lake, El Capitan, Yosemite Falls, Sentinel Falls, Ribbon Falls, Bridalveil Falls, and all the rest of Yosemite's stellar attractions, head out of the park via the Big Oak Flat station. Just beyond the boundary, pick up Evergreen Road, which leads through Mather and winds down 9.5 miles to the Hetch Hetchy Reservoir sitting atop the valley of the same name. About half the size of Yosemite Valley, the Hetch Hetchy was once, according to John Muir, "one of nature's rarest and most precious mountain temples." It was also the scene of one of California's most bitterly fought conservation battles.

Beginning in 1900, San Francisco embarked on a determined campaign to sink this national park valley beneath an 8-mile-long reservoir. In 1913 dam forces finally got the break they needed when San Francisco city attorney Franklin K. Lane, the man who had submitted many of the key city briefs in the legal battle to inundate Hetch Hetchy, was appointed secretary of

the interior by Woodrow Wilson. In Washington, he was able to persuade Congress to pass the Raker Act, which authorized flooding the valley. John Muir, who had fought relentlessly to block the project, was devastated by the defeat. He died a few months later of what some described as a broken heart.

Today, you can walk over the M. M. O'Shaughnessy Dam, named for the San Francisco city engineer whose supplemental appropriation requests for the project led city supervisors to inquire if his initials meant "More Money." On the other side of the dam, there's a trail that leads along the northern edge of the reservoir. Fishing is allowed from the shore only.

While you're in the area, you may want to give some thought to a small movement that's developed to drain Hetch Hetchy. Writer Tom Devries has pointed out that San Francisco no longer needs the reservoir. Downstream on the identical Tuolumne River is the Don Pedro reservoir, six times the size of Hetch Hetchy. By merely adding another 200 feet of water to Don Pedro, the entire Yosemite Park reservoir could be

Yosemite Falls. (*Hutchings' California Magazine, from "Scenes of Wonder and Curiosity," Howell-North Books*)

drained. In this way Hetch Hetchy could gradually be restored to its original beauty and provide more space for some of the crowds that overwhelm Yosemite.

On the way back from Hetch Hetchy, be sure to stop at Poopenaut Valley View (road marker H3). There's a good panorama here of the Tuolumne River Canyon below the dam. For an even better view, drive 1 mile up the road to the head of a trail that drops 1275 feet into the valley in just 1 mile. It takes three times as long to climb back up as it does to get down, which is why local people refer to this as the ''poopin' out'' trail. You can camp or fish in the valley, but you'll need permits for both activities. Also bear in mind that this area is a favorite with students of reptiles owing to its abundance of Pacific rattlesnakes.

North of the Yosemite region, several trans-Sierra highways offer additional access to the high country. Among them is S.R. 4, which cuts through popular Calaveras Big Trees State Park. Here, you can camp on the edge of a meadow, roam the giant sequoia groves, and swim in Stanislaus River pools. Among the leading attractions is the stump of a giant tree measuring 24 feet in diameter. Five men spent twenty-three days cutting it down in 1853 as part of a contest. Subsequently, the broad stump surface was used as a dance floor.

Farther up S.R. 4, stop off at Bear Valley, best known for its skiing, but also popular as a summer resort. Heading over Ebbetts Pass (closed in winter) and up S.R. 89, you soon reach Markleeville. This onetime mining center is the seat of sparsely populated Alpine County. A few years back, gay activists proposed moving in and taking over this county, which has a population of 700. But the idea was abandoned after an advance party showed up and found out about the fierce winters.

The best thing about this region is Grover Hot Springs State Park, 3.5 miles east of Markleeville. Located in a meadow at the base of two bare granite peaks, this park is popular with backpackers, who

PACIFIC SLOPE.   SIERRA.   PLATEAU REGION.   ROCKY MOUNTAINS.

Lake Tahoe.

frequently retreat here at the end of a mountain hike to soak out aches and pains. The uncovered concrete pool is fed by runoff from six mineral springs and is kept between 102 and 105 degrees year around. During the summer, an adjoining swimming pool also remains open. Although most will find it too cold for camping here during the winter, some skiers actually enjoy using the springs during freezing weather.

Northwest on S.R. 89 is Picketts Junction, which offers easy access to the Hope, Faith, and Charity valleys. There's good fishing at the nearby Blue Lakes, and by heading west on S.R. 88 you'll soon be atop Carson Pass. From here, trails lead into the nearby Mokelumne Wilderness and such destinations as Fourth of July Lake. Farther down at Peddler Hill, you can cut off to a number of remote campgrounds on the Mokelumne River.

After exploring these remote areas, return to Picketts Junction and pick up S.R. 89, which leads to California's mountain lake metropolis, South Lake Tahoe and its Nevada neighbor, Stateline. Together these overgrown twin cities have become the Gary, Indiana, of western resorts, funneling bumper-to-bumper traffic into a hideous urban strip that blights the lake with high-rise casinos. The largest share of Tahoe visitors usually stays here in one of the many hotels, motels, or condominiums. But unless you want to gamble or ski (see Part Eight, under Skiing), skip this area and head over to the lake's southwestern shore on S.R. 89.

Mark Twain once observed that "three months of camp life on Lake Tahoe would restore an Egyptian mummy to his pristine vigor and give him an appetite like an alligator." Turning off to the white sands of Pope Beach, you see what he had in mind. Here, just a few minutes away from the lake's urban center, you can sunbathe, bird-watch, or comb the shore. Although the clear waters are a bit cool for serious swimming, the beach is free of commercial intrusion.

Nearby, you can pick up area trail maps and wilderness hiking permits at the Forest Service visitors' center. Although information is available for all parts of the Tahoe area, you're probably best off concentrating your visit in the relatively unspoiled region extending from Pope Beach to Sugar Pine Point State Park and back into the adjacent Desolation Valley Wilderness. Traditionally this has been the part of Lake Tahoe favored by the moneyed few.

For example, Baldwin Beach, just up from the visitors' center, was once the site of the elegant Tallac House, which maintained a private vegetable garden and dairy herd to supply wealthy visitors who spent their days gambling, bowling, playing croquet, and taking hunting trips with an Indian guide. Among the employees was Erich Von Stroheim, who eventually moved to Hollywood, where he became rich and famous.

Before they were given park protection, some of the Sierra's giant Sequoia were chopped down by entrepreneurs. (*Hutchings' California Magazine, from "Scenes of Wonder and Curiosity," Howell-North Books*)

Farther on, at Emerald Bay State Park, you'll want to stop for a look at Vikingsholm, the replica of an old Norse fortress built in 1929. The thirty-eight-room mansion was occupied by Lora J. Knight of Santa Barbara until her death in 1945. Many of the furnishings she sought for the home were so important historically that the Norwegian and Swedish governments forbade their export. So she had them precisely reproduced right down to the texture of the wood.

Adjacent to Emerald Bay is the D. L. Bliss State Park, where you'll want to visit Rubicon Point. Here you can see several hundred feet down into the water. And nearby Sugar Pine Point State Park offers good lakeside camping as well as a museum in the old Ehrman Mansion. But no matter which of these parks you choose, make it a point to take one of the trails back into the Desolation Wilderness. At the south end of Fallen Leaf Lake Road, there's a good 5-mile trail to Aloha Lake that runs along bubbling soda springs. You can take an easy 1-mile hike from Eagle Falls (near Emerald Bay State Park) up to Eagle Creek. And at Meeks Bay there's an 8-mile hike along Meeks Creek to several mountain lakes. Don't miss this back country. No California wilderness area is more accessible than this one. And as you look down at the lake, you'll understand why Mark Twain called a good view of Tahoe "the fairest picture the whole earth affords."

Continuing along the lakeshore, you'll soon come upon the motels and condominiums of Tahoe City, Kings Beach, and Incline Village. Although this area is not nearly as built up as South Lake Tahoe, it is no match for the unspoiled region you just left. And if you turn away from the lake and continue up S.R. 89, you'll soon reach Truckee, a community surrounded by resort subdivisions. An unpretentious town, Truckee's greatest asset is nearby Donner Lake. There's a state park and museum here commemorating the Donner party, which made the mistake of getting a late start over the Sierra in the fall of 1846. Trapped by a snowstorm on November 2, the eighty-seven travelers were forced to camp at the lake for the winter. The bitter cold and lack of food drove party members to madness, murder, and cannibalism. By the time rescue efforts finished, only forty-seven members remained alive. The lake has long since lived down its evil past and become one of the Sierra's more popular resorts. There are cabins, motels, and cottages here, but none of South Lake Tahoe's rampant commercialization. You'll be welcome here as long as you lay off the bad jokes about Donnerburgers.

Sierra Nevada Notes

Reservations are a good idea for all national park lodges and cabins during the summer. For Sequoia and Kings Canyon, write to Sequoia and Kings Canyon Hospitality Service, Sequoia National Park, CA 93262. At Yosemite, lodging is handled by the Reservation Department, Yosemite Park and Curry Company, Yosemite National Park, CA 95389. In California you can call, toll-free, 800-692-5811. From out of state, call 209-372-4671.

A wide variety of hotel, motel, and condominium accommodations can be found in the Lake Tahoe area. Write the Greater North Lake Tahoe Chamber of Commerce, P.O Box 884, Tahoe City, CA 95730 (or telephone 916-583-3461) or the South Lake Tahoe Chamber of Commerce, P.O. Box 3418, South Lake Tahoe, CA 95702. Information on other popular Sierra recreation areas can be obtained from Sonora Pass Vacationland, Inc., P.O. Box 607, Columbia, CA 95610; Alpine County Chamber of Commerce, Markleeville, CA 96120; Eldorado County Chamber of Commerce, 542 Main Street, Placerville, CA 95667; and Placer County Chamber of Commerce, Auburn, CA 95603.

Bears

In 1953 the state legislature decided to recognize the California grizzly bear as the state's official animal. Unfortunately, this decision didn't do much for the grizzlies; they had all been wiped out a generation earlier. Citizens anxious to have a look at the official state animal will have to settle for those depicted on the state flag.

Extinction of the grizzly leaves just one bear species alive in the state today, the black bear. These animals, which average 200 to 300 pounds, come in two varieties. One is the northwestern black bear found, naturally, in the northwestern part of the state. The other

is the Sierra Nevada black bear, found in the Sierra Nevada range south to Kern County and in portions of the Coast Range. Black bears living at higher elevations hibernate in winter; those in the southern part of the state and at lower elevations remain active year-round.

Although they are generally shy of people, bears can become dangerous, particularly when people make the mistake of trying to feed them. Although troublesome bears in the California national parks are trapped and removed to remote areas, the majority are allowed to roam free. Since these animals make frequent nocturnal visits to campsites, it's important not to keep food in your tent. Seal all food in airtight containers and store it in your car's trunk along with your ice chest. Be sure to keep the windows of your car rolled up. If you have a station wagon, throw a blanket over your ice chest, as rangers in Sequoia National Park report some perceptive bears can recognize coolers by their shape. These gourmets actually break into your car and tear the chest open to see what you've brought for them. Never keep food in a convertible. And if you're hiking overnight in the back country, be sure to suspend all food between two trees, away from your tent and out of bear grasp.

Mark Farmer Catalogue. Anyone with an interest in dolls will want a copy of the fifty-page catalogue of this firm, which offers, either in assembled or unassembled form, all thirty-nine first ladies* ($43 per kit), Louisa May Alcott's little women, the Prince of Wales, Florence Nightingale, Mary Stuart, and dozens of other china and porcelain dolls, many of which are of historical or literary interest. A special bonus in each new edition of the firm's catalogue is an updated account of the Farmer family, which has run this enterprise for twenty-eight years. You'll get the rundown on the Farmer children—Ann, Scott, and Mark, Jr.—each the inspiration for a doll that bears its name. You can save by ordering the Ann and Scott 12-inch doll kits together for a combined price of just $14. For your copy of the catalogue, send 50¢ to the Mark Farmer Company, 36 Washington Avenue, Point Richmond, CA 94801.

* President Woodrow Wilson was married twice while in the White House.

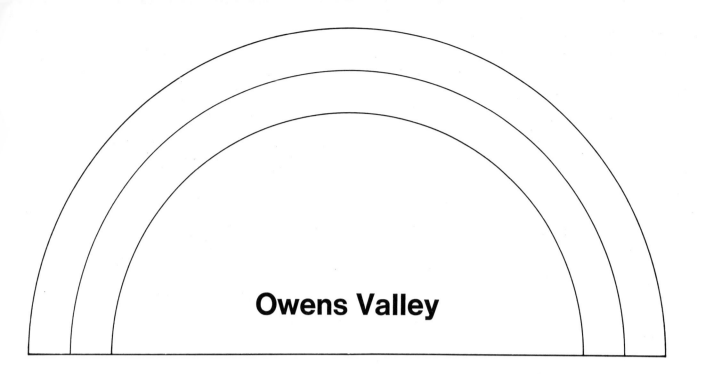

Owens Valley

The Best of Owens Valley

Trees: Bristlecone pine forest
Camping: Bishop Creek; June Lake
Hiking: Mammoth Lakes area
Backpacking: Minarets Wilderness (strenuous)
Mountain climbing: Mount Whitney
Swimming: Crowley Lake
Waterskiing: Crowley Lake
Snow skiing: Mammoth Mountain
Geological formation: Devil's Postpile
Rock formations: Alabama Hills
Craters: Mono
Obsidian dome: Glass Mountain
Petroglyphs: loop trip off U.S. 6 north of Bishop
Rock formations: Alabama Hills
Birds: Petroglyph Loop trip off U.S. 6 north of Bishop
Wildflowers: Bristlecone pine forest
Ghost town: Bodie
Railroad museum: Laws
Regional museum: Eastern California Museum, Independence
Mountain view: Minaret Vista, Mammoth Lakes
General Owens Valley view: Sierra View, Bristlecone pine forest
Drive: S.R. 168 to Bristlecone pine forest (steep)

The Owens River Valley east of the Sierra Nevada has long been California's stepchild. This region, extending roughly from Olancha to Bridgeport, has suffered countless indignities. Its major tributary has been siphoned off to fill Los Angeles swimming pools. Its rich farmland has been dried up into barren wasteland. Its great railroad lines are now museum pieces. And what were once its most prosperous towns now stand abandoned.

The region's only major body of water, Mono Lake, is so alkaline that it cannot support fish life. Many of the roads traversing the arid countryside are soft pumice that can easily trap the visiting driver. And the last sudden population influx came during World War II, when the federal government forced thousands of Japanese-Americans behind barbed wire at the Manzanar internment camp.

Nonetheless, the largely unknown Owens Valley should not be missed by anyone with a serious interest in California, its people, and its history. In the mountains overlooking the region you'll find forty-century-old groves of bristlecone pine, the oldest known living things. Just north of Mono Lake is Bodie, which many consider western America's leading ghost town. Here also are the Alabama Hills, one of Hollywood's favorite locations, plus easy access to some of the state's best mountain lakes, fishing, and backpacking.

Your best introduction to this once prosperous mining and agricultural region is the gleaming 20-mile-long dry bed of Owens Lake itself. Before engineers diverted its water to Los Angeles via a 233-mile-long aqueduct, the Owens Valley had a growing economy dominated by vast orchards and wheatfields and supplemented by active silver and lead mining.

The beginning of the end of Owens Lake came in 1905, when Los Angeles residents, terrified by summertime droughts, passed a bond issue to finance construction of the new water system. This plan was bitterly fought by Owens Valley residents, who saw it as a scheme to expand Los Angeles and irrigate San Fernando Valley fields at the expense of their region. They appealed to the federal government, but President Theodore Roosevelt decided that Los Angeles' growth was more important than the rights of the Owens Valley settlers. As historian Walton Bean explains: "In 1908 to prevent homestead entries in the path of the proposed aqueduct, Roosevelt ordered the extension of the Sierra National Forest eastward to include the prospective right of way, even though the only trees in the region were those planted by settlers themselves."

After the aqueduct was opened, Los Angeles gradually began appropriating more of the Owens River water. By the early 1920s a new drought in Los Angeles led the community to drain away nearly all the river flow. In 1924, some Owens Valley residents started making their opposition heard by sabotaging, and eventually dynamiting, portions of the aqueduct. But the damage was quickly repaired, and the opposition eventually died out.

Today you can speed past the onetime lake on U.S. 395, stopping only at Cottonwood Canyon for a look at the remains of the beehive kilns that produced

charcoal to power a local silver and lead smelter. Or if you're not in a hurry, circle around the lake bed by cutting off on S.R. 190 and then returning left on S.R. 136 back to U.S. 395. Beginning this loop at Olancha, your first stop is the Dirty Sock Hot Spring, where miners used to come from miles around to do their wash in the warm waters.

Next you'll pass through Keeler, terminus for the regional Carson and Colorado freight railroad, where a few buildings remain, including the depot. Train buffs will be able to find some of the old, narrow-gauge C&C roadbed in nearby Dolomite. Here too are a number of old movie sets. But an authentic regional landmark, the once prosperous Cerro Gordo silver-lead-zinc mine, is closed to visitors. The entire drive provides an excellent view of the lake, but don't consider exploring the dry bed (now mined by chemical companies) without a four-wheel-drive vehicle.

Continuing north on U.S. 395, you'll soon pass along the backside of some of the Sierra's major peaks, including California's highest point, Mount Whitney. The knobby rocks in the foreground are the Alabama Hills, and you can reach them by cutting west out of Lone Pine on the Whitney Portal Road. These domes, small buttes, and other rock formations were named during Civil War days by a group of drunken southern miners celebrating attacks made by the Confederate battleship *Alabama* against the Union. Hundreds of films have been made here; one of the most popular locations is Movie Flat, just off the Whitney Portal Road. At the portal itself, there's a panoramic view of the entire region. You'll find fishing, picnicking, and camp-

During World War II, the Federal Government forced thousands of Japanese Americans behind barbed wire at the Manzanar detention camp. (*Courtesy, The Bancroft Library*)

Memorial Day, 1942, at Manzanar. (*Courtesy, The Bancroft Library*)

ing at this site, which serves as a base for thousands who hike to Mount Whitney's summit each summer.

Returning to the main highway, your next stop should be Manzanar, about 10 miles north of Lone Pine. Today all you'll find of this infamous World War II internment camp are a few streets and sidewalks and two oriental gatehouses designed to make the Japanese prisoners feel at home. Acting on the irrational notion that the 112,000 Japanese nationals living on the West Coast posed a threat to American security, the federal government sent them off to ten "relocation" camps sited in some of the nation's remotest regions. In addition to the big Manzanar unit, a second California internment facility was built at Tulelake, near the Oregon border.

The decision to intern the Japanese was based more on mass hysteria than military necessity. For example, William Randolph Hearst was so worried that Japanese submarines might pull up to the coast and shell San Simeon that he moved inland to his Northern California retreat for much of the war. After the war the United States Army admitted that "little support for the argument that military necessity required a mass evacuation of the Japanese can be found in contemporary evidence." Instead, official army historians argue that without bowing to public pressure to lock up the Japanese, "the cooperation of the white population of the Pacific states in the national defense effort could not have been assured."

From Manzanar it's a short drive north to Independence, where you'll want to stop at the Eastern California Museum, which is filled with extensive displays depicting the Owens Valley heyday. Then con-

tinue on to Big Pine and take S.R. 168 right toward Westgard Pass. The highway climbs a canyon for 13 miles before reaching White Mountain Road. Here you should cut off to the north and drive up through the pinyon pine forests, stopping briefly at the Sierra View promontory, where you can see much of the central Sierra, the Owens Valley, the White Mountains, and the neighboring Deep Springs Valley. As you continue up the winding slopes, you'll soon reach the Schulman Memorial Grove.

Here, at 10,100 feet up in the White Mountains Range, are the bristlecone pines, all carefully protected by the U.S. Forest Service. These short, gnarled trees seldom exceed 25 feet. Physically they are no match for the giant redwoods and sequoias found elsewhere in California. But over a 4000-year span they have managed to survive every possible danger, including mountain winters, sandstorms, and fires. Indeed, it is these elements that have sculptured the gnarled trees into a kind of living driftwood.

As you walk through this grove, you'll find 4500-year-old trees that were alive before construction of the great Egyptian pyramids. Thanks to their remarkable ability to adapt to a rugged environment, they have lived longer than anything else on earth. Although the trees often add less than 1 inch in diameter per century, they cling to life so fiercely that some have actually grown parallel to the ground.

Many of the older trees you'll see here scattered amid the landscape covered with red Indian paintbrush, blue lupine, white desert sweet, and hundreds of other plants, are partially dead. Herein lies the secret of their endurance. Only a small vein of living tissue is needed to keep the tree alive. Thus, part of the pine dies, while the living portion remains in balance with the natural elements. Incredibly, even some of the oldest trees still drop pinecones bearing fertile seeds.

Any visit to this ancient forest and the sibling Patriarch Grove 12 miles up the road should begin with a full tank of gas, as there are no services here. If you plan ahead and bring your own water, you can camp in this remote region where some of the vast open spaces resemble a moonscape. Most visitors leave by 5 P.M.; then virtually nothing interrupts your mountaintop privacy amid the bristlecones.

If you're not pressed for time, consider continuing east on S.R. 168 after your visit to the forest. Here you'll follow the path of a nineteenth-century toll road that heads over Westgard Pass and drops quickly into the Deep Springs Valley. Off to the right you'll see the dry white bed of Deep Springs Lake. And further up the road there's two-year Deep Springs College, where the all-male student body works with the school-owned cows and cattle while also pursuing a traditional academic curriculum. Nearby is the ghost town of White Mountain City, which includes a series of stone corrals, a stone chimney, and the remains of a few houses.

After examining the Indian petroglyphs at adjacent Wyman Canyon, return west on S.R. 168 to U.S. 395, head north to Bishop, and then take the 4.5-mile drive northeast on U.S. 6 to the Laws Railroad Museum. This 11-acre site once formed the railroad yards of the Carson and Colorado, which ran 300 miles from Mound House, Nevada, to Keeler, the town you just visited on your trip around Owens Lake.

Supplementing the original depot, church, post office, and pump house in Laws are a number of other structures built for a Paramount movie set. One of these buildings is the reception center and museum, where the staff does much of its work on vintage office equipment. After visiting the depot, agent's office, and hand-operated turntable, stroll through the old caboose, baggage, and passenger cars en route to engine No. 9.

Even if you have no interest in trains, consider this side trip mandatory. For here are a number of other items of general historical interest, such as a horse-drawn hearse, a 1931 Model A Ford coupe, and a branding iron collection found in the depot freight room. Be sure to visit the old station agent's residence that includes such rare antiques as a free-standing Murphy bed.

Before leaving Laws, stop back at the museum to pick up a brochure on the 50-mile-long Petroglyph Loop trip. This drive leads north on U.S. 6 and then brings you back to Bishop via Fish Slough Road, once the old stage route linking Bishop with the mining boom towns of Bodie and Aurora. About half this trip is on a dirt surface, and no water or roadside service is available en route. But as you explore this volcanic tableland, you'll find pictures of deer, insects, snakes, and people and handprints and footprints carved into the rocks by ancestors of the Paiute Indians. Many of the geometric designs found here are as wide as 4 feet across.

Climbing through the wildflowers to examine these pictures, you'll find remains of old Indian camps and see deer, white-tailed antelope, roadrunners, kingfishers, red-shafted goldfinches, flickers, and quail. Look carefully at the marshes, and you'll probably see herons, egrets, ducks, or geese feeding. And be sure to get out at Panorama Stop, where there's a 360-degree view of the Sierra crest to the west, Owens Valley to the south, the White Mountains (where you visited the bristlecone pines) to the east, and the Benton Range and Blind Springs Hill to the north.

If you drive Petroglyph Loop on a hot summer day, consider cooling off afterward by heading up Bishop Creek. Take S.R. 168 west out of Bishop, and you'll soon be up on the eastern slope of the Sierra, where you can camp by the streams, fish the lakes, and explore the ruins of the old Cardinal Mine. Access to a similar region can be gained by heading north on U.S. 395, cutting west at Tom's Place, and heading up Rock Creek Canyon.

Continuing north on U.S. 395, you'll soon come to the major resort-recreation area of Owens Valley, Mammoth Lakes. This historic mining region has long been a favorite spot for campers as well as backpackers, who use the area as a base for their ascent into the popular Minarets Wilderness. More recently Mammoth Mountain has become a leading California ski resort (see Part Eight, under Skiing), which has turned the area into a popular year-round vacation center.

So far, most of what you've seen in the Owens Valley has remained unspoiled by commercial development. Indeed, much of the region suffers from depopulation. This is not the case at Mammoth. Poor zoning has led to wholesale condominium development, creating a hectic tourist town atmosphere in the community of Mammoth Lakes. Unless you're a skier, don't consider vacationing here in the winter. In the summer, however, it is a must.

How you approach the town of Mammoth Lakes depends on your travel biases. If you prefer avoiding urban pressure on a vacation, simply consider it as the town you pass through en route to some of Owens Valley's leading sites. However, if you seek the luxuries you left at home, consider renting a relatively inexpensive condominium ($170 a week for a two-bedroom unit with loft) where you can relax in a sauna or whirlpool following a tiring day of hiking. Here there are swimming pools, tennis courts, Ping-Pong tables, dishwashers, garbage disposals, maids, supermarkets, and other creature comforts perfect for families that don't want to rough it.

But whether you camp, stay in a motel, or choose a condominium, be sure to start your visit with a trip to the Mammoth Visitors' Center for an Inyo National Forest Map. Here, too, you can sign up for a historic tour that includes a look at the ruins of nearby Old Mammoth. This area was the site of a busy mining camp thrown up in 1878 by settlers who had come expecting to find the biggest bonanza outside Virginia City. Mammoth City, as it was called then, was busy enough to support two breweries and twenty-two saloons, while potatoes sold at $1 a pound.

Expectations exceeded reality, and by 1879 stock in the year-old Mammoth Mining Company had fallen from $20 a share to nothing. Two years later, the mining property was sold off by the sheriff. Aside from various excavations and stone foundations, virtually all that remains of the firm's mill is the flywheel found just beyond the Mill City campground.

Returning to the center of town, pick up S.R. 203 and take the cutoff to the nine bodies of water that give the town its name, Mammoth Lakes. They range from mile-long Lake Mary to tiny Crystal Lake. You'll want to stop at Twin Falls and perhaps rent a fishing boat on Twin Lakes or Lake George. Although a swimming beach has been set aside at Horseshoe Lake, the water is too cold for much beyond a quick dunking. The best way to see these mountain lakes is to take some of the easy hikes, such as the 1-mile-long path that links Twin Lakes with Lake Mamie via Twin Falls.

After heading back toward town, once again pick up S.R. 203 and turn off toward the ski area. En route stop and take the self-guiding trail through a crack in the earth called earthquake fault. Actually the name is a misnomer; the split is not a true fault because there is no vertical or horizontal displacement. In point of fact, you're being led through a fissure. In any case, be careful since ice and snow often lie at the bottom of this deep fracture even during the summertime.

Shortly beyond ski area headquarters (where there are gondola rides to the 11,053-foot summit), you can turn out to Minaret Vista, one of the best viewpoints in the state. Beyond this point, a narrow, rough, winding, dirt road will bring you to Devil's Postpile. It's a short hike from the parking lot to this weird formation produced by lava that poured through a vent in the vicinity of Mammoth Pass. As the lava cooled, it solidified and cracked apart, making a series of three- to seven-sided columns 40 to 60 feet high. Later, huge glaciers exposed and polished these posts of basaltic rock.

Devil's Postpile is the jumpoff point for everything from monumental hikes up the John Muir Trail to short walks in nearby Red's Meadow. Before you do any serious hiking, check with the Forest Service. Nearby Minarets Wilderness features some of the Sierra's steepest trails, and first-time visitors frequently overestimate their endurance.

North of Mammoth Lakes, you may want to turn off U.S. 395 to visit the two Inyo Craters. Although neither of these depressions is as impressive as the Mono Craters near Mono Lake, they are far more accessible. The latter chain of twenty obsidian domes was shaped by a series of explosions that dumped a layer of soft pumice over the surrounding area. Today only four-wheel-drive vehicles and trucks can make it over the sandy pumice roads. However, a few miles north of the Inyo Craters, you can easily reach another obsidian dome known as Glass Mountain. Here it's possible to walk through the volcanic glass flow and examine the glistening black boulders once used by the Indians for arrowheads.

Not far from Glass Mountain is another popular Owens Valley spot, June Lake. Even if you can't get into the busy campgrounds here, you may want to stop for a picnic or to sunbathe on the beach. S.R. 158 forms a 13-mile loop past a number of other lakes in the region, eventually linking up with U.S. 395 just south of Lee Vining. This small community sits on the edge of California's dead sea, Mono Lake. The 6430-foot mountain-rimmed lake contains two small volcanic islands and is about 15 miles across and 20 miles long.

Devil's Postpile.
(*Cecil W. Stoughton, U.S. Department of the Interior*)

Although pumice roads do run along the north and south shores of Mono Lake, they are not recommended for passenger vehicles. The best way to approach the shore is on the main highway just north of Lee Vining.

Because it has no outlet, Mono Lake is actually saltier than the ocean. Thousands of years of evaporation have concentrated the water's mineral content, making it particularly alkaline. All this was pointed out by Mark Twain in *Roughing It* a century ago following a boat ride on the sterile waters: "This lake is two hundred feet deep, and its sluggish waters are so strong with alkali that if you only dip the most hopelessly soiled garment into them once or twice, and wring it out, it will be found as clean as if it has been through the ablest washerwomen's hands. While we camped there our laundry work was easy. We tied the week's washing astern of our boat, and sailed a quarter of a mile and the job was complete, all to the wringing out."

When you've finished looking at this lake Mark Twain called the "loneliest tenant of the loneliest spot on earth," consider a detour east on S.R. 120, just south of the lake. Soon you'll be driving through a pine forest toward Mono Mills, where you'll find the remains of a lumber camp that supplied the mining town of Bodie north of Mono Lake.

From here, it's about an hour through rolling volcanic tableland, dominated at points by sculptured red rock, to the tiny historic town of Benton Hot Springs. Some 6 miles farther on you'll reach Benton and U.S. 6, where you can head south and pick up the Petroglyph Loop trip if you missed it first time around. At the end of that side trip, it's easy to rejoin U.S. 395 for the return north. This is a good one-day excursion if you happen to have run out of sights to see while staying in the Mammoth Lakes area.

By now you have seen much of the Owens Valley. But before leaving the region, there's one more important turnoff on U.S. 395 about 18 miles north of Lee Vining. This is the road to Bodie. Although the state designated the abandoned gold mining town a historic park in 1962, no effort has been made to promote it. And Bodie Road, the 13-mile-long washboard into the ghost town, is impassable from Thanksgiving to Easter, when it's blocked by snowdrifts as high as 20 feet.

As a result, the vacationing hordes speeding by on U.S. 395 tend to skip Bodie. And that's just fine because it leaves room for ghost town aficionados, who approach the place with the zeal of Renaissance art majors on their first trip to Florence. What appeals to them most is the ghost town's purity. The state has not developed a motel, put in a gas station, cleared a campsite, opened a single store, or licensed so much as one hot dog stand. All there are in Bodie are drinking fountains, seventy-five splendidly preserved russet-colored wooden structures, the Standard Mine, and a cemetery.

Miraculously, Bodie's remote location has protected it from thieves. You'll see students' papers still lying on school desk tops, homes with their original furniture, glasses still set up on bars, and apothecary bottles filling the drugstore windows. The whole place has an *On the Beach* look, as if the residents simply decided to pull up stakes and leave en masse. This is just about what happened in the summer of 1932, when the last remaining Bodie citizens left in the wake of a disastrous fire.

Gold was first discovered here in 1859 by Waterman S. Bodey, who died shortly thereafter in a blizzard. During the town's heyday in the late 1870s, more than 10,000 residents kept 700 mining locations going, plus 70 mills, hoisting works, and other production enterprises. It took 2000 men, spread out over 150 camps in the hills, just to chop the wood necessary to power these operations. By the time the town was abandoned, more than $100 million worth of gold and $8 million in silver had been taken from local mines.

But today Bodie is remembered more for its rough frontier life style than for its gold and silver. "A sea of sin lashed by the tempest of lust and passion," was how one minister characterized this town that claimed sixty-five saloons. During the peak of the gold rush, residents liked to boast that their community had "the wildest main street . . . the wickedest men . . . and the worst climate out of doors." Daily killings were tolled on the fire bell; robberies, stage holdups, and street fights became so commonplace that townspeople frequently just turned the other way. When the parents of one young Aurora girl told her they were moving to Bodie, she ended her nighttime prayers by saying, "Goodbye, God, I'm going to Bodie."

When visiting here today, be careful not to disturb anything you see and not even to consider taking anything with you. Much of Bodie's distinction is explained by the fact that it is one of the few western ghost towns that has not been vandalized. Plan on spending at least a couple of hours here. And if you're heading south after you leave, take the Cottonwood Canyon Road to S.R. 167 and out to U.S. 395. It's downhill and smoother than the Bodie Road.

Owens Valley Notes

No serious trip into this region can begin without Russ Leadabrand's *Exploring California Byways, VI, Owens Valley* (50¢, Ward Ritchie Press, 3044 Riverside Drive, Los Angeles, CA 90039). Also valuable is Genny Schumacher's *Deepest Valley: Guide to Owens Valley and Its Mountain Lakes, Roadsides and Trails* (Wilderness Press, 24440 Bancroft Way, Berkeley, CA 94704). *The Mammoth Lakes Sierra* ($4.95), offered by the same author and publisher, provides extensive detail on the most popular part of this region. Mark Twain's *Rough-*

ing It (Signet, New American Library, Inc., 1301 Avenue of the Americas, New York, NY 10019) has an amusing section on Mono Lake. *Gold, Guns and Ghost Towns* ($4.95, Stanford University Press, Palo Alto, CA 94305) offers an excellent historical perspective on the region by a man who edited *Bishop's Inyo Register* for fifty-five years.

For additional travel information, contact the Bishop Chamber of Commerce, 690 North Main Street, Bishop, CA 93514, or the Mammoth Lakes Chamber of Commerce, P.O. Box 123, Mammoth Lakes, CA 93546. Condominium rentals can be arranged through the Mammoth Reservation Service, P.O. Box 277B, Mammoth Lakes, CA 93546. There is also scheduled air service from Los Angeles to the Mammoth Lakes Airport via Sierra Pacific Airlines (telephone 800-232-2121).

Rare and Endangered Species

Table 22 lists the wildlife species in California that have been designated rare or endangered by the state Fish and Game Commission. They may not be taken at any time.

TABLE 22. RARE AND ENDANGERED SPECIES

Species	Status	General location
Mammals		
Morro Bay kangaroo rat	Endangered	Morro Bay
Salt marsh harvest mouse	Endangered	San Francisco Bay salt marshes
San Joaquin kit fox	Rare	South Coastal Range, west side foothills
Island fox	Rare	Santa Barbara Channel islands
Wolverine	Rare	Remote high country, Northern California
California bighorn sheep	Rare	Sierra Nevada crest from near Mammoth Mountain to Mount Langley
Peninsular bighorn sheep	Rare	Santa Rosa Mountains
Guadalupe fur seal	Rare	Last California sighting on San Nicholas Island
Mohave ground squirrel	Rare	Part of Mohave Desert
Fresno kangaroo rat	Rare	Fresno County
Stephens kangaroo rat	Rare	San Jacinto Mountains
Birds		
California condor	Endangered	South Coastal, Tehachapi, south Sierra Nevada ranges
American peregrine falcon	Endangered	Coastal and Sierra Nevada ranges
Southern bald eagle	Endangered	Along coast, mountain lakes
California brown pelican	Endangered	Santa Barbara Channel islands
California least tern	Endangered	San Francisco Bay, coastline of Orange and San Diego counties
California clapper rail	Endangered	San Francisco Bay, Elkhorn Slough
Yuma clapper rail	Endangered	Southern Colorado River
Light-footed clapper rail	Endangered	South coastal marshes
Belding's savannah sparrow	Endangered	Southern California estuaries
California black rail	Rare	Lower Colorado River
California yellow-billed cuckoo	Rare	Dense streamside growth
Reptiles		
Blunt-nosed garter snake	Endangered	San Joaquin Valley, west side
San Francisco garter snake	Endangered	San Francisco Peninsula, west half
Giant garter snake	Rare	San Joaquin Valley
Alameda striped racer	Rare	Contra Costa and Alameda counties
Southern rubber boa	Rare	Kern, San Bernardino, and Riverside counties
Amphibians		
Santa Cruz long-toed salamander	Endangered	Monterey Bay
Desert slender salamander	Endangered	Santa Rosa Mountains
Black toad	Rare	Inyo County
Siskiyou mountain salamander	Rare	Siskiyou County
Limestone salamander	Rare	Along Merced River
Shasta salamander	Rare	Shasta County
Kern Canyon slender salamander	Rare	East of Bakersfield
Tehachapi slender salamander	Rare	East of Bakersfield
Fish		
Colorado squawfish	Endangered	Colorado River
Thicktail chub	Endangered	Sacramento Valley, Sacramento Delta
Tecopa pupfish	Endangered	Near Death Valley
Bonytail	Endangered	Colorado River
Humpback sucker	Endangered	Colorado River
Shortnose sucker	Endangered	Along Klamath River and Boles Creek
Lost River sucker	Endangered	California-Oregon border, along Klamath River, Tulelake
Unarmored three-spine stickleback	Endangered	Santa Clara River, Los Angeles County
Owens tui chub	Endangered	Owens Valley
Owens pupfish	Endangered	Owens Valley
Mohave chub	Endangered	Mohave River
Modoc sucker	Rare	Modoc and Lassen counties
Rough sculpin	Rare	Shasta County
Cottonball Marsh pupfish	Rare	Death Valley

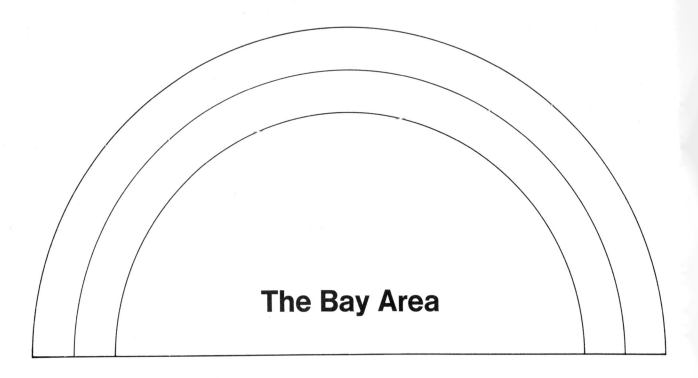

The Bay Area

The Best of the Bay Area

State park: Angel Island
Redwood grove: Muir Woods
National seashore: Point Reyes
Camping: Samuel P. Taylor State Park, Marin County
Tidepools: Point Reyes
Urban park: Golden Gate
Mountain: Mount Tamalpais
Hiking: Point Reyes; Mount Tamalpais
Beach: Stinson
Nude beach: San Gregorio
Sailing: San Francisco Bay
Garden: Berkeley Rose Garden
Japanese Tea Garden: Golden Gate Park
Art museum: M. H. de Young, Golden Gate Park
Historical museum: Fort Point
Museum architecture: Oakland
Victorian building: Haas-Lilienthal House
Victorian neighborhood: Pacific Heights, San Francisco
Bridge: Golden Gate
Airport: Oakland
Public university: University of California, Berkeley
Private university: Stanford, Palo Alto
Repertory theater: ACT, San Francisco
Arboretum: Villa Montalvo, Saratoga
Haunted house: Winchester Mystery House, San Jose
Observatory: Mount Hamilton

Hardware store: Ace Foothill Hardware, Oakland
Newsstand: De Lauer news agency, Oakland
Ice cream: Bud's
Stadium hot dog: Polish sausage, Candlestick Park, San Francisco
Steam beer: Anchor
Hot fudge sundae: Ghirardelli Square
Historical library: Bancroft, University of California, Berkeley
Night view: San Francisco from Sausalito
Day views: Mount Tamalpais; Mount Diablo
Drive: S.R. 1 in Marin County from U.S. 101 to Point Reyes

There are many ways to tour the Bay Area. You can charter a limousine, take a bus, buy a cassette tape, or follow a Convention and Visitors' Bureau self-guided tour. But really to understand the area, you have to get off the traditional tourist circuit and experience some of the region's more valuable and lesser known attributes.

A good place to begin is Angel Island in the middle of San Francisco Bay and easily accessible via boat from Pier 43½ on Fisherman's Wharf. Come supplied with a lunch, as there are no concessions at this state park, long a favorite with hikers. It was here that the *San Carlos,* the first ship to enter San Francisco Bay, landed in August 1775 while on a Spanish expedition. Biking around the island, you'll be able to visit a number of old buildings dating from the late nineteenth century when it served as a military staging area, fort,

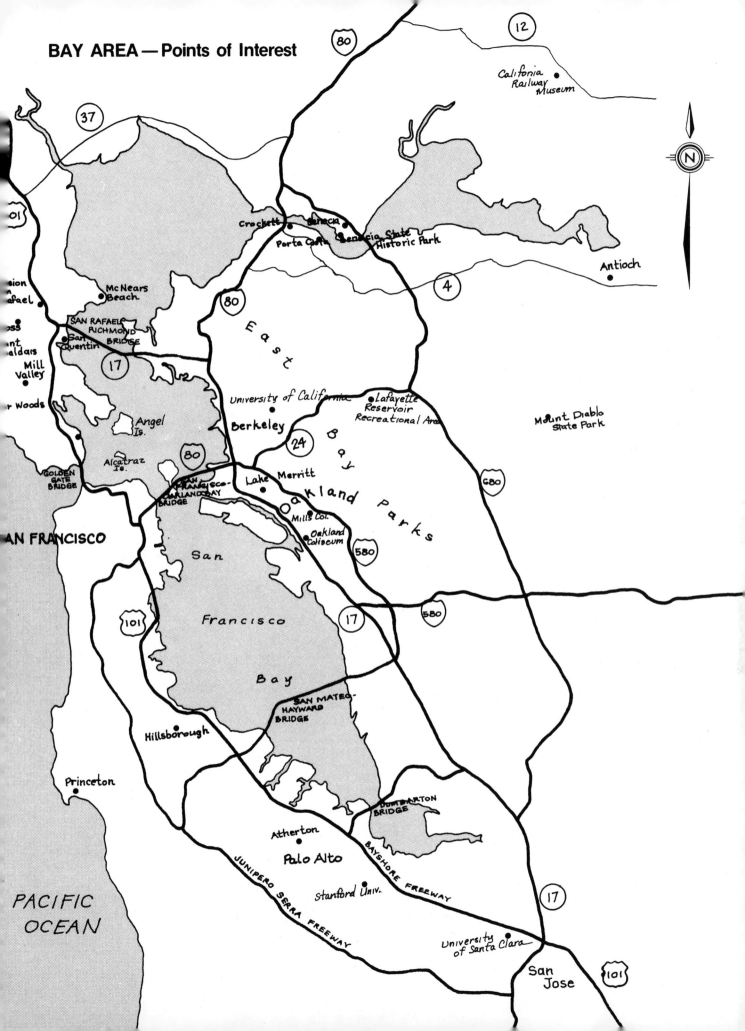

BAY AREA — Points of Interest

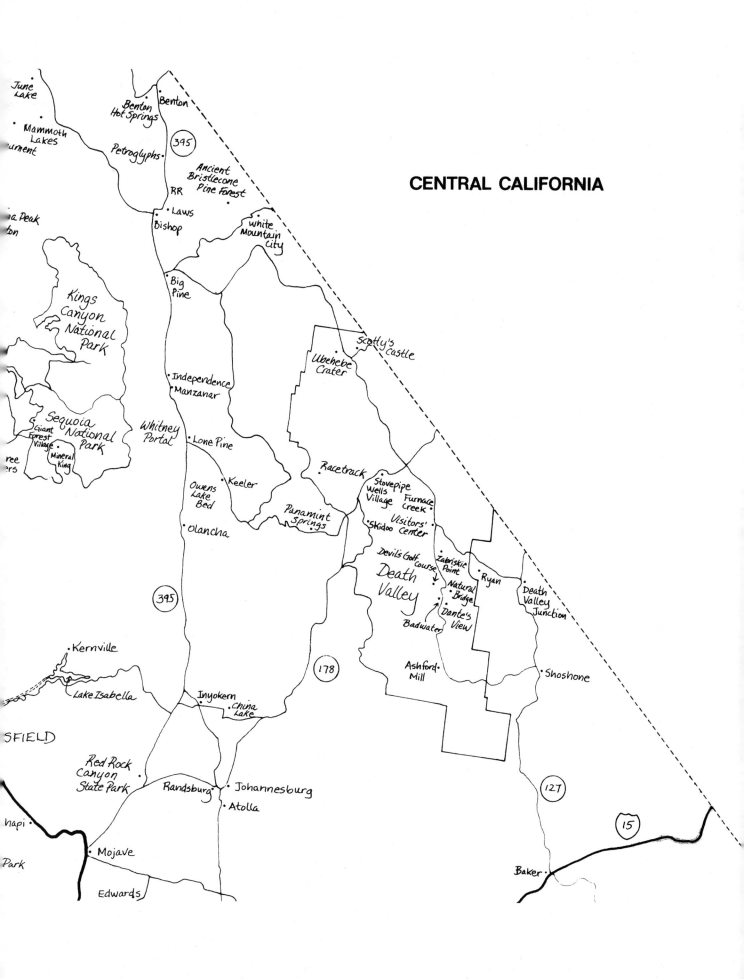

CENTRAL CALIFORNIA

June Lake

Mammoth Lakes

Benton Hot Springs

Benton

395

Petroglyphs

Ancient Bristlecone Pine Forest

RR

Laws

Bishop

White Mountain City

Big Pine

Kings Canyon National Park

Scotty's Castle

Ubehebe Crater

Independence

Manzanar

Sequoia National Park

Giant Forest Village

Mineral King

Whitney Portal

Lone Pine

Racetrack

Stovepipe Wells Village

Furnace Creek

Keeler

Owens Lake Bed

Panamint Springs

Visitors' Center

Skidoo

Olancha

Devil's Golf Course

Zabriskie Point

Death Valley

Natural Bridge

Ryan

Death Valley Junction

395

Dante's View

Badwater

178

Ashford Mill

Shoshone

Kernville

Lake Isabella

Inyokern

China Lake

SFIELD

Red Rock Canyon State Park

Randsburg

Johannesburg

Atolla

127

15

hapi

Park

Mojave

Baker

Edwards

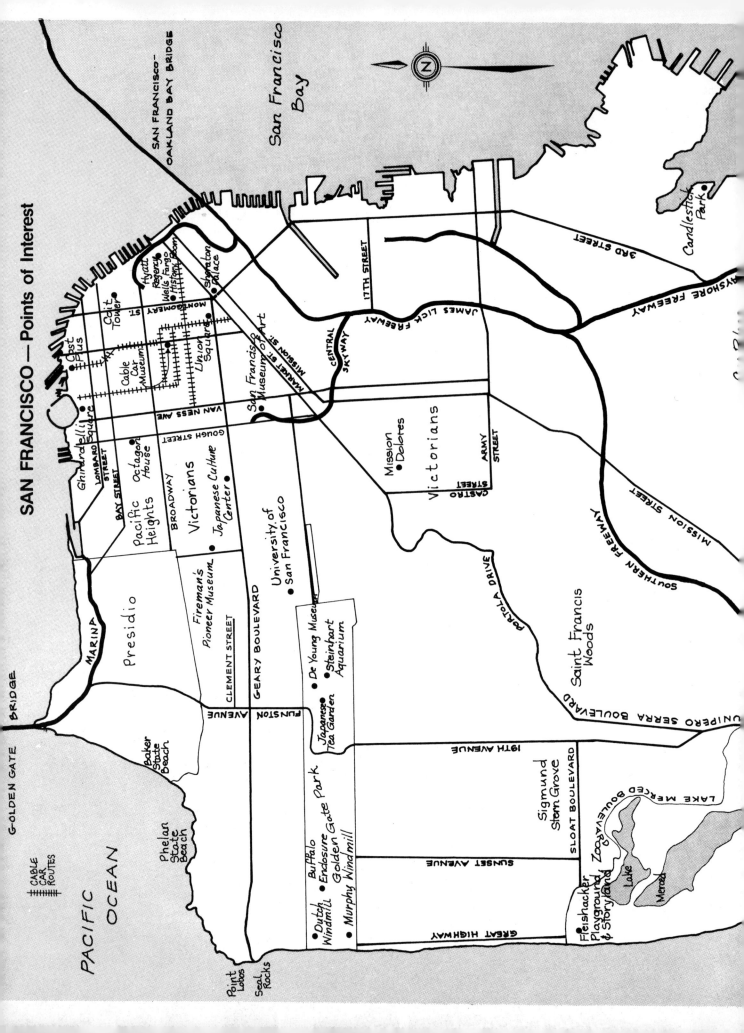

SAN FRANCISCO—Points of Interest

and immigration station. The Sunset and North Ridge trails will take you around the entire island—a trip of about 5 miles—and provides you with excellent introductory views of the Bay Area.

Returning to San Francisco itself, you'll do well to see as much of the city as possible on foot or bike. One good starting point is the Golden Gate Bridge, where a special path has been set aside for cyclists and pedestrians. This trip is best made on weekends early in the morning, when adjacent highway traffic is light. Not only will you get some good views, but you can also check out the side of the bridge from which nearly 500 people have jumped to meet their maker.

Another San Francisco must is Golden Gate Park, the sand dune that has been transformed into one of the nation's outstanding urban retreats. Inside this 1017-acre site, you'll find more than 5000 kinds of plants, 27 miles of hiking trails, eleven lakes, a 7-mile-long bike path, two major museums, a fly-casting pool, a hall of flowers, a pioneer log cabin, a redwood grove, buffalo, elk, and deer paddocks, windmills, tulip gardens, a planetarium, and an aquarium. Most visitors flock to the south end of the park in the vicinity of the

de Young Art Museum, the Japanese Tea Garden, and the California Academy of Science. But perhaps the best entertainment in the park is people-watching. The colorful natives will be happy to provide pathways to the latest in religion (organized and unorganized), meditation, politics, fashion, and takeout restaurants. A grassroots center of the arts, Golden Gate Park also serves as the spawning ground of musicians, artists, actors, and mimes who try out their acts on a non-paying public.

Not far from the north end of the park is the stately Palace of the Legion of Honor, a museum well worth visiting for its French Impressionist paintings and Rodin sculpture. From here, you can drive west to Point Lobos, walk the Lands End Trail overlooking the ocean, and see the old Sutro Baths site. Or you can go in the opposite direction through the posh Seacliff area down to the scenic, seldom crowded Baker Beach or Phelan Beach.

Returning south to the Richmond District, you'll soon come to Clement Street, one of the last remaining Bay Area shopping districts that remains blissfully unspoiled, unfranchised, and undiscovered. San Fran-

San Francisco's financial district. The tallest tower is the Transamerica Pyramid at the left.
(*San Francisco Convention and Visitors Bureau*)

Golden Gate Bridge.
(*San Francisco Convention and Visitors Bureau*)

Avocado Starter/Planter. A must for every would-be Californian. Only $9.50 from Le Saisons, 3027 Fillmore, San Francisco, CA 94123.

Patio Furniture. Hundreds of outdoor furnishings are available through the Patio Company catalogue. A complete range of modern and traditional chaises, coffee tables, loveseats, floor coverings, garden torches, hammocks, and ottomans is offered. Pool furniture includes inflatable chaises, artificial rainbow fish, twinkling water lilies, and a floating love lounge that the company claims is "wide enough to cuddle two who love each other and/or the sun." For a copy of the catalogue, send $1 to the firm, 550 Powell, San Francisco, CA 94108.

Canyon Cinema. This nonprofit cooperative distribution center for independent film makers rents and sells hundreds of pictures ranging from 1-minute shorts to 118-minute features. Among the offerings are *Day of the Muni Love Bus,* a satire on X-rated films, shot with the cooperation of the San Francisco Municipal Railway (which later disavowed its participation); a documentary on barbed wire; a visual study of a single bathroom; a seven-minute study of rust; and a short on the shooting of the film *Cool Hand Luke,* which the director explains should be shown "with sound from side one of 'Sketches of Spain'" by Miles Davis. Also in the catalogue is a wide number of films dealing with major political and social causes of the 1960s and 1970s. For a copy, send $2 to Canyon Cinema Co-Operative Catalogue Department, Room 220, Industrial Center Building, Sausalito, CA 94965.

---

cisco abounds with all sorts of commercial areas that have been converted into tourist shopping complexes. There are renovated warehouses and converted chocolate factories as well as the high-priced spreads that now dominate Union Street. But if you want to get some feel for a traditional neighborhood street, try Clement with its unpretentious Russian bakeries, antique shops, used-book stores, fish markets, poultry shops, etc.

A few blocks away is Presidio Heights, which links up with Pacific Heights, the swankest residential areas in the city. Although there are steep hills, here it's worthwhile driving by to look at the carefully preserved Victorian dwellings. One, the Haas-Lilienthal House, a Queen Anne Victorian at 2007 Franklin at Washington Street, is open for inspection. And when you're done, you might consider sampling some of the ex-

---

The Goodfellow Catalog of Wonderful Things. This, California's leading independent crafts catalog, features a wide array of handmade mail order items, including banners, ceramic drums, looms, hummingbird feeders, deerhorn pipes, dulcimers, mountain pipes, granny puppets, flutes, toys, weaving, batik, terrariums, jewelry, and giant macrame wall hangings. Product descriptions are accompanied by lively autobiographical sketches of the craftspeople. For a copy, send $3.50 to the Catalog, P.O. Box 4520, Berkeley, CA 94704.

Taylor and Ng Catalogue. Taylor and Ng makes a wide line of products designed to fill gaps in the housewares and gardening marketplace. For instance, the 12-inch flat-bottom wok set is designed to cope with small or electric stoves, achieving greater heat than the round-bottom wok. There's also a 13-inch-deep steel paella pan (good for pasta, lasagna, cacciatore, sautées, and flambées too), a steel tempura deep fryer, a stoneware fish cooker, and a hummingbird feeder. Among the firm's most popular items are the complete Chinese kitchen set, with ten essential tools for preparing any dish, and steel crêpe pans with built-in hooks for hanging. The catalogue is available from the firm, 666 Howard Street, San Francisco, CA 94105.

China Books. This firm, the American importer and distributor of Chinese publications, operates a West Coast center in San Francisco. The thirty-two-page catalogue is an excellent source for English-language publications ranging from Mao's selected military writings to a collection of famous Chinese poultry dishes. For a copy, write China Books and Periodicals, Inc., 2929 Twenty-Fourth Street, San Francisco, CA 94110.

The Japanese Tea Garden, Golden Gate Park.
(*San Francisco Convention and Visitors Bureau*)

cellent, lesser known museums scattered through the city, such as the Cable Car Museum, Dr. Gardner's Museum of Witchcraft and Magic, Pioneer Museum, Fireman's Pioneer Museum, Fort Point, the Wine Museum, the Octagon House, and the Wells Fargo History Room.

Golden Gate Park's glass conservatory is modeled after the royal greenhouses in Kew Gardens, London.
(*San Francisco Convention and Visitors Bureau*)

Cable Car Clothiers Catalogue. Well known for the quality of its British and domestic menswear, Cable Car Clothiers/Robert Kirk, Ltd., San Francisco, offers a remarkably complete eighty-page catalogue. Although its emphasis is on Harris tweeds, rep ties, Burberry raincoats, touring caps, and other traditional styles, you'll also find specialty items like brass Rolls Royce belt buckles, Stetson hats, and half-sleeve referee shirts. A few women's items, such as short-sleeved safari bush jackets, are offered as well. Thanks to the services of the firm's shopping adviser, it's easy to get advice on sizes and style by letter or phone. For a catalogue, write the firm, 150 Post Street, San Francisco, CA 94108.

Williams-Sonoma Catalogue. This catalogue for cooks offers such items as lemon reamers and strippers; Indian mountain whetstones; ice cube splitters; tomato knives; cookie guns; copper butter melters; rolling mincers; chicken bricks; copper fish poachers; and potato nest baskets. Traditionally, the store has specialized in imported French cookware of professional quality, but in recent years they've been adding equipment from Germany, Italy, England, China, and North Africa. For a copy of the catalogue, write the mail order department, 532 Sutter Street, San Francisco, CA 94102.

Gump's Catalogue. One of California's most exclusive stores, Gump's is a San Francisco institution offering a wide array of art goods, diamonds, antiques, utensils, jewelry, and other gift items. From the $35,000 jadeite vessels of the Tao-Kuang period (1821–1850) to the $10 silver-plated piggy bank, everything at Gump's is in the best of taste. The emphasis is on Oriental art objects, but you can also find Italian silver, French crystal, German beer glasses, and sculptures by a number of California artists. For a copy of the catalogue, send Gump's a card at 250 Post Street, San Francisco, CA 94108.

This last stop brings you downtown, where the Hyatt Regency Hotel has become one of the hottest free attractions in town. People flock in for a look at the atrium dominating the vast open lobby of this building that resembles a partially eaten wedding cake. But this hotel is still no match for the classic elegance of the garden court of the nearby Sheraton Palace.

Although most major hotels are in the downtown area, you should give some thought to a number of other places worth staying at. You might enjoy, for instance, the Oriental luxury of the Miyako in Japan Town, the Alta Mira in Sausalito, or the Claremont in Berkeley. The advantage in staying outside San Francisco is that you'll probably enjoy better weather for less money.

But if you do decide to stay in the central city area, you'll find a number of low-cost motels on Lombard Street, west of Van Ness Avenue, and plenty of classic choices in the Union Square area and on Nob Hill. Although Union Square is somewhat more convenient to the best shops (be sure to visit elegant Gump's),

theaters, and transportation, Nob Hill has the best views and the ambience you tend to expect in San Francisco. The Mark Hopkins, Fairmont, Stanford Court, and Huntington collectively make Nob Hill a perennial favorite with those who are traveling on someone else's money.

While you are in the city, be sure to take a ride on BART, the nation's most luxurious and controversial mass transit system. Although performance is irregular over an inadequate route, BART is a must for jaded straphangers from the IRT and other New York cattle cars. Clean, comfortable, and relatively quiet, BART sets a new standard for mass transit excellence, at least when the computer isn't having one of its periodic breakdowns.

After completing your BART round trip, return to

Sourdough Starter. Sourdough bread is a favorite in San Francisco. A natural leavener, sourdough has been used since biblical times to make light bread. Until the development of commercial yeast, it was the only way to make leavened bread. The Gold Rush Sourdough Company, Inc., makes an authentic sourdough starter you can use in your own baking. By following simple directions, you can keep the starter perpetually alive and ready for use. The starter (and recipe folder) sells for $1.75, and you can also get a pair of sourdough cookbooks from the firm. For information on these items and a complete sourdough kit ($12.66), write the company, 65 Paul Drive, San Rafael, CA 94903.

Shambhala Review. This journal, offered by Shambhala Publishers and Booksellers, carries a wide range of articles on Eastern religions, meditation, yoga, alchemy, magic, psychic phenomena, and related subjects. At the back of each issue is an updated list of titles available through the Shambhala Bookstore, which is worth a visit if you happen to be in Berkeley. This establishment has the atmosphere of a scholarly library; you're encouraged to sit down and study contemplated purchases in a leisurely fashion. This admirable read-before-you-buy policy has won the store many friends. A six-issue subscription to the review is $3, but if you just want the store catalogue, Shambhala will supply it free. The operation is located at 2482 Telegraph Avenue, Berkeley, CA 94704.

Chinatown, as it was and is. (*Courtesy, The Bancroft Library*)

(*San Francisco Convention and Visitors Bureau*)

downtown and take a relaxed tour via foot and cable car of the popular tourist areas. These may include Chinatown, Jackson Square, the topless nightclubs of Carol Doda fame, and City Lights. San Francisco is blessed with a number of unusual bookstores, among them Philobiblon on Maiden Lane, where you can simultaneously eat and browse, thanks to a management that is always experimenting with new cookbook recipes in the kitchen adjoining the bookstalls. There are also excellent stores specializing in the occult, women's literature, radical politics, Chinese and Spanish culture. But amid all this competition, City Lights endures as one of the community's most important cultural institutions. A second home to the beat generation, today the City Lights basement still features tables and chairs where you are welcome to sit and browse for hours through some of the thousands of books on hand. And if, after spending half a day there, you decide to buy nothing, no one on the management end will even think of questioning you on the way out.

From there, you will come to the North Beach area, beginning with Broadway and progressing to upper Grant Avenue, with its cafés, boutiques, bars, and reasonably priced restaurants. This area once really was a beach until it was buried under landfill that pushed the city out into San Francisco Bay. Today you'll want to visit the old bakeries, delicatessens,

Fisherman's Wharf. (*San Francisco Convention and Visitors Bureau*)

ravioli firms, and wine companies. And when you are done, continue up to Coit Tower on top of Telegraph Hill or head back through Chinatown to Washington and Powell, where you can catch a cable car to Fisherman's Wharf. This is the place where tourists come thousands of miles to stop at sidewalk stands for "fresh" shrimp that has actually been shipped down from Oregon in cans. Overcommercialized though it may be, this district still maintains a number of important shopping establishments like Cost Plus, a discount import store. Among the other noteworthy attractions are the Buena Vista (birthplace of Irish coffee), Ghirardelli Square (home of outstanding hot fudge sundaes), and Scoma's (probably the wharf's best known seafood restaurant). Lines are long at all these nonreservation establishments.

There are, of course, times when every serious vacationer needs a rest. Many San Francisco visitors make the obligatory pilgrimages to the Sausalito waterfront as well as the Muir Woods National Redwood

Lunching in Tiburon, across the Bay from San Francisco. (*Redwood Empire Association*)

Monument. But there are other pleasant alternatives in Marin County. Consider, for instance, taking S.R. 1 to Muir and Stinson beaches and then continuing on to the Audubon Canyon Ranch, which is open from March 1 to July 4. This 1000-acre bird sanctuary offers a good look at egrets and great blue herons from well-designed hiking trails.

After stopping off at nearby Bolinas, an artists' colony on a mesa overlooking the ocean, head north into the Point Reyes National Seashore. Although roads do lead out to the ocean and the site where Sir Francis Drake landed the *Golden Hind* in 1579, be sure to take time to enjoy one of the many hiking trails on this 64,000-acre peninsula. Hiking through the forests and meadows to the beach, you'll see some of the more than 300 bird and 72 animal species that live in this region.

If you're looking for a short hike, consider taking the self-guiding earthquake nature trail. Geologically Point Reyes is an island separated from the mainland by the San Andreas fault. As a result, rocks on the peninsula are totally different from those on the mainland. During the 1906 earthquake the land on Point Reyes shifted northward as much as 21 feet. You can see excellent visual evidence of this offset on the earthquake trail.

If you don't have time to go all the way out to Point Reyes, consider visiting a couple of other excellent Marin County retreats, Mount Tamalpais or McNear's Beach. The latter is located on San Pedro Road out of San Rafael and often remains sunny when the rest of the bay is fogbound. Although the water's much too cold for swimming, there's a good pool here surrounded by a broad lawn where you can simply rest.

Leaving this area, you can take U.S. 101 north to the cutoff to the Richmond–San Rafael Bridge. Just before reaching this span you'll pass infamous San Quentin, the aging state penitentiary that just about everyone in and out of state government would like to see closed. On the other side of the bay, S.R. 17 will lead you to the celebrated college town of Berkeley. This community of 120,000 is best known for its University of California campus. Backed up against the East Bay hills and laced by creeks, the place gives little hint of its riot-torn past. Just south of campus is Telegraph Avenue, the scene of many marches and the gateway to controversial People's Park and its adjoining parking lot. Once a center for the counterculture, Telegraph Avenue now seems somewhat seedy, as panhandling families work to put together enough money to treat themselves to a round of Orange Julius.

After the university probably Berkeley's most important asset is its architectural heritage. The community has done an admirable job of holding onto the brown shingle classics left by prominent California architects Bernard Maybeck, Julia Morgan, and others. Maybeck himself lived at a house at 2701 Buena Vista Way. Walking tours lead along some of the creeks that come down from the hills. Starting at Live Oak Park, you can follow a series of paths and streets to the city rose garden. Immediately behind the city is Tilden Park, one of several units in the East Bay Municipal Park District that provides an extensive greenbelt system for this region. Some Bay Area residents actually prefer rugged Tilden to Golden Gate Park because it offers swimming, a terrific merry-go-round, and superior bongo drummers. Leaving this park, you can continue south into the adjoining regional parks or head down into Oakland, where Rod McKuen was born and Jack London was raised.

Because it sits in the shadow of San Francisco, Oakland has traditionally enjoyed second-city status. Attempts at civic improvement, such as the waterfront Jack London Square, are hardly serious competition for San Francisco's many attractions. Yet Oakland does have some fine residential districts and a beautiful new museum featuring western and California art that should be a part of any trip to the Bay Area. Even less well known is the adjacent island of Alameda, which includes the Robert W. Crown Memorial State Beach and some of the finest Victorian homes in the entire Bay Area. While you're in this general area, you also might want to make a side trip to the Emeryville waterfront, where you can see the weird collection of large makeshift driftwood sculptures that have become a community tradition. They're clearly visible from the southbound lanes of Interstate 80 just before the Bay Bridge.

Returning to San Francisco, pick up U.S. 101, which leads south past Hillsborough and some of the region's other exclusive residential areas to Palo Alto and Stanford University. If you're interested in seeing one of the few major universities that has managed to maintain a consistent architectural theme, a stop here is

Point Reyes. (*U.S. Department of the Interior, National Park Service Photo*)

mandatory. The Memorial Church, knocked down in the 1906 earthquake and subsequently rebuilt, is a prime attraction, as is the Hoover Library, where Solzhenitsyn came to study on a recent visit. Nearby is the medical center where Dr. Norman Shumway perfected the techniques that made human heart transplant a reality. And in the Stanford Museum you'll find the golden spike driven at the junction of the Union Pacific and Central Pacific railroads at Promontory Point, Utah.

Continuing south on U.S. 101, cut off on S.R. 85 to Saratoga, where Route 9 leads east to the 175-acre Villa Montalvo Arboretum. Once the home of the late Senator James D. Phelan, this estate is now maintained as a county park. The mansion has been converted into a small art museum that overlooks one of California's most beautifully landscaped formal gardens. There are a number of self-guiding nature trails designed to acquaint you with Montalvo's diverse plant and floral community.

After a visit to the nearby Los Gatos old town, take S.R. 17 back into San Jose, where you'll want to visit the Rosicrucian Egyptian Museum and Art Gallery. Here you'll find the biggest collection of Egyptian and Babylonian antiquities in western America. Immediately adjacent are the Rosicrucian Science Museum and Planetarium. Astronomy buffs may also be interested in making the 20-mile trip southeast of town to the Lick Observatory atop Mount Hamilton. Home of the world's second largest reflector telescope, this observatory was originally built with funds donated by James Lick, a piano tuner who turned to real estate and made a killing. Lick, who also has a major San Francisco freeway named in his memory, is buried directly under the 120-inch telescope.

You may also want to consider making the side trip south of San Jose to New Almaden, once site of America's richest quicksilver mine. Although all that's left of the mine are the furnace chimneys and powder house, you can still visit several old adobe buildings, the New Almaden store, the Casa Grande Mansion, and the privately owned New Almaden Museum.

Other interesting stops in the rapidly growing Santa Clara Valley area include the Alum Rock Part, Mission Santa Clara, and Winchester Mystery House. Don't let the name of this last attraction scare you off. For a modest admission charge, you get a look at the greatest home improvement project in American history. The original seventeen-room structure was purchased by Sarah Winchester after the death of her husband, heir to the Winchester rifle empire. Taking the advice of spiritualists who convinced her she would be immortal as long as the house remained uncompleted, she sank millions of dollars into expansions. The place was filled with stairways leading nowhere, secret passages, and rooms surrounding other rooms. Her own private

quarters were completely furnished in white satin. Although Mrs. Winchester kept the construction going for thirty-six years, the spiritualists turned out to have misled her. She died in 1922, leaving the 160-room house you can visit today. One other possibility in this area is Marriott's Great America, the only major amusement park in Northern California. It is located in Santa Clara on Great America Parkway, off U.S. 101.

Although all these urban attractions south of San Francisco are worthwhile, you may also want to give some thought to taking Skyline Boulevard (S.R. 35) down the peninsula. This route, easily accessible via Interstate 280, heads south into the Santa Cruz Mountains and offers good panoramas of both San Francisco Bay and the ocean. Steep, winding side roads give access to state and county parks and hook up with S.R. 1. If you prefer sticking to the coast, you can take S.R. 1 out of San Francisco over Devils Slide and through the Half Moon Bay area (be sure to visit the pumpkin fields here in the fall) en route to Santa Cruz. But at times fog makes this route a disappointment, particularly if you're going to check out the beach for nude bathing at San Gregorio.

Bay Area Notes

Probably the most worthwhile guides to this region are the walking tour books by Margot Pattern Doss. *San Francisco at Your Feet* ($2.95, Grove Press, 53 E. 11th Street, New York, NY 10003), *The Bay Area at Your Feet* ($2.95, Chronicle Books, 870 Market Street, San Francisco, CA 94102), and *Golden Gate Park at Your Feet* ($2.95, Chronicle Books) provide excellent advice on how to see the region without being dependent on a car. *San Francisco Free and Easy* ($3.85, Headlands Press, Inc., 243 Vallejo Street, San Francisco, CA 94111) offers a wide variety of advice not found in more traditional guidebooks. Two older, out-of-print guides worth a trip to the library are Jim Benet's *A Guide to San Francisco and the Bay Region* (Random House) and *Diablo's Complete Guidebook to the East Bay and the University of California* (Diablo Press). A more up-to-date general guide is Curt Gentry's *Dolphin Guide to San Francisco and the Bay Area* ($1.95, Dolphin Books, Doubleday, Garden City, NY 11530). For advice on places for children, *Where To Go and What To Do With the Kids in San Francisco* ($2.95, Price, Stern, and Sloan, 410 North La Cienega Boulevard, Los Angeles, CA 90048) is helpful. Bikers will find a number of San Francisco trips in *California Bike Tours* ($2.95, Goshua Publications, % Crown Publishers, Inc., One Park Avenue, New York, NY 10016. If you plan to follow the coast route south from San Francisco, consider getting *Combing the Coast: San Francisco Through Big Sur* by Ruth A. Jackson ($2.95, Chronicle Books).

Glide

Trying to find the Lord? Well, of course you can contact him at numerous traditional houses of worship throughout the state. But there's also an interesting alternative available every Sunday at Glide Memorial United Methodist Church, 330 Ellis Street, in the heart of San Francisco's seedy Tenderloin. About ten years ago, this dying parish decided to replace services with "celebrations" that included rock music, light shows, and sermons delivered by guests like Sammy Davis, Jr. Today over 3000 people show up for the religious festivities every week, and it's often hard to find a seat.

You can spend a lot of money on entertainment in California and not have nearly as much fun as you will at Glide's free celebrations on Sundays at 9 A.M. and 12 noon. Don't worry if you're not Methodist. Only 5 percent of the congregation's current parishioners are. Today the place regularly welcomes Catholics, Baptists, Lutherans, Presbyterians, Christian Scientists, Zen Buddhists, Mormons, Muslims, and agnostics.

Interestingly, the largest share of Glide's parishioners (23 percent) are Jews. Helping represent their interests is Glide's seventy-six-year-old rabbi-in-residence, Abraham Feinberg, who passes the plate and struts around the altar with a cane given him by his late friend, Ho Chi Minh. The man in charge of the parish is Minister of Celebration and Involvement A. Cecil Williams, who is determined to change the church into a vehicle for "rapid, significant, social change where the unheard voices, the untouchables like prisoners, ex-prisoners, the poor and the elderly can come together and act."

Although traditionalists have denounced Glide as America's "only Sunday morning nightclub," Williams has turned it into the center of San Francisco's counterculture. On any given Sunday you can hear guest speeches by such political celebrities as Benjamin Spock, Jane Fonda, Angela Davis, or Dick Gregory. For Glide is the home base for demonstrations supporting the rights of students, blacks, Indians, skycaps, prisoners, papermill workers, senior citizens, mental patients, and dozens of other groups seeking everything from parole to better bus service. Few major protests get going in San Francisco without its support.

One of the best things about Glide is that every Sunday is different. After you are ushered to your seat by a paroled rapist (ex-cons are an integral part of the church staff), you may hear Rev. Williams read a few "quotations from Chairman Jesus" or be asked to join in a chorus of "She's Got the Whole World in Her Hands." Then Bill Cosby may rise to deliver a few words: "I needed God and I called him. He put me on hold."

As you sit among the junkies, psychiatric patients, convicted felons, winos, and homosexuals who attend the church each Sunday, you will probably smell the faint aroma of marijuana. Rev. Williams may have to stop his sermon to tell a derelict to quit chugging Ripple out of a paper bag: "Hey, man, you ain't got enough in there for all of us. And if you did, we'd call it communion." And when women start celebrating by pulling off their blouses, Cecil gets down from the pulpit and helps them put their clothes back on.

People come from everywhere to see this religious extravaganza, and Glide's activities have been publicized by the print and electronic media worldwide. In part, this notoriety comes from Glide's status as an extraordinary power broker. When Patty Hearst is kidnapped, George Jackson is murdered, or Indians seize Alcatraz, Glide becomes a focal point once again. This is where the Symbionese Liberation Army sends underground communiqués, where the mayor makes a good-faith offer and the negotiations carry on past dawn.

Those who decide to join Glide permanently find its program does have limitations. It is not ordinarily possible to get married or buried through Glide, although Rev. Williams will take time out to join homosexuals in holy matrimony or do a memorial service for a radical figure like United Prisoners Union leader, Popeye Jackson. The church has no Sunday school program. But then Glide is probably not the kind of place you'd want to send your teenage daughter for divine guidance. Rev. Williams, who was named one of the ten sexiest men in San Francisco by a local magazine last year, says: "Some of the most important relationships going are out of wedlock. I think it's important for people to live together for a while before they get married."

Sea Lions

Two kinds of sea lions can be found barking on the rocks and islands off the California coast. One is the stellar or northern sea lion, distinguished by its tawny coat. The other is the smaller California sea lion, which has a brown coat. The female of this latter species is frequently captured and trained for the amusement of circus crowds. But in California you can catch acts by untrained seals of both species on numerous points, offshore islands, and an occasional secluded beach. Perhaps the most convenient place to see them in action is Seal Rock, just off the San Francisco coast.

Although sea lions were hunted widely in the nineteenth century, legislative protection has succeeded in keeping their population stable. A recent census estimated that more than 23,000 sea lions live off the coast of California. The islands in the Santa Barbara Channel are one of several breeding grounds used by the California sea lions each summer. Here thousands of sea lions and elephant seals crowd one another for space amid the raucous crying of the new pups. The males go hungry for as long as two months while standing guard over the breeding ground. The females head out to search for food, swimming back every couple of days to nurse their young. Unfortunately, more than half the newborns are crushed in this hopelessly crowded mob scene.

San Francisco to Los Angeles

The fast way: From downtown, take Interstate 80 over the Bay Bridge, pick up Interstate 580 to Interstate 5 southbound, exit onto the Pasadena Freeway (S.R. 11) southbound to the Harbor Freeway, and get off at Second Street.

Drawbacks to this route are (1) much of the way you are stuck going down the dull west side of the San Joaquin Valley, and (2) it's very hot in summer. For diversions, see under San Joaquin Valley.

The truckers' way: From downtown, take Interstate 80 over the Bay Bridge, pick up Interstate 580, exit onto S.R. 120 eastbound, pick up S.R. 99 at Manteca southbound to Interstate 5, exit onto the Pasadena Freeway (S.R. 11) southbound to the Harbor Freeway, and get off at Second Street.

Heavy diesel traffic is a drawback on this route, which is longer than following Interstate 5 all the way through the valley and is just as hot during the summer. But there are some interesting side trips along the way, discussed under San Joaquin Valley.

The old way: From downtown, take U.S. 101 and follow it to the Spring Street exit in Los Angeles.

A good compromise between speed and scenery. The route down the Salinas Valley is attractive in springtime, and the second half takes you through interesting towns like San Luis Obispo and Santa Barbara. You also get some coastal landscapes thrown in. A good choice when the San Joaquin Valley is fogged in; Salinas Valley gets very hot in summer. For sightseeing details, see under Central Coast.

The scenic way: From downtown, take U.S. 101 to Interstate 280, exit westbound on S.R. 92 to S.R. 1 and follow it to Santa Monica, where you take the Santa Monica Freeway (Interstate 10) eastbound to the Harbor Freeway northbound, and exit at Third Street.

This is the slowest of all, but it takes you through the popular Big Sur region. To do it right you must allow at least two days. See under Central Coast for additional information.

A Walking Tour of the Berkeley Revolution

Throughout California you will find historic markers commemorating obscure wheat transactions, old ferry crossings, and pioneer butcher shops. Yet no brass plaques can be found in Berkeley denoting one of the most significant periods in the state's history. For it was here in 1964 that Mario Savio stood on the steps of Sproul Hall and yelled the shout heard round the world. The academic revolution was on.

If you're visiting the Bay Area, you may want to take a few hours to inspect some of the famous sites that have figured in various chapters of the campus warfare. The logical place to begin is at Sproul Plaza, located at the intersection of Bancroft Way and Telegraph Avenue. It was here that Joan Baez sang to radical students sitting in, Eldridge Cleaver chewed out the white middle class, and the National Guard sprayed tear gas from a helicopter. Heading south down Telegraph Avenue, you can turn left at Haste and walk up half a block to what is now People's Park. In 1969 the University regents wanted to turn this property into a dormitory. But the students felt otherwise. They marched down Telegraph Avenue and were met by Alameda County sheriff's deputies, who opened fire. One young man, James Rector, was shot to death while watching the action from the roof of what was then the Telegraph Theater near the intersection of Telegraph Avenue and Dwight Way. Subsequent demonstrations led to the arrest of 482 protesters, shoppers, reporters, and one mailman, who were herded into the Bank of America parking lot downtown near the intersection of Shattuck and Center.

Telegraph Avenue has been the scene of countless other demonstrations aimed at everything from stopping the draft to ending the Vietnam War. Two other popular sites for political rallies in the city are Provo Park at Center and Grove and Willard Park at Derby and Regent (which radicals have renamed Ho Chi Minh Park). This was the place where SLA member Emily Harris made contact with Kathy Soliah, who allegedly helped the fugitive kidnappers hide from police. (Her brother Steve Soliah later became a friend of Patty Hearst.) Just a block away from the park, you'll find the apartment house at 2603 Benvenue where the SLA kidnapped Patty Hearst. She lived in unit 4. Please do not disturb the tenants.

Another stop worth adding on your tour is the corner of Parker and Milvia streets. To the left of 2006 Parker you'll find an unnumbered house with a large flashing sign reading "Smash the State." Pictures are allowed, but loitering is discouraged.

Finally, you may want to head over to People's Park annex at Hearst and Grant streets. In 1969, Weatherwoman Bernadine Dohrn made one of her last public appearances here before going underground.

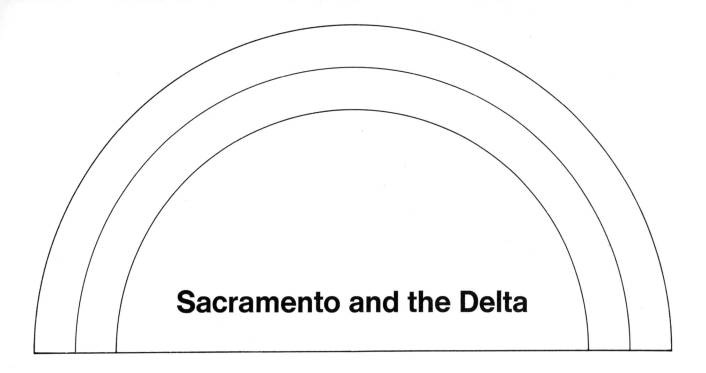

Sacramento and the Delta

The Best of Sacramento and the Delta

Camping: Brannan Island State Recreation Area
Houseboat rental: Brannan Island; Rio Vista
Waterskiing: Frank's tract
Swimming: Seven Mile Slough
Biking: Brannan Island to Locke
Historic buildings: Port Costa
Antique shops: Benecia
Old hotel: Washington House, Benecia
Railroad museum: California Railway Museum, S.R. 12 west of Rio Vista
Fort: Sutter's Fort, Sacramento
Small town: Locke
Indian museum: State Indian Museum, Sacramento
Steamer: *Delta Queen,* Sacramento
Urban park: state capitol grounds, Sacramento
Victorian building: governor's mansion, Sacramento
Drive: S.R. 160, Antioch to Sacramento

Long a favorite hideaway for Bay Area residents, this region, about an hour's drive northeast of San Francisco, is one of California's leading sleepers. The Delta's decidedly unspoiled, uncrowded, unhurried way of life makes it a favorite with many who could afford to go elsewhere. Perhaps its best known fan was the late Erle Stanley Gardner, who wrote three books about this region reminiscent of the Deep South. It's also a popular choice of location for Hollywood producers.

A visit to this region opens a wide variety of recreational opportunities. You can explore 800 miles of waterways by houseboat, waterski and swim in the placid sloughs, rent a skiff, fish for bass, and visit old river towns. You can also drive, bike, or hike through this level territory, relying on free ferries to get you between islands.

It's easy to combine a trip to the scores of Delta rivers and sloughs with an excursion to notable nearby sites of historic interest. Perhaps the best way to approach the region is from the Bay Area via Interstate 80. Cutting off at Crockett, you can head east to the tiny community of Port Costa, once a great grain port. A number of stores in the well-preserved commercial district have been turned into antique shops, and you can stay at the old Burlington Hotel. Before visiting this community, you may want to read *Mrs. Munck,* a fascinating novel written by San Francisco's Ella Leffland. She makes excellent use of this setting for a story as terrifying as anything Hitchcock has ever produced.

From here, wind down the Carquinez Scenic Drive into Martinez, where you can pick up Interstate 680 across the Carquinez Straits and then head west on Interstate 780 to Benecia. In 1853, citizens of this community persuaded the state legislature to leave Vallejo and make their town California's capital, with the lure, so gossip had it, of introductions to "twenty or thirty marriageable young ladies." Although the politicians moved on to Sacramento the following year, you can still visit the old Benecia capital.

The town is also the home of America's first west coast arsenal, first Episcopal church, first Masonic church—and some twenty-five antique shops. Even if you're not in a buying mood, be sure to visit Washington House, an antique store that has been a bordello, a speakeasy, a Chinese lottery, and a hotel. This prefabricated building was built in Maine and assembled here in 1848.

Leaving Benecia, double back across the Carquinez Straits on Interstate 680 and pick up S.R. 4 eastbound. You'll pass the U.S. Naval Weapons Station near Concord, where 322 dock workers were killed by an accidental explosion in July 1944. Expansion of the facility in the 1950s and 1960s raised serious questions about the safety of 3000 residents in the community of Port Chicago, immediately adjacent to the weapons station. Instead of limiting the size of the arsenal to conform with federal regulations, the government bought up and leveled the community.

Continuing east on S.R. 4, you pass through Oakley and Brentwood before reaching the cutoff to Byron. Once a shipping center, Byron was also the home of a popular hot springs resort. Although this spa on Byron Hot Springs Road, south of town, is now private property, present owners may give you permission to visit the old hotel and mineral bath houses.

From here, you can head back to S.R. 4, which leads to Stockton, a port and agricultural center that has in recent years become a popular location for Hollywood

---

John Muir House Model. San Francisco architect Roy Kileen has executed paper replicas of historic American buildings, including the Martinez home of the famed naturalist (now a national historic site). Models are printed in color on heavy paper and come ready to cut out and construct. The kit includes a heavy cardboard base, instructions, and history of the building. Also available in this series are the Victorian-period Dickey House in Tiburon, the Old Lighthouse in San Diego, and Los Angeles' Old Plaza Firehouse. To order any of these mini mansion kits, send $4.95 to 101 Productions, 834 Mission Street, San Francisco, CA 94103.

---

films like *Fat City*. Although the old waterfront section of the city has been lost to urban renewal, you can visit the new Chinese Center and the ten-story Filipino Community Center, the largest found outside the Philippine Islands. Home of University of the Pacific, the state's oldest private college, Stockton also has an unusual Buddhist temple worth visiting.

Doubling back on S.R. 4, you can cut off to the major Delta resort center of Bethel Island a few miles beyond Brentwood. If you don't want to stay on land at one of the many hotels, cottages, or campsites, rent a houseboat here and head out into the sloughs. Houseboat rentals start at $50 a day for a fully equipped boat during the summer, but are less in the off-season, when you'll be able to avoid uncomfortably hot weather. Although some of the major waterways are crowded with power boats and sailboats from local anchorages and the Bay Area, you'll find plenty of remote sloughs with the help of the rental agencies and Delta Regional Harbor Chart No. 5527. You can purchase it for $1 from the U.S. Coast and Geodetic Survey Chart Distribution Division, Washington, D.C., 20235.

Returning to the mainland, S.R. 4 leads to S.R. 160, which heads north toward Brannan Island State Recreation Area. A popular bass fishing site, the park also offers camping, a sandy beach for swimming in Seven Mile Slough, and a boat-launching ramp. A few miles north on the opposite side of the Sacramento River is Rio Vista, another major Delta resort center. This community of 3000 boasts a number of Victorian houses. A good attraction west of town via S.R. 12 is the California Railway Museum, featuring a wide variety of old electric and steam railroad cars as well as a short excursion ride.

Returning to S.R. 160, the highway leads north through two of the most important towns in the Delta's history, Locke and Walnut Grove. Both were once home to substantial Chinese communities that helped settle the region, run local stores, work the river docks, and farm nearby islands. Neither town prospers today. Locke's population has fallen to less than 100. Over in the old lumber and port town of Walnut Grove there's a little more action. Here you can get a beer at the Gato Negro or shop at one of the groceries run by descendants of the original Chinese residents.

Winding north along the Sacramento River, you'll pass the Chicano community of Courtland and the tiny village of Hood before reaching the outskirts of the state capital. Hot, flat, and scarcely a tourist mecca, Sacramento has, nonetheless, a pleasant midwest feeling, particularly in the central part of the city, where the streets are lined with tall shade trees and people seem more relaxed than they do in the state's other major urban centers.

Most people who visit Sacramento come to see the state capitol surrounded by a 40-acre park where

Squeaky Fromme tried to shoot President Ford in 1975. Tours of the capitol are available, and you are free to wander about the lobby of the governor's office under the open-door policy of Jerry Brown. Guides will not take you into the old capitol building, which has been declared unsafe in the event of a major earthquake, but it does remain open to individual visitors at their own risk.

Unfortunately, many leave town after seeing the capitol, thereby missing other significant Sacramento sites such as the old governor's mansion. This fifteen-room Victorian-Gothic structure was built for a hardware store owner in 1877. Later it was owned by dry-goods merchant Joseph Steffens, father of muckraking author Lincoln Steffens. The state purchased the place in 1903, and it served thirteen governors over the next sixty-four years, until the Ronald Reagan family left in 1967 in favor of a modern dwelling. Although all the mansion's furniture looks as though it had been ordered from a mid-1940s Sears catalogue, the building remains an important part of the state's architectural heritage.

Another important landmark is Sutter's Fort, reconstructed on the site of the settlement founded in 1839 by Captain John A. Sutter. The German immigrant, who became a Mexican citizen, built the fort to protect 48,000 acres given him by Governor Juan B. Alvarado. Two years later, he purchased Fort Ross and subsequently built the American River Sawmill where James Marshall discovered gold in 1848. The ensuing gold rush put him deep into debt, as borrowers failed to meet their obligations. Defending his property rights against squatters added to Sutter's financial burden. He moved into a farmhouse near Marysville and lived there until it burned down in 1865. Subsequently, Sutter left California for Lititz, Pennsylvania, and died in Washington, D.C., in June 1880.

Adjacent to Sutter's Fort is the State Indian Museum established in 1940. The numerous exhibits deal with such subjects as archaeology, featherwork, pottery, mythology, ceremonies, and basketry. All told, there have been at least forty distinct Indian tribes or groups in California, with some believed to date back 15,000 to 20,000 years. It is estimated that at least 275,000 Indians lived here when the Spaniards began establishing their settlements in 1769. Many of these native Californians succumbed to diseases introduced by the white man, and their numbers dwindled drastically. Today about 40,000 Indians live in California, about 7000 on the state's roughly 100 reservations and small rancherias.

Before leaving Sacramento, you may want to visit the Old Sacramento area now being renewed on the edge of the downtown section. Forty-one gold rush era buildings are being restored over a thirteen-block area near the Sacramento River. Nearby you can see

Locke, once home to a substantial Chinese community, now has fewer than one hundred residents.

the decaying steamer *Delta Queen,* which made overnight trips between Sacramento and San Francisco in the 1920s and 1930s.

Sacramento and the Delta Notes

Mike Hayden's *Guidebook to the Sacramento Delta Country* (50¢, Ward Ritchie Press, 3044 Riverside Drive, Los Angeles, CA 90039) provides excellent information on this region. Additional information is available from the Benecia Chamber of Commerce, 737 First Street, Benecia, CA 94510; the Stockton Convention and Visitors' Bureau, 1105 North El Dorado Street, Stockton, CA 95202; and the Sacramento Convention and Visitors' Bureau, 1100 14th Street, Sacramento, CA 05814.

Forty-one gold-rush era buildings, like these, are now undergoing restoration in Old Sacramento. (*California State Resources Agency, Department of Parks and Recreation*)

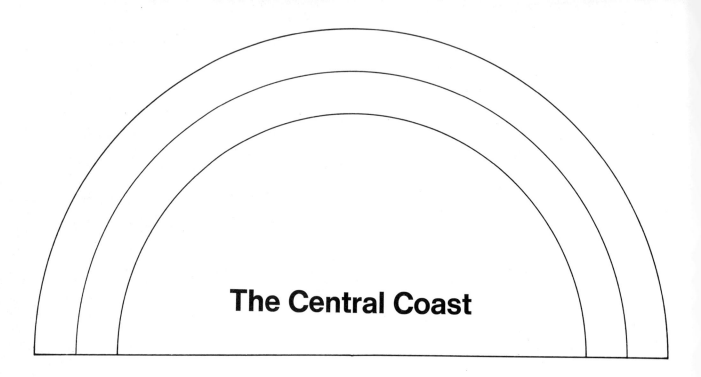

The Central Coast

The Best of the Central Coast

State park: Pfeiffer–Big Sur
State historic monument; San Simeon
National monument: the Pinnacles
Redwoods: Big Basin State Park
Camping: Pfeiffer–Big Sur; Big Basin
Hiking: Ventana Wilderness
Backpacking: Ventana Wilderness
Swimming: Carpinteria Beach
Sailing: Monterey Bay
Wildflowers: S.R. 1, Big Sur region; J1, San Benito
   County east of Pacines
Hot Springs: Tassajara (access difficult)
Rock formations: the Pinnacles
River: Arroyo Seco
Sea lions: Point Lobos
Tidepools: Point Lobos
Bird-watching: Point Lobos
Victorian buildings: Santa Cruz; Capitola; Mon-
   terey
Rest rooms: Madonna Inn, San Luis Obispo
Historic tavern: Mattei's, Los Olivos
Roller coaster: Santa Cruz
Boardwalk: Santa Cruz
Ghost town: New Idria
Utopian community: Holy City
Mission: San Antonio de Padua
Adobes: Monterey
Shopping: Carmel
Road: S.R. 1
Hotel: Biltmore, Santa Barbara

Parking lots: Santa Barbara
Zoning: Santa Barbara
Rock: Morro
Clamming: Pismo Beach
Urban ocean view: Santa Barbara Biltmore lawn at
   dusk
Rural ocean view: S.R. 1, Big Sur region

Flying from San Francisco to Los Angeles, you can pass over the Central Coast in slightly more than half an hour. As the plane heads past Santa Cruz and on down the Salinas Valley, you can glimpse some of the state's better known attractions, among them Monterey, where tourists shop the boutiques carved out of extinct fish factories on Cannery Row. Immediately south is Robinson Jeffers's Carmel and the fabled Big Sur region, which has been home to such notables as Henry Miller and Kim Novak. And if your pilot is good enough to tip the wing on a northbound flight, you just may be able to make out William Randolph Hearst's San Simeon.

Most people come to this region for a look at the rugged coastal landscape. There is excellent camping here, but you can also stay in one of several moderate-size communities that have done an admirable job of resisting the wholesale development that has destroyed so much of California's character. Once you're in the area, you'll probably find yourself tempted to explore nearby inland attractions, such as the Pinnacles and New Idria. Although not widely known, these un-crowded places are well worth a special trip.

Santa Cruz. (*University of California, Santa Cruz*)

This region begins at the Santa Cruz County line, where you may want to visit Big Basin Redwoods State Park, the oldest unit in the state system. Although it is less than a two-hour drive from San Francisco, this park offers much of the serenity found in the faraway redwood groves of the North Coast. Established in 1902, Big Basin includes 35 miles of hiking trails where you'll see a number of waterfalls, as well as an abundance of birds, flowers, and wildlife.

Heading out of Big Basin, you can pick up Highway 9, which leads directly through the San Lorenzo Valley and Cowell Redwoods State Park to Santa Cruz. Highway 17 out of San Jose provides another way to reach the same destination. If you follow this latter route, consider turning off about 5 miles beyond Los Gatos to the site of yet another of California's utopian experiments, Holy City. Established in 1918 by Father William E. Riker as seat of the "world's most perfect government," this community prospered by establishing a roadside gas station, grocery, and restaurant, which served tourists en route to Santa Cruz. Although Father Riker devoted his life to the cause of world peace, Holy City was constantly at war with the outside world because of Riker's racist philosophy. As historian Robert V. Hine explains, Riker "assigned positions corresponding to parts of the human body to the ethnic groupings of mankind; the head for the Jews, the trunk for the Gentiles, the arms for the yellow races, the legs for the black. The white race was meant to direct mankind; all others, merely to serve." Four times the Holy City leader campaigned for governor on a platform proposing that Negroes and Asiatics be banned from running their own enterprises. He believed they should be limited to serving the master white race. According to Hine, Riker also predicted that when Armageddon came, the state would be hit by massive earthquakes that would kill everyone except the Gentiles and the Jews. Although these views kept Holy City in constant controversy, the community endured into the 1950s; today you can still walk past many of the old homes and stores.

Heading on down S.R. 17, you'll soon come to Santa Cruz, home of California's oldest functioning full-size roller coaster. This fifty-one-year-old structure, situated by the city's extensive boardwalk, is considered one of the best in the country and gives you a good aerial view of this old resort town that is now home to a modern branch of the University of California. Most people come here to enjoy the beaches, where they can fish, clam, sail, explore tidepools, sunbathe, or even swim if they don't mind the cold water. Although the Santa Cruz area got some bad publicity a few years back due to the handiwork of a mass murderer, people are friendly here, and many of the local enterprises have been taken over by purveyors of organic oils, nostalgia, and handicrafts. Part of the fun of visiting here is walking into a plastic-looking restaurant and discovering it has been taken over by natural food advocates who have removed hamburgers from the menu. There's also a good self-guiding tour past some of Santa Cruz's admirable Victorian buildings. Don't fail to visit the downtown mall, where the old courthouse has been outfitted with shops, a bar, and an outdoor café. This yellow building, known as the Cooper House, serves as a leading local meeting place.

South of Santa Cruz is Capitola, another popular old beach resort distinguished by its Victorian architecture. Farther on, there is camping at several of the state beach parks along Monterey Bay. Seacliff State Beach is probably the best of these units, but unfortunately it's almost always full. Inland just a few miles is the Forest of Nisene Marks, a state park. This facility's blessed state of undevelopment makes it a natural for those seeking an alternative to overdeveloped recreational facilities. Be sure to check out the rain forest here.

From this point, it's a short drive down S.R. 1 to the Monterey Peninsula. However, if you have a couple days to spare, a circuitous route will take you to the same destination via a number of the state's lesser known, yet eminently worthwhile, attractions. Turning east at Watsonville on S.R. 129, you'll head along the Pajaro River to the San Juan Highway, which leads to San Juan Bautista. One of the state's most popular mission towns, this community includes old hotels, homes, barracks, stables, and adobes left over from the days of Spanish and Mexican rule. Built on a plateau created by the San Andreas fault, San Juan Bautista was the home of Tiburcio Vasquez, another self-styled western Robin Hood. In between robbing the rich and helping the poor, this bandit took time out to become intimate with countless beautiful women. Vasquez was finally caught and hanged on the San Jose gallows in 1875.

Much of San Juan Bautista's prosperity as a commercial and transportation center in the mid-nineteenth century was due to the discovery of quicksilver (mercury) at New Idria, 60 miles to the southeast. This community's mines were in continuous operation from 1850 until 1972, when environmental regulations undercut the market for the mineral. Virtually a ghost town today, New Idria is worth visiting. To reach it, take S.R. 156 east to Hollister and then head south on S.R. 25, turning onto County Highway J1 at Paicines (where you should get gas for the remainder of the trip). From here, it's a delightful 50-mile drive through rolling ranchland as you pass through the Panoche Valley and cut off on New Idria Road. In the small town,

you'll find old homes, dormitories, schools, and stores completely intact. Although the mill and mines are closed, you can still inspect much of the equipment, including the headframes, ore carts, hoppers, and rail lines.

Make the trip in the spring, when the fields are covered with poppies and hundreds of yucca bloom on the hillsides. Aside from a few old buildings and a blacksmith shop in Panoche Valley, there's no development here. As you drive through the countryside, past wooded valleys and along the clear streams, you'll probably have the road to yourself. Most people return to S.R. 25 by doubling back on New Idria Road. But if you're adventurous and not driving an oversized vehicle, you can take Clear Creek Road back to S.R. 25. Be sure to inquire locally about the route, since it crosses several creekbeds.

Once you reach the state highway, it's an easy drive north to the Pinnacles National Monument, which should be a basic part of everyone's California geology education. These jagged, 1000-foot-high volcanic remnants are laced with popular hiking trails that are ideal in the spring. Carved by the elements, the Pinnacles provide an excellent vantage point for the surrounding countryside. Here you can also visit a number of caves and canyons that are home to a wide variety of wildlife. In the evening several bat species patrol the skies searching for insects. Although park facilities are open year-round, 100-degree weather can make a summer visit uncomfortable.

Leaving the Pinnacles, you can return to the Monterey Peninsula by doubling back to Hollister and taking S.R. 156 and U.S. 101 to Salinas. Here you can visit John Steinbeck's birthplace (where lunch is served on weekdays), grave, and a library named in his memory. Inside the library you'll find a room filled with Steinbeck's pictures, manuscripts, and memorabilia. From here, it's a short drive on S.R. 68 to Monterey.

Another route into Steinbeck country from the Pinnacles leads south on S.R. 25, west on G13, and north on U.S. 101. Heading up the Salinas Valley, you can take G16 westbound to the popular Arroyo Seco campground. If you don't mind cold water, there's a nearby picnic area that offers good swimming in the Arroyo Seco River. And nearby is a trailhead into the Ventana Wilderness, where you can hike your way over to the Big Sur Coast.

Following the road beyond the campground, you can wind through the mountains into the Hunter Liggett Military Reservation. The first part of this trip abounds in switchbacks and steep grades; it is not recommended for oversize vehicles or during wet weather. Picking up Milpitas and Del Venturi roads inside this scenic 170,000-acre tract purchased by the government from Hearst's San Simeon estate in 1940, you'll soon come to Mission San Antonio de Padua. Unlike a number of the outposts in the Spanish chain, this one was completely self-sufficient. Carefully restored, this mission sits just a few miles from sites now used by the army for developing new combat techniques. It is also accessible from S.R. 1 south of Lucia via the Nacimiento-Fergusson Road and from U.S. 101 via G14 or G18. Unless you like rough back-country driving, take one of the last two routes.

Resuming your trip from the Arroyo Seco area, pick up G16 westbound, which leads toward the Carmel Valley. Take the cutoff on Cachagua Road, and you'll soon reach the turnoff to Tassajara Hot Springs, now a Zen Buddhist retreat. Although California abounds in fine hot springs, this hard-to-reach retreat has become increasingly popular in recent years. Jerry Brown retreated here after winning the California gubernatorial race in 1974. During summer months, the Zen practitioners offer vegetarian food and lodging to a limited number of guests, but these fairly expensive accommodations are almost always booked months in advance. A cheaper way to enjoy the hot baths and cold streams is to visit for the day.

Peaceful though this resort may be, the 16-mile-long Tassajara Road is not really suited to four-wheel vehicles. More than one person has set out on this road to nirvana and wound up with burned-out brakes or a ruined transmission. Instead of taking this rough route, consider backpacking in from Arroyo Seco. Then you can stay overnight for free at a nearby campsite.

After passing the cutoff to another Ventana Wilderness trailhead, Cachagua Road leads back to G16 and through exclusive Carmel Valley Village toward the coast. About 3 miles before reaching S.R. 1, you'll find the Thunderbird, a bookstore dedicated to the intelligent proposition that it's a good idea to read part of a book before buying it. To that end, customers are encouraged to browse through a volume or two during lunch or dinner at the store's own restaurant.

Turning north on S.R. 1, you'll soon come to Monterey, where the Chamber of Commerce offers a map that leads you on the 3-mile-long "Path of History." Along the way you'll want to visit some of the community's old adobes that include the Custom House, California's first theater, and Colton Hall, site of the state's first constitutional convention. One of the most popular old buildings here is the Stevenson House on Houston Street. Robert Louis Stevenson lived in this boardinghouse in 1879 and divided his time between writing and trying to persuade Fanny Osbourne to leave her husband and marry him. He succeeded the following year. If you're intrigued by the Stevenson memorabilia found here, you may want to visit the Silverado Museum at Saint Helena (see under Wine Country).

Of course, every visit to Monterey requires a stop at Cannery Row, once a world-renowned sardine-packing capital. The sardines disappeared from local waters in 1945 and remain missing and unaccounted for to this day. As a result, all eighteen canneries have gone out of business, leaving the door open for stores selling English antiques, Parisian fashions, and authentic Japanese ashtrays. Although every third seafood restaurant here is named after Steinbeck, today's Cannery Row has lost most of its ties with the book of the same name. Even the building that formed the basis for Doc's laboratory has been turned into a private club.

Just beyond Monterey is Pacific Grove, home of the "butterfly trees" that each winter attract vast numbers of monarch butterflies from thousands of miles around. Heading past this town's notable Victorian buildings, you'll reach Point Pinos, where Juan Rodríguez Cabrillo first landed in 1542. From this point you can drive along the beach and loop back through Pacific Grove, past the historic Monterey Presidio, and on down to Carmel. Or you can take the private 17-mile drive through scenic Pebble Beach, one of the state's most exclusive residential areas. Probably best known for the Crosby Open, this area abounds in golf courses, country clubs, private schools, and riding trails. But what sticks in the minds of most visitors is the fact that they must shell out $3 just for the privilege of making the 17-mile excursion through this affluent little society world.

No matter which way you choose to reach Carmel, you'll probably be impressed by the tight zoning that has allowed this small residential community to accommodate gracefully over 150 shops. Strict sign limitation ordinances, extensive use of malls, and intelligent landscaping all enhance this tourist community. Many inns, motels, and hotels are within walking distance of the shopping district and the beach. There's another mission here, situated on the edge of a coastal bird sanctuary.

Just south of Carmel off Highway 1 is Point Lobos State Reserve. Northernmost breeding ground of the California brown pelican and inhabited by two sea lion species, this 1250-acre site is one of California's most important wildlife sanctuaries. On the headlands amid the increasingly rare Monterey cypresses you can watch migrating whales, hear sea lions barking, visit the nation's first underwater tidepool reserve, see over 250 animal species and 300 kinds of plants, and maybe even glimpse a California sea otter.

Continuing on S.R. 1, you'll soon pass into the Big Sur region, which is at its best in springtime when wildflowers dominate the coastal mountains. If it's not too wet, Coast Road makes a good side trip through wooded canyons and provides easy access to a number of creeks that are hard to reach from the main highway. This old route cuts off the highway near Bixby Creek Bridge, largest of the many graceful spans found in Big Sur Country. In a state notorious for its wretched

Point Lobos.

highway construction excesses, these bridges provide a notable example of intelligent design that helps minimize the main road's intrusion on the coastal landscape.

Heading on past the Point Sur lighthouse, the road leads away from the coast along Andrew Molera State Park and into the modest Big Sur settlement. There is no town here per se, since local residents live in homes scattered over this forested locale. But there are a variety of lodges as well as the Pfeiffer–Big Sur State Park, where you can camp, take day hikes through the redwoods, or head off into the adjacent Ventana Wilderness. Although ocean access is somewhat limited by steep, rugged cliffs, you can reach Pfeiffer Beach via a 2-mile road that cuts off Highway 1 at Sycamore Canyon (get directions from a park ranger). Travel the entire California coast and you probably won't find a better place to watch the sun set.

Continuing down the coast, you'll come to Julia Pfeiffer Burns State Park, where a hike out to the headlands will frequently yield a view of sea otters. From here, the road leads past the Esalen Institute, a private human development center that does wonders for those who can afford the fairly steep prices. After passing through Lucia, you'll see the New Camaldoli Hermitage cutoff. Visitors are welcome at Sunday mass, and, all days of the week, at the guest house and the gift shop, where they can purchase souvenirs made by some of the order's forty resident Benedictine monks.

Should you want to stop overnight in this area, there are private and public campgrounds at Lime Kiln Creek and nearby Kirk Creek. Just beyond the latter is the Nacimiento-Fergusson Road mentioned earlier in this section. This narrow, steep, winding road offers access to a number of inland campgrounds as well as to the Hunter Liggett Military Reservation. But it should not be attempted at night or in the rain.

Continuing south on S.R. 1 you'll shortly reach that mecca of California coastal travelers, San Simeon. In the belief that this historic site is a basic part of everyone's California education, we have devoted an adjacent section to San Simeon and its environs. Although we have tried to remain reasonably restrained about the state's attractions in these pages, it is impossible to be low key about this one. Don't miss it.

After your visit to the castle, you can take S.R. 46 east to Paso Robles, home of Mission San Miguel Arcangel, distinguished by remarkably well preserved wall paintings by early nineteenth-century missionary artists. Or you can continue south on S.R. 1 to San Luis Obispo, home of another important mission as well as the campus of California State Polytechnic University. As in Monterey, a "Path of History" takes you past the county museum, old commercial buildings, and Victorian dwellings. There are also remnants of a once-prosperous Chinatown which met the needs of thousands of coolies who helped dig nearby railroad tunnels in the late nineteenth century.

San Luis Obispo is also home of the bizarre Madonna Inn, which, at 214 Madonna Road, has long caught the eye of travelers along Highway 101. Its gingerbread architecture and colorful interior design combine to give the place a Christmas feeling year around and put Howard Johnson to shame. Every one of the 109 rooms and suites (ranging from $14 to $60) has its own decor. Postcards of each room are sold in the gift shop.

But what makes the place unique is its matchless bathrooms. Handsome brick, polished wood, and fine wallpaper combine beneath subdued lighting for a clean, natural look. In the men's room, a waterwheel is mounted at the ceiling. On the wall is a sheet of copper that sweeps down to form a trough. To approach the urinal, you must pass through an electronic eye that sends water shooting out of the wheel and down into the trough. But be careful. We know one person so astounded by this flushing mechanism that he kept darting back and forth, tripping the electronic eye repeatedly. The fifth time through a maintenance man rushed in screaming: "Stop! Stop! People are always messing up the system."

From San Luis Obispo, the highway heads back out to the coast, where you can choose between the relaxed atmosphere of Avila Beach or head on to busy Pismo Beach, a favorite with clam diggers and dune buggy drivers. A few miles south is the tiny beach town of Oceano, which includes the Coffee T. Rice Victorian home, now surrounded by a hideous trailer park. Just beyond Oceano, you can visit the remnants of the Temple Home utopian colony at Halcyon. Located just south of Fair Oaks, this turn-of-the-century collective consists of small cottages surrounding half a dozen community buildings. The settlement is distinguished by a decaying three-story Victorian sanatorium built by a physician member of the group who believed love and harmony were the keys to conquest of disease.

If you're not in a hurry, take a leisurely drive down S.R. 1 into the Lompoc Valley, which produces over half the world's garden flower seed supply. The best time for a visit is spring, when thousands of acres come into bloom. Millions of blossoms are put to use in the area's flower festival each June. Lompoc is also the home of La Purisma Mission, which has been restored under state auspices. If you time your visit right, you just might walk out of the sanctuary and see a missile lifting off at nearby Vandenberg Air Force Base. Headquarters for the Air Force Western Test Range, this is the place where the military tries out new missiles by firing them 5000 miles out into the Pacific. On a clear night the glow from these launches can be seen hundreds of miles away.

Head east from Lompoc on S.R. 246, and you'll soon cross over U.S. 101 into the Santa Ynez Valley. This region was first settled by the Spanish, who established a mission to convert nearby Indians. Damaged by floods, earthquakes, and Indian uprisings, the structure has been carefully restored. Inside the chapel, you'll find the original Indian murals and a vestments collection that is considered outstanding.

Mission Santa Ynez is located on the edge of Solvang, a Danish settlement that has become a popular tourist town filled with galleries, antique shops, and bakeries. At nearby Ballard, there's a charming old schoolhouse built in 1883. And a few miles on in Los Olivos is Mattei's Tavern, a historic bar and restaurant that once served as a stage and railroad terminal. From here, you can head to U.S. 101 and continue south toward Santa Barbara. Your route will lead past Nojoqui Falls County Park, a good picnic site, and then along the first of a number of beaches still slightly tainted by oil from controversial offshore drilling. Or you can take S.R. 154 down San Marcos Pass into the Santa Barbara region.

No matter which gateway you choose, chances are you'll find Santa Barbara measuring up to almost every standard of the American dream. Home to such distinguished California citizens as the author Ross McDonald, this city is a model of intelligent community planning. Sign ordinances, building height limitations, malls, wood-paneled parking lots, mosaic-adorned mailboxes, and freeway restrictions make this coastal town a world favorite among those who can afford to live anywhere. Here immigrants find the California they have dreamed of.

The place to begin a look at Santa Barbara is the opulent oceanfront Biltmore Hotel at sunset. Probably no place in the entire state better symbolizes the California image. By the time you have rented a bike and peddled along the shoreline, walked the downtown mall, visited the mural-filled Moorish courthouse, stopped off at the Santa Barbara Mission, and driven through the exclusive Montecito and Hope Ranch residential areas, you will see why one travel magazine

Tillotson's Roses. The seventy-two-page catalogue published annually by this Watsonville firm is a work of art. Hundreds of roses, including many you are doubtless unacquainted with, are offered for sale by this firm. The descriptions are filled with historical allusions and endorsements from satisfied customers around the nation. For the connoisseur or dilettante, Tillotson's catalogue is a must. Write for it at 802 Brown's Valley Road, Watsonville, CA 95076. The $1 charge is refundable when a purchase is made.

Santa Barbara's Biltmore Hotel. Perhaps no place in the entire state better symbolizes the California image. (*Santa Barbara Chamber of Commerce*)

has called this area "America's replica of the old Riviera."

But, alas, even here in paradise things aren't what they used to be. Ever since the big 1969 oil spill off Santa Barbara, life here has been somewhat unsettled. First, there were the students at the local University of California branch who torched a Bank of America branch. Then the Loud family punctured the California dream by breaking up on national television. Smog levels have been worsening. One of the community's most distinguished institutions, the Center for the Study of Democratic Institutions, has been forced to close due to a cash shortage (even the infusion of royalties from *The Joy of Sex* by center fellow Dr. Alex Comfort failed to stave off the demise of the Santa Barbara office). And late in 1975, the federal government auctioned off more oil leases in the Santa Barbara Channel. A community that has already grown used to scraping tar from its feet following an ocean dip now shivers as offshore drilling resumes.

Central Coast Notes

Combing the Coast by Ruth Jackson ($2.95, Chronicle Books, 870 Market Street, Suite 508, San Francisco, CA 94102) offers good information on the Santa Cruz and Monterey county shoreline. For a booklet on Steinbeck country traveling, send fifty cents to Salinas Chamber of Commerce, 119 East Alisal, Salinas, CA 93901.

You can get additional information from the Santa Cruz Convention and Visitors' Bureau, P.O. Box 921, Santa Cruz, CA 95060; the Monterey Peninsula Visitors' and Convention Bureau, P.O. Box 1770, Monterey, CA 93940; the Paso Robles Chamber of Commerce, P.O. Box 457, Paso Robles, CA 93446; the San Benito County Chamber of Commerce, P.O. Box 381, Hollister, CA 95023; and the Santa Barbara Chamber of Commerce, P.O. Box 299, Santa Barbara, CA 93102

Sea Otter

Once one of the most abundant marine mammals found off the California coast, the sea otter was driven nearly to extinction before special legislation fostered replenishment of the species. Pursuit of the otter's prized fur was a primary reason for Russian colonization at Fort Ross during the eighteenth century. Between 1741 and 1911, hunters took more than 200,000 otters from coastal waters off California and Baja

California. Finally, the signing of a treaty by the United States, Great Britain, Russia, and Japan preserved the few remaining sea otters. Additional protection was provided by passage of a state law in 1913 and subsequent establishment of a sea otter refuge, which extends along the coast from Carmel to Cambria.

Today an estimated 1700 California sea otters live in the waters extending from Santa Cruz to Point Buchon in San Luis Obispo County. From a boat, it's possible to catch a glimpse of these fascinating animals, who keep relatively near the coast and live on sea urchins, rock crabs, clams, and other shellfish. If you're very lucky, you may catch sight of an otter resting on its back using a rock to crack open an abalone shell for dinner.

San Simeon

No matter how many times you've seen *Citizen Kane* or read *Citizen Hearst,* it's difficult to visualize California's Taj Mahal, San Simeon. Driving along the Pacific coast midway between Los Angeles and San Francisco, you can catch a glimpse of the twin-towered Hispano-Moorish mansion standing high on a 2000-foot hill, 5 miles to the east. But only after purchasing your ticket at the gate near S.R. 1 and starting the bus ride up toward La Casa Grande do you begin appreciating the scale of what Hearst was able to accomplish with $30 million.

En route, you pass hillsides that took all twenty of his gardeners to cover with wildflowers. It wasn't enough that guests (who arrived each weekend by private plane, train, and car) could look out in any direction from San Simeon and see nothing but Hearst property. No, there had to be some color to break up the 240,000-acre ranch that stretched back toward the Santa Lucia Mountains and was half the size of Rhode Island. Farther up the hill, you may spot some of the wild zebra and barbary sheep descended from animals in Hearst's private zoo, which also included lions, leopards, cheetahs, and polar bears housed in special enclosures. And near the top you'll see how $1 million worth of landscaping has turned the castle grounds into an arboretum.

From here, there's a good view of the ornamented ivory-colored towers rising above the 100-room mansion with its 38 bathrooms, 31 bedrooms, and 14 sitting rooms. These are not the original towers. Hearst had the originals torn down and replaced at enormous expense because they were too bare looking to suit his taste. The chief continued tinkering with his dream castle for thirty-two years, and it remained unfinished at the time of his death in 1951. Because the Hearst family could not afford to maintain this monument, they gave the castle and its adjacent 123-acre grounds to the state in 1959. Today, visits cost $3 to $14, depending on how much of the mansion you want to see.

These are very reasonable fees for a look at one of the most remarkable castles ever built. The entire place was designed to accommodate the rooms, floors, ceilings, walls, and other knickknacks Hearst bought on his epic antique-collecting journeys about the world. In 1919, with his warehouses bulging, he commissioned architect Julia Morgan to assemble his baroque, medieval, renaissance, Moorish, Greco-Roman, Hispano, Florentine, Persian, and other acquisitions into one home. Much of what couldn't be accommodated in the castle was put into the forty-six rooms of three lavish guest houses. And leftover odds and ends, like sarcophagi, were simply placed along the walkways for decorative effect.

Because of the castle's vast size, the state has wisely elected to divide the viewing into three tours. Tour 1 gives you a look at the grounds, one of the guest houses, and rooms on the lower level. Tour 2 shows twenty-six rooms in Hearst's inner sanctum on the upper levels. Tour 3 looks at thirty-six rooms in the north guest wing, completed shortly before his death. If possible,

San Simeon.

The Gothic Suite, San Simeon.

try reserving for all of them. San Simeon is endlessly fascinating, and if you're like most people, you'll wish the tours were longer. Although it is possible to take all three two-hour tours in a single day, consider staying overnight at one of the campgrounds, trailer parks, or motels in the area. Not only will you be able to divide up your mansion visit, but you'll have time to take a closer look at this picturesque coastal region.

Among other things, you should make a point of visiting the little village of San Simeon across Highway 1 from the castle entrance. This community, with its abandoned schoolhouse, has a row of Spanish-style houses that have been the homes of Hearst ranch employees for many decades. The Sebastian Store, constructed in 1868, is the oldest building in the area and a historic landmark. And on the waterfront you can still see the old dock where ships lined up to unload pieces of Hearst's jigsaw castle. Nearby are Hearst warehouses still filled with rare walls, ceilings, fire-places, and other objects that could not be built into San Simeon before the chief's death.

San Simeon is also conveniently close to Morro Bay, distinguished by its towering landmark, Morro Rock. One of the most popular ocean communities of the Central Coast, the town's seafood restaurants draw visitors from hundreds of miles around. Morro Bay State Park at the south end of town is a good camp-site; it borders one of California's largest natural coastal marshlands, a haven for more than 250 bird species that frequent the area. The park also in-cludes a golf course and an excellent natural history museum at White Point, which is a great blue heron rookery. If you camp at Morro Bay, be sure to visit nearby Montana De Oro State Park, with its unspoiled hiking trails along the oceanfront cliffs and headlands. Swimming, rock hounding, skindiving, abalone picking, and fishing are popular here, but you need a sport fish-ing licence to pursue the last two activities. There is also good clamming on the sand spit wild area that separates Morro Bay from the ocean.

San Simeon tickets: Reservations are a good idea for the castle during the summer and holidays. You can make them by writing the Hearst Reservation Office, Department of Parks and Recreation, P.O. Box 2390, Sacramento, CA 95811. Information is available by telephone (916-445-8828), but all reservations must be made in writing. Tickets for Tours 1 and 3 are $4 for adults and $2 for children six through twelve. Tour 2 costs $5 for adults and $2.50 for children. Children under six get in free if they sit on a parent's lap for the bus ride. Tour 3 operates on weekends and holidays only, from October 1 through June 30.

The Pismo Clam

Perhaps the most widely pursued clam in California is the pismo. Not only are these mollusks good eating, but they also make terrific bait. How does the pismo differ from all other clams? Where can it be found? What are its origins? What is the best way to find one? For answers to these and other questions we turned to the State Department of Fish and Game.

Distinguishing characteristics: Famous throughout California is the pismo clam, a native diligently sought each year by thousands of diggers from Monterey Bay to southern Baja California. Pismos are found on wide, exposed, sandy beaches from just below the high tide line to depths as great as 80 feet. They are large clams, attaining more than 7 inches in length and over 3 pounds in weight.

They are characterized by thick, heavy, almost triangular shells covered with a varnishlike periostracum. Generally they are tan or buckskin colored, but range from this to a dark chocolate. Some are striped, with markings originating near the point of the shell and radiating out toward its margin or lip.

The hinged point of the shell, called the umbo or beak, contains a tough ligament and a set of interlocking teeth. These teeth and the impressions left by the mantle and muscles on the shell's interior are used to identify clams. The ligament is under tension when the shells are closed and forces the shell to gape open when the adductor muscles relax or are cut.

Range: Pismo clams occur on long stretches of exposed, sandy beaches from Half Moon Bay south to Magdalena Bay in Baja California. They are most accessible to the digger at Hueneme, Pismo Beach, Morro Bay, and between Elkhorn Slough and Santa Cruz. They do occur in other localities, but digging is slow at most of these.

Life history notes: Pismo clams have been residents on our coast since the last Ice Age. They have been found in Pleistocene deposits laid down as long as 25,000 years ago. Their name is a corruption of the Indian word *pismu*, meaning "tar." Bitumen seeps are abundant in the area around Pismo Beach, giving rise to the name "Pismo."

Planktonic animals, plants, and small drifting pieces of decaying animal and vegetable matter are sucked into the clam through an "incurrent" siphon. Food particles are retained and the water is expelled through an "excurrent" siphon.

Respiration occurs simultaneously with food gathering.

Growth rings mark the shell with alternating light and dark bands, and it is possible to determine the age of pismo clams by counting each pair of light and dark bands.

These clams lie just under the surface of the sand with the hinged side toward the surf (offshore) and the open side toward the beach. The large, raised hinge faces up and sometimes a colony of hydroids, *Clytia bakeri,* will make a home on the upper edges of the valves.

Sexes are separate in pismo clams; males and females being found in about equal numbers. A few hermaphroditic individuals have been found, but in every case these were in their first spawning season.

Spawning usually starts in late July or early August with the release of sperm and eggs, probably triggered in both sexes by a rise in water temperature.

The mature eggs are 1/350 inch in diameter and are spawned in tremendous numbers. An average of 15 million eggs is produced by a 5-inch female.

It was estimated in 1949 that on the 9.4 miles of clam-producing beach at Pismo, somewhat over 112 trillion eggs were spawned. Of this huge total, only 33,000 clams resulted, representing considerably more than 99 percent mortality. What happens to the tiny, free-swimming larvae after they hatch is almost a complete mystery. Ocean currents may move them up to 100 miles along the coast before they metamorphose and settle on a beach.

Gulls, sharks, rays, drill snails, and some fish take their toll of young clams. If the clam can live through all these perils, and man's depredations too, it has a bare chance of living to an age of thirty or thirty-five years.

Capture and use: Usually a six-tined potato fork is used to dig pismo clams. At any low tide, clam beaches will be covered with sportsmen, probing for these succulent bivalves. Some clammers walk backward, dragging a rake through the sand. If digging implements are unavailable, the clammer can expose clams by rotating his feet back and forth on the bottom, allowing the receding surf to wash away the sand.

Since pismo clams are regulated by fish and game laws, be sure to check for the current size and bag limits before indulging in the sport.

The pismos found in the local bait shop are shipped in from Mexico; our local stocks cannot be sold.

Legal-size pismo clams are taken primarily for food but make excellent bait for barred surfperch, calico surfperch, spotfin croakers, and cabezon. They work quite well when fishing that deep rockpile for rockfish,

---

Clam Cookbook. The Pismo Beach Chamber of Commerce has solved all your clam culinary problems with the publication of their valuable clam cookbook. For your copy, send $2.75 to the Pismo Beach Chamber of Commerce, 581 Dolliver Street, Pismo Beach, CA 93449.

sculpin, or lingcod. A cut piece of the foot or gut is considered best by many fishermen, but others prefer the siphons.

The California Condor

One of the state's most precious resources is the California condor, an Ice Age relic with a 9-foot wingspan. One of only two species remaining alive in the world (Andean condors can still be found in South America), this bird continues to hold out in the Ventura and Santa Barbara county mountains.

Sometimes mistaken for the smaller turkey vulture, the California condor is distinguished by its large size, featherless neck, pinkish orange head, red eyes, black feathers, and white wing bars. Surviving on carrion, condors raise their young in tree hollows or clefts in mountain ledges. The female lays only one egg every two years. The proximity of human beings causes the parents to abandon the nest for hours, exposing either the egg or the young to the elements and hunger, which can lead to death.

During the nineteenth century, many condors were shot for their quills, and collectors snatched the birds' pale green eggs from their nests. By 1901, the decline in the number of birds led to passage of legislation establishing the condor as a protected species. Despite the subsequent establishment of two condor sanctuaries within the Los Padres National Forest (both are closed to public use), the number of birds has dwindled to less than forty. Today conservationists and government officials are working continuously in hope of staving off the eventual extinction of this majestic bird.

The California Brown Pelican

Every year about 20,000 California brown pelicans visit the state's coastline between August and November. This large, long-billed grayish brown bird is distinguished by the grandiose high dives it makes in pursuit of fish. After swooping straight down into the ocean, the pelican surfaces, tips its bill down to drain all the water out, and then tilts the bill up into the air so it can swallow the fish.

Although most brown pelicans nest off the Mexican coast, some breed at Anacapa Island off the Santa Barbara coast. A few years back, the buildup of DDT in coastal waters was making it difficult for this colony to replenish itself. Scientists found that pesticide pollution caused the pelicans to lay thin-shelled eggs that fell apart during incubation. By 1970, just one new pelican was born in 552 Anacapa nests.

The drastic drop in the pelican birth rate on Anacapa was one of many factors that helped persuade state and federal agencies effectively to ban use of DDT in 1971 and 1972. This decision, plus the closing of public access to the western portion of the island during the nesting season, has had an immediate effect. More than fifty pelicans are born on Anacapa each year; conservationists anticipate a continued increase in the near future.

Steinbeck Country

While visiting the Central Coast region, you'll pass many of the settings in the Monterey Peninsula–Salinas Valley area that appear throughout Steinbeck's novels.

- *East of Eden.* Based in the Salinas Valley, this novel made heavy use of the King City area, with a ranch in Hamilton Canyon serving as the model for the Trask family property. The Ford dealership mentioned here is currently Stateside Motors on Broadway Street in King City.

- *Of Mice and Men.* Steinbeck also made use of King City in this novel, set on the Arroyo Seco River near Soledad.

- *Cannery Row.* Western Biological Laboratory, 800 Cannery Row, was the model for Doc's lab. Edward Ricketts, who served as the model for Doc, collected specimens at nearby Asilomar Beach and Point Lobos.

- *Tortilla Flat.* Impoverished characters in this novel stole vegetables from the old Hotel Del Monte, which is now the Naval Postgraduate School, Sloat and 3rd streets. Steinbeck's experiences during a brief career at the Spreckels Sugar Factory near Salinas also figure in this book.

- *Sweet Thursday.* This book used Monterey's San Carlos Cathedral, Cannery Row, and Pacific Grove's China Point area (the setting for Chin Kee's squid yard), which is now occupied by Stanford University's Hopkins Marine Station.

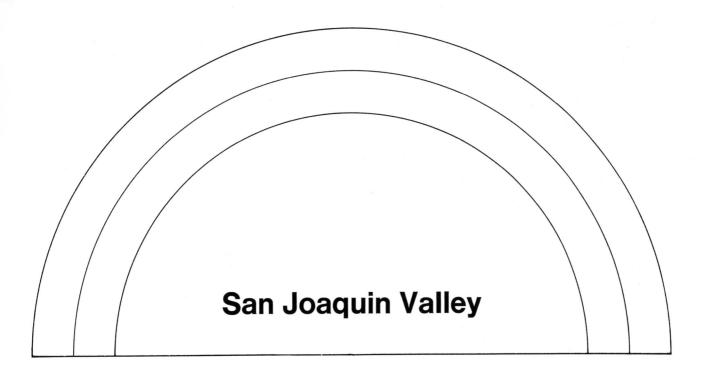

San Joaquin Valley

The Best of the San Joaquin Valley

Swimming: McConnell State Recreation Area
Fishing: Kern River Canyon
Underground gardens: Forestiere, Fresno
Museum: Tulare County, Mooney Grove Park
Adobe: Burell Mansion
Mansion: Chateau Fresno, Kearney Park
Pioneer village: Bakersfield
Oil well pumps: S.R. 198 from Interstate 5 to Coalinga
Armenian bakeries: Fresno
Fort: Tejon
Historic Chinese buildings: Hanford
Elk: Tule Elk State Reserve, off Interstate 5 west of Bakersfield

Most travelers tend to look upon this rich agricultural region as a place to speed through en route to the Sierra Nevada or the northern mountains, yet it, too, has a goodly share of recreational and historic attractions. Immortalized in Steinbeck's *Grapes of Wrath,* it has moved into the spotlight in the last few years owing to continuing labor strife between farm workers and growers. More recently, rivalry between Cesar Chavez's United Farm Workers Union and the Teamsters has added a new dimension to the controversy.

If you're serious about seeing the valley, you should follow S.R. 99, the lesser of two main routes leading through the region. Although this road is no match in speed for modern Interstate 5, it cuts through all the valley's major cities and runs close to most of the key attractions.

The best time to visit the region is in the spring, since the summer heat can be oppressive. Entering from the north, you'll note the vast network of irrigation canals that has been instrumental in turning this desert into a world-renowned agricultural center. Intensive cultivation here is a key reason why California supplies nearly 40 percent of the nation's fruit and nuts and about 25 percent of its vegetables. The first major town you'll pass through is Modesto, home of E. and J. Gallo, the state's largest winery. Although there are no tours here, you can see some of the firm's huge storage tanks towering over the vineyards at Livingston. Unlike some of the pastoral wineries you may have visited in the Napa Valley, this mammoth installation has all the warmth of a refinery.

In Modesto, the center of a vast fruit-growing and

livestock region, you'll find the McHenry Museum, which has recreations of an old blacksmith shop, dentist's office, and other rooms of historical interest. At Delhi, you can take a short side trip east to McConnell State Recreation Area, where there is excellent swimming in the Merced River, which glistens with gold dust. This is one of a number of streams and lakes found throughout the valley where you can cool off on a hot summer day.

As you approach Madera, you'll drive past cotton fields, vegetable farms, vineyards, wheat fields, and feed lots that continue on down to Fresno, the valley's largest city. A few miles north of Fresno is the Forestiere Underground Gardens, where you can see trees, vines, shrubs, and vegetation planted in sixty different rooms and grottoes. While in the area, you may want to visit Roeding Park, one of the community's distinguished Armenian bakeries (try Valley Bakery, 502 M Street), or the old mansion at Kearney Park. The last structure, west of town on Kearney Boulevard, was built by estate owner M. T. Kearney to accommodate servants of his dream home, Chateau Fresno. Unfortunately, he died in 1906 before the main house was finished.

Back in Fresno, take S.R. 41 south, make a westward turn on Elkhorn Avenue, and you will come to one of the state's most expansive old adobes, the century-old Burell Mansion. Still occupied by a farming family today, this structure boasts walls 18 inches thick. Resuming your trip south on S.R. 41, turn east on S.R. 198 to Hanford, where you can visit an old Chinese settlement with half a dozen well-preserved buildings. There are two restaurants here; one is the Imperial Dynasty, where part of the facilities are located in a former opium den; the other is the Chinese Pagoda. The side-by-side restaurants are operated by descendants of Chow Gong Wing, who opened a restaurant here in 1883. The elaborate Continental menu of the Imperial Dynasty features everything from escargots to veal sweetbreads.

From Hanford, take S.R. 198 east to Visalia and head south 5 miles on S.R. 63 to Mooney Grove Park and the Tulare County Museum. In this 155-acre park, you'll find a number of vintage buildings, vehicles, and pioneer relics, as well as peacocks and a small lake. Continuing south on S.R. 63, you'll link up once again with S.R. 99. At J15 you can head west to S.R. 43, which leads south to the tiny settlement of Allensworth. This community, founded at the turn of the century by Colonel James Allensworth, was envisioned as a black utopia. Although this ambitious plan was never realized, a number of blacks still live here today, and the state is in the process of turning the community into a historic park.

Continuing south on S.R. 43, you'll soon reach Garces Highway. Turn east here, and you'll come to the head-quarters of Cesar Chavez's United Farm Workers Union. Although there are no visitors' facilities here, you can stop for a look at the union hall. Just beyond union headquarters is Delano, central battleground of the protracted fight to organize California's agricultural workers. While traveling through this region, you will see a number of fruit stands offering premium grapes in season. Buy them as long as they carry the United Farm Workers Union label. Frequently this is first-quality fruit not ordinarily seen in California stores. An irony of California agriculture is that nearly all the top-flight table grapes are shipped to major eastern cities. California markets usually end up with second-quality grapes, the ones not considered likely to survive the transcontinental train trip in good shape.

Not far south of Delano is Bakersfield, the state's country music capital. Merle Haggard lives here; so does Buck Owens, who maintains his own studio and production, recording, music publishing, and talent company in town. This community is also the home of the Kern County Museum and Pioneer Village, which includes the county's first courthouse as well as an old saloon, hotel, and caboose. East of town is the popular Kern River Canyon Recreation Area. In the late nineteenth century there was a major gold rush on this stream, and you can still find a few mining buildings in the ghost town of Keysville.

Although most of the attractions in this region lie along S.R. 99, Interstate 5 has several side trips to offer. The 12-mile stretch from the freeway to the town of Coalinga provides a real treat for kids. Here you'll find some forty-six oil pumps painted by local artist Jean Dakessian to resemble such diverse creatures as Snoopy, Woodstock, cowboys, and a skunk. Farther south on Interstate 5 is the Tule Elk State Reserve near Tupman. And as you leave the valley and head up into the Tehachapi Mountains, you'll come upon Fort Tejon, an old army post that has been turned into a state historical park. Although there was no significant fighting here, the fort is distinguished by the fact that it was the home of the first camels used by the U.S. Army. Unfortunately, the animals, imported with great difficulty, proved to be of minimal utility in the California climate.

San Joaquin Valley Notes

For information write the Modesto Chamber of Commerce, P.O. Box 844, Modesto, CA 95353, or the Fresno County Chamber of Commerce, P.O. Box 1469, Fresno, CA 93716. The Bakersfield area is covered by the Kern County Board of Trade, P.O. Box 1312, Bakersfield, CA 93302.

Elk

Like the buffalo of the Great Plains, California's elk

herds once seemed a limitless resource. Prized for their meat, skins, and antlers, these graceful animals abounded in many parts of Northern and Southern California. Most common were the dwarf or Tule elk in the San Joaquin Valley, the somewhat larger Rocky Mountain elk in the central and northern part of the state and, in the north coast counties, the largest of the state's species, the Roosevelt elk.

Pioneers had no qualms about picking off these animals. The Tule elk proved particularly vulnerable, and by 1873 hunting had turned to slaughter. To prevent the elk from being wiped out, the state put them off limits and threatened offenders with a jail sentence. Although this native California species has survived, agricultural development has forced the remaining Tule into just a few areas. Most accessible is the herd found inside the Tule Elk State Reserve at Tupman off Interstate 5 near Bakersfield. Another herd introduced in the Owens Valley is also under protection, while a small group of about 100 roam free in Colusa County.

Finding the other two species is a bit more difficult. The 1000 remaining Rocky Mountain elk are in the back country of Kern, Monterey, and San Luis Obispo counties as well as in the Mount Shasta area. And another 1000 of the Roosevelt elk species are concentrated in Humboldt and Del Norte counties. Although their numbers are limited, overpopulation has led to some crop damage. As a result, the state does periodically sanction elk hunting to control the size of the herds.

Tours for the Hungry

Many hungry travelers make a point of stopping off at food plants, figuring they can pick up free samples while on tour. This strategy doesn't always work, but the production operations are fun to watch, particularly for children. Here are a few to keep in mind while heading through the state. Remember that virtually all

are closed on holidays and that it's a good idea to call ahead.

- California Almond Growers Exchange, 1802 C Street, Sacramento, offers tours at 10 A.M. and 2 P.M. weekdays. Telephone: 916-442-4618.
- The Cheese Factory, 7500 Red Hill Road, Petaluma, offers tours weekdays from 10 A.M. to 4 P.M. Telephone: 707-762-6001.
- China Noodle Factory, 308 Hazelton Avenue, Stockton, is open weekdays, except Tuesday, from 9 A.M. to 11 A.M. Telephone: 209-462-1387.
- Hershey Foods, Albers Road, Oakdale, is open Monday through Friday, 8:15 A.M. to 3:30 P.M. Telephone: 209-847-0381.
- Peter Paul, Inc., 1800 South Abbott Street, Salinas, offers tours on Tuesday and Thursday at 9, 9:30, and 10 A.M. Plant is closed the first three weeks of July. Telephone: 408-424-0481.
- Sun-Maid Raisin Growers of California, 13525 South Bethel Avenue, Kingsburg, offers weekday tours from June 1 to April 1 from 8:30 to 11:30 A.M. and from 1 to 3 P.M. Telephone: 209-897-5861.

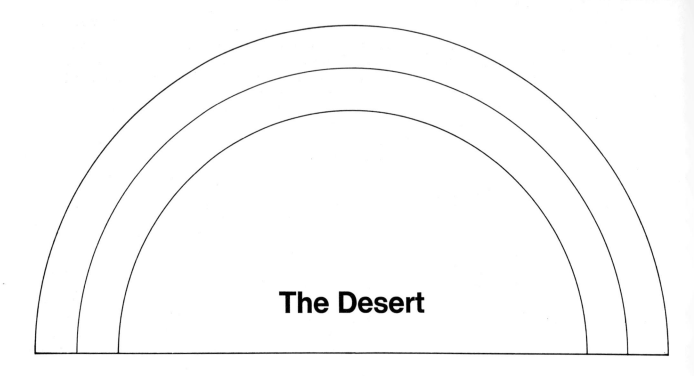

The Desert

The Best of the Desert

State park: Anza-Borrego
National monument: Death Valley
Desert preserve: Joshua Tree
Botanical garden: Moorten's Desertland Botanical Gardens, Palm Springs
Camping: Anza-Borrego State Park (not recommended in summer)
Houseboating: Colorado River
Mud hills: Zabriskie Point
Canyon: Titus, Death Valley (access extremely treacherous)
Crater: Ubehebe, Death Valley
Pinnacles: Trona Pinnacles
Rock hounding: Red Rock Canyon State Park
Caves: Providence Mountains State Recreation Area
Gorge: Topock Gorge, Colorado River
Wildlife: Anza-Borrego State Park
Museum: Roy Rogers, Apple Valley
Ballet: Amargosa Opera House, Death Valley Junction
Mine tour: Burton's Tropico
Indian petroglyphs: China Lake Naval Weapons Station
Old jail: Randsburg
Marsh birds: Salton Sea
Drive: Artist's Drive, Death Valley
View: Font's Point, Anza-Borrego State Park
Shopping: El Paseo Drive, Palm Desert

Although roughly 25 percent of California is desert, residents and visitors alike tend to avoid it in favor of the state's more temperate regions. Those who do frequent the area usually limit themselves to spas like Palm Springs, resorts like the Colorado River, and landmarks like Death Valley. Perhaps you recall that Part One of this book even discouraged vacationers from entering the state via the southeastern desert.

We stand by this judgment primarily because the majority of tourists drive into California during the summer, when this region is simply too hot for comfortable touring. But in the other three seasons, and particularly in the late winter, California's Mojave and Colorado deserts are worth exploring. Within this part of the state the history buff can find everything from the stuffed hide of Roy Rogers's old mount Trigger to a trailer park commemorating Wyatt Earp. And as you make your way through the back country, you'll come upon forests of Joshua trees, fields of wildflowers, collapsed utopias, mining ruins, Indian caves, and sand dunes.

One of the best features of this region is its proximity to the population centers of Southern California. It's possible to see a number of major Desert attractions in a single day. For instance, if you take S.R. 14 northeast from the Los Angeles region to S.R. 138, you can visit the remains of one of California's most ambitious, and for a time successful, utopian experiments, Llano Del Rio. This village, which usually shows up on maps as Llano (it's near the intersection of S.R. 138 and 65th Street), was organized in 1914 by socialist visionary Job Harriman. Over 900 people joined this desert agricultural enterprise, which was producing 90 percent of its own food by 1916. Divided into sixty departments ranging from hogs to a soap factory, Llano's aim was to finance a socialist utopia from profits derived from sales of food and handicrafts to the capitalist world. But in 1917 a water shortage persuaded Harriman it was time to move the community to a new site in Louisiana, where it lapsed into receivership in 1935.

Beyond Llano, S.R. 138 leads into S.R. 18, which takes you into Apple Valley, best known for the Roy Rogers Museum and Stockade. Here you'll find the late Trigger and other memorabilia from the television series. Continuing east into the Lucerne Valley area, you can visit Tegelberg Cactus Gardens or one of several hydroponic farms, where plants are grown in water rather than soil. Doubling back on S.R. 18, you can turn off on Bear Valley Road and visit the Apple Valley Museum, distinguished by its Indian relics.

Another easy one-day trip from the Los Angeles area leads north on S.R. 14 to Rosamond, where you turn west to Burton's Tropico Mine. Over $8 million worth of gold was extracted here between 1894 and 1956. Two years after the mine was closed, Dorene Settle, daughter of one of the mine's original owners, and her husband, Glen, reopened it to the public. Today you're welcome to join the guided tours through the hard rock tunnels, explore the collection of old mining buildings, and examine artifacts collected by the Settles. Every March there's a world gold-panning championship with contestants coming from as far away as the Yukon.

If you enjoy day trips, consider setting aside more time for a comprehensive look at the desert region. From Rosamond, you can head north through the town of Mojave to Red Rock Canyon State Park. Popular with rock hounds, who come here to hunt agate and quartz as well as petrified wood, this picturesque area has formed the backdrop for many motion pictures. Unimproved campsites are being developed here, not far from the site of Ricardo, an old stage stop.

From this point you can head to Inyokern Road, which leads east to the China Lake Naval Weapons Center. Pick up a pass at the main gate to visit rocket displays at the exhibit center as well as Indian artifacts at nearby Maturango Museum. By calling or writing ahead, you can arrange to explore via jeep some of the thousands of Indian petroglyphs on this military reservation.

If your next destination is Death Valley, pick up S.R. 178, which leads past the dry bed of Searles Lake and the Trona Pinnacles (you can see them from the highway, but a bad road makes direct access difficult). If you're heading south, you'll find one of California's most prosperous mining districts, the Rand Mountains, directly south of China Lake. Today there's still some

life in the old communities supported by thousands who flocked here during successive booms. You can visit Red Mountain, Atolia, Johannesburg, and Randsburg, where there's a mining museum, art gallery, and old jail. Above the town you'll see a few tailing piles that are the sole remains of the Yellow Aster Mine, which produced $16 million worth of gold between 1895 and 1942. Unfortunately, visits to the old mine have been banned for safety reasons.

Continuing on S.R. 395, you'll soon reach S.R. 58, which heads west along the edge of Edwards Air Force Base. Here test pilots break in advanced aircraft like the F-111 and B-70, which have been instrumental in unbalancing the federal budget. Although the flight line is open to the public just once a year, on Armed Forces Day in May, you can see the aircraft movements from some of the roads in and around the base.

Doubling back east on S.R. 58 will bring you to Barstow, home of the Mojave Valley Museum. This area has become increasingly popular with motorcyclists and dune buggy owners, banned for ecological reasons from zooming about most Desert areas. South of town, the Bureau of Land Management has set aside a special 15,000-acre "off-road vehicle playground" where trail riders are free to drive. North of town you can visit the Rainbow Basin area, where twenty-five fossil beds offer evidence of 40-inch-high horses, dogbears, sabertooth cats, and other species of an earlier age. Digging is forbidden here.

A few miles to the east of Barstow is the well-publicized—but deplorably plastic—ghost town of Calico, restored by Walter Knott of berry farm fame, who later gave the place to San Bernardino County. Skip it. Instead, continue east on Interstate 15 to the Calico archeological dig, reached via the Minneola Road exit and a well-marked dirt road. There are tours here every day except Tuesday.

Farther on, at the Afton exit, turn off to colorful Afton Canyon, where there's a small campsite and good hiking. At Baker you can head north about 35 miles on S.R. 127 to the vicinity of the Dumont Sand Dunes, and continue on to Shoshone and Death Valley Junction. Or if you continue on Interstate 15 over Halloran Summit, the Kelso-Cima road leads through the Providence Mountains and gives you a long look at Kelso Sand Dunes, the largest in the state. Wildflowers abound here in springtime.

An alternate route out of Barstow is east on Interstate 40. This will lead you past the Mount Pisgah and Amboy Crater cinder cones. Farther east, Essex road, heading north, will bring you to Providence Mountains State Recreation Area. Daily tours lead through Indian caves and limestone caverns, where you'll find rock castles, temples, domes, and good desert viewpoints. Hot in summer, cold in winter, the best months to come here are May, June, October, and November.

SOUTHERN CALIFORNIA

Just before Interstate 40 crosses into Arizona, you'll come to Needles, an old steamboat port that has become a commercial center for the Colorado River resort region. This muddy river once characterized as "too thick to drink and too thin to plow" has been cleaned up, thanks to an extensive network of dams. There are several nearby marinas where you can rent houseboats, ski boats, or skiffs. But before you head off down the river, take time out to visit some of the old mines, Indian ruins, and historic military sites such as Fort Piute. Check with the Needles Chamber of Commerce near the two-story railroad station for information on all these activities. Here rock hounds can acquire maps that will help in their search for jasper, quartz, feldspar, and other stones in the nearby Turtle Mountains.

After you've finished exploring the Desert Region, rent a boat or canoe and take the 20-mile ride down through the Topock Gorge area. Along the way you'll pass a stretch of pinnacles known as the Needles. Further down, you'll be able to beach near Picture Rock, where there are Indian petroglyphs. You may observe wild burros drinking at the water's edge or spot mustangs among the cattail growth. At Lake Havasu you can camp in designated riverfront campgrounds (for one night only) and float beneath London Bridge. Originally constructed over the Thames in 1831, this structure was taken apart a few years back, shipped to Arizona, and reassembled stone by stone. South of Lake Havasu you can visit giant Parker Dam and nearby Earp, named for Wyatt Earp, who is said to have lived here years after his famous O.K. Corral shootout. The gunman's abandoned house sits in the midst of Wyatt Earp Trailer Park.

From Earp, head south to Blythe, an agricultural center founded by an ambitious Englishman oblivious to the annual floods that inundated this fertile landscape. The subsequent construction of dams along the Colorado has corrected the problem, and today the community is the center of a prosperous farming region. If you're looking for adventure, consider launching a boat in the Colorado here and floating down through Picacho State Recreation Area. Although floods have wiped out Picacho, a nineteenth-century town developed by Mexican gold miners, you can still visit the remains of a major stamp mill here. With the help of a rock hound map acquired from the Imperial County Chamber of Commerce, you can set out from here to find a wide variety of stones as well as petrified wood. And when you're done, float on down to Imperial Dam, where your river trip ends. (This same recreation area is also accessible by Picacho Road off S.R. 24, a few miles north of Winterhaven. Summer visits are not recommended.)

Leaving this southeast corner of the state via Interstate 8, you'll parallel the route of an abandoned plank road that was the first highway to carry autos over the California Desert. It linked the Imperial Valley with Yuma, Arizona. If you cut off the Freeway at Ogilby Road (S.R. 34) and head north for about 11 miles, you'll come to the ghost town of Tumco and its adjacent mine. Today only a few remnants are left of this town that once had 3000 residents. But the area is still frequented by rock collectors. Returning to the freeway, you'll head through the 40-mile-wide Imperial Sand Dunes (a popular dune buggy habitat once used for tank training by General George Patton's forces) before passing into one of California's richest agricultural regions, the Imperial Valley.

El Centro and Brawley are the commercial centers here, but your priority should be nearby Anza-Borrego Desert State Park. Accessible by either Interstate 8 or S.R. 78, this 500,000-acre refuge offers easy access by road and trail to some of the state's best desert scenery. This park, located on the old Butterfield overland route (you can visit the original Vallecito stage station here), gives you a chance to explore barren badlands, narrow canyons, sandstone formations, waterfalls, pictographs, elephant trees, and an old Yaqui Indian well. As you climb from the desert floor into the 8000-foot-high Santa Rosa Mountains, you may come across bighorn sheep, antelope, mule deer, and roadrunners. Be sure to see Font's Point overlook for a view of the surrounding Borrego badlands.

To the east of the park is the Salton Sea, a resort area located 232 feet below sea level. Once a part of the Gulf of California, this region was cut off from the ocean by the accumulation of silt from the Colorado River. The region slowly turned into a dry lake bed, which was subsequently replenished by floods from the Colorado. Now a second-home and retirement area, the sea is kept alive with irrigation runoff from nearby farms. Fishing, swimming, and boating are pleasant here as long as you avoid the hot summer months.

Directly north of the Salton Sea is another of the state's outstanding desert preserves, Joshua Tree National Monument. On the border between the Mojave and Colorado deserts, this park was formerly the home of the Serrano and Chemehuevi Indians, who mastered the art of desert survival. Remnants of their campsites, grinding holes, pottery, and other artifacts have been found throughout the monument. A number of old mine shafts and mill sites left by gold prospectors who arrived before the turn of the century are also here.

But the monument's primary attraction is the vegetation, particularly spring wildflowers and Joshua trees, which grow to a height of 40 feet and bear cream white blossoms in clusters 8 to 14 inches long. Here you'll also find a number of palm-shaded oases, cactus gardens, and ocotillos. East of the monument—6 miles north of Desert Center on Desert Center–Rice Road—

is a desert lily preserve that abounds with wildflowers in the spring. Keep in mind that any time you set out to see desert wildflowers, you should inquire ahead about conditions. Frequently the blooms are at their peak for only a few weeks.

West of Joshua Tree is the Palm Springs region, California's most popular desert retreat. A heavy influx of smog in recent years has failed to discourage a steady migration into this affluent area. Here you can visit the Palm Springs Desert Museum, which sponsors hikes to nearby oases, and Moorten's Desertland Botanical Gardens, or take the aerial tramway up to Mount San Jacinto, where you'll get a fine overview of the surrounding desert. You can shop at Saks or join the investment community watching the ticker tape at Merrill-Lynch.

But face it, most people come here for one of two reasons: to see or to be seen. At the height of the winter season, the town probably has more celebrities than any resort in America. This is where Spiro Agnew came to play golf with Frank Sinatra before resigning the vice-presidency. And after being pushed out of office, Richard Nixon came here to console himself at Sunnylands, the home of his friends, the Annenbergs.

However, seeing celebrities here isn't all that easy. Yes, there is a good chance you can run into Gene Autry if you stay at his hotel. But you probably won't find big names like the Firestones, the Kissingers, the Billy Wilders, the Bop Hopes, Truman Capote, Greer Garson, Frederick Loewes, Gloria Swanson, all four Gabors, and the other celebrated residents mingling with common folk here. For that, you'll have to stop off at Smoke Tree Ranch, Melvin's Restaurant at the Ingleside Inn, or such private country clubs as the Thunderbird and the Eldorado. The elite shops on El Paseo Drive in Palm Desert, 13 miles east of Palm Springs, are also a good bet. Be sure to stop off at Beau James's elegant specialty shop, where there's free champagne in the tearoom.

Desert Notes

Choral Pepper's *Guidebook to the Colorado Desert of California* (50¢; Ward Ritchie Press, 474 South Arroyo Parkway, Pasadena, CA 91105) provides a good overview of the Desert Region. Also helpful is *The California Deserts* by Dr. Edmund C. Jaeger ($4.95, Stanford University Press, Stanford, CA 90039).

Informative tour guides on the Mojave Desert and the Colorado River region are available free from the San Bernardino County Economic Development Department, 175 West Fifth Street, San Bernardino, CA 92415. You can also contact the Palm Springs Convention and Visitors' Bureau, Municipal Airport Terminal, Palm Springs, CA 92262; the Needles Chamber of Commerce, P.O. Box 705, Needles, CA 92363; and the El Centro Chamber of Commerce, 660 State Street, El Centro, CA 92243.

For information and authorization to explore the China Lake area for petroglyphs, write Commanding Officer, China Lake Naval Weapons Center, China Lake, CA 93555.

Death Valley Days and Nights

Like Disneyland, Yosemite, and San Simeon, Death Valley is a California name instantly recognized worldwide. Its historic past inspired a television series hosted by Ronald Reagan. Its natural features, embracing all the great divisions of geological time, have been the backdrop for everything from Antonioni pictures to *Oui* magazine photo spreads. And today, more than 500,000 visitors come annually to explore the valley's volcanic craters, dry lake beds, fault scarps, alluvial fans, and other features created by contortions, tiltings, risings, lowerings, and other changes in the earth's crust.

Virtually all these tourists come during the winter and early spring, since the Death Valley heat is unbearable during the summer months. Within this 2-million-acre monument that spills over into Nevada are the hottest (over 130 degrees), driest (as little as 1.5 inches of rainfall annually), and lowest (282 feet below sea level) places on the North American continent. These extremes of climate and geography have given rise to many legends about hundreds of pioneers who perished crossing the valley. But the fact is that only one early emigrant, Captain Robert Culverwell, died in 1849 after making the mistake of striking off on his own when his party was temporarily lost during a valley crossing.

Although you can travel for hours in this region without seeing another person, it is difficult to get lost in Death Valley today. Assuming you come in the winter (February and March are the best months) and follow the marked roads and trails, you'll be able to explore this remote world safely. Stop at the Furnace Creek Visitors' Center, and you'll be able to find out if any bad storms are coming that could trigger a flash flood.

Most visitors to this region come in their own cars. But since the national monument's bumpy roads and sandstorms can rough up your vehicle, consider flying to Las Vegas and renting a car for the drive (150 to 200 miles depending on your route) to Death Valley. If you are coming from the Las Vegas area, you might want to refer to information in Part Three, under Radiation, before selecting a route.

The valley offers a variety of accommodations ranging from comfortable inns to campgrounds at four widely scattered locations. Because of its central location, the Furnace Creek area (site of a historic ranch) is usually the first choice for overnight visitors. But

Death Valley. (*U.S. Department of the Interior, National Parks Service Photo by George A. Grant*)

this region can be crowded, particularly during winter holidays, when hotel reservations are essential. It's also a good idea to check ahead for information on campground availability.

One advantage of staying at Furnace Creek is the ranger talks and slide shows, which provide an easy way to orient yourself to this 130-mile-long valley. Rangers will lead you on walks and car caravans, or you can pick up some of the self-guiding auto tour and trail leaflets. They'll also help you explore remnants of the region's mining heyday.

Rough roads and long distances between key valley sites make the visit to some attractions an all-day trip. In the immediate Furnace Creek area, you'll want to see Zabriskie Point, an upended group of yellow mud hills best viewed shortly after sunrise or late in the afternoon. This site was named after Christian Brevoort Zabriskie, who ran a borax mine here years ago. More recently, it inspired the title of an Antonioni movie. A private group has now filed claims that could lead to strip mining in this scenic region. Environmentalists working to block the excavation are being stymied by a 1933 law opening the region to extractive

industries. Even worse, publicity about the Zabriskie Point controversy has drawn a whole new group of prospectors, anxious to file claims before a mining moratorium can be enacted.

Just beyond Zabriskie Point is Twenty-Mule-Team Canyon, where borax was also once mined. Although the mules never actually worked this region, they did haul boxcars from the Harmony Borax Works north of Furnace Creek to Mojave 165 miles away. It was a three-week round trip over a miserable road frequently obscured by sandstorms. The mules were given a vacation during summer months because the borax works closed after temperatures exceeded 115 degrees (excessive heat interfered with the refining process).

While in this central part of the monument, you can also visit the ruins of the Eagle Borax Works, a salt pan known as Devils Golf Course, and Artist's Drive, which leads you through colorful washes and mud hills (be sure to stop at Artist's Palette along the way). Nearby are Badwater, Natural Bridge, and Dante's View, a great place to watch the sun rise.

Enroute from Dante's View back to S.R. 190, a turn-

Zabriskie Point, Death Valley. (*U.S. Department of the Interior, National Parks Service Photo by George A. Grant*)

off leads to the old company town of Ryan, founded in 1914 and abandoned in 1930. A few homes and buildings still remain. Once back on S.R. 190, you can either head farther into the national monument or drive out of it in the opposite direction to Death Valley Junction, home of the rustic Lila C Café, named after a borax mine located a few miles southwest.

Once a commercial center for the eastern Death Valley mining region, this settlement is now best known for its Amargosa Opera House. Thanks to this institution, Death Valley Junction (population 50) is the smallest town in America regularly offering live ballet. The opera house is the work of ballerina Marta Becket, who performs at 8:15 P.M. on Friday, Saturday, and Monday from mid-October through April, with or without an audience. Because it's impossible to count on a crowd at such a remote location, Ms. Becket has taken the liberty of painting pictures of assorted royalty, nuns, monks, and cherubs on the wall. This silent audience keeps her company on those evenings when no one else can come. If you're in the vicinity of the opera house, make a point of seeing Ms. Becket's remarkable one-woman show.

From here, you can double back on S.R. 190 through Furnace Creek and head north to Stovepipe Wells, the only other site within the monument offering overnight lodging. Located on the edge of the often photographed Death Valley Sand Dunes, this village is the site of an old waterhole once kept open by a piece of stovepipe. Nearby, you can walk along the polished rocks of Mosaic Canyon. Farther south, there's a rough road leading to ruins of the old mining town of Skidoo. Like many other Death Valley settlements, this city was nurtured by a mining boom, with lots going for as much as $1000 each. Settled in 1906, this community's local mining enterprise turned out more than $3 million worth of gold by 1917, when operations closed. All that remains today of this town of 500 is the graveyard.

Continuing south on S.R. 190, you can turn off at Wildrose Station to visit the beehive kilns used to produce charcoal for the Modoc Mine owned by George Hearst. Built by Chinese workers in the 1870s, these 30-foot kilns were supplied with wood by Indian laborers.

Doubling back once again on S.R. 190, you can pick up S.R. 58 at Sand Dunes Junction, which leads east

Thanks to the Armagosa Opera House, Death Valley Junction is the smallest town in America regularly offering live ballet. (*Paul Provins*)

prospectors down a nearby canyon that now bears his name. The three men were never found, and today, a rugged, one-way road leads through this area, which some consider the most scenic locale in all Death Valley. The trip is recommended only for four-wheel-drive vehicles and should not be attempted without prior ranger consultation.

What you'll see on the all-day trip through Titus Canyon are beautiful multicolored rocks that have been sculptured and polished by flash floods. Along the way, you can stop at Leadfield, a lead mining town promoted by hustler C. C. Julian who suckered newcomers in 1926 with special trains from Los Angeles, buffet lunches, jazz bands, and other inducements. But lead taken from the mines didn't measure up, and the town collapsed in 1927.

At the end of the Titus Canyon, you'll reach the main road, where a right turn leads north to a Moorish mansion known as Scotty's Castle. In 1925, Chicago insurance man A. M. Johnson teamed up with local prospector Walter Scott to begin construction of this desert showplace. Six years and $1.5 million later, they had finished a home that included eighteen fireplaces, a two-story living room complete with fish pond, an organ taking up a full room, and a 185-foot swimming pool. Johnson died in 1948; Scott died six years later; today the castle is owned by the National Park Service, which runs daily tours.

A few miles west of the castle you can visit 400-foot-deep Ubehebe Crater as well as half a dozen other pits produced by volcanic explosions. From here, a jeep

to ruins of another old mining boom town, Rhyolite. At one time this community had four papers, two magazines, a symphony, several churches, and numerous bordellos competing for the attention of 6000 residents, who began arriving in 1905 to take advantage of offers of free land.

One of Rhyolite's better known citizens was miner Morris Titus, who got lost while leading two other

Murals in the interior of the Armagosa Opera House guarantee this remote theatre an audience for every performance. (*Paul Provins*)

trail leads on the all-day trip to the Racetrack, supposedly the onetime site of Indian horseracing. Although historians have debunked this claim, geology students can profit from a visit to this dry lake bed as well as to nearby Hidden Valley, where there's an abandoned asbestos mine.

After completing the visit to the monument, most visitors head out via S.R. 190 toward Panamint Springs. But if you're adventurous, consider the remote dirt road that leads north from the Ubehebe Crater region through the Eureka Valley to Owens Valley. Although this route should not be attempted in summer heat, it can be worthwhile during winter and early spring, provided you check first with the rangers about driving conditions. Be sure to stock up with extra gas, food, and water.

Death Valley notes: The basic reference for any trip to this national monument is *Exploring Death Valley* by Ruth Kirk ($2.25, Stanford University Press, Stanford, CA 90039). *Death Valley Ghost Towns* by Stanley W. Paher ($4.95, Nevada Publications, Box 15444, Las Vegas, NE) provides good historical information.

Bus service to Death Valley is offered daily, except Monday, from Las Vegas by the Las Vegas–Tonopah–Reno Stage Line.

Desert Tortoise

Turtles outlive all other vertebrates, including human beings. One of the most fascinating species is the desert tortoise, which has adapted completely to the hardships of life in the barren, arid sections of the Southwest.

When visiting the California desert, keep an eye out for one of these tortoises (completely protected by law) which are up to 12 inches long and can move at speeds up to 20 feet per minute. Because they can't regulate their own body temperature, they hibernate in winter, emerging in spring to forage on grass and plants. Although they can live without food for as long as a year and without water for months, they gorge themselves when an opportunity presents itself. Desert tortoises have been known to increase their body weight by over 40 percent with just one long drink of water.

Adept at hiding, these reptiles are often hard to spot. After they come out of hibernation, they tend to move about when it's cloudy or during the early part of summer days. Generally, the female builds her nest in the summer or fall, and the young hatch between August and November. Although records are not available on the life span of the desert tortoise, it is known that one turtle remained alive in captivity for more than 150 years, and finally died in an accident.

Desert Travel

Many of the dangers associated with desert travel can be eliminated by not exploring this region during the summer. But whenever you go, be sure that your car's cooling system and tires are in top shape. It's a good idea to carry extra water for both yourself and your radiator. If you plan on doing any exploring away from settlements, carry no less than 1 gallon per person per day. Emergency equipment such as flares, first-aid kit, matches, and a compass is mandatory. It won't hurt to take along a shovel, tire pump, and extra gas.

Never try to carve your own road through the desert. This practice, which is outlawed in Death Valley, is a mistake no matter what kind of vehicle you are driving. In an area where it's often a challenge to make it over existing dirt roads, trailblazing is craziness.

If your car's engine overheats, don't turn it off; turn the front end toward the wind and pour some water on the front of the radiator. If you're going into an area where there is any chance of getting stuck in the sand, ask a ranger or gas station attendant ahead of time for tips on how to dig your way out.

You may have read some of the stories about macho types who insist on walking or biking through Death Valley in the summer. So far, three people have killed themselves this way. No matter what anyone tells you, Death Valley is miserable in the summer; you'll be much better off someplace like San Francisco.

Since the valley can get hot other times of year too, be sure to bring sunglasses and a hat and to wear long pants (shorts lead to sunburn). Despite what you may have heard, tarantulas, spiders, and scorpions living in California are not poisonous. Rattlesnakes are and should never be cofronted. Keep a careful eye out for them, particularly in rocky areas, mining ruins, or around wood debris.

Try to begin your trips early in the day, avoid excessive exposure during the middle of the day, travel in pairs, and watch for sunstroke signs such as dizziness or nausea. If you notice these symptoms, feel weak, and stop sweating, it's time to get to a doctor.

And don't forget to also bring along warm clothing, since winter nights in Death Valley can be cold.

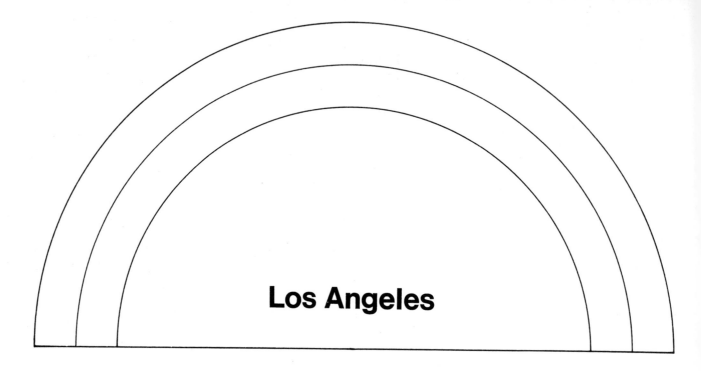

Los Angeles

Best of the Los Angeles Area

State historic park: Will Rogers

Beaches: Zuma; Malibu; Will Rogers; San Clemente City Beach

Urban park: Griffith

Hiking: San Gorgonio Wilderness

Surfing: The Wedge, Balboa Peninsula

Sea lions: Santa Barbara Island

Alligators: California Alligator Farm, Buena Park

Mortuary: Forest Lawn, Glendale

Miniature golf course: Gittelson Brothers, Hollywood

Studio tour: Universal, Universal City

Tar pits: La Brea

Amusement park: Disneyland

Rolls Royce collection: Robert D. Valley Classic Cars, Ltd., Beverly Hills

Parking lot: Home Savings and Loan, downtown Los Angeles

Towers: Watts

Library: Huntington, San Marino

Botanical gardens: Huntington, San Marino

Museum collection: Los Angeles County Art Museum

Small museum: Getty Museum, Malibu

Mission: San Juan Capistrano

Hotel: Bel Air

Sports columnist: Jim Murray

Cartoonist: Paul Conrad

Pizza: La Barbera's, Los Angeles

Delicatessen: Canter's, Los Angeles

Shopping: Beverly Hills

Stadium: Chavez Ravine

Fans: Los Angeles Dodgers

Amtrak station: Union

Overpass: intersection of Harbor, Pasadena, Santa Ana, and San Bernardino freeways

Off-ramp: Santa Monica Freeway westbound to San Diego Freeway southbound

Drive: S.R. 1, Palos Verdes to Malibu

Day views: from Mount Baldy or Malibu Canyon

Night view: San Diego Freeway southbound overlooking west central region from Westwood area

Pinball arcade: Knott's Berry Farm

Newcomers making a reasonable attempt to acquaint themselves with the Los Angeles area soon discover why the petroleum industry characterizes it as the world's greatest gasoline market. The auto is so firmly entrenched here that the local transit company tries to win business by telling the public to look on buses as an "extra car."

Although this region does have an extensive public transit system (see Part Two, under Common Carriers), cars are indisputably a basic necessity here. People think nothing of traveling more than 100 miles a day over the 680-mile freeway system that links the over 100 communities that make up the metropolitan area. And unless you plan carefully, you may well end up spending more time driving than sightseeing in the Los Angeles area.

Unlike most cities, Los Angeles' major attractions

are spread out. It's not practical to try to take in Frederick's of Hollywood, the California Alligator Farm, and Magic Mountain in a single day. Sensible basic sightseeing strategy in Los Angeles dictates that you carefully organize each day's travel into a single locale and avoid, at all costs, driving during the rush hour.

To apply this strategy, you must avoid the temptation to stay in an outlying area. Unless you have come primarily to enjoy one of the beach towns, you'll do well to base yourself in the west central part of the city. Hollywood, the Wilshire District, Beverly Hills, and Westwood are important tourist destinations in themselves. And in each of these areas it's possible to find plenty of entertainment on foot.

We stress these localities because collectively they embrace many of the cultural and commercial features unique to Southern California. Also, they provide a fairly central base for regional sightseeing. Unfortunately, many of the region's leading innovations, such as freeways, drive-ins of all description, and sub-

urban tracts have been so widely imitated nationwide that they no longer impress the newcomer. Most of the promotional emphasis here is on man-made attractions like Busch Gardens, Disneyland, Knott's Berry Farm, and Magic Mountain.

Don't get us wrong: everyone who comes to Los Angeles should sample at least one of these family entertainment centers. But be wary of overcommitting yourself to this programmed world. For in Los Angeles you can enjoy yourself simply checking out the incredible show business billboards on Sunset, lazing on the lawn at Will Rogers State Park, or stopping off downtown on Spring Street at the home of America's only kosher burrito stand.

A good place to start your visit to Los Angeles is the information center of the Southern California Visitors' Council at Seventh and Hope streets, but be wary of their hyperbole about the virtues of visiting an array of skyscrapers nearby. Downtown Los Angeles has long been second-rate, and the city is trying to overcome

Mid-nineteenth-century Los Angeles. (*Courtesy, The Bancroft Library*)

LOS ANGELES,

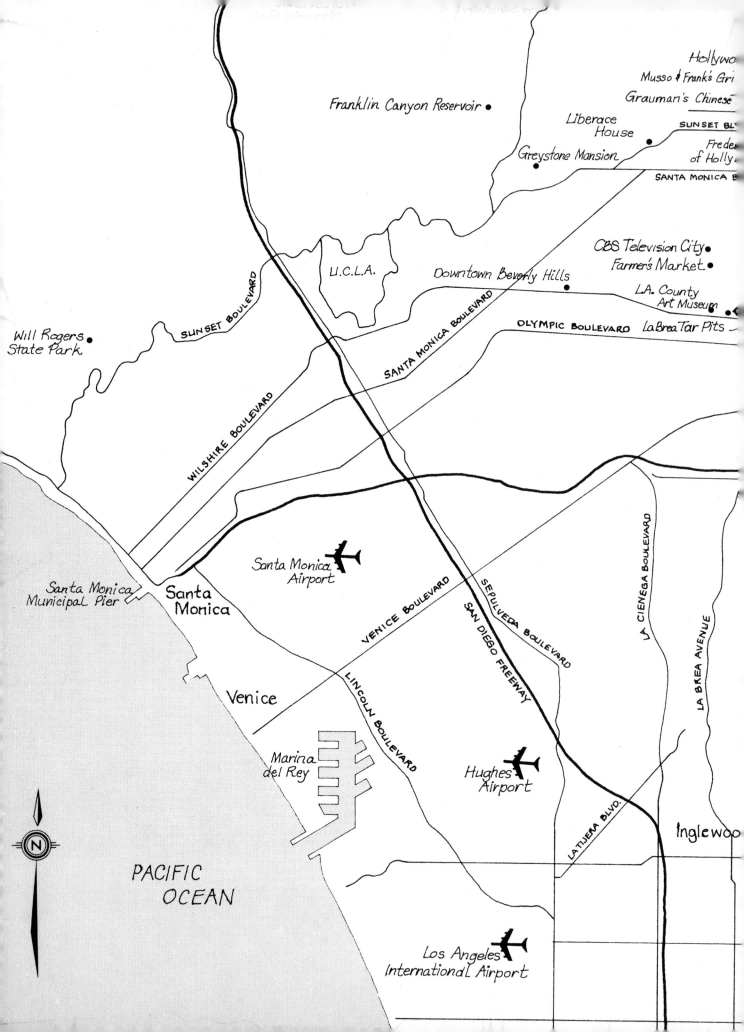

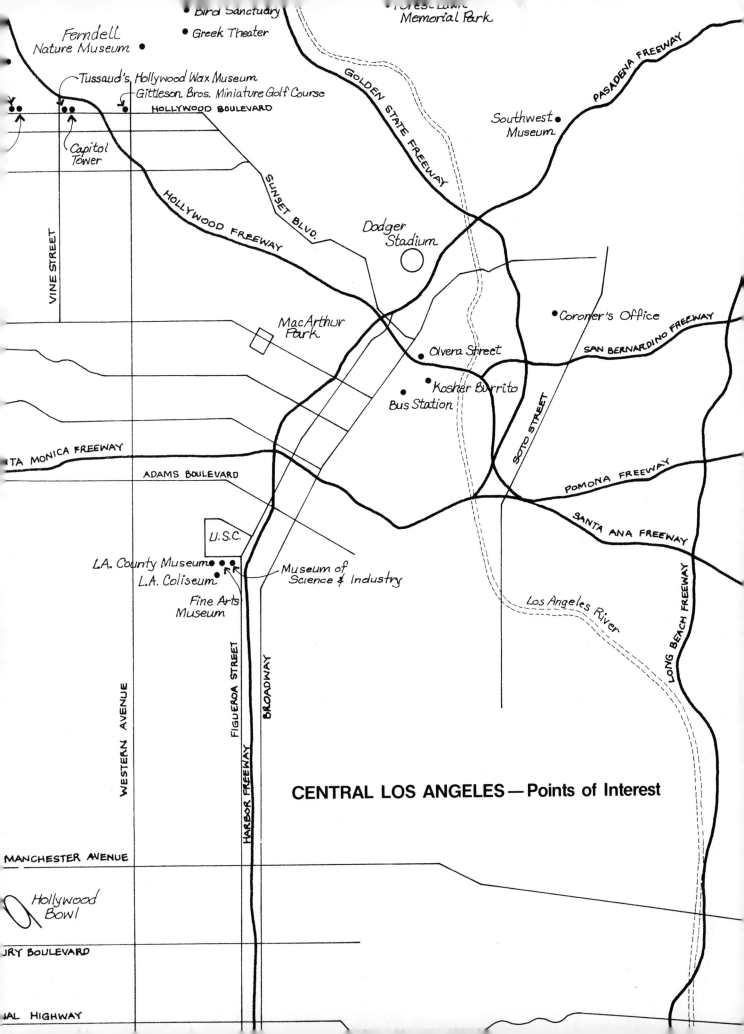

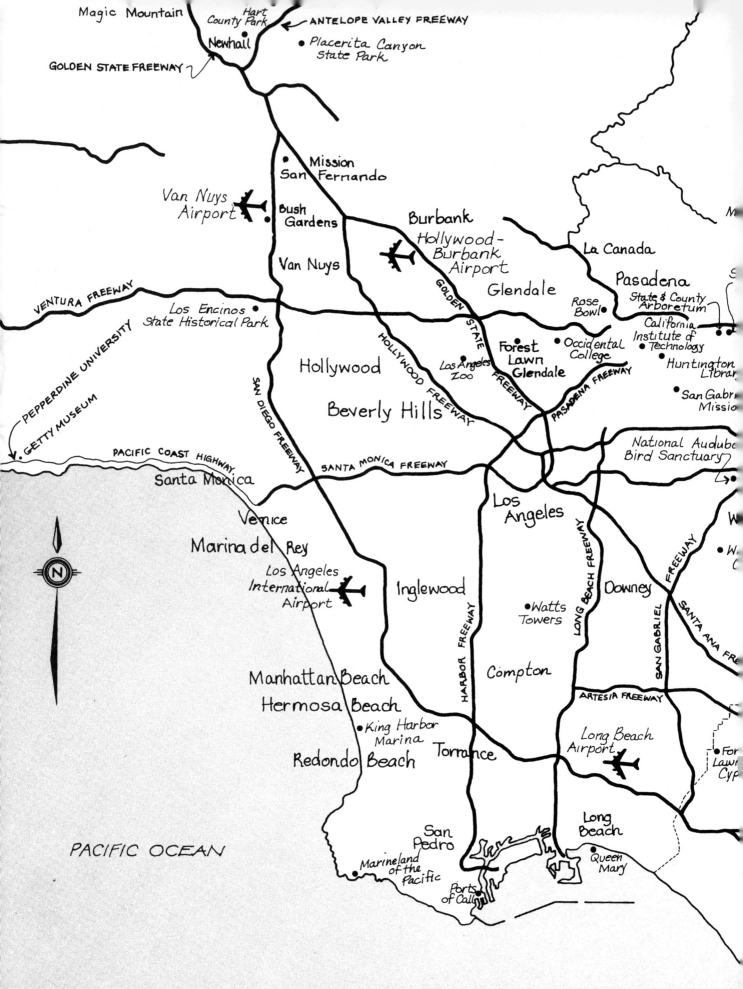

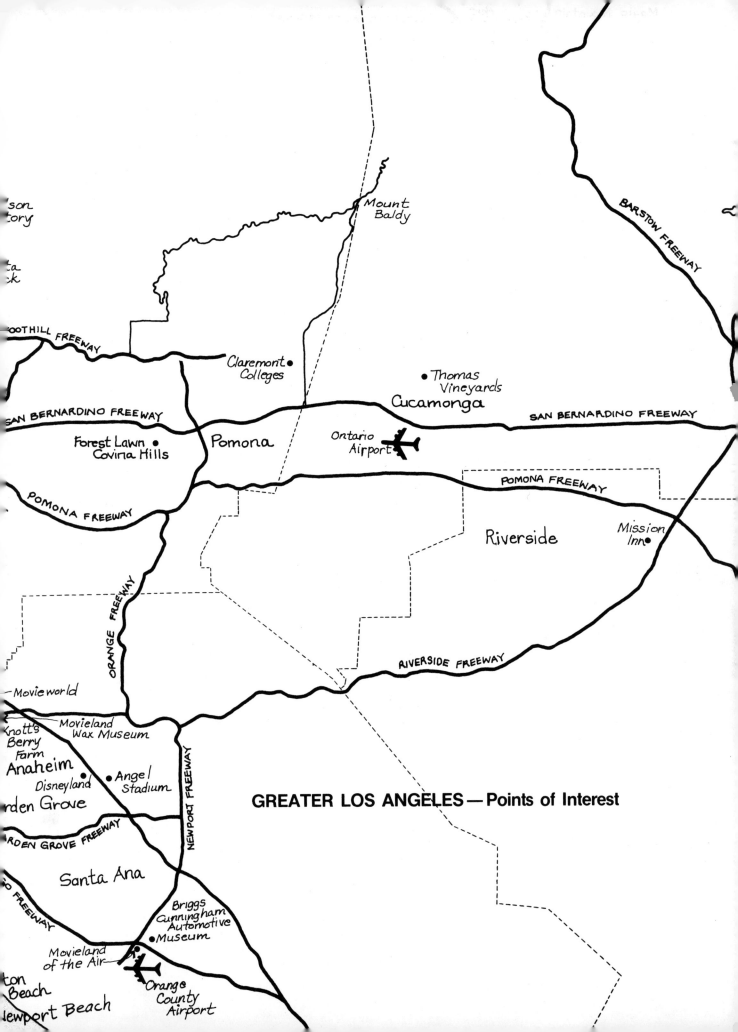

son
tory

a
k

OOTHILL FREEWAY

Claremont •
Colleges

Mount
Baldy

• Thomas
Vineyards

Cucamonga

BARSTOW FREEWAY

SAN BERNARDINO FREEWAY

Forest Lawn •
Covina Hills

Pomona

Ontario
Airport

SAN BERNARDINO FREEWAY

POMONA FREEWAY

POMONA FREEWAY

Riverside

Mission
Inn•

ORANGE FREEWAY

RIVERSIDE FREEWAY

Movieworld

Movieland
Wax Museum

Knott's
Berry
Farm

Anaheim

Disneyland

• Angel
Stadium

den Grove

NEWPORT FREEWAY

GREATER LOS ANGELES — Points of Interest

RDEN GROVE FREEWAY

Santa Ana

FREEWAY

Briggs
Cunningham
Automotive
• Museum

Movieland
of the Air

ton
Beach

ewport Beach

Orange•
County
Airport

Astrological Compatibility Reading and Financial Report. Just about anyone will do your horoscope. But the California Astrology Association will give you a compatibility reading plus a financial report for the low package price of just $7.50 (including postage and handling). Send your name, address, birth date, birthplace, and time of birth to the association, P.O. Box 810, North Hollywood, CA 91603.

Fountains. No home is complete without a fountain, and Rain Jet Corporation of Burbank makes units suitable for every home. From the basic one-tier Crystal Cone ($199.50) to the deluxe three-tier Dancing Jewels ($1887.00), these bowl fountains will delight your friends and astonish your neighbors, particularly when you light them at night. Also available are a line of aquavator submersible assemblies engineered for installation in your own decorative pool or bowl. With these units you can create geyser domes, trumpet jets, crystal canopies, etc. Although some of the larger units are designed for commercial installation, they can be used by homeowners as well. For information, write the firm, 301 South Flower Street, Burbank, CA 91503.

its inferiority complex by touting new commercial, residential, and performance centers. Confine yourself to the old tourist centers like the Mexican shops of Olvera Street as well as the restaurants of Little Tokyo and Chinatown (all accessible via a ten-cent minibus). And be sure to check out the downtown office of Home Savings and Loan, 761 South Broadway, where you'll find the only known grassy parking lot in America. A remarkable new concept called "Grasscrete" allows the company to maintain a lawn on the parking lot which can withstand the traffic.

If you follow Macy Street out of the downtown area to Mission Road and turn left, you'll soon pass beneath the Golden State Freeway and arrive at the office of Los Angeles County Coroner, Thomas Noguchi, who

Frederick's of Hollywood. For a catalogue from this world-famous lingerie shop, send fifty cents to the firm, 6608 Hollywood Boulevard, Hollywood, CA 90028.

Steam Driven Scale Model Trains. Why be tied to Amtrak when you can run your own railroads? Little Engines of Lomita makes a full line of steam-driven locomotives, cars, and tracks suitable for private operation and large enough actually to carry passengers. The scale model kits come with everything necessary to build a miniature line. Among the trains available are the American, C. P. Huntington, Atlantic, Pacific, Northern, and Camelback. For an illustrated catalogue, send $2 to Little Engines, 2135–37 250th Street, Lomita, CA 90717.

has done autopsies on such luminaries as Bobby Kennedy, Sharon Tate, Janis Joplin, Cinque, and Lenny Bruce. Call from the gate and you may be able to visit the modest morgue museum. Exhibits and display cases offer pictures of multiple stab wounds, skulls, and jaws, as well as nooses, hoses, knives, and other items left by suicide victims. For a slightly different perspective on this subject, take the Golden State Freeway north to the Glendale Boulevard exit, where you can drive up to Forest Lawn Memorial Park (see pages 209–210 for details).

Bonsai. One of the nation's best known bonsai dealers, Western Arboretum, offers scores of bonsai with all the supplies necessary to keep them growing. These containerized trees include conifers, palms, bamboo, maples, oaks, elms, and the Chinese scholar tree. Camellias and azaleas are also available. For a catalogue, send $1 (refundable with any order) to the firm, P.O. Box 2827, Pasadena, CA 91105.

Bronze Bagel. This classic paperweight comes packed in its own flannel bag for $14.90 from Propinquity, a Hollywood mail order house specializing in novelties, memorabilia, antiques, and trinkets. Among the specialty items are gold-plated jacks, a 24-karat gold-plated kazoo, high-wheeler bicycles, a finger-paint that turns into bubble bath when hit by water and then washes away completely, as well as a Civil War drum music box that plays the "Battle Hymn of the Republic." To get your catalogue, send 25¢ to Propinquity, 8915 Santa Monica Boulevard, Los Angeles, CA 90069.

Just across the Golden State Freeway from Forest Lawn is Griffith Park, where you'll find the Los Angeles Zoo, an observatory, a Greek theater, a bird sanctuary, and good views of the Los Angeles area on a clear day. The best way to see this carefully protected park is via one of the hiking or riding trails. One of the most pleasant takes you to a nature museum via the brooks, waterfalls, and pools of Ferndell Canyon.

From here, you can drive south to Hollywood Boulevard to visit Grauman's Chinese Theater, the Hollywood Wax Museum (where subjects range from Mahatma Gandhi to Ringo Starr), and F. Scott Fitzgerald's favorite California drinking spot, Musso and Frank's. Heading over to Hollywod and Vine, you'll find landmarks like the Brown Derby and the Pantages Theater amid a motley assortment of massage parlors, topless bars, and X-rated bookstores that local police chief Ed Davis is dedicated to stamping out.

While you're here, you'll find many stores hawking maps that claim to give you the addresses of nearby movie stars' homes. But what with present-day mobility and the high California divorce rate, this information is frequently inaccurate. But one star, Liberace, has opened his Hollywood Hills home to visitors. For $5 you can take the guided tour through the thirty-room residence that includes seventeen grand pianos and a pipe organ. Nothing is off limits. Those who wish can even have a look at the hand-painted toilet seats. There's also a gift shop here where you can buy everything from a 12-inch-high electric candelabrum for $69.95 to a $24.95 hot nut dispenser. (A zoning dispute has forced temporary stoppage of the tour. At press time the matter was before the Los Angeles City Planning Commission, which must decide if and when the tour can be reopened. For information contact Starline Tours, which runs the excursions, at 213–463–3131.)

Another important part of any Hollywood visit is a stop at Gittelson Brothers Golf Course at Hollywood and Western. Here you'll find one of virtually every tree growing in California, as well as big fountains and water hazards on several holes. There's a good assortment of pinball machines too.

Star Homes. If you can't take a tour of the great mansions in Hollywood, Beverly Hills, and Bel Air, then consider buying a copy of the *Stars' Homes Souvenir Magazine.* The color guidebook includes candid shots of the stars and their houses as well as their addresses, astrological signs, birth dates, and real names. Send $2.50 to Starline Sightseeing Tours, Inc., 6845 Hollywood Boulevard, Hollywood, CA 90028.

Los Angeles County Museum of Art Bookshop. Permanent and special exhibition catalogues, audio cassettes of conversations with masters of modern art, slides, prints, posters, reproductions, and postcards are available by mail from the county art museum. These items, which range from the works of the pharaohs to those of Mies van der Rohe, Chagall, Henry Moore, Calder, Claes Oldenburg, and Degas, are listed in a brochure available from the bookshop, 5905 Wilshire Boulevard, Los Angeles, CA 90036.

From Gittelson's, take Hollywood Boulevard west to Fairfax and turn left to the Farmer's Market, which has 160 shopping stalls and a variety of outdoor cafés. Next door is CBS Television City, and south on Fairfax you'll run into the heart of the Los Angeles delicatessen belt. At Wilshire, turn left to the Los Angeles County Art Museum. Immediately behind this building are the La Brea Tar Pits, for thousands of years a death trap for animals. Wildlife mistook the shiny black pools for water and got stuck in the oozy tar. Fortunately, from the archeological standpoint, this heavy asphalt was a superb preservative. Exploration began in 1906, and since that time over 500,000 specimens representing more than 200 different plants, birds, reptiles, insects, and mammals have been recovered. More has been learned about North American Ice Age animals and plants from these pits than from any other single site.

Try to combine a pit tour with a visit to the Museum of Natural History in Exposition Park, where you can see skeletons of the imperial mammoth, mastodons, giant ground sloths, sabertooth cats, camels, bison, and other animals uncovered at La Brea. (While here you can also visit the neighboring Fine Arts Museum and Museum of Science and Industry). Those interested in taking part in future discoveries may want to volunteer their efforts in the current dig at Pit 91. Details on the training and work requirements are available from guides at the La Brea site.

Leaving the museum, take Wilshire west to La Cienega. Turn right and you'll pass through the city's leading restaurant district en route to Sunset, where you should turn left again. This boulevard winds through Beverly Hills (see special section) to the UCLA campus. While here, be sure to visit the botanical garden, which boasts over 3500 species including the impressive bunya-bunya tree from Australia. You should also stop off at the Franklin D. Murphy Sculpture Garden. Fifty major twentieth century works by such sculptors as Rodin, Jacques Lipchitz, and Gaston Lachaise are on

Will Rogers State Park.

ens of stores along the west side of the Los Angeles harbor channel that make up the Ports O'Call shopping complex. In nearby Long Beach harbor, you can tour the *Queen Mary,* which now serves as a floating hotel. Don't put off a visit here if the ship interests you, because financial problems have raised questions about the future of the tourist-hotel complex. Another worthwhile stop is Rancho Los Cerritos, 4600 Virginia Road, where you'll find a beautifully restored Spanish adobe open for tours.

From here, return to the San Diego Freeway westbound, then pick up the Harbor Freeway and head north. If you take the Imperial Highway exit eastbound to Compton Avenue, turn left to 108th Street, turn right to Willowbrook, and left to 107th Street, you'll come to the Towers of Simon Rodia, better known as the Watts Towers. For more than thirty years, this Italian-born tile setter devoted his life to the construction of these remarkable towers covered with bits of pop bottle glass, shells, clay, cement, bathroom tile,

display in this relaxed setting, which doubles as a park.

Resuming your trip west on Sunset, you'll reach Will Rogers State Park, which embraces the ranch of the late columnist, movie star, writer, and humorist. After visiting his home, stables, barn, and polo field, you can head on down to the Pacific Coast Highway. Turning south along the oceanfront (for details, see under San Diego), you'll soon pass Santa Monica's Palisades Park. Home to such celebrities as Jane Fonda, Tom Hayden, and Richard Zanuck, this community's enterprises include everything from Lawrence Welk's headquarters to the Rand Institute. The local pier is one of the Los Angeles area's most popular fishing sites.

To the south you'll find Venice, a community designed in the late nineteenth century to resemble its Italian counterpart. Unfortunately, visions of gondoliers chauffeuring everyone about via canals fell apart due to design problems. Persistent efforts to upgrade the place and improve the canals failed. This was fine with low-income and retired people, who appreciated the reasonable cost of living in this beachfront area. But in recent years the city has undergone a renaissance; the condominium set moved in and plans are being pushed to upgrade the canals. Next door you'll find Marina Del Rey, the site of countless singles complexes as well as more lavish residences that have been home to married folk like the Mark Spitzes. Continuing south on S.R. 1, past the airport, you'll head through two more communities popular with the singles set, Manhattan Beach and Hermosa Beach. The latter community is distinguished as the surfboard manufacturing center of North America. From here you pass into Redondo Beach, a more family-oriented community, and on to posh Palos Verdes Peninsula, the home of Marineland of the Pacific, a major sealife park.

Continuing on to San Pedro, you can visit the doz-

Watts Tower, the remarkable lifework of Simon Rodia.

and other castoff items. Ignoring the taunts of neighbors convinced he was out of his mind, Rodia let nothing stop his progress, not even a wave of earthquakes that jolted the Los Angeles region during the 1930s. The towers survived the seismic shocks and Rodia kept working until in 1954 ridicule turned to harassment. Tired of being persecuted by neighbors who tossed their garbage over his walls, Rodia left Watts, giving the towers to a friend. For four years these remarkable pieces of folk art were persistently vandalized. Finally, in 1958 a committee was established to protect and preserve the towers. Rodia never did come back to Watts. But before his death in 1965, his belittled towers had gained stature as remarkable pieces of folk art. It costs fifty cents to see the towers today, and children will appreciate the fact that visitors are actually encouraged to touch the remarkable monument.

Leaving the towers, resume your trip north on the Harbor Freeway which merges into the Pasadena Freeway (S.R. 11). This, California's original superhighway, will take you to Highland Park, where you should exit west at 43rd Street to Figueroa Street, where you turn left to 42nd Street. Then turn right to Marmion Way and take another right to the Southwest Museum, which contains an extensive collection of Indian artifacts. Nearby, you'll find more Indian objects at El Alisal, the Lummis home, and at Casa De Adobe, a replica of a Spanish era ranch house.

Huntington Library Reproductions and Books. San Marino's distinguished Huntington Library offers reproductions of a wide number of significant items in its book, manuscript, and art collections by mail. Particularly useful are moderately priced Christmas and note cards with color reproductions of popular art works. Facsimiles of proclamations, playbills, posters, and other significant American historical documents are available, as well as needlepoint kits adapted from eighteenth-century needlework in the collection. The Huntington also publishes scholarly books, occasional exhibition catalogues, and facsimiles of books in the library collection, such as Davy Crockett's *Almanack* for 1873, *Cinderella,* and William Blake's *Songs of Innocence and of Experience.* The publication catalogue includes a number of scholarly volumes on California and the Southwest. To obtain the library's lists of books in print and reproductions from the Huntington collections, write the Huntington Library, San Marino, CA 91108.

Returning to the freeway, head into Pasadena, where the Arroyo Parkway leads north to California Boulevard. Here you should turn right to Allen Avenue, where another right turn will take you to the Huntington Library, Art Gallery, and Botanical Gardens. This complex is best known for its remarkable gardens, where there are plants in bloom at every season of the year. For instance, in the North Vista, you'll find seventeenth-century Italian statues bordering a lawn surrounded by azaleas and camellias. The Rose Garden features hundreds of varieties, including America's largest collection of tea roses. The Japanese Garden is actually a 5-acre landscaped canyon that includes a furnished Japanese house and a Zen garden. Best of all is the 12-acre desert garden, which embraces the largest outdoor desert plant collection in the world. Be sure to visit the library, which houses over 500,000 books and is regularly used by scholars from all over the world. The art gallery, which was originally the residence of the Henry E. Huntington family, focuses primarily on eighteenth- and nineteenth-century British art. Among the famed paintings in this collection is Gainsborough's *Blue Boy.*

While in the area, you may also want to stop off at the San Gabriel Mission in nearby San Gabriel, where there's an extensive collection of paintings by Spanish and Mexican artists. Also in the area are two wildlife sanctuaries, the Audubon Center in El Monte and the Los Angeles State and County Arboretum in Arcadia. At the latter, be sure to visit the Lasca Lagoon, which has formed the backdrop for numerous Tarzan movies.

Next, consider visits to some of the major sites in Los Angeles' outlying districts. Since you're probably going to Disneyland, we've set aside an adjoining section on the subject. While in Orange County, you may also want to stop off at Knott's Berry Farm, where you can visit a nineteenth-century ghost town, Independence Hall, Knott's Lagoon, Gypsy Camp, and the John Wayne Theater. The only berries you'll find on the farm are in pies and jellies. Walter Knott's famed vines have all been torn out to make way for more tourists.

Across the street from Knott's is the California Alligator Farm, which has one of the world's largest reptile collections. Nearby, at 7711 Beach Boulevard in Buena Park, you'll find Movieland Wax Museum and Palace of Living Art. Here under one roof are likenesses of 125 great stars plus reproductions of 70 famed paintings and sculptures. On display you'll find the world's only wax copies of the Mona Lisa, Venus de Milo, and Whistler's Mother. A few miles away, at 6900 Orangethorpe Avenue in Buena Park, you can visit the allied Movieworld Cars of the Stars and Planes of Fame museums. In the former, you'll find Al Jolson's 1929 Mercedes; at the latter, German Messerschmitts and a Japanese Zero. More World War I and II fighters as well as planes used in many feature films are on display at Movieland of the Air at the Orange County Airport in Santa Ana. And nearby, at 250 Baker Street in Costa Mesa, you can see the vehicle collection at Briggs Cunningham Automotive Museum.

Farther south, at Irvine, you'll find one of the nation's first drive-in wildlife parks, Lion Country Safari. Here visitors take their own cars past elephants, rhinos, giraffes, ostriches, lions, and many other species. Picking up Interstate 5 south, head on to San Juan Capistrano, where you'll find the most picturesque of all the California missions. Unfortunately, developers have had a heyday here erecting a thicket of gaudy shops.

From here, you can head south to San Clemente or west to Dana Point (where Richard Henry Dana did his on-the-job research for *Two Years Before the Mast*) and visit some of the oceanfront shops at Mariner's Village before returning north on S.R. 1. After passing through Laguna Beach, you'll come to the Newport Beach–Balboa area, home to such celebrities as H. R. Haldeman and John Wayne. Here you can take the harbor cruise or ride the ferry over to Balboa Island, crowded with shops catering to the tourist trade.

After completing your visit to Orange County, set aside some time to visit the San Gabriel and San Bernardino mountain areas to the east of Los Angeles. Take S.R. 2, the Angels Crest Highway, out of La Canada to the Wrightwood resort area, where you can link up with S.R. 138 and head on toward Crestline. Here you can pick up the Rim of the World Highway to the popular Lake Arrowhead area as well as nearby Big Bear Lake. To the north is Holcomb Valley, site of Southern California's richest gold field, accidentally discovered in 1860 by a bear hunter. A few mine structures remain in the area. Looping back on S.R. 38, you'll reach one of Southern California's most popular hiking regions, the San Gorgonio Wilderness. On your return to Los Angeles, detour through Riverside to see the expansive Mission Inn, once a favorite spot for vacations and celebrations (the Richard M. Nixons were married here in 1940). Another good stop is Thomas Vineyards, 8916 Foothill Boulevard, Cucamonga. Built in 1839, this winery is the first in California and the second oldest in the United States. There's also a cutoff in Claremont leading to the top of Mount Wilson. Here you can visit the renowned observatory and enjoy the Los Angeles view.

Heading north from Los Angeles, you'll find a good variety of historic sites, recreation areas, and amusement parks. Take the San Diego Freeway (Interstate 405) to the Ventura Freeway westbound (U.S. 101) and head south at the Balboa Boulevard exit to Moorpark Street, where you turn left to visit the De La Osa Adobe at Los Encinos State Historic Park. From here, take Balboa Boulevard northbound to Roscoe Boulevard and turn right to Busch Gardens, an entertainment

center featuring a free-flight aviary with more than 200 rare and endangered species of birds. Next take Interstate 405 north to the San Fernando Mission Boulevard exit, where you head east to visit Mission San Fernando. The church is all that remains today of the original complex. The other structures were demolished in 1887 at the behest of a padre who had succumbed to the boom generated by the railroads.

Leaving the mission, take Interstate 5 north to S.R. 14, where you can exit at Newhall Avenue to William S. Hart County Park. Named for the silent-screen star who left this ranch to the county, the park is popular with children, who come to see a variety of farm animals. Hart's old ranch house complete with Indian rugs, old movie props, antique guns, and paintings by Charles M. Russell is open to visitors. From here, you can take San Fernando Avenue over to Placerita Canyon Road and head east to Placerita Canyon State Park. Some now claim California gold was first discovered here in 1842—six years before James Marshall made his famous find at Sutter's Mill. While historians try to straighten out the record, you can pan for gold here, hike to a waterfall, and visit the nature center. Returning to Interstate 5, you can drive on to yet another Southern California amusement park, Magic Mountain. Some of the rides here, such as the roller coaster, are a bit wilder than anything you'll find at Disneyland.

One more corridor worth exploring in the Los Angeles area leads northwest from Santa Monica along S.R. 1. At Malibu is the remarkable J. Paul Getty Museum situated on a hill overlooking the Pacific. An expanded collection in a new building has drawn so much interest that it's advisable to call ahead (213-459-2306) to make sure parking space is available. Visitors drive in over a Roman cobblestone road, park in the garage, and are transported to the villa, which has a 300-foot-long pool, formal gardens, abundant statuary, marble stairways, Corinthian columns, bronze doors, tapestries, French chandeliers, etc. Unlike San Simeon, the art work here has been carefully divided into three collections: Greek and Roman antiquities, Western European paintings, and the French decorative arts.

Continuing north along the coast, you'll reach Ventura, the jumpoff point to the Channel Islands. Tight restrictions have effectively closed all but Santa Barbara and Anacapa islands to the public. Because there are no docking facilities here for private vessels, virtually all visitors come via tour and charter boats. If you take the trip, you'll find abundant wildlife on these islands, which have been designated a national monument. Hundreds of sea lions live on Santa Barbara, while Anacapa has abundant birdlife. Modest camping facilities are available on Anacapa's East Island under permit from the Channel Islands National Monument

Avalon Harbor and casino on Catalina.

Office, 1699 Anchors Way Drive, Ventura, CA 93003. For information on boats leaving for the Channel Islands from Ventura and nearby Oxnard, write the Island Packer Company, P.O. Box 993, Ventura, CA 93001.

From Ventura, consider taking the long way back through the Ojai Valley. Follow S.R. 33 to S.R. 150, which leads to the town of Ojai, where local artists exhibit their work outdoors every Sunday. From here, continue on S.R. 126 to Interstate 5, where you turn south toward Los Angeles.

Los Angeles Notes

The Southern California Visitors' Council, 705 West Seventh Street, Los Angeles, CA 90017, is a good general source of information on this area. Also helpful are the Anaheim Area Visitors' and Convention Bureau, 800 West Katella Avenue, Anaheim, CA 92802; the Long Beach Convention and News Bureau, Inc., 555 East Ocean Boulevard, Suite 718, Long Beach, CA 90802; and the Greater Ventura Chamber of Commerce and Visitors' and Convention Bureau, 785 South Seward, Ventura, CA 93003.

The What, When and Where Guide to Southern California, by Basil C. Wood ($2.95, Doubleday, Garden City, NY 11530) provides valuable route information on how to reach many of the major regional attractions. Also helpful are Russ Leadabrand's *Exploring California Byways, II, In and Around Los Angeles* as well

as his *Guidebook to the San Gabriel Mountains of California* (each 50¢, Ward Ritchie Press, 474 South Arroyo Parkway, Pasadena, CA 91105). Another helpful guide is George Lowe's *Where Can We Go This Weekend?* ($2.95, J. P. Tarcher, 9110 Sunset Boulevard, Los Angeles, CA 90069).

Catalina

This 76-square-mile island located 21.8 miles southeast of Los Angeles Harbor is one of the few places in California where the automobile isn't king. In Avalon, Catalina's sole town, strict legislation limits the number and size of cars, and visitors find it impossible to rent anything bigger than a motorized golf cart. Speed limits are sharply enforced, the main drag is a pedestrian mall, and back roads that traverse the mountainous terrain are open only to those who purchase expensive permits. In short, Catalina is California without traffic.

Catalina's many ardent admirers tout the place as a south sea idyll. This seems excessive. Although the island is blessed with lovely coves, good skindiving, abundant wildlife, and fine views, it is hardly a lush, subtropical paradise. The climate is dry, the mountainsides are usually brown, the water is chilly much of the year, the scenic cliffs are frequently buried in fog, and it is not easy to get out of Avalon, where the narrow beach fronts on a compact swimming area squeezed into the harbor. Unless you have your own oceangoing boat or are willing to make the arduous hike into the back country, you'll find it difficult to reach the island's marvelous, secluded beaches.

But if you hit Catalina right, the place can be splendid. In the spring when the hills turn green or in the early fall when the crowds are gone and the ocean is still fairly warm, Catalina is one of California's finest refuges. You'll find Avalon, a town of 2000, blessed with lovely gardens, fine houses, and good fishing as well as a variety of rides and cruises that will keep you busy rubbernecking for days. You can stay at one of thirty-eight hotels, inns, and lodges, ranging from $50-a-day bungalows at Las Casitas to $8-a-night rooms at the modest Hermosa Hotel. Although Avalon offers the only year-round accommodations, you can also backpack to campsites in the island's interior, where you'll be virtually by yourself. For although Catalina is easily accessible to the mainland (an hour and forty-five minutes by boat or fifteen minutes by plane), most of the 500,000 annual visitors limit themselves to Avalon during the hectic summertime.

It was Juan Rodríguez Cabrillo, the Portuguese-born navigator, who found Catalina for Spain in 1542, shortly after discovering the California mainland. Ownership of the island passed through numerous hands until chewing-gum magnate William Wrigley, Jr., bought it in 1919 for $3 million. He was so impressed with his acquisition that he began bringing his Chicago Cubs here for spring training. Sportswriters began talking it up, and soon Catalina's reputation spread throughout the country. In 1929, Avalon built a vast casino ballroom that hosted all the big band names—Benny Goodman, Bob Crosby, Kay Kyser—during the 1930s. On a hill overlooking the casino, Zane Grey mass-produced his western novels. And all the while the island kept attracting leading Hollywood stars like Charles Laughton and Clark Gable, who made *Mutiny on the Bounty* here.

To this day, Catalina's remote areas remain a favorite location for California film directors searching for a convenient island setting. Indeed, it is Hollywood that has left Catalina one of its more interesting legacies. In 1924, a small herd of buffalo was brought over to form part of the supporting cast for a film called *The Vanishing American.* To save the expense of freighting his buffalo back to the mainland, the producer donated these animals to the island. Over the years they have multiplied to a herd of more than 300. Frequently these buffalo come down to graze on inhabited sections of the island.

Three other animals introduced to the island—deer, boar, and goat—have unfortunately denuded much of the Catalina landscape. To limit the proliferation of these species, some hunting is allowed in fall and winter. However, the valuable buffalo herd is off-limits. A hunter who shoots one accidentally is fined $2000 and required to provide a replacement buffalo.

All these animals, plus a few llamas, can be seen on the 66-mile (three hour and forty-five minute) Inland Motor Tour, which includes stops at Catalina's mountaintop airport, the Wrigley ranch, and an old stage coach stop. This $7.25 bus trip is the only way to get a good look at the island's interior short of hiking or camping in this rugged back country. Happily, just about everything you see on the trip will continue to be preserved in its natural state. That's because in 1975 the Wrigley family donated 86 percent of the island (42,135 acres) to a nature conservancy. Besides protecting most of Catalina from development, the gift land includes an open-space easement that broadens opportunities for hiking, camping, and backpacking.

Of course, the Wrigleys' gift netted them a big tax break. But at the same time, they have ensured that the island will not be overcommercialized like the rest of Southern California. The two family residences, one in Avalon overlooking the harbor and the other at El Rancho Escondido in the back country, are plush yet unobtrusive. (You can walk to the former and see the latter on the Inland Motor Tour.) And back at the head of Avalon Canyon, they have built the Wrigley Memorial and Botanic Gardens. Beneath a monument to the late William Wrigley, Jr., is the garden, featuring cacti, succulents, and over 100 of the other 393 species of plant life native to the region. Six of these—Catalina ironwood, Saint Catherine's lace, Catalina mahogany, wild tomato, Catalina manzanita, and live forever—are native only to the island itself.

Like most of Avalon, the memorial garden is easily accessible by bike. But you'll probably find it easier to walk rather than bike uphill to the Zane Grey pueblo, where the prolific western novelist lived the last years of his life. After the writer's death in 1939, new owners converted the expansive home into a hotel. Instead of numbering the rooms, they named each of them after a Grey novel. This involved some complicated decision making, because the author's eighty-nine books are more than triple the number of rooms. On your visit be sure to drop by the lounge, which used to be Grey's living-dining room. It's distinguished by a hewn-plank door, log-mantled fireplace, and a beam ceiling made from teak the writer brought back from Tahiti on one of his periodic fishing trips.

After you've finished exploring the town and grown tired of horseback riding, golf, and tennis, consider taking one of the island's numerous cruises. Catalina likes to boast that it launched the first successful glass- bottom boat in 1896. The island Visitors' Bureau claims that the present-day version of this trip "can be compared only with the glass bottom boat trips of Bermuda and the Great Barrier Reef of Australia." Such exaggeration aside, Catalina does boast clear waters that reveal a wide variety of marine life. In the evening there's also a special nocturnal fish boat trip in which 40-million-candlepower searchlights bring fish soaring out of the water. Watch your step, as some of the fish usually land on deck. After the ride ends, you can stop off for a drink at the town's only nightclub, the Chi Chi.

Perhaps a more worthwhile boat trip is the 14-mile ride to Two Harbors. This small village is the base for many of the camping, backpacking, and hunting trips. Good beaches, a restaurant, and limited accommodations are available. A University of Southern California Marine Science Laboratory offers occasional tours and has a decompression chamber that will help you avoid the bends should you get careless while scuba diving. Two Harbors, incidentally, is the place where Howard Hughes's *Glomar Explorer* retreated after it was revealed that the vessel had been digging up Russian submarines for the CIA.

At Two Harbors you'll also see some of the many yachts frequenting Catalina year around. They come by the thousands to explore the various coves. This is the ideal way to see the island's largely undeveloped coast. Even the backpackers climbing up and down Catalina's mountains can't reach all these picturesque locations. But if you don't have your own boat, Catalina still offers a welcome contrast to the kind of high-pressure tourism that abounds in much of Southern California. Here is one place where you can relax without being bored. Catalina is no Maui, but then again it's a long way from the Pomona Freeway.

Catalina Notes

Catalina is reached by Long Beach–Catalina Cruises from Long Beach Harbor and Catalina Motor Cruisers (summer only) from the San Pedro Harbor. Air service is offered by Air Catalina, Catalina Air Lines, and Golden West Airlines (summer only). For hotel information, reservations, and general information, write the Catalina Chamber of Commerce, Avalon, CA 90704, or phone 213–547–2030. Tour reservations, tickets, and information are also available from the Visitors' Information and Services Center, Box 1159, Avalon, CA 90704 (phone Avalon 1111). Camping reservations can be made through the Visitors' Center, Santa Catalina Island Conservancy, P.O. Box 1547, Avalon, CA 90704 (phone Avalon 1421) and the Los Angeles County Department of Parks and Recreation, 155 West Washington Boulevard, Los Angeles, CA 90015 (phone 213–749–6941, Ext. 822). In addition, camping and hunting reservations are handled by the Catalina Cove and Camp Agency, P.O. Box 1566, Avalon, CA 90704 (phone Avalon 303 or 213–547–4882).

Disneyland

From the second you arrive in the parking lot, Disney-

land's management is shouting at you over the public address system to get in line for one of the trams headed toward the front gate. There you pay $5 or $7 to get past guards who refuse to let you bring in your picnic lunch. Inside you walk down Main Street, where you can get a free look at a reproduction of Walt Disney's personal office, buy plastic flowers, have your personal portrait painted simultaneously with fourteen other people, or pay a quarter to enter a seatless theater showing six silent movies on different screens.

Farther down in the plaza, a midget named Little Oscar slips you a ring with a red plastic Oscar Mayer hot dog on it. Then you walk over to take a picture at one of the designated spots on the GAF photo trail. There is no need to consult your light meter because professionals have already predetermined the appropriate setting for various films under any lighting condition. You can take perfect pictures, just like the 140 million people preceding you.

Being adventurous, you decide to try the people mover, a futuristic transportation system designed to help relieve urban traffic congestion. But you give up after finding the wait is twenty-five minutes. Hungry, you head back to a restaurant, where there's a half-hour line, and you curse the guard who made you dump your lunch. So you sit down in the plaza until you find the street being roped off for a parade of giant Disney characters. There's Mickey Mouse, his spouse Minnie, Snow White, the dwarfs, and Donald Duck. And damn it if that isn't Goofy riding along on a float waving the American flag while the PA system blares a chorus of "This Land Is Your Land." Woody Guthrie in Disneyland! Why, he would have never been around in Walt's day.

But the founder has been gone for nearly a decade now, and the $150 million Anaheim amusement park off the Santa Ana Freeway at Harbor Boulevard is a bigger, more polished place. And as the park and crowds grow, the lack of practical advice from man-

Mickey Mouse and friends. (*Disneyland Publicity Department*)

agement makes it a tricky place to visit. But anyone, even a person who comes prepared to hate it, can have a good time if he plans ahead.

It's important to understand that Disneyland is not just another amusement park, but a semiautomated environment that must be appreciated selectively. You have to pick and choose while being sure to relax occasionally to take in some of the free attractions. One of the most remarkable is the army of enthusiastic young cleanup crews who keep the place squeaky clean. Somehow they manage to snatch up every piece of paper instantly.

There is endless debate on the matter of how long you should allow to take in Disneyland's attractions. Chances are you've heard the propaganda about how "you can't see it all in one day." That's true, but who in his right mind would want to see everything? One day every couple years is enough for anyone but a Disneyland junkie.

If possible, your visit should not be during the peak summer period, mid-June through September, when the park is open from 8 A.M. to 1 A.M. Come, instead, during a non-holiday, off season period when the park is open on a Wednesday-Sunday schedule from 10 A.M. to 6 P.M. The best days are Wednesday and Thursday. Assuming things are slow, you can peacefully work your way up Main Street, move in through Tomorrowland, and then work your way across through Fantasyland, Frontierland, Bear Country, New Orleans Square, and Adventureland. But during the summer, weekends, and holiday periods, you need to adopt special line-beating strategies to avoid the 45 minute (and longer) waits at the popular rides.

First bear in mind that the park is popular with families and children during the morning and early afternoon, while teenagers tend to arrive in droves during the late afternoon and evening. If you're on your own, without children in tow, a good approach is to arrive early, skip the Main Street stores (you can buy mouse ears at the Disneyland hotel or outside the park without wasting precious time) and head straight for the most popular teenage rides, like the Pirates of the Caribbean and the Haunted Mansion. After riding on the Matterhorn Bobsleds, go back to the Adventureland-Frontierland-New Orleans Square-Bear Country side of the park. Next stop at Tomorrowland (lines drop off during lunch and the mid-afternoon parade) and end up over at Fantasyland, the kiddie favorite, late in the day after most families or small children have gone. Use the evening to catch up on attractions you couldn't make during the day. Variations of this basic strategy are good for families too.

On entering the park, adults should probably get the 15 ticket book for themselves ($7) and the 11 ticket book for any children they have with them ($5 to $5.50, depending on age). The books are divided into five types of coupons, increasing in value from A (10¢) through E (85¢).

Using all your tickets on a busy day can be a challenge, so first familiarize yourself with the park layout. The heaviest concentration of major rides is found in Fantasyland and Tomorrowland. There are some other key rides scattered throughout other sections, but in those much of the emphasis is on exploring treehouses and islands as well as on a variety of boat trips and shooting galleries.

No matter what your preference, you'll do well to arrive when the gates open and head straight for the popular E rides such as the Submarine Voyage, the Haunted Mansion, the Pirates of the Caribbean, It's a Small World, the Country Bear Jamboree, and the Matterhorn Bobsleds.

Since you don't want to get ripped off on the high-priced Es, be sure each of these attractions is for you. Tomorrowland's Submarine Voyage was an early E ticket and popular from its inception in 1959. Disneyland likes to boast that these eight passenger vessels give the famed park one of the largest submarine fleets in the world. But unfortunately, the plunge is simulated, and you don't even submerge completely. What you get is a ride around a shallow lagoon where plastic sealife dangles outside the window. In a state that has fine tidepools plus outstanding marine parks like Sea World in San Diego and Marineland in Palos Verdes, such artificiality seems shabby. Disney's attempt to make it an adventure with mermaids and sea serpents only adds to the phoniness.

In Fantasyland, the Matterhorn Bobsleds are Disney's

Disneyland at dusk. The Matterhorn, the Monorail, and the Submarine Voyage. (*Disneyland Publicity Department*)

major concession to the amusement park tradition. Four passenger sleds on two different runs wind in and out of the artificial mountain. On the drop down, they skim waterfalls and offer good views of the park before splashing into glacier lakes at the bottom. You'll wait thirty to ninety minutes for this brief ride. But most people find it hard to miss. No real steep falls. Just a lot of fast fun.

Fantasyland's other big E attraction is It's a Small World. Originally designed for the 1964–1965 New York World's Fair, this trip carries passengers by boat through the 1400-foot-long Seven Seaways and features 297 miniature model children representing 100 nations. All are singing about the virtues of world friendship. This extremely popular attraction has been seen by 40 million and goes over big with kids, but some adults find it like swallowing a bottle of saccharin. And even people who enjoy the ride are turned off by the Small World Gift Shop that greets them just after emerging from this world of brotherly love.

Across the park in New Orleans Square, you'll find one of the park's best E tickets, the Haunted Mansion. A decade in the making, this $7 million spook house opened in 1969. You ride through the place in "doom buggies," while hordes of Disney terrorists come rushing at you. Although the trip is not really frightening, keep in mind that it might scare a small child. Another good ride in this part of the park is the Pirates of the Caribbean. For this ride, you board a flat-bottomed bateau, plunge down a waterfall, pass through pirate caves and into the midst of an all-out war. You see fighting, plundering, looting, shooting, and just about every form of mayhem short of rape.

The Country Bear Jamboree in nearby Bear Country offers a chance to see Disney's patented Audio-Animatronics that synchronizes voice and body movements to give animated objects lifelike qualities. This comical music show, sponsored by ubiquitous Wonder Bread (corporate sponsors are everywhere at Disneyland—even the park's memorial to Walt Disney is backed by Gulf Oil), is good for children as well as adults who enjoy listening to the antics of eighteen bears, a raccoon, buffalo, stag, and moose.

If you enjoy the Country Bear Jamboree, consider also the Enchanted Tiki Room (Adventureland) and America Sings (Tomorrowland) which, between them, feature more talking animals, loquacious birds, flowers, and tiki gods. They sing, tell legends, do western numbers, and otherwise carry on in the stage show format. But you can probably live without them, at least until later in the day when you've had a chance to finish up high-priority rides.

Neither of the remaining E tickets, Adventureland's Jungle Cruise and the Monorail that links Tomorrowland with the Disneyland Hotel, can be considered crucial. One of the park's original rides, the Jungle

Trip, carries passengers down a man-made river filled with artificial alligators, fake hippos, and spear-chucking natives. Such prestigious Disneyland alumni as Ron Ziegler have guided tourists through this land, where lions, elephants, and rhinos wail in the background. But the trip's a drag. Any smart six-year-old will see the cruise for the phony hype it really is.

You can also consider the $5.6 million Monorail optional unless you think you'll be charmed by a panoramic view of the Disneyland parking lot. The train, inaugurated in 1959 by Richard Nixon, doesn't show you much more of the park than you can see from the skyway linking Tomorrowland and Fantasyland (a D ticket and worth it). And a good share of the ride doesn't reveal anything but the roofs of cars as you speed over the parking lot toward the Disneyland Hotel. If you happen to be staying here, this is the logical way to get back and forth to the park. Otherwise, skip it.

Should the lines make it impossible to get on the E rides of your choice, turn to some of the less crowded attractions for the rest of the morning. This might be a good time to try the Flight to the Moon (D) or Adventure Through Inner Space (C), both in Tomorrowland. You could also take a ride on the Santa Fe and Disneyland Railroad (D), which circles the park (other stations are at Main Street and New Orleans Square). The train provides a view of the park, although the tunnel ride past the Grand Canyon diorama fails to measure up to advance billing.

Since ride lines generally slack off during lunchtime, you should skip the crowded restaurants and grab a hot dog or sandwich at one of the fast-food outlets. Then immediately make an effort to squeeze in some more E trips. If the waits remain long, head to Frontierland and take a ride on the Mark Twain Paddle-wheel Steamboat (D) or the Mike Fink Keel Boats (C). Both these trips are particularly good when you're traveling with grandparents or small children.

Another good bet for families is Frontierland's Tom Sawyer Island linked with the mainland via raft (D). This is perfect for kids, so plan to spend an hour here as they crawl through tunnels, forts, and mining shafts, play on a teeter-totter rock, or run across the barrel bridge. The island is also a fine place for parents to rest because it's impossible to lose kids unless they decide to sneak back to the mainland alone.

After finishing up on the island, have lunch (Casa de Fritos in Frontierland is a good choice) and decide whether you want to stay around the plaza for Disneyland's daily parade. (Check with the park for parade times.) What you'll see is a flock of flag-waving Disneyites march in from Fantasyland en route to Main Street. What you'll hear blasted out the PA system is preprogrammed music mixed with a Moog synthesizer. What you'll feel is the elbows of people around you as they jockey for a better view of Donald Duck. What you'll miss is a good shot at the popular rides while most visitors are watching the procession.

During summer months the best parade is in the evening, when there's also a special fireworks show. But if you won't be staying until evening and insist on seeing the afternoon march, be sure to line up well in advance of the 3 P.M. starting time to assure yourself a good view. Otherwise, you may miss seeing the dwarfs entirely.

Those who are able to skip the afternoon parade should head straight for Fantasyland. This is an ideal time to get your children into some of the best attractions. For here the park has effectively used themes to make rides entertaining rather than simply bumpy or frightening. Although there are some good amusement-park-type rides, all are done with imagination. For example, instead of the traditional scrambler, Disneyland has put cups and saucers into a Mad Tea Party (C). And instead of just soaring around in planes, you get to ride in Dumbo Flying Elephants (C). And the Casey Jr. Circus Train (B) puts children in traditional circus gondolas for an interesting ride past Geppetto's Village, Cinderella's Dream Castle, Mr. Toad's Mansion, and other miniature settings from Disney's animated films.

Fantasyland also has a variety of other good offerings. The Alice in Wonderland (B) attraction is the best of the spook house rides for small children. The Peter Pan Flight (C) and Mr. Toad's Wild Ride (C) are good, while the King Arthur Carousel (no two animals here are identical) is the perfect location to use up your A ticket.

By late afternoon, families with small children will want to begin winding up. From the plaza you can walk back up Main Street or catch a ride on one of several vehicles (A). Take a look in the shops if you want, but skip the Main Street Cinema (B) because there's no place to sit down. In the town square near the entrance, you'll find *The Walt Disney Story*, featuring *Great Moments with Mr. Lincoln!* A collection of Disney artifacts, including the founder's old Burbank office, are on display here. After making you stand up to watch a film about the founder's life, the park lets you sit down and listen to Honest Abe. Unlike most other major attractions in the park, this one's free. And that's a good thing because who would really want to pay to see old Walt's grand piano?

If you have older children, try staying into the evening, when lines for most rides are shorter. Be sure to revisit Tomorrowland, which really jumps at night. The place is dominated by teenagers catching the fireworks from the skyway, holding hands in the space bar, and necking in the Coca-Cola Tomorrowland Terrace (free). All this excitement may tempt you to come back the next day for another visit. But remember what we told you about avoiding a Disneyland overdose. Not only

is it expensive to return right away, but you may sap your strength and have no energy left to tackle Knotts Berry Farm.

Beverly Hills

A century ago two southern California entrepreneurs formed a corporation aimed at subdividing an open field into a new town called Santa Maria. But when the public refused to snap up the 5-acre residential lots at $10 apiece, the land was purchased by two businessmen, who put it to use growing lima beans for their United States Hotel. It wasn't until 1907 that an entrepreneur named Burton E. Green began successfully merchandising this neighborhood. Even then, progress was slow until Mary Pickford and Douglas Fairbanks moved in to build their mansion, Pickfair, in 1919. Finally the celebrities began flocking to Beverly Hills.

Today the community of 33,000 offers some of the best free entertainment in California. After New York's Fifth Avenue, probably no area in the nation can boast a larger concentration of chic shops than downtown Beverly Hills. Here women can shop at Giorgio's Boutique (Rodeo and Dayton streets) while their husbands kill time at the store's billiard table. At Robert D. Valley Classic Cars, Ltd., across from the Beverly Wilshire, you can see the fleet of Rolls Royces that rent at $65 per day and sixty-five cents per mile (most major credit cards honored). At places like Saks, Bonwit-Teller, or Robinson's, you can frequently sip champagne while watching a fashion show. And shops out of the central area, like Adele's Boutique at 8815 West Pico Boulevard, will even send a limousine to pick you up at your hotel.

Another popular diversion here is simply driving up through the affluent (prices for homes generally *start* at around $100,000 here) neighborhoods to the Franklin Canyon Reservoir. Along the way you may pass the fifty-five room Greystone Mansion at Doheny and Loma Vista. Built by the Doheny family and now city-owned, this building is currently headquarters of the American

---

Beverly Hills Guide. No one should come to California without his own guide to Beverly Hills. A twenty-eight page booklet offered by the city's Chamber of Commerce at no charge provides complete information on all the city's shops, restaurants, hotels, galleries, and other attractions. It's especially useful for those who want to orient themselves on shopping opportunities. For a copy, write Beverly Hills Chamber of Commerce, 239 South Beverly Drive, Beverly Hills, CA 90212.

Film Institute. The local Visitors' Bureau runs weekend tours here by reservation. Inside you'll get a look at servants' quarters for thirty-six, a children's wing with its own kitchen, and a doll house converted into a guest house. Large enough to support its own fire station, the Greystone property also encompasses a city reservoir. For tour information, contact the Beverly Hills Visitors' and Convention Bureau, 239 South Beverly Drive, Beverly Hills, CA 90212. For a general driving tour of the stars' homes, contact Starline Sightseeing Tours, 6845 Hollywood Boulevard (telephone: 213-463-3131).

The Studios

Getting tickets to TV shows or tapings is often difficult. If you're interested, send a stamped, self-addressed envelope to the studio's ticket division as far ahead as possible. Specify the show you want to see and list several alternate dates. Address CBS at 7800 Beverly Boulevard, Los Angeles, CA 90036; NBC at 3000 West Alameda Avenue, Burbank, CA 91523; and ABC at 4151 Prospect Avenue, Hollywood, CA 90027.

If you can't get tickets to the shows you want, consider taking one of three film and television tours available in the Los Angeles area. The best and most expensive ($5.40 for adults) is the Universal Studios Tour located off the Hollywood Freeway at Lankershim. In addition to getting a look at television and film production, you'll also be taken via tram through rock slides,

torpedo attacks, flash floods, glaciers, and a parted Red Sea, all courtesy of the Universal lot. NBC studios offer daily tours ($1.75 for adults), and at CBS you can join a free studio tour on most weekday afternoons.

Nobody Doesn't Like Forest Lawn

No trip to the Los Angeles area is complete without a visit to one of the four Forest Lawn memorial parks conveniently located in Glendale, Hollywood Hills, Covina Hills, and Cypress. Unique in all the world, Forest Lawn opens its memorial gardens, museums, and art work to the public at no charge. Visiting Forest Lawn, Glendale, you'll see some of the many features that inspired Evelyn Waugh to write *The Loved One.* This park is distinguished by *The Last Supper* window, a stained glass recreation of the Da Vinci masterpiece. Other highlights include Jan Styka's monumental five-story work *The Crucifixion* (the world's largest religious painting), Gutzon Borglum's *The Dying Chief* as well as the inspirational *Wee Kirk o' the Heather.*

At the Hollywood Hills park you'll find the Court of Liberty presided over by the bronze figure of Abraham Lincoln. Honest Abe seems to be reflecting on America's largest historical mosaic, *The Birth of Liberty,* composed of twenty-five scenes taken from American paintings covering the 1619–1787 period. Here too is a monument to George Washington, which includes busts of his favorite generals: Lafayette, Knox, Greene, and Benjamin Lincoln. Don't forget also to see the exact

Beverly Hills, looking north from Santa Monica Boulevard, 1924.

duplicate of England's crown jewels on display in the Hall of Liberty.

At the Covina Hills park you'll want to visit the elegant Church of Our Heritage along with the Court of Masters, which includes the statues of David, Venus, and Saint George. And at the Cypress branch are the Ascension, Church of Our Fathers, and nativity mosaics as well as the memorable statue *Suffer the Little Children.*

More than just mortuaries, the Forest Lawn parks are also available for wedding ceremonies. While here you can also make your own funeral arrangements. But of course there's no obligation. For further information, call Forest Lawn headquarters in Glendale at 213-254-3131.

Visit San Clemente—You Paid for It

Whatever happened to the Western White House? It's still there, of course, and so are the Nixons. Here's how to find it. Take the San Diego Freeway (Interstate 5) to the Avenida Califa exit in San Clemente. Turn west onto Avenida Del Presidente (there has been talk of changing the name of this street to Avenida Del Ex-Presidente) until you reach the coast guard station. Turn right, and you'll be there. The only problem, of course, is that the Nixon residence, La Casa Pacifica, is not open to the public. However, you can visit the nearby Nixon museum that has been established at the San Clemente Inn, 125 Avenida Esplandian. The motel owner has filled a large room with memorabilia ranging from Peking to Watergate.

How to Buy a Swimming Pool

Everyone comes to California assuming life is incomplete without a swimming pool. Everywhere you turn there are contractors who will happily start digging out your backyard tomorrow. But before you sign a $5000 to $10,000 contract, be sure you're ready to assume all the obligations a pool entails. Talk to a few owners, and you'll find out about maintenance expenses running over $600 annually, as well as the burden of constantly watching neighborhood children in your pool. You'll also learn of the special California geological problems that can jeopardize even the most carefully built pool. Shifting soil in this seismically active state can ruin just about any pool deck.

If these facts don't discourage you, pick three large, reputable contractors and check their reputations with the nearest office of the state contractor's licensing board. Assuming none of these firms has a bad complaint record, invite each to submit plans and estimates. Be sure to specify that you want a diatomaceous earth filter and separation tank as well as a solar heater. The latter item costs $700 to $800, about 25 percent more than a gas heater. But you'll save $60 a month or more on heating costs.

When discussing plans with the contractors, don't let them know whom they are competing against. "The worst thing a customer can do," says one suburban San Francisco pool dealer, "is to tell a salesman who else is bidding on the job. You're also crazy to show one company's drawing to another firm. As soon as they have that information, they know what kind of prices you've been quoted and they cease being truly competitive."

The second biggest mistake you can make is buying your pool in the summer. The big bargains are available during the fall and winter, when you can save hundreds of dollars. You'll pay more and wait as long as two months to get your pool if you buy during the summer rush. Another common error is failing to check with a contractor before purchasing a new home or lot. If you plan to install a pool, have a salesman survey the place to make sure there is sufficient space for the kind you want. Real estate agents are not always knowledgeable on the subject, and swimming pool companies are generally happy to do a free site survey. Also bear in mind that your pool costs will probably rise sharply if your lot is on a hillside. The extra engineering and construction fees can double pool cost in some cases.

After you've worked out the siting details and decided on a tentative design, review your plans. Visit a couple of swimming pool showrooms, talk with pool owners, and be sure you're buying what you need. Don't make the mistake of building a pool that's deep all around. At least 90 percent of the fun is in the shallow end. It's tiresome playing catch when you're treading water all the time.

When you've confirmed your choice, review the details carefully with your contractor. Try to get a guaranteed completion date, insist on a written lifetime structural guarantee, and be sure the contractor agrees to clean up all the debris after construction. Shop for your own financing and you'll probably save money. When the pool is done, there is no reason why you can't handle the skimming yourself. But have a pool service put in the chemicals. They charge roughly $18 to $20 a month to do the job, which is probably cheaper than you can do it yourself. More important, it will eliminate a common problem that develops when owners mess up. If the pH value is not low enough, the calcium in the water is attracted to the calcium in the plaster. Eventually, this forms a rough cover on the pool surface which can cut your feet. One final warning. Insist on self-closing gates that will keep small children out of the pool area. At the same time consider investing in a pool alarm that will sound if a kid should accidentally fall into an unattended pool. It happens more often than you'd imagine.

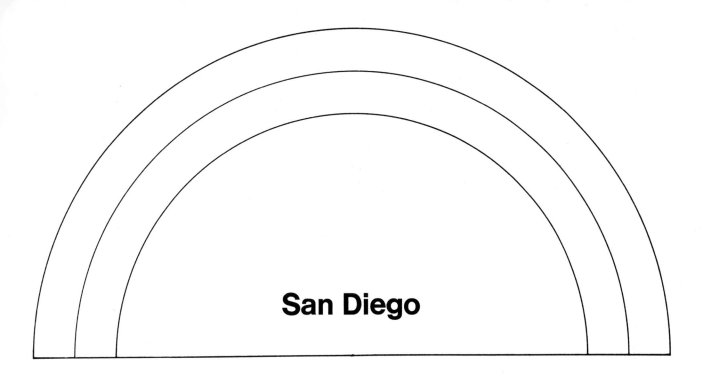

San Diego

The Best of San Diego

State park: Torrey Pines
Beaches: Torrey Pines; Silver Strand
Snorkeling, scuba diving: La Jolla Cove
Hang-gliding: Torrey Pines
Whale-watching: Point Loma
Nude beach: Black's Beach, La Jolla
Sailing: San Diego Bay
Urban park: Balboa
Sealife park: Sea World
Zoo: San Diego
Aquarium: Scripps Institute, La Jolla
State historic park: Old Town, San Diego
Adobe buildings: Old Town State Historic Park
Victorian building: Hotel del Coronado, Coronado
Indian museum: Cuyamaca Rancho State Park
Old hotel: Julian Hotel
Hot springs: Warner Springs
Bakery: Dudley's, Santa Ysabel
Small town: Julian
Observatory: Mount Palomar
Organ concerts: Spreckels Organ Pavilion, Balboa
   Park (Sunday)
Shakespeare: Old Globe Theater (summer)
Architecture: El Prado, Balboa Park
Airplane-watching: from Mr. A's restaurant, San
   Diego
View: Mount Soledad, La Jolla

Navigator Juan Rodríguez Cabrillo was tired when he rowed ashore in San Diego Bay on September 28, 1542, with several sailors and a priest. Arriving after three months of illness and stormy weather, Cabrillo claimed the new land for Spain; then he took six days off to rest and explore the countryside.

Surveying the San Diego region today it's hard to understand what motivated Cabrillo to leave after this brief visit. Had he stayed put, the explorer might well have enjoyed a long life in the balmy coastal climate. But instead he weighed anchor and headed up the coast as far as Point Reyes before returning to the Channel Islands, where he died on January 3, 1543, from injuries sustained in a fall weeks earlier.

Following Cabrillo's death it took Spain 226 years to get around to colonizing the city with Mission San Diego de Alcala, the first of twenty-one established in California. Subsequently burned down by Indians, the mission was rebuilt only to be knocked over in an earthquake. Finally, in the mid-1830s, with the structure in ruins, secularization took away the mission lands and redistributed them among Indians and settlers. The missions themselves were reduced to the status of parish churches.

Slowly the city began establishing itself as a trading center. But unlike Los Angeles to the north, this community made an effort to control growth and protect its environment. The result is that today San Diego, the birthplace of California, headquarters of the Eleventh Naval District, and home of the world's largest zoo, is a hard place to leave. There's a great deal to do here, particularly in the way of sightseeing at Old

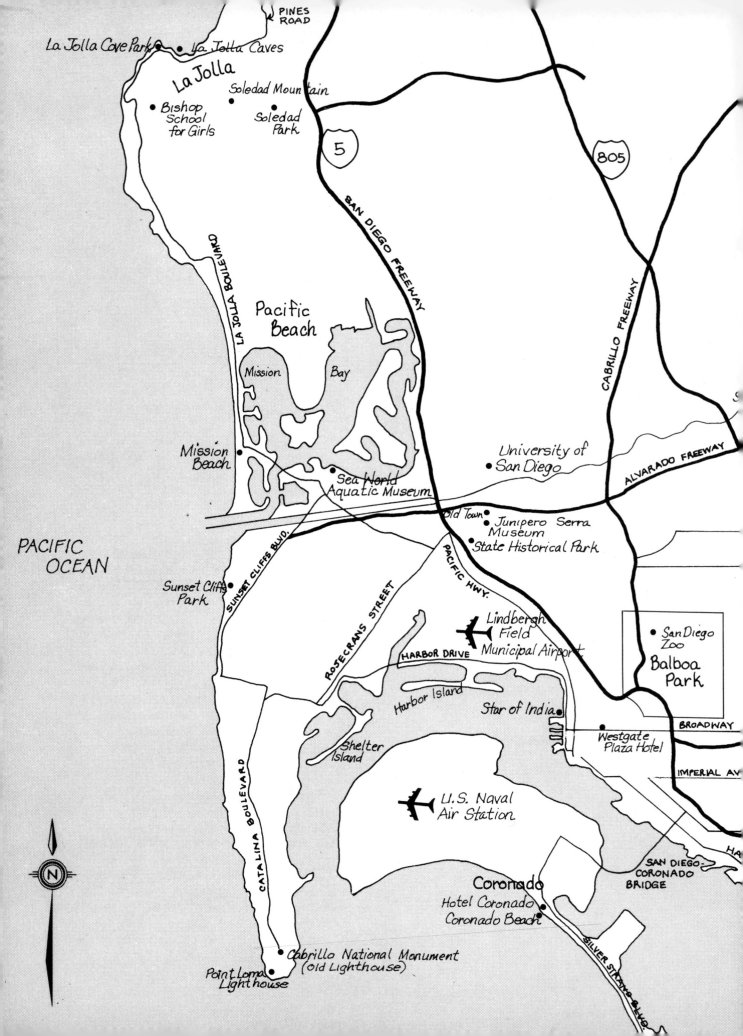

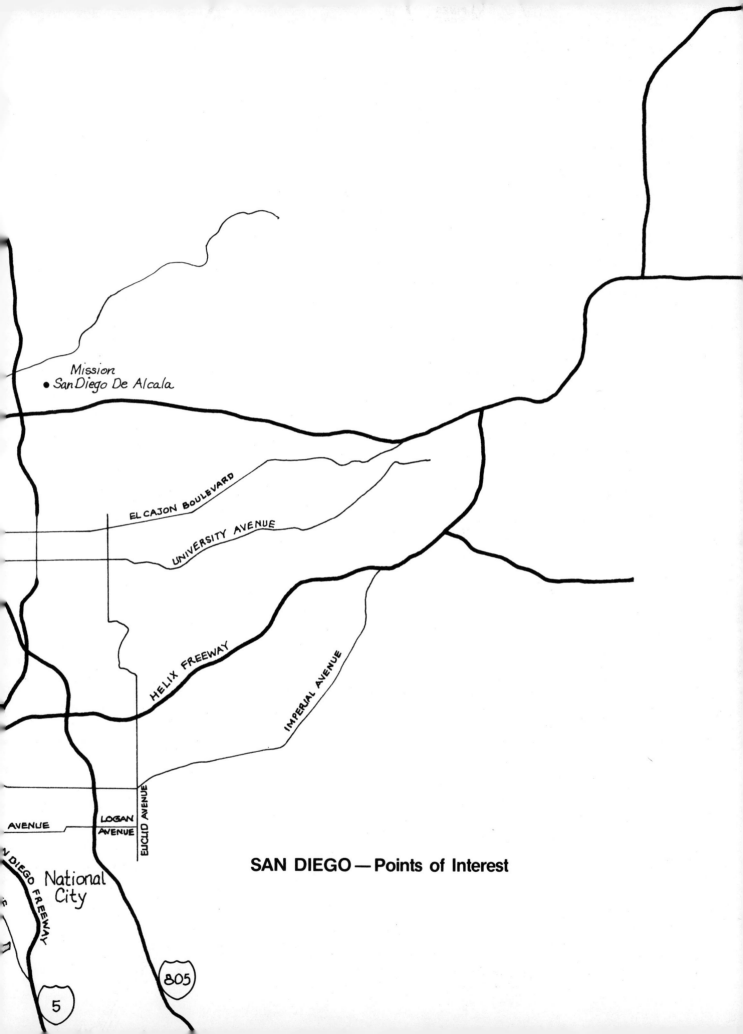

Mission
● San Diego De Alcala

EL CAJON BOULEVARD

UNIVERSITY AVENUE

HELIX FREEWAY

IMPERIAL AVENUE

EUCLID AVENUE

LOGAN AVENUE

AVENUE

N DIEGO FREEWAY

National City

SAN DIEGO — Points of Interest

805

5

San Diego waterfront and skyline. (*San Diego Convention and Visitors Bureau*)

Town, Sea World, Balboa Park, Torrey Pines Park, the Salk Institute, Mission Bay, and Mount Soledad. But this is also a place to do nothing more strenuous than sunbathing or trolling. For this informal, unpretentious, low-key community almost forces you to relax. Of all the city's popular attractions, the local zoo is clearly the most significant. If you're on a quick visit with time enough for only one site, this should be your choice. Located in the midst of 1400-acre Balboa Park, this zoo has the world's largest collection of wild animals—over 5000 specimens of 1400 species are on display. Besides the elephants, snakes, lions, and other animals you'll find at most major zoos, this one has such rare and vanishing species as Prezewalski's horse, the giant Galápagos tortoise, golden marmosets, pigmy chimps, Indian rhinos, golden-shouldered parakeets, and proboscis monkeys. And thanks to open-moated, natural-habitat enclosures many of the animals are displayed without bars or fencing.

A forty-minute guided bus tour provides a good orientation to this lush 100-acre zoo. You can also get an overview from the gondola ride that passes above the park. A special children's zoo scaled to the size of a four-year-old offers direct contact areas where children may pet baby animals. Here, too, you'll find a glass-fronted nursery, where attendants bottle-feed and diaper young primates. There are also extensive

educational activities including a full program of summer classes for schoolchildren. In addition, the zoological society has recently opened the San Diego Wild Animal Park 30 miles north of downtown. About 1000 animals roam freely in this 1800-acre preserve. It's located east of Escondido off S.R. 78.

After visiting the San Diego Zoo take some time out to explore adjacent Balboa Park, where many of the attractions are housed in buildings erected for world expositions held in 1915–1916 and 1935–1936. Among the major attractions are the Fleet Space Theater, aerospace museum, natural history museum, and the Old Globe Theater, where there's a Shakespeare festival during summer months. Most of the cultural attractions are found along El Prado, a narrow street within the park dominated by Spanish colonial architecture. Try to attend one of the Sunday afternoon concerts at the Spreckels Organ Pavilion. In most cities, temperature variation makes it impossible to keep an organ in tune out of doors. But thanks to San Diego's fairly consistent temperatures, open-air concerts can be offered here weekly on this, the world's largest outdoor organ.

A few miles northeast of Balboa Park near the intersection of Interstate 5 and Interstate 8 you can visit the Old Town State Historic Park. Here one may see restored adobes, several museums, stables, interpretive displays, and the ancestral home of Leo Carillo, who played Pancho in "The Cisco Kid." There are also a number of handicraft shops here as well as restaurants specializing in early California food. Walking tours led by park rangers depart from the Visitors' Center, 2660 Calhoun Street, at 2 P.M. daily. The local historical society also offers a tour of twenty-five historic sites at 1:30 P.M. on Saturdays, leaving from the Whaley House, 2482 San Diego Avenue.

While in the Old Town region you can also visit the Presidio Hill ruins of Mission San Diego de Alcala established in 1769 (also here are the ruins of Old Fort Stockton). But to find the mission itself you'll have to drive about 6 miles east on Friars Road to a site near San Diego Stadium. That's because the Franciscan establishment was shifted upriver in 1774 to assure a good water supply.

Leaving this old city center, head downtown, where you should pay your respects to the posh Westgate Plaza Hotel (where prints of Emperor Nero hang in the bathrooms), before heading over the Coronado Bay Bridge to Coronado Island, where you can visit the oceanfront Hotel del Coronado. This Victorian hotel, built in 1887, is distinguished by its turrets, tall cupolas, hand-carved wooden pillars, and gingerbread features. A hit from the day it opened in February 1888, the del Coronado has accommodated eight American presidents, the Astors, the Vanderbilts, the Tiffanys, the Armours, and the Lennon sisters. It was also the location for Billy Wilder's *Some Like It Hot.* Near the hotel is 5-mile-long Silver Strand Beach, which offers good swimming in both the ocean and San Diego Bay.

Doubling back over the Coronado Bridge, pick up Harbor Boulevard, which leads along the waterfront, where you can board one of the excursion boats that will take you on one- or two-hour trips through the harbor. This is an easy way to see the port area and such man-made attractions as Harbor and Shelter islands, which offer major resort and marina facilities. After completing your trip, head up the wharf to visit San Diego's three-vessel maritime museum, featuring the *Star of India* (the oldest sailing vessel afloat), an old San Francisco ferryboat, and a 1904 luxury yacht called *Medea.*

From here, drive around the bay to the Cabrillo National Monument on Point Loma and then head north to Sea World Aquatic Museum on Mission Bay. Many consider this to be the best of California's marine life parks. Here you can watch trainers waterski on the backs of charging bottlenose dolphins, see killer whale Shamu walk on his tail, and view sea maids swim with sea lions in the Star-Kist Undersea Experience. After the show, you may want to explore some of the 27-mile-long shoreline along man-made Mission Bay. This resort area is an excellent place to rent everything from a $2-an-hour kayak to a $25-an-hour ski boat complete with licensed driver. Sailing is good here, with boats and lessons available at several locations. The flat expanse of the shoreline is also ideal for bikers.

Picking up Mission Boulevard, you'll pass the popular oceanfront swimming areas of Mission Beach and Pacific Beach en route to affluent La Jolla. After visiting the elegant downtown shopping district, La Jolla Cove (a popular skin diving spot), and the Mount Soledad Viewpoint, head north to the Scripps Institute of Oceanography for a look at San Diego's best known fish, Harvey, the gulf grouper. Major feeding times are 1:30 P.M. on Wednesdays and Saturdays.

Near the north end of the University of California campus is the handsome Salk Institute, designed by architect Louis Kahn to the immunologist's precise specifications. While touring the institute, you may note local hang-glider enthusiasts swooping off nearby cliffs. Their landing strip is an oceanfront reserve set aside to protect a rare stand of gnarled Torrey pines. Swimming is good here and at a number of other La Jolla spots such as Black's Beach (for nude bathing) near the University campus.

Farther from the immediate San Diego area are a number of attractions. Certainly the most popular is the border town of Tijuana just thirty minutes away. But perhaps a more worthwhile town is Ensenada, about an hour farther south. There are good, un-

Killer whale Shamu performs at Sea World.
(*San Diego Convention and Visitors Bureau*)

crowded beaches here that are fine for skin diving. Immediately to the north of San Diego are posh resort developments like La Costa and beach communities such as Del Mar, Cardiff, and Carlsbad. At Oceanside, you can cut inland on S.R. 76 to visit Mission San Luis Rey, a Franciscan seminary that was once the largest and richest of all twenty-one California missions.

Another good trip is east into the San Diego County back country via S.R. 94. This route takes you through picturesque little towns like Dulzura, Campo, and Boulevard, home of the remarkably diversified Wisteria Candy Cottage, where you can buy such homemade items as chop suey brittle. Cut south farther on to visit Jacumba, an old stage stop on the Yuma–San Diego plank road, where you'll find a noteworthy Chinese castle.

Doubling back on Interstate 8, turn north on County Route S1 for the fine drive up Mount Laguna, where there's a good view of the nearby Anza–Borrego Desert State Park (see under Desert for more details). You can stop at one of several campsites here or head on down the Sunrise Highway to Cuyamaca Rancho State Park, where there's an Indian museum. A few miles north of the park is the old gold mining boom town of Julian. Today the rustic community is surrounded by rich apple-growing country. While here, you'll want to visit the Julian Hotel built by freed Georgia slaves in 1887, the museum—featuring local artifacts, including tools, mining equipment, buggies, and a fireplace made from Indian grinding rocks—a library in the former one-room school, and the old Eagle Mine. Come in late August and you can catch the unique Julian Weed Festival. Residents compete with one another by presenting displays of homegrown weeds.

At Julian you can head east on S.R. 78 to Anza–Borrego State Park and the resort community of Borrego Springs or turn west to Santa Ysabel, where you can visit Mission San Diego de Alcala. The bells that once tolled here were stolen in 1926 and have yet to be returned. Before leaving, be sure to pick up one of the many varieties of bread baked at distinguished Dudley's Bakery.

Heading north, you can visit Warner Springs, once a stop on the Butterfield overland mail route and today the home of a popular hot springs resort. Returning south to Moretti's Corner, take S.R. 76 north to Palomar Mountain State Park cutoff. Blessed with the climate of the Sierra Nevada, this park was once a favorite hideout for nineteenth-century cattle and horse thieves, who kept their stolen animals in the remote mountain meadows before taking them across the border. Nearby is the Mount Palomar Observatory, home of a 200-foot telescope, the world's largest. There's an exhibit hall here with various photos of nebulas, constellations, the sun, and other galaxies.

San Diego Notes

Carol Mendel's *San Diego on Foot* ($1.95, Carol Mendel, P.O. Box 6022, San Diego, CA 92106) plus Leander and Rosalie Peik's *Discover San Diego* ($1.50, Peik's Enterprises, Box 17271, San Diego, CA 92117) provide good introductory information on this area. For information on the back country, consult Russ Leadabrand's *Guidebook to the Mountains of San Diego and Orange Counties* ($1.95, Ward Ritchie Press, 474 South Arroyo Parkway, Pasadena, CA 91105). The San Diego Convention and Visitors' Bureau, 1200 Third Avenue, Suite 824, San Diego, CA 92101, is also a valuable resource. For information on trips down the Baja peninsula, contact the Mexican Government Tourist Office, 245 Westgate Plaza Mall, San Diego (telephone: 714-232-6758).

Whales

More than a dozen whale species frequent California coastal waters. They range from the giant 100-ton blue whale (the largest animal known) to the dwarf sperm whale, only about 6 feet in length. With luck, you may hear the singing of the humpback whale (the voice of one has actually been used as the background for a modern symphony), see a fearsome killer whale or view a sperm whale, distinguished by its massive squared-off head.

Although catching a glimpse of most varieties is chancy, you should have a fairly easy time sighting California gray whales making their annual migration from the Bering Sea to breeding lagoons off Baja California. Over 9000 of them make this 12,000-mile trip, passing south between Christmas and mid-February. The return trip to Alaskan waters usually begins in April.

These whales, which are protected under international treaty, can be seen from numerous coastal locations. Probably the best observation area is in the San Diego region, where as many as eighty whales per day can be sighted during late January. You can watch for free from the whale observation station at Cabrillo National Monument on Point Loma or catch a ride on one of several commercial boats that take you out into the Pacific for a closeup look.

Often the first sign of an approaching whale is its spout or blow, actually a warm breath that condenses into a vapor plume when exhaled into colder air. Usually a whale blows about three times in a five-minute period. Generally it surfaces from a cruising depth of 100 feet to take its first breath. Then it swims about 20 feet underwater, rises for a second breath, cruises again, and follows a third breath with a deep dive. The way a whale flips its tail on this plunge can help you establish its species.

After an initial venture at whale-watching, you may

be interested in taking one of the day-long trips offered by the San Diego Natural History Museum. And if you have the time, consider taking one of several six-day charter cruises down to the Scammon's Lagoon breeding ground, where the whales congregate by the thousands each winter. This is the ultimate experience for the whale voyeur and well worth the expense. For information on all these trips, contact the whale information desk of the San Diego Convention and Visitors' Bureau, 1200 Third Avenue, Suite 824, San Diego, CA 92101.

How to Swim in the Pacific

California has some of the world's best ocean beaches. But the coastal waters also pose some special hazards for people who have spent their lives swimming in lakes and pools. To begin with, the majority of the state's Pacific coastline is not generally used by swimmers. Although you'll find people jumping in the water as far north as Santa Cruz, most people don't go in north of the Santa Barbara region.

Of course, if you are unusually hardy or own a wet suit, it is possible to swim in the ocean all the way up to the Oregon border. But you should bear in mind that unusually strong current, riptides, and undertows make many Northern California coastal waters off limits for everyone. Some of these dangerous beaches are posted "no swimming," but many are not. When you consider the rough waters, lack of lifeguard services, and higher shark attack rate (see Part Three, under Jaws), it makes sense to stay away. For even when the water looks calm, unexpected currents may make it difficult if not impossible to swim.

The situation is much better in Southern California, where generally excellent swimming conditions prevail. You can keep risks to the absolute minimum by taking a few simple precautions. First, never swim alone. Even on what may seem like the best of days any number of problems from cramps to unseen logs and strong currents can pose serious hazards.

Second, always try to swim on a guarded beach. Generally excellent Southern California lifeguards make thousands of rescues each summer. Since they can be found on most of the principal beaches, there's really no reason to swim without their protection. California waters are generally colder than those you may have enjoyed off Hawaii, Florida, or in the Caribbean. This means you'll probably tire faster here and have less energy to respond to an emergency.

If you are swimming with a partner on a guarded beach, you need keep only a few other simple principles in mind. Perhaps the most common mistake made by novice ocean swimmers is trying to fight the water. No matter what is going wrong, you'll do best by relaxing and exerting as little energy as possible. For example, if you find a giant wave crashing over you, don't make the common mistake of trying instantly to fight your way to the surface. Instead go limp, let the breaker push you around a bit, wait until it passes by, and then calmly work your way to the surface.

If an undertow is sucking you down, don't fight it. Let yourself be taken under and then come back up on the very next wave. Similarly, if a rip is pulling you out to sea, go along or start swimming across the current. Don't make the mistake of trying to swim against the tide; you'll just wear yourself out and get nowhere. This principle of swimming across rather than against the tide is also the best way to prevent being swept away from the location where you entered the water.

But even if you follow all these precautions, unusually rough seas can pose special dangers. If you're in trouble, don't flail your arms for help. Red Cross experts say you're much better off leaving your arms in the water (where they weigh less) and slowly waving them up and down. You'll still be able to attract attention and not wear yourself out as fast. While waiting for help, employ the principles of drownproofing promoted by the U.S. Public Health Service. Hang vertically, and keep your face underwater. Exhale slowly through your nose, cross your arms before your face, and spread them out palms down. Then by simply tilting your head back your mouth will break the surface and allow you to breathe. Then drop your head and arms to resume bobbing until you want to take another breath. As you begin to feel more confident, shift your body into a swimming position and begin moving toward shore. Revert to the drownproofing technique whenever you begin feeling frightened or tired. Stay with this system, and you should have little trouble getting back on the beach.

Hotel del Coronado, a success from the day it opened in February, 1888. (*San Diego Convention and Visitors Bureau*)

The Amateur Sailmakers Catalogue. Anyone thinking about making his own replacement sails should start with this forty-four-page booklet. In it, you'll find everything you need to know about putting together your own spinnaker, jib, main, and storm sails. The catalogue is produced by Sailrite Kits, which sells all the materials necessary to do it yourself. For a copy, send $1 to the firm at 2010 Lincoln Boulevard, Venice, CA 90291.

Trimaran. If you want an oceangoing vessel, but can't afford the current prices, consider making your own with plans leased by Tri-Star Trimarans, of Venice. Naval architect Ed Horstman offers everything you need to make vessels from 18 to 65 feet in length. Basic woodworking ability and shop tools are all you need. For a brochure listing the various plans available, write Tri-Star, P.O. Box 286, Venice, CA 90291.

Sierra Designs Catalogue. From mukluks to glacier tents, few manufacturers can boast a better line of outdoor gear than Sierra Designs. This firm's catalogues, always works of art in themselves, offer just about everything necessary for a trip to the outback. Unusually complete product descriptions and manufacturing specifications simplify your shopping. A number of specialty items, like chestnut walking canes (resistant to heat, cold, dryness, and humidity), boot scrapers (there's no excuse for muddied floors with this item), and Kel-lite flashlights (totally indestructible), are available. For a copy of the catalogue, write the firm at 4th and Addison Streets, Berkeley, CA 94710.

The North Face Catalogue. First-rate outdoor equipment has brought about steady growth for this Berkeley-based manufacturer. A full line of wilderness travel equipment as well as such exotic items as a geodesic shelter for backpackers are offered. A special Nordic ski equipment package is available for $100. For a copy of the firm's catalogue, write to 1234 5th Street, Berkeley, CA 94710.

The Smilie Company. Yet another camp-and-trail gear specialist, the Smilie Company offers first-rate cookware, packs, tents, clothing, fishing tackle, and books for those who frequent the back country. For a copy of the thirty-two-page catalogue, write Smilie's at 575 Howard Street, San Francisco, CA 94105.

California Explorer. A valuable guide for those who enjoy backpacking and ski touring, this monthly provides information about little-known trails not in the standard guides. Articles treat such subjects as springtime hiking in the Los Padres National Forest, the Grand Canyon of the Tuolumne, Nordic skiing in June, and the best months for hiking and touring. A year's subscription costs $12, but you can get a free sample copy by writing to California Explorer, 119 Paul Drive, San Rafael, CA 94902.

Sportsworld. The state's most extensive program of camps for competitive sports is run by an enterprising firm called Sportsworld. There's Bill Sharman's basketball camp for boys in Grades 3 through 11 (guest lecturers include Kareem Abdul-Jabbar, Lucius Allen, Cazzie Russell, and Sidney Wicks); John Wooden's basketball camps for boys and girls; Billy Casper's golf camp; as well as soccer, track, and tennis camps at several locations. For a brochure, write Sportsworld, Dept. LA8, 8245 Ronson Road, Suite D, San Diego, CA 92111.

State Forest Maps. The California Division of Forestry sells administrative maps covering portions of the state for which it has fire responsibility. These maps provide information on picnic areas, campgrounds, jeep and hiking trails, rivers, streams, boating and fishing access, etc. Printed on special tear-proof paper, they are available through the State Forester's Office, 1416 9th Street, Sacramento, CA 95814.

PART EIGHT: SPORTS

Gliding at Torrey Pines Park, near La Jolla.

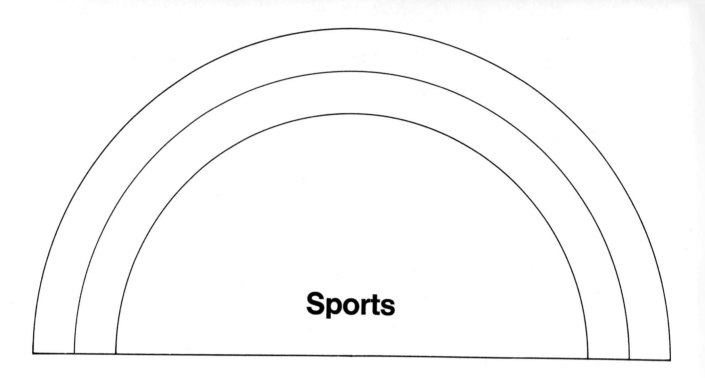

Sports

Sports in California is a year-round business. Spectators and weekend athletes never really have an off-season. An abundance of professional and college teams in major metropolitan centers means there's virtually always a home game. Tennis, backpacking, golf, and sailing are a reality every month of the year. Skiing at Mammoth Mountain frequently extends into June. And if the rain starts pouring in one region, you can almost always find the sun shining in another. The whole state is seldom socked in.

Fans who like their action live are seldom forced to stay home and depend on television. During the baseball season, it's possible to see a game nearly every day in Los Angeles and the Bay Area. When the Dodgers are away, the Angels are home. The same is true for the Giants and the A's. During football season, Bay Area residents can choose between the Raiders and the '49ers; Southern Californians, between the Rams and the Chargers. Basketball fans can spend winter months with Golden State and the Lakers; hockey enthusiasts, with the Seals and the Kings.

On top of all this professional competition is the heaviest schedule of collegiate games anywhere in the country. During the fall and winter months, Los Angeles fans can see a major home football and basketball game virtually every weekend at USC or UCLA. The same is true in the Bay Area, thanks to Stanford and Berkeley. In addition to these schools, residents can follow teams fielded by twenty-five other state universities and colleges as well as by private universities like San Francisco, Santa Clara, Loyola, and Pepperdine.

Over the years, these professional and collegiate teams have given California more than its fair share of sports dynasties. UCLA, of course, has led in basketball; USC has been big in both football and baseball. Charles O. Finley's Oakland A's took three successive World Series—in 1972, 1973, and 1974—while Golden State won the basketball title in 1975. This talent for winning creates a good atmosphere for instructional training. Where, besides California, can high school students have their choice of basketball camps run by John Wooden (he runs one for boys and another for girls), Bill Sharman, and Rick Barry? In Northern California, the Santa Clara swim center has been instrumental in the development of such competitors as Mark Spitz. Even if you don't want to train, you can come here in the summer to see the Santa Clara Invitational, a major international swim meet. The Bay Area also has a top indoor track meet, the Examiner Games, held at the Cow Palace every winter. And Los Angeles has two major track meets—the Times Invitational and the Sunkist. In September you can see the Pacific Southwest Tennis Tournament in Los Angeles. And, of course, there's the regular series of golf tournaments at Pebble Beach, the Silverado Country Club (Napa), the Riviera, La Costa, etc.

After they're done competing, many athletes remain in California to take advantage of the mild climate that generally makes outdoor training a reality year-round. The weather is also an important asset for major recreational sports. There's no need to reserve a private tennis court at $15 an hour in the winter, since public courts found in most cities keep their nets up year-round. Of course, many hotels have private facilities for guests, and there are some private tennis resorts like the Gardiner Ranch in Carmel Valley. Likewise, sailors need take their boats out of the water only for repairs. Although snow makes backpacking inadvisable in the Sierra Nevada during the winter months, you can always turn to exploring lower elevations within the Ventana Wilderness and the Santa Barbara area. Hikers must contend with the rains during these times, but trails are generally free of the crowding experienced in the dry summer months.

Ocean swimming is, of course, limited to the summer months; the warmest temperatures are generally found in the San Diego area and Catalina. When the weather turns cold, you can head for one of several hundred hot springs located throughout the state, particularly in the Napa and Sonoma valleys. Among the best are Nance's Hot Springs, one of five local establishments in the little town of Calistoga, Grover Hot Springs, located in the state park of the same name (see Part Seven, under Sierra Nevada), Sespi Creek in the Santa Barbara area, and Orange County's posh Murrieta Hot Springs.

Like ocean swimming, whitewater rafting is limited to the summer months. Increasingly popular in recent years, whitewater rafting should be attempted only in the company of experienced guides. Ideas about where to pursue these and other activities are covered below, under Top Recreational Sports Areas. But regardless of your preference, bear in mind, once again, that you'll have a better time pursuing almost every recreational activity in California (except skiing) if you avoid the peak summer months. This is particularly true of backpacking, which is at its best in the late spring or early fall.

Sport Notes

The definitive series of California backpacking guides is published by Wilderness Press, 2440 Bancroft Way, Berkeley, CA 94704. Bikers can profit from *California Bike Tours* ($2.95, Goshua Publications. Order % Crown Publishers, Inc., One Park Avenue, New York, NY 10016. In addition, the state Department of Transportation's District 10 *Bicycle Touring Guide* shows access routes to Lake Tahoe, Yosemite, the Central Valley, and the Bay Area for bikers (who are frequently banned from using freeways). For a free copy, write Caltrans, Box 2048, Stockton, CA 95021. You can also get a map of the 70-mile California Aqueduct Bikeway (the state's longest) by writing Department of Water Resources, 1416 Ninth, Sacramento, CA 95814. Bikers who want to have all their gear hauled for them can join trips run by Tours Unlimited, 5844 Paddon Circle, San Jose, CA 95123. The firm takes you to starting points inside Death Valley, Yosemite, the Gold Country, and the Feather River Country. Then you bike along the tour route, while the company trucks your gear to a pre-designated campground or motel. When the trip ends, you are driven back to San Jose.

Charles Martin's *Sierra Whitewater* ($5.95, Fiddleneck Press, P.O. Box 14, Sunnyvale, CA 94088) provides good information for those who want to run Sierra River rapids. A number of companies sponsor raft trips down the Stanislaus and American rivers. Among them are American River Touring Association, 1016 Jackson Street, Oakland, CA 94607, and Outdoor Adventure River Specialists, P.O. Box 67, Angels Camp, CA 95222.

U.S. Army Corps of Engineers' Reservoirs. Free brochures with information on recreational opportunities at corps reservoirs in California are available from the Public Affairs Office, U.S. Army Corps of Engineers' Sacramento District, 650 Capitol Mall, Sacramento, CA 95814.

Bureau of Reclamation. The U.S. Bureau of Reclamation offers two pamphlets on recreation opportunities at its reservoirs within the state. Brochures and leaflets describing the larger units are also available. To obtain this material, write Regional Information Officer, Mid-Pacific Region, U.S. Bureau of Reclamation, 2800 Cottage Way, Sacramento, CA 95825.

Fish and Game Publications. A broad list of inexpensive periodicals, booklets, maps, leaflets, and technical publications are made available by the California Fish and Game Department. The species booklets, covering such categories as marine mammals, waterfowl, and fur bearers, are a particularly good bargain at seventy cents each; the fifty-seven wildlife leaflets (four cents each) are also a good bet. Anglers' guides provide detailed information on all categories of lake, stream, and ocean fishing. Also available are the department's quarterly magazine (with many fine articles devoted to wildlife conservation) and special bulletins of scientific interest concerning fish. For a copy of the Department of Fish and Game publications price list, write Office of Procurement, Documents Section, General Services Agency, P.O. Box 20191, Sacramento, CA 95820.

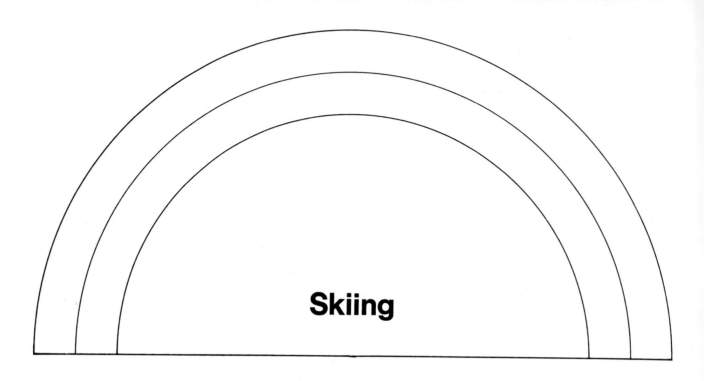

Skiing

After the Rocky Mountain region, California probably offers the best skiing in the nation. Although the state's resorts lack the dry, light powder that makes skiing in Colorado, Utah, Wyoming, and New Mexico such a pleasure, they do have a number of important attributes. Conditions are fairly dependable because of the unusually heavy snowpack (over 100 inches some years) that builds up almost every winter. Many of the areas are situated in some of the state's most scenic locales, such as Yosemite, Lassen, Mount Shasta, and Lake Tahoe. The heaviest concentration of ski development is found in the last area, which offers inexpensive accommodations, ample nightlife, and casinos to relieve you of spare change. And most of them are easily accessible via interstate highways.

Although there are several dozen good areas to choose from, most skiers would probably agree that the state's two most important resorts are Heavenly Valley on the south edge of Lake Tahoe and Mammoth Mountain on U.S. 395 at Mammoth Lakes. Heavenly is one of the nation's largest ski resorts, with 20 square miles of skiing terrain that spills over into Nevada, where you'll find a 7-mile run. This area's greatest asset is a splendid view of Lake Tahoe, which you can enjoy from many of the California runs.

While Heavenly is a favorite with Northern Californians, skiers from the southern part of the state tend to favor 11,000-foot-high Mammoth Mountain, which generally remains open until June. Located on the eastern slope of the Sierra Nevada, this resort has accommodations for over 20,000 visitors. And when you tire of Mammoth, you can ski nearby June Mountain, which boasts 20 miles of skiable terrain.

Another popular California area is Squaw Valley U.S.A. built for the 1960 Winter Olympics on a site about 7 miles west of Lake Tahoe. You would think this area's outstanding terrain, three ski jumps, ice rink, and historic past would make it an ideal winter resort. But Squaw Valley has been plagued by more than its share of difficulties. Happily, the area has taken notable steps to clear up its problems. Today, the biggest difficulties here are the long weekend lift lines and skiers who overestimate their abilities. The area gets more than its share of amateurs who try to pass themselves off as olympians. As a result, the ambitious skiers make the mistake of setting out for some of the more challenging runs, like KT-22, where they can end up over their heads. Ski here during the week and proceed cautiously.

Not far from Squaw Valley are a number of excellent family areas. Some of the best are Alpine Meadows, blessed with fine skiing through glades and bowls; Northstar, a resort development geared to intermediates; and Homewood, a relatively inexpensive resort that's a bargain midweek. Back over Donner Pass you'll find night skiing at Boreal Ridge and posh Sugar Bowl, one of the state's older ski areas favored by the socially prominent. There are no cars at the resort itself, which is reached via a short tramway. Although half the area's runs are for the expert, there are some good slopes for the novice or intermediate. Keep Sugar Bowl in mind when conditions are marginal. Owing to its location and high base elevation, this resort generally has more snow than nearby Lake Tahoe resorts. But be prepared to stay down the road at Truckee because the limited accommodations here are fairly expensive.

If you're heading for the Tahoe area on a crowded weekend, give some thought to trying Slide Mountain and Mount Rose. One lift ticket is good at both these areas, which share a mountain between Lake Tahoe and Reno. Snow-making equipment helps extend the season at Slide, which offers a free beginners' lesson and has night skiing on Friday and Saturday. A number of smaller areas like Incline, Tahoe-Donner, Echo Summit, Sierra Ski Ranch, Powder Bowl, Papoose, and Tahoe Ski Bowl help soak up the overflow.

Although most skiers reach these Tahoe resorts by car, several areas are easily accessible by bus or train. Take Amtrak or Greyhound to Truckee and catch a shuttle to Northstar or Tahoe-Donner. Public transportation is also available to several areas in the North Lake Tahoe area, and a bus ride to South Lake Tahoe puts you within a couple of miles of Heavenly Valley's front door. There is also bus service to Yosemite, where you can catch a shuttle to Badger Pass, one of the state's original ski areas, which is geared to beginners and intermediates.

Most of California's other ski areas are accessible only by private transportation. Among them are two growing developments: Kirkwood, south of Lake Tahoe, and Bear Valley, on S.R. 4. Kirkwood, primarily for intermediates (there's a free rope tow for beginners), is one of the Sierra's most scenic ski areas, although heavy winds often make skiing uncomfortable in the exposed bowls. A similar problem at Bear Valley leads to closure on bad days. Two other Sierra resorts that have a big following among San Joaquin Valley skiers are China Peak, east of Shaver Lake, and Dodge Ridge, off S.R. 108. Both these areas offer reasonably priced packages for groups, but can get uncomfortably crowded on weekends.

Often overlooked by the state's skiers are three Northern California areas. The smallest is Plumas-Eureka, part of a state park on the edge of the historic mining town of Johnsville. Limited facilities are open on Wednesdays, Saturdays, and Sundays at this area, which claims to be the cradle of American skiing and home of the world's first chair lift. In the mid-nineteenth century, Scandinavian miners introduced the sport to their American friends, who were soon racing on 12-foot-long boards. To spare themselves the ordeal of climbing back uphill, men working the Eureka Mine here grabbed a ride back up the mountain on the chain tramway used to transport ore buckets.

Farther north at Lassen National Park, there's skiing until Easter on terrain suited primarily to beginners and intermediates. And at Mount Shasta, skiers are drawn by 6-mile-long runs, a 4500-foot vertical drop, and reasonably priced lift tickets.

Although most of California's ski areas are in the northern part of the state, several operations are within 100 miles of Los Angeles. Thanks to snowmaking, these facilities in the San Bernardino and San Gabriel mountains offer fairly dependable conditions over diverse terrain. Close in are Mount Baldy (49 miles east of town) and Mount Waterman (55 miles northeast). But if you're willing to make the two-hour drive up to Big Bear Lake, you'll have a choice of several areas, all good places for beginners. Among them are Snow Valley, which offers six chair lifts; Snow Summit, which has an extensive ski school; Goldmine, which has a 1500-foot vertical drop; and modest Green Valley Snow Bowl. In the Wrightwood area off Highway 2, you'll find several smaller areas, including Ski Sunrise, Blue Ridge, Holiday Hill, and Kratka Ridge. Try visiting these areas during the week, as lines can be long on weekends.

The limitations of these resorts have led many residents in Southern California to press for a development within easy driving distance. For many years their effort has been spearheaded by the Disney interests, who want to put in a major ski area at Mineral King, south of Sequoia National Park. But this project has been stymied by Sierra Club legal opposition, and the Disney interests have now shifted their energies to a new site at Independence Lake, north of Truckee. However, this project has also come under fire from environmentalists, who object to the entertainment corporation's grandiose plans.

Conservationist pressures are one of several factors that have helped promote development of cross-country skiing at many California winter resorts. The sport is inexpensive, relatively easy to pick up, and a good way to escape the crowds while enjoying the back country. Many resorts such as Kirkwood, Tahoe-Donner, Bear Valley, and Sugar Bowl offer touring instruction. Yosemite, Lassen, and Sequoia national parks also have cross-country programs. All are fine places to get started because you can put in practice time amid some of the state's best winter scenery.

If downhill or cross-country skiing seems like too much work to you, there's no reason to be left out in the cold with nothing to do. There are plenty of good places—including Mount Shasta, Mount Lassen, Yosemite, Sequoia National Park, Boreal Ridge, and North Lake Tahoe Regional Park—to go sliding on a sled or inside a saucer, tube, or toboggan. On Lake Tahoe's south shore there is an excellent toboggan run on Busy Bee Hill, and Camp Sacramento, on S.R. 50 west on Echo Summit, is a good bet. In Southern California you'll find tobogganing facilities at Goldmine and a sledding area at Holiday Hill. For ice-skating, try the rink at Squaw Valley.

Skiing Notes

The automobile club offers a winter sports guide free to members, and you can purchase the *Skiers Alma-*

nac, a guide to western skiing, for $1 at some newsstands or by writing to 2066 Potomac Way, San Mateo, CA 94403. Dave Beck's *Ski Tours in California* ($4.95, Wilderness Press, 2440 Bancroft Way, Berkeley, CA 94704) is a useful guide to cross-country skiing. The Far West Ski Association (1313 West 8th Street, Los Angeles, CA 90017) offers a wide variety of services and benefits, including a biweekly paper.

Never set out for a California ski area without chains in the trunk of your car. The highway patrol *strictly* enforces the use of chains on the mountain passes during winter storms. Although crews will gladly put your chains on for $4 to $5, you may want to save money by doing it yourself. Fine. But practice before leaving home and carry rainwear and a plastic mat. It's no fun trying to figure out chain installation directions while lying under your car at night as passing trucks spray you with slush.

National Forests. For general information on national forests within the state, write U.S. Forest Service, Division of Information and Education, 630 Sansome Street, San Francisco, CA 94111. A map of one national forest and campground directory will be sent free upon request. There is a charge for additional maps. This office will also supply, for each of the national forests within California, an address where you can get more specific information.

U.S. Geological Survey Maps. These topographic maps of California are sold at stores throughout the state or may be ordered direct from the Distribution Section, Geological Survey, Federal Center, Denver, CO 80225. They are also sold over the counter (but *not* by mail) by Geological Survey offices at 345 Middlefield Road, Menlo Park; 7638 Federal Building, 300 North Los Angeles Street, Los Angeles; and 504 Custom House, San Francisco. Indexes showing the maps available may be obtained free of charge at the above offices.

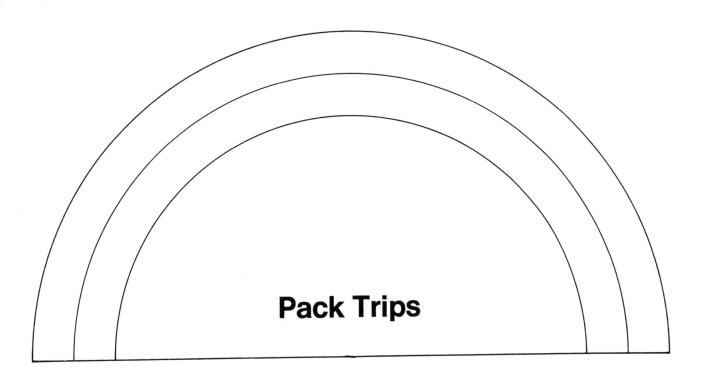

Pack Trips

One of the most convenient ways to reach the back country is through the services of one of California's many pack stations. You can join a pack trip with an experienced guide or take a "spot" trip, where you and your gear are dropped off at a predesignated location and then picked up on a specified day. Some packers will even drop you off with horses on a spot trip. Prices range widely, depending on the type of trip you choose, the amount of equipment brought along, and your willingness to share the work load. Generally, spot trip prices start at around $40 per person; overnight pack trips run $30 to $50 per day (per person). A day-long trip for a group of four costs about $100. For details, write the packers listed below:

Minarets Wilderness: Agnew Meadows Pack Train, Box 395, Mammoth Lakes, CA 93546

Sonora Pass area: Leavitt Meadows Pack Station, Bridgeport, CA 93517

Mineral King: DeCarteret Pack Train, 30547 Mehrten Drive, Exeter, CA 93221

King's Canyon: King's Canyon Pack Train, Cedar Grove (mailing address: A. R. Simmons, Star Route, Squaw Valley, Fresno, CA 93646

Huntington Lake Area: D & F Pack Station, P.O. Box 82, Raymond, CA 93653

Lake Tahoe area: Camp Richardson Corral, Emerald Bay Road, Camp Richardson, CA 95705

Marble Mountain Wilderness: Ed Burton Pack Trips, R.F.D. 60, Fort Jones, CA 96032

Feather River region: Greenhorn Creek Guest Ranch, P.O. Box 11, Spring Garden, CA 95971

For additional information on pack trips, contact the High Sierra Packers Association. The Western Unit is at Box 123, Madera, CA 93637; the Eastern Unit is at Box 147, Bishop, CA 93514.

Top Recreational Sports Areas

Biking: San Diego's Mission Bay area, La Jolla Coast, Palos Verdes Coast, Santa Cruz, Santa Barbara, San Francisco–Sausalito, Russian River, Sacramento River Delta, Napa Valley, Davis.

Canoeing: Russian River.

Hiking: Minarets Wilderness, Desolation Wilderness, Sequoia–Kings Canyon National Park, Yosemite National Park, Lassen National Park, Marble Mountain Wilderness.

Sailing: Mission Bay, San Diego Bay, Marina Del Rey, Monterey Bay, San Francisco Bay.

Snorkeling, scuba-diving: La Jolla Cove.

Swimming: The San Diego Coast, from Torrey Pines south.

Surfing: The Wedge, Balboa Peninsula.

Tennis: Best hotel courts at the Claremont Hotel, Berkeley.

Whitewater rafting: Stanislaus River, Camp 9 to Parrot's Ferry; south fork of American River, Chile Bar to Folsom Lake (experienced guides required on both routes).

PART NINE:
HIGHER EDUCATION

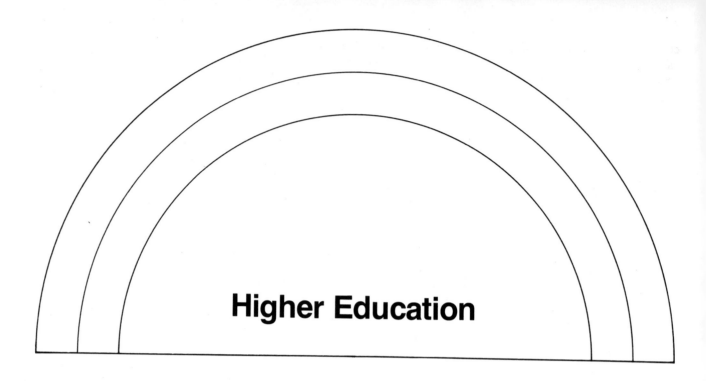

Higher Education

No state has done more to make higher education accessible than California. There are no tuition charges at the state's ninety-eight community colleges. At a number of campuses, free or low-cost child care is available for mothers. Working people can schedule twelve-hour weekend class loads. Those who want to get a Ph.D. without giving up their regular jobs can do classwork during summer vacations and correspond with a thesis adviser the rest of the year. Other correspondence courses make off-campus training possible through television and cassette tape instruction. Specialized programs have been developed for prison inmates, minorities, the handicapped, senior citizens, and foreign-language-speaking students. You can also get credit through job internships, South American cruises, or African photographic safaris. Here are some ideas for finding the educational program best suited to your needs.

University of California

Campuses are located at Davis, Berkeley, San Francisco, Santa Cruz, Santa Barbara, Los Angeles, Riverside, Irvine, and San Diego.

The state's prestige public institution, UC provides some of the best graduate training found anywhere in the world. The nine-campus system enrolls about 124,-000 students annually in regular academic programs. Prestige campuses like Berkeley are good places for undergraduates with specific career goals such as medicine, law, or dentistry. However, students who don't arrive with clear vocational objectives will prob-

ably not appreciate being squeezed into introductory lecture courses with 500 other students. If you're after a general liberal arts education, consider a more congenial, less crowded undergraduate atmosphere such as can be found at the Davis campus (near Sacramento). Other campuses at Santa Cruz, San Diego, and Santa Barbara also draw students trying to escape the depersonalized nature of big, research-oriented schools like Berkeley or UCLA. Minority students show a decided preference for certain UC branches. For example, the highest percentage of black and Spanish-speaking students is found on the Riverside campus, Berkeley has the greatest Asian representation, and American Indians tend to favor Davis.

In addition to the regular campus instructional program, UC offers a vast extension program throughout the state. These courses, which range from weekend seminars on paranormal phenomena to twelve-day expeditions to the Galapagos Islands, are ideal for working people who want to devote weekend or vacation time to educational courses and expeditions. A remarkably diversified program includes an art study tour of Venice, a course on marriage and family contracts, and lectures on building and investing in earthquake country. Not all courses are offered for credit in this excellent program that is open to all state residents. Fees for the nontravel courses are frequently under $100, and day-care facilities are available at some branches. A limited number of extension students may take selected on-campus courses with the general student body.

Other educational choices offered by UC include

correspondence courses for independent study as well as cooperative education at Berkeley and Davis in which students get credit for supervised on-the-job experience. About half the 2000 students at Davis are part of this system. A variety of other programs helps the educationally disadvantaged through scholarships, special seminars, counseling, and university-financed tutors. Berkeley and Riverside provide special aid to the handicapped, and Berkeley, Davis, UCLA, and Santa Barbara all have active women's centers, which offer special financial and career counseling, set up seminars on women's issues, and arrange for child care.

California State University and Colleges

Campuses are located at Bakersfield, Chico, Dominguez Hills, Fresno, Fullerton, Hayward, Humboldt, Long Beach, Los Angeles, Northridge, Pomona, Sacramento, San Bernardino, San Diego, San Francisco, San Jose, San Luis Obispo, Sonoma, and Turlock.

Almost 300,000 full-time and part-time students are enrolled on the nineteen campuses of the state university and college system, which is administered separately from the University of California. With courses running from 8 A.M. to 10 P.M., the CSUC units cater to working people by the tens of thousands. Most urban campuses keep administrative and student service offices open after 5 P.M. to accommodate night students. Some units, such as San Diego State University's Imperial Valley campus in Calexico, have extensive weekend programs in which students can earn up to twelve credits per semester. In addition, about 127,-000 adults study part-time through extension courses, special summer sessions, and external degree programs. About half the 5000 extension courses are taught off-campus. The twenty-eight external degree programs taught at forty-two off-campus sites make wide use of late-afternoon, evening, and weekend scheduling. Independent study is often coupled with intensive on-campus instruction as well as TV broadcasts, tape cassettes, phone networks, and on-the-job training. The state system also offers cooperative education programs that give academic credit for work activities, individualized instruction with self-paced curriculums, and compensatory education for disadvantaged students. Five of the nineteen CSUC campuses have women's centers, and additional services are provided on a number of campuses for senior citizens and the handicapped.

Independent Colleges and Universities

California has eighty-three accredited independent two- and four-year colleges and universities with a combined enrollment of 141,000. Through participation in academic consortiums, many of these schools rival the facilities offered by large state university systems. For example, Stanford shares its library resources with the University of Southern California and the California Institute of Technology, while also serving as the base for a regional university computing network in Northern California. California College of Arts and Crafts in Oakland belongs to a ten-member consortium of independent art colleges. Los Angeles–based Immaculate Heart has cooperative programs in special areas with Cal Tech and Antioch College/West in San Francisco.

At least fifteen of the state's private colleges offer extended degree programs that let students study off-campus. In addition, Golden Gate University in San Francisco, Johnston College in Redlands, University of the Pacific at Stockton, and the University of Southern California offer cooperative education that allows students to gain credit for working in law offices, schools, hospitals, probation departments, drug rehabilitation centers, and welfare departments. Seventeen schools also permit students to develop highly individualized curriculums and proceed at their own pace.

Perhaps the most attractive feature of many of the smaller private schools is their innovative approach to education. For example:

- The new resources program at Pitzer College (Claremont) is specially designed for returning or older students seeking undergraduate degrees, with degree requirements partially dependent upon life experiences.

- La Verne College (La Verne) gives credit for life experience in an accelerated adult program that combines on- and off-campus work with independent study.

- Loyola Marymount (Los Angeles) runs an ENCORE program offering supportive services for women over twenty-five who are resuming their education at the freshman level.

- Lone Mountain College (San Francisco) offers off-campus tutorials taught by nonfaculty professionals. Masters programs in community development and public service involve workshops, internships, as well as service activities.

- Chapman College (Orange) runs classes aboard the S.S. *Universe Campus*. Typical cruises to the Caribbean and Latin America examine cultural, economic, political, and religious aspects of life in assorted ports of call.

- University of San Francisco has a weekend college offering twenty-one courses. The terms last eight weeks.

- The University of San Diego Evening College offers complete undergraduate degree programs in business administration, history, political science, and religious studies.

- Azusa Pacific College (Azusa) offers off-campus courses based around video cassette materials. On enrollment, each student is given a video playback machine to use for self-paced study.
- Johnston College at University of Redlands runs a model community action program in which students get credit for contracting to spend a year in community service. This approach concentrates on tutoring and counseling disadvantaged students in conjunction with local school districts, legal aid clinics, senior citizens' groups, and probation departments. Students get a modest living stipend.

In recent years a variety of new, nonaccredited colleges have opened up. Among them are:

- Common College (Woodside), a two-year school that operates without courses, units, or grades. Students perform self-evaluations in terms of personal goals. Typical goals range from improving Bay Area ecology to speaking up in groups, learning to follow an extended metaphor, and transferring to UC.
- International Community College (Los Angeles) operates a liberal arts program in which students apply directly to such professors as Buckminster Fuller, Anais Nin, and Ivan Illich to develop independent study courses.
- World College West (San Rafael) offers a work-study program in which students attend class fifteen hours a week and work an additional twenty. Classes include a work seminar in which students relate course work to their jobs.
- Nairobi College (East Palo Alto) offers a two-year program for black students that stresses career skills. The school runs cultural programs for the local black community. About one-third of the student body is over thirty.

Community Colleges

California's seventy community college districts operate ninety-eight campuses with enrollment exceeding 1.1 million. A variety of programs makes these schools accessible to all segments of their commu-

nities. For instance, College of Marin (Kentfield) runs an emeritus college where senior citizens are taught by noncredentialed retirees. In the Oakland area, Merritt College has community development programs that actively involve ethnic minorities.

Private Specialty Schools

About 750 privately owned schools provide vocational training beyond the high school level to 200,000 California students. A national study by the Center for Research and Development in Higher Education concludes that the instructional level in these private specialty schools is comparable to that in public institutions teaching similar vocational subjects. Significantly, instructional costs were generally lower at specialty schools than at public colleges. Although most graduates of these privately owned establishments found work, the national study showed "only about 20% (of those) who chose professional or technical-level training (higher-status and higher-paying jobs such as accounting, computer programming and electronic technician) actually got the jobs they trained for, or jobs of equivalent pay and status. The other 80% of the (private school) graduates took lower-level, lower-paying jobs, some of which could be considered related."

Higher Education Notes

The *Directory of California Colleges and Universities,* published by the State Coordinating Council for Higher Education, 1020 12th Street, Sacramento, CA 95814, provides a comprehensive listing of state schools. More detailed information about these institutions is provided in *Choosing a College in California* by Norman Charles and Donald Ridenour ($7.95, Chronicle Books, 870 Market Street, Suite 508, San Francisco, CA 94102.

The University of California is headquartered at 2200 University Avenue, Berkeley, CA 94720; the state university and college system is based at 5670 Wilshire Boulevard, Los Angeles, CA 90036. Statewide administration for the California community colleges is headquartered at 825 15th Street, Sacramento, CA 95814. The Association of Independent California Colleges and Universities is at One Wilshire Building, Suite 2120, Los Angeles, CA 90017.

PART TEN:
MISCELLANEOUS
INFORMATION

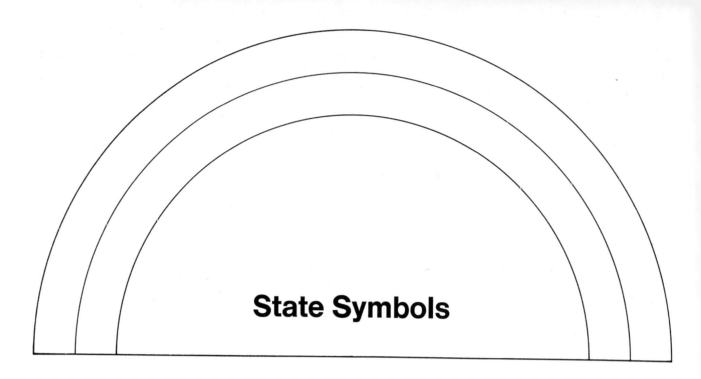

State Symbols

State flag: Adopted by the state legislature in 1911, the flag shows a grizzly bear on a white background with a red striped border on the bottom and is patterned after a flag designed and flown by a group of American settlers who revolted against Mexican rule in California on June 14, 1846, at Sonoma, north of San Francisco Bay. The original flag was made of odds and ends of cloth and colored matter. The government of the Bear Flag men, which extended over only a part of northern interior California, was short-lived, for on July 7, 1846, naval forces of Commodore John D. Sloat landed at Monterey, raised the Stars and Stripes at the old customhouse there, and proclaimed California a United States conquest. For years the original Bear Flag was preserved in San Francisco, but was lost in the earthquake and fire of 1906.

Governor's flag: This symbol, which accompanies the chief executive at all official state occasions, is emblematic of his rank as commander in chief of the California National Guard. It is of blue silk, trimmed with gold fringe. The Great Seal of California, in the center, is embroidered in several colors of silk.

State bird: The state legislature in 1931 gave official recognition to the California Valley quail (*Laphortyx californica*). The California Valley quail is found in many sections of the state, is social in nature, and is noted for its hardihood and adaptability. It is about the size of a dove or small pigeon and belongs to the same order of birds as the domestic chicken, though it is much trimmer and able to run much more swiftly. Much of the brushland where quail once lived is now occupied by farms, houses, and gardens, but quail frequently penetrate into these areas. Here they are secure from hunters and hawks, but have found a new enemy in the common house cat. If not disturbed too much, however, they will often nest about the shrubbery of country houses. The nest, merely a hollow scratched in the ground and concealed by foliage, holds about a dozen white eggs, thickly spotted and patched with golden brown.

State flower: In 1903 the state legislature officially adopted the golden poppy (*Eschscholtzia californica*), which can be found blooming in some portion of the state on any day throughout the year. It once grew in great profusion the length and breadth of California, and the flaming glow it lent the hills could be seen from far out at sea.

State seal: The design for the Great Seal of California was adopted October 2, 1849, by the convention that framed the Constitution of the State of California. The thirty-one stars around the bend of the ring represent the number of states in the union after the admission of California, on September 9, 1850. To symbolize the fact that California was admitted to the union without going through the usual probationary period, the goddess Minerva, who sprang full-grown from the brain of Jupiter, is included. The grizzly bear has long been considered emblematic of the state. The wheat and grapes are emblems of the agricultural and horticultural products. The miner represents a leading industry, and the shipping scene typifies commercial greatness. The snowclad peaks in the background represent the Sierra Nevada. The Greek motto *Eureka* ("I have found it") applies either to the principle involved in the admission of the state or to the success of the miner at work.

State motto: "Eureka."

State nickname: The Golden State.

State colors: Blue and gold.

State tree: The California redwood was designated by the state legislature in 1937 as the official state tree. It grows to greater height than any other living thing, its natural distribution is limited almost wholly to California, and it is one of the best known and most beloved of all trees. The ancient forests of redwoods that once flourished over most of the northern hemisphere have reached their last stand on the Pacific Coast. Many of the finest groves are reserved as public parks. There are two species of redwoods: *Sequoia sempervirens,* a straight towering tree found along the north and central coastal areas, and *Sequoia gigantea,* a tree of tremendous girth found in the central Sierra Nevada. The maximum recorded height of a coast redwood is the 367.8 feet of a tree at Redwood Creek in Humboldt County. The largest tree is the General Sherman Tree in Sequoia National Park; it is 272 feet in height and has an estimated age of 3000 to 4000 years.

State mineral: Native gold was designated by the 1965 legislature as the state mineral. It is the mineral that first brought fame to California and gave it the designation of the Golden State. California has produced more gold than any other state in the union, though in recent years production has been greatly curtailed. However, gold can still be panned from streambeds and found in many rocks.

State rock: Serpentine was designated by the 1965 legislature as the official state rock. California has more serpentine within her borders than any other state. It is a distinctive rock, with shiny outcrop surfaces in many shades of green and blue. It is the host rock for such minerals as asbestos, chromite, magnesite, and cinnabar.

State song: California's official state song is "I Love You, California," written by F. B. Silverwood, a Los Angeles merchant. The music was composed by A. F. Frankenstein, also of Los Angeles. The song was introduced publicly by Mary Garden in 1913. It was the official song of the San Francisco and San Diego expositions of 1915, and was played aboard the first ship to go through the Panama Canal.

State animal: In 1953 the legislature named the California grizzly bear (*Ursus horribilis Californicus*) as the official state animal. It appears on the state flag and the great seal. A bear frequently represents California in cartoons and serves as a symbol for the state university. The California grizzly was a large, particularly fierce animal which, in early days, was frequently forced into bull-bear fights popular with the pioneers. It is now extinct.

State fish: In 1947 the state legislature adopted the brilliantly colored South Fork golden trout (*Salmo aquabonita*) as the official fish of California. It is one of several species of beautiful golden trout native only to the upper waters of the Kern River tributaries in the High Sierra country. Less than 10 inches long, and usually about 8 inches, it is a type of rainbow trout.

State insect: No state insect has been adopted by the legislature, but the California dog-face butterfly or dog head (*Zerene eurydice*) is supported by the California Conservation Council. This insect was selected in 1929 by a vote of entomologists in the state. The California dog-face butterfly is found from the San Francisco Bay region to San Diego. A small, attractive butterfly about 2 inches across, the male is orange with black border markings, and the female is orange-yellow without pattern except for a small black spot on the upper wings.

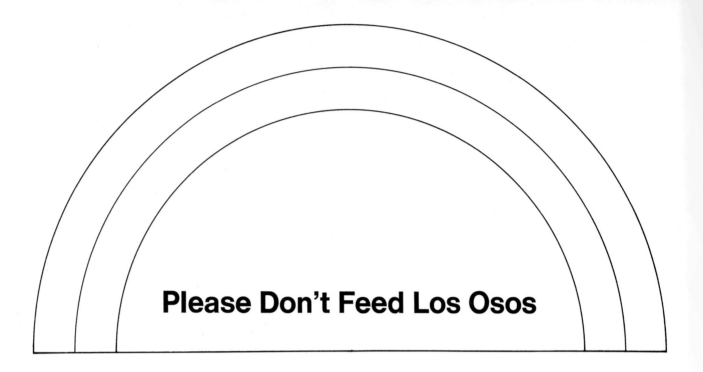

Please Don't Feed Los Osos

Many California names are Greek to those who aren't fluent in Spanish. Here are the English translations of some of the better known place names left by the state's original settlers:

Agua Caliente: hot water
Alameda: poplar grove
Alta Loma: high hill
Arroyo Grande: big stream
Atascadero: muddy place
Brea: tar
Calabasas: pumpkins
Carpinteria: carpenter
Chico: little
Chino: Chinese
Chula Vista: good-looking view
Corona del Mar: crown of the sea
Corte Madera: cut timber
Descanso: rest
El Cajon: the narrow canyon
El Centro: the center
El Cerrito: the little hill
El Monte: the mountain
El Nido: the nest
El Portal: the entrance
El Rio: the river
El Segundo: the second
El Toro: the bull
El Verano: the summer
Escalon: step
Escondido: hidden

Fortuna: fortune
Gaviota: seagull
Goleta: schooner
Hornitos: little ovens
Indio: Indian
La Honda: the slingshot
La Jolla: the jewel
La Mesa: table
Lome Linda: small pretty hill
Los Alamos: the poplars
Los Altos: the heights
Los Banos: the baths
Los Gatos: the cats
Los Molinos: the mills
Los Olivos: the olive trees
Los Osos: the bears
Los Robles: the oak trees
Madera: wood
Manteca: lard
Mariposa: butterfly
Merced: mercy
Montecito: small mountain
Pajaro: bird
Palo Alto: tall tree
Palos Verdes: green trees
Paso Robles: oak pass
Sacramento: sacrament
Salton: jumping
Sausalito: little willow
Tiburon: shark
Ventura: happiness

Environmental Organizations

As you travel about the state and watch its natural resources being systematically greased by oil spills, splintered by loggers, covered by subdividers, and buried by road builders, you may find yourself motivated toward preserving unspoiled portions of the California environment. Here are some organizations you can join that are working toward that end:

- California Wildlife Federation, P.O. Box 9504, Sacramento, CA 95823. Works for the preservation of wildlife and other natural resources.
- California Committee of Two Million, P.O. Box 2046, San Francisco, CA 94126. Works to maintain freely flowing rivers within the state.
- California Conservation Council, Box 5572, Pasadena, CA 91107. Promotes conservation through a variety of educational programs.
- California Tomorrow, 681 Market Street, San Francisco, CA 94105. Works on planning that permits growth without adversely affecting the environment.
- Council for Planning and Conservation, Box 228, Beverly Hills, CA 90213. Focuses on environmental concerns in Southern California and serves as an informational clearinghouse.
- Ecology Center, 2179 Allston Way, Berkeley, CA 94704. A major California ecological clearinghouse that helps citizens' groups organize on a wide variety of conservation projects.

- Friends of the Earth, 529 Commercial Street, San Francisco, CA 94111. Major national environmental organization active in a wide variety of causes, such as the nuclear power issue.
- Friends of the Sea Otter, Big Sur, CA 93920. Devoted to protection of California's rare remaining sea otters.
- General Whale, 9616 MacArthur Boulevard, Oakland, CA 94605. A leader in the whale conservation movement.
- Save the Redwoods League, 114 Sansome Street, Room 605, San Francisco, CA 94104. Tries to keep the big trees standing.
- Sierra Club, 220 Bush Street, San Francisco, CA 94108. America's largest conservation organization; headquartered in San Francisco; plays a major role in state environmental issues.

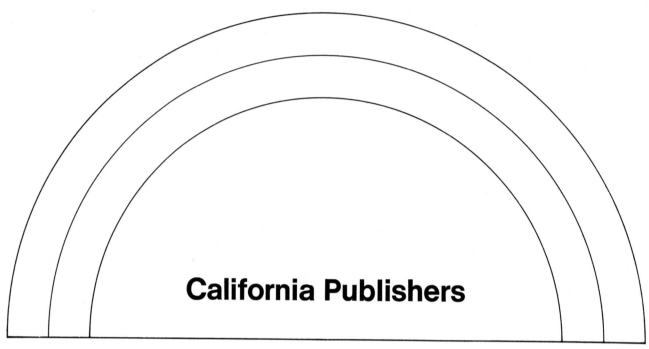

California Publishers

Practical information on living, working, and vacationing within the state is available from a variety of California publishers. Most of them prefer selling through bookstores, but all will fill mail orders. To avoid complications due to price fluctuations and shipping costs, you may want to write first for their catalogues. California residents must add 6 percent for sales tax (6.5 percent in San Francisco, Alameda, and Contra Costa counties).

- Chronicle Books, 870 Market Street, Suite 508, San Francisco, CA 94102. An arm of San Francisco's Chronicle Publishing Company, this firm offers such valuable titles as Margot Patterson Doss's walking guides, Peter Yanev's *Peace of Mind in Earthquake Country,* plus a variety of other special interest books on travel and recreational activities.

- Howell-North Books, 1050 Parker Street, Berkeley, CA 94710. Nationally known for its railroad books by such authors as Lucius Beebe, Howell-North also offers a number of good, reasonably priced, illustrated histories of California cities, counties, and mining regions.

- Lane Publishing Company, Willow and Middlefield Roads, Menlo Park, CA 94025. California's largest publishing house, Lane currently offers some 122 titles under its Sunset imprint, including the authoritative *Western Garden Book,* which many landscape architects consider a basic reference work. Specialized books dealing with the Wine Country, Southern California, Northern California, the Gold Country, San Francisco, Los Angeles, the missions, the coast, and back roads provide valuable travel information. The firm also publishes Robert Iacopi's excellent *Earthquake Country.*

- Sierra Club Books, Box 7959, Rincon Annex, San Francisco, CA 94120. This conservation society publishes an extensive list of ecology- and wilderness-oriented publications with a 10 percent discount to members. Although volumes deal with subjects ranging from the Everglades to Alaska, many of the best focus on California. You can learn about whales (*Mind in the Waters*), read about the state's great environmental battles (*John Muir and the Sierra Club*), or acquire handy pocket-sized totebooks for your next outdoor adventure (*Climber's Guide to Yosemite Valley*).

- Stanford University Press, Stanford, CA 94305. This firm offers a strong line of western Americana books, including Edmund C. Jaeger's definitive *The California Deserts* and *Desert Wild Flowers,* as well as a handbook for exploring Death Valley. *Gold, Guns and Ghost Towns,* by W. A. Chalafant, is a valuable study of the gold rush era.

- Wilderness Press, 2440 Bancroft Way, Berkeley, CA 94704. Publishers of the definitive line of Sierra hiking guides, this company also offers useful books on climbing Yosemite, hiking the San Bernardino Mountains, ski touring, and fishing. Anyone with a serious interest in exploring the California back country will want to check out Wilderness Press's valuable line.

- Ward Ritchie Press, 474 South Arroyo Parkway, Pasadena, CA 91105. Until recently, this firm published the leading line of California regional guidebooks, but has elected to discontinue its western travel and leisure series. Many titles are still available through bookstores and the publisher, which is remaindering its present stock at fifty cents. Quantities are limited, so move quickly for the regional guide of your choice.

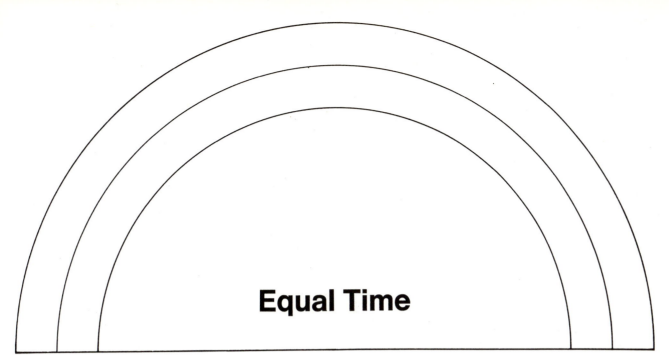

Equal Time

One problem with writing a book about California is that it ends up sounding too good to be truthful. Although it's a marvelous place to visit, the state has its share of problems from the residential standpoint. Without asking us to choose sides, let us give you a bit of background on why there is no longer a mass migration into the state. The truth is that many dissatisfied residents are packing up and heading east.

The primary problem is California's substantial unemployment rate (see Part Five). With the exception of selected professional categories, the work outlook is dismal. For example, one day in early 1976 over 30,000 people showed up to be interviewed for $2.25-an-hour jobs being offered at a new San Jose amusement park. The crush caused massive traffic jams, and police were finally forced to divert prospective applicants away from the park. When a San Francisco restaurant decided to hire a new host to seat customers, applications poured in by the hundreds for the $3.00-an-hour job. The winner: a lawyer from Boston.

You simply can't expect miracles if you don't have a job lined up ahead of time. And even when you do get work, chances are the pay scales will lag behind those in many major eastern cities. Why should your employer give you top dollar when he has hundreds of applicants willing to take less just for the privilege of working in California?

Job stability is another problem. Consider this. When *Saturday Review* Magazine moved its editorial offices to California, more than 16,000 people wrote in seeking work. And those lucky few who did land positions moved out to participate in a venture that failed in just one year. After the magazine was sold, many of the unemployed editors found themselves being dunned for moving bills the bankrupt company refused to cover.

Even those who conquer the job market are put off by other problems like smog, freeway congestion, and the two-season weather. If you've lived in a four-season climate all your life, adjusting to California's meteorological monotony may be difficult. Another problem is that most of the state's picturesque resort areas have been, are being, or will soon be overrun. Housing prices are soaring to the point where it is difficult to get into the market unless you already own property that you can sell to raise cash for a downpayment on a new purchase. For instance, in recent years San Francisco prices have doubled in many areas. In suburbs near the city people are paying $60,000 for a two-bedroom house. In Greater Los Angeles, you can't even consider looking in places like Beverly Hills for under $100,000. To buy lower-cost housing in urban areas, you generally have to accept outlying areas that require long, increasingly expensive commutes.

New offshore oil-drilling leases are scarcely encouraging to those who recall the depressing Santa Barbara Channel oil spill of 1969. Scientists worry about plutonium migrating into the state from the Nevada test site. Skyscraper proliferation makes San Francisco look a little more like Manhattan every day. The governor is threatening to curb new admissions to the state university. Doctors are leaving rather than pay the highest malpractice premiums in the country. Seismologists believe a major earthquake along the

San Andreas fault may come before the end of the century.

Perhaps none of these arguments are sufficient to change your mind. Fair enough; but why not take a few minutes and commit some of them to memory. Use them the next time you're in New York and someone starts putting California down. And while you're at it, add a few more discouraging words of your own. Mention that people on the coast are lazy and shiftless. Refer to Squeaky Fromme, Sara Jane Moore, Sirhan Sirhan. Point out that you frequently can't play tennis because of smog alerts. Talk about the neighbor who fills his pool at night with water from your hose. And if someone is actually thinking of moving to the state, tell him about the teams of menacing German shepherds that sniff for drugs carried by incoming passengers at California airports. Invent, fantasize, lie. The place is already overcrowded, and the more people you can discourage from moving into the state, the better.

Index